YOUT GLOBALIZATION, AND THE LAW

ORGANIZED BY THE SOCIAL SCIENCE RESEARCH COUNCIL
COLLABORATIVE RESEARCH NETWORK ON YOUTH
AND GLOBALIZATION

YOUTH,
GLOBALIZATION,
AND THE LAW

EDITED BY

SUDHIR ALLADI VENKATESH

AND RONALD KASSIMIR

STANFORD UNIVERSITY PRESS · STANFORD, CALIFORNIA 2007

Stanford University Press
Stanford, California

Printed in the United States of America on acid-free,
archival-quality paper

Library of Congress Cataloging-in-Publication Data

  Youth, globalization, and the law / edited by Sudhir Alladi
Venkatesh and Ronald Kassimir ; organized by Social Science
Research Council Collaborative Research Network on Youth and
Globalization.
      p. cm.
  Includes bibliographical references and index.
  ISBN-13: 978-0-8047-5473-6 (cloth : alk. paper)
  ISBN-13: 978-0-8047-5474-3 (paper: alk. paper)
    1. Juvenile justice, Administration of. 2. Youth—Legal status, laws,
etc. 3. Youth—Social conditions—21st century. 4. Social control.
5. Globalization—Social aspects. I. Venkatesh, Sudhir Alladi.
II. Kassimir, Ronald. III. Social Science Research Council (U.S.).
Collaborative Research Network on Youth and Globalization.
  HV9069.Y67 2007
  305.235—dc22   2006012938

Typeset by BookMatters, Berkeley in 11/15 Adobe Garamond

Original Printing 2007

CONTENTS

Preface and Acknowledgments

The roots of this project rest in some casual conversations between two New Yorkers in Cape Town, South Africa, in the spring of 1999. Kassimir, then director of the Africa Program of the Social Science Research Council (SSRC), organized a symposium on behalf of SSRC's Africa Regional Advisory Panel (RAP) on youth in Africa and the ways in which global changes were shaping their lives and futures. The meeting also served as a forum to explore issues related to one important subset of Africa's young population—young intellectuals and publicly engaged researchers. Young Africa-based scholars spoke about the difficulties of knowledge production and research (including knowledge about young people even less privileged than themselves), citing challenges that ranged from lack of library books to classes interrupted by civil war. A lively debate emerged not only about what African youth are seeking, but also about the ways in which globalization was affecting their needs, aspirations, and capacities.

At the suggestion of Jean Comaroff (a member of the RAP who helped design the agenda of the symposium and was a key participant in it), Venkatesh was invited to the symposium to be a comparative voice because he had worked on the plight of African-American communities in U.S. inner cities and young people's varied responses. His engagements with African social scientists centered on the similarities and differences of marginalized youth in developed and developing countries, as well as the global economic, political, and cultural interconnections that were part of the marginalizing processes and the responses of youth to them.[1] Sitting on a bench outside the high-end Waterfront Mall in Cape Town (also, and ironically, where the ferry boats leave for tours to Robben Island, former "home" to many apartheid-era political prisoners, including Nelson Mandela), we started imagining a project in which scholars working on different sets of young people around the world (including those in Africa and the United States, but also beyond) would collaboratively take on the intersection of globalization and youth.

Planning meetings in New York and London allowed us to narrow down our interests into (at least relatively) more manageable social sites, processes, and institutions for which globalization has high stakes for young people and that required interdisciplinary and cross-regional partnership and debate. The law, legal institutions, and the governance structures and strategies devised for and by young people became a key arena that met these criteria for reasons we elaborate in the first chapter of this book.

The chapters in this volume represent much of the work generated by the social scientists and legal scholars who were subsequently invited to participate in a working group on Youth, Globalization, and the Law mobilized by Kassimir at the SSRC with Venkatesh as its chair. The group met twice—once in Paris (at Columbia University's Reid Hall), and once in New York—to present and critique papers while discussing the broader questions of how their interests intersected. All participants were working on connections between two of our three key terms of youth, globalization, and law. For the purposes of this project, we asked each to turn his or her dyad (e.g., youth and the law) into a triad, considering how the third term not explicit in his or her research agenda (e.g., globalization) affected or inflected how one might think about the dyad both analytically and practically.

Importantly, both the Cape Town symposium and the activities and meetings of the working group were supported by grants to the SSRC from the Johann Jacobs Foundation. The foundation, based in Zurich, Switzerland, is a key supporter on innovative research and practice in the youth field and is open both to the need for comparative and transnational conversations and to unconventional approaches. We are grateful for its support and for the substantive suggestions of its staff and board.

We are also grateful for the participation of others whose work is not represented in this volume, but who took part in the activities of the working group: Klaus Boehnke, Philippe Bourgois, John Comaroff, Mamadou Diouf, John Hagan, Alcinda Honwana, Barbara Ibrahim, Eric Klinenberg, Patricia Marquez, Magaly Sanchez, and Geraldine van Bueren. The talented and intrepid freelance journalist Sasha Abramsky was an especially important contributor to the project as a whole. Encouraged by the Jacobs Foundation to find ways to get some of the issues and research results of the project to broader audiences, we asked Abramsky to take part in the working group and collaborate with some of its members, including visiting them at their research sites in different places around the world. The results were a series of magazine articles and op-ed pieces that brought the issues of youth, globalization, and the law to a wider public. Abramsky's expertise on young people's experiences in the prison system, and the effects of that system on democracy, was influential to many of the other participants in this project.[2]

Many thanks are owed to several program assistants at the SSRC who worked long and hard on the logistics and complex networking required for this project and publication: Funmi Vogt, Ada Umezurike, and Sion Dayson. At Columbia University, Alexandra Murphy worked long hours to steer the manuscript toward completion while also co-authoring a chapter in this book with Venkatesh. Eva Rosen provided invaluable help in the final stages of editing. Columbia's Institute for Social and Economic Policy Research graciously co-hosted the project in its formative stages, and we thank Peter Bearman and his staff for supporting the initiative with kindness and manpower. And the Columbia University Institute for Scholars at Reid Hall provided key support for the project—in the form of a fellowship to Venkatesh and resources for an early convening of contributors. We extend our gratitude to Dr. Danielle Haase-Dubosc and Dr. Mihaela Bacou. Stanford University Press editor Kate Wahl has been a great resource for improving the book's content and structure, and her colleagues at the Press have been extremely helpful and patient. Last, thanks are due, of course, to all the contributors to the volume, who put up with the editors' entreaties and quirks with rapid response and good humor.

We were finalizing the volume in the fall of 2005 when the riots occurred among marginalized migrant youth in Paris and elsewhere in France. In an immediate sense, the riots were sparked by the death of two young people rumored to have been fleeing the police. But they had clearly been structured by a generation or more of a lethal combination of neglect, containment, and harassment. Sadly, it drove home the point that the authors in the volume (two of whom present case studies on migrant youth in Paris) have hit upon something important—that there is a real need to address how young people's lives are shaped by the intersection of local circumstance and global flows and forces. From migration patterns to international economic shifts that constrain local labor markets (and perhaps, reinforce their segmentation), from the circulation of policing strategies, the regulation of public space, and juvenile justice laws to the idioms and actions related to youth protest and violence around the globe, the knowledge provided and the analyses offered here are relevant to understanding the sources of disaffection for youth (which will certainly look different in different places) and the resources young people draw on in shaping their futures or expressing their concerns about their lack of one.

SUDHIR ALLADI VENKATESH

RON KASSIMIR

NEW YORK CITY, APRIL 2006

ENDNOTES

1. A book edited by Alcinda Honwana and Filip de Boeck that draws on work presented at the Cape Town symposium was recently published as *Makers and Breakers: Children and Youth in Postcolonial Africa*, Oxford: James Currey, 2005.

2. See, for example, his latest book, *Conned: How Millions Went to Prison, Lost the Vote, and Helped Send George W. Bush to the White House*, New York: New Press, 2006.

I

Youth, Globalization, and the Law:
Overviews

1

Youth and Legal Institutions: Thinking Globally and Comparatively

SUDHIR ALLADI VENKATESH

AND RONALD KASSIMIR

PROLOGUE

On a wet December morning in Bobigny, a suburb of Paris, a group of youth stand around a corner café, sipping espresso, sharing cigarettes, and discussing the aftermath of *l'émote*, their term for the autumn 2005 events that engrossed France and much of the world for nearly a month. There are only a few signs left of the disturbances in their immediate neighborhood. From the café, one can see a nearby school that has been set on fire and that is being repaired; the destroyed cars—also set on fire—have been removed, leaving only eerie black scars on the pavement. But the traces are enough to remind, and so the conversation turns back around to those two weeks, when the world was gripped by young Frenchmen—some immigrant, some native-born—who took to the streets in frustration and release.[1]

These particular young Frenchmen are impatient. "Is there anything that has changed?" they ask rhetorically. "It's 11 AM," another one instructs. "Come back at 3 PM, I'll still be here. No work, you see. Nothing. Only for the French." The last statement is particularly curious because these young men are of Algerian background, but they are all born and raised in France. Indeed, from their clothes, musical tastes, sport, and passions, one cannot discern an immigrant's guise. But they share a feeling of being stuck in *les banlieues*, those swaths of land tracts on the outskirts of French cities most notable for

3

their high-rise public housing developments and their entrenched poverty. (See the chapters in this volume by Bonelli and Terrio for rich detail and analysis of life for young people in these districts and their encounters with the police and justice system.)

Like the emotions and fires that spread quickly to fuel civil unrest and rebellion in the city suburbs—in Paris and beyond, discussions of their socioeconomic opportunities move abruptly and unforgivingly to the subject of their civic status. "Am I French?" one asks rhetorically, pointing to his clothes and then his skin. "I was born here! When will I count [as French]?!" For them, economic mobility, civic engagement, and the capacity to be a citizen are not separate; the conversation quickly and forcefully turns to the subject of French citizenship as they discuss the revolts. The opportunities to move into adulthood, provide for family and household, and realize dreams and aspirations seem blocked at every turn by the past and the present, by the branches of ethnicity, colonialism, and nationhood. The young man tugs at his olive skin, as if it is a prison from which he cannot escape while also a source of pride and meaning. Smiling, he turns and says, "Until we figure out who is French, the rest is bullshit."

These young French youth, and millions of others like them throughout Europe's urban centers, are part of a new wave of global citizens. Their ethnicity has no multicultural resting place, no melting pot ideal that promises an eventual embrace in the nation (we can, of course, debate whether, in practice in countries such as the United States, this cloak actually facilitates assimilation). They live in a Bantustan-like urban region set off socially and politically from the wider nation, but they also live in their skin, which places them closer to their country of origin than the heart of the city they inhabit. Finding a meaningful job in Paris, Brussels, Berlin, and so on, may be geographically proximate, but it is remote in its likelihood.

The conflagrations that swept French cities—and that were rumored to have reached other parts of metropolitan Europe—were French in character, but they had perceptible regional and global dimensions. French *banlieues* are comprised of families, the majority of whom have arrived recently from, or trace their background to, North and West Africa—that is, from countries such as Senegal and Morocco that have had historic and historically troubled connections with France. These are also neighborhoods that are impoverished, where families face exclusion from the social mainstream and yet simultaneously are publicly portrayed and viewed as taking advantage of the social welfare arm of the French state.

The immediate events said to have precipitated the riots were, from one perspective, identifiably "local" in character. In response to the death of two youngsters outside Paris at the hands of the police, in a context in which many youths daily encounter police harassment, youths took to the streets, burning police cars, vandalizing schools, and destroying public property—that is, they targeted the symbols of the State.

Yet the extra-local aspects of this are all too clear, not least because of the transnational character of the migrants, whether they are French citizens or not. The conflagration spread widely across French cities, a feat that is popularly believed to have been facilitated by communication advances such as cell phones and the Internet—used by a population that other French view as not quite "modern." And, of course, for those who lived a few miles away or in other parts of the world, the revolts were broadcast by a global media industry that spread highly engrossing, often provocative images of brown and black bodies intent on destroying everything in their path. What these large media conglomerates rarely conveyed were the challenges for youth (and their families and communities) seeking to find a place and a voice in a society imbricated within global economic structures that increasingly shape long-term employment prospects in France, as they do elsewhere.

Not least, *l'émote* reveals the comparative and global dimensions of the law enforcement and governance of marginalized young populations across the world, especially although not exclusively in urban and peri-urban settings. Issues of relationships of these populations to the police and justice systems are not new, but models of policing and of juvenile justice are both changing in more punitive directions and spreading through old and new transnational institutions, networks, and media. At the same time, other global institutions, networks, and media promote ideas and instruments for supporting the rights of young people in unprecedented ways.

Our volume engages this dynamic. In doing so, it intends to bring fresh reflection on the structural aspects of marginalized youth's pathways, their deferred aspirations, that are occasionally revealed in rebellion—whether these outbursts take the form of protest, delinquency, or violent revolt. We also call attention to those daily interactions that take place in less dramatic institutional arenas—such as the courts, schools, social service facilities, churches, and public spaces—where a wide range of actors work in less noticed ways to shape youth, and sometimes help them make successful transitions to adulthood.

INTRODUCTION

This volume addresses the impact of globalization on young people by focusing on a critical but poorly understood dimension of global social processes: the role of legal institutions and discourses as they shape the life experiences of young people. The legal arena is a central sphere in which youths integrate into the social fabric and through which their possibilities for meaningful transitions to adulthood, active civic engagement, and self-expression arise. The use of the law as a vehicle to deal with youth integration has been a longstanding challenge in advanced industrialized nations.[2] And, in developing and post-colonial societies, it is via new constitutions and national legislation that questions about the rights of young people are taken up.[3] In these nation-building projects, the interests of young people are framed by drawing on local traditions and notions of universal rights and ideas of citizenship.

In recent years, this arena has been re-aligned as ideas and practices about justice, rights, and maintaining order travel the globe. The contemporary promotion and transmission of zero tolerance and redistributive justice programs across international boundaries, the near ubiquitous acceptance of United Nations Convention on the Rights of the Child, and the transnational migration of street gangs between industrialized and developing countries are some of the most prominent examples of socio-legal practices that reach across societies, cultures, and states. Although these global legal phenomena are typically based in the work of courts, police, and prison systems, they also directly involve international aid and advocacy organizations (that support practice and implementation), media actors (who disseminate information, create knowledge, and shape public opinion), and other institutions that have daily impact on young people's lives—families, schools, political organizations, and so on.

The global structures and flows that dominated the front pages of newspapers during the Paris riots, the youthfulness of the faces on the television screens, while always locally inflected, are consequential for young people in cities throughout the world. This includes the American ghetto, where highly localized social phenomena are part of wider systemic processes (see chapter 5 by Venkatesh and Murphy in this book). Among other things, the riots made it impossible to avoid United States–Europe comparisons on issues of socio-economic exclusion, cultural difference, security, and the life chances of young people. Numerous European inner cities face challenges long associated with the United States, including entrenched urban poverty, inadequate integration of ethnic minorities into the labor force, and the fragile legitimacy of their respective criminal justice institutions.

Yet the similarities among and the connections across the Atlantic do not erase or make meaningless the distinctiveness of each locality in terms of their cultural, political, and historical landscapes—a point that recent research on global processes has made quite evident, and that complicates any simplistic notions of homogenization.[4] Indeed, a central contribution of the chapters in this book is to provide an analysis of local patterns, to show that local specificities are not rendered entirely derivative or epi-phenomenal by virtue of their placement in encompassing social structures.[5] Whatever utility remains in framing key social questions under the rubric of "globalization," calling attention to the structuring role of external influences (whether they enable or constrain local ideas and action) need not replicate the hubris of past systemic/functionalist analyses in which the spirit and curiosity of life lived locally is reduced to the dictates of institutional logics operating here, there, and everywhere. What the authors in this volume emphasize are the overlaps, interminglings, and clashes of such logics in ways that matter for how young people are governed and protected.

The relationship between governing and protecting, between controlling and enabling the lives of the young is the central focus on this book. And it is here where globalization, as it affects youth, "happens" via legal discourses and institutions. Although the antecedents are clear, the 1990s accelerated two trends related to youth and the law, clearly in tension if not outright contradiction. At national levels, we have seen a punitive turn in juvenile justice and the treatment of young people in public space. So-called success stories and the ideologies behind them (e.g., the "broken windows" approach to policing) have been part of neoliberal trends in the global political economy. These trends include the ways in which urban security issues have become central to city governments starved for investment, and a general breakdown in social welfare policies within which juvenile justice issues have been embedded. John Muncie's chapter articulates this broad trend while rightly calling attention to local differences as well as to how older welfare approaches and more recent criminalizing ones can be juxtaposed within national legal and governance regimes.

At the same time as these criminalizing approaches have increased, the 1990s also witnessed an explosion of new legal instruments, discourses, and organizations around the rights of children and young people. Emanating out from the Convention on the Rights of the Child that took shape within the international space of the United Nations, the protection—even the empowerment—of young people through legal means has been one of the more powerful sites for rights talk and rights mobilization.[6] The chapters in the final section of the book address these developments, including the limits of law-based strategies to achieve the goals of protection and empowerment.

It is this moment, one in which the pushes and pulls of criminalizing youth and of enabling them are juxtaposed, that we attempt to capture in the book. It is intended to call attention to those social structures commonly identified with an interconnected world and, at the same time, to open up the possibilities for locally based research and analysis of the world's young people. Although the contributions vary in the degree to which they directly engage debates on globalization, as a whole we do argue that global social dynamics, in the form of background context or analytic constructs, must be incorporated into social analysis.

GLOBAL PROCESSES, INSTITUTIONAL SITES, EVERYDAY PRACTICES

Globalization and *youth* are overused terms that have taken on multiple connotations. Both have entered popular and academic discourse with ferocity and, in part as a result of their speedy integration into numerous fields of study, have lost much of their specificity. For example, two decades ago, in different circles, one might have found a working consensus on the conceptual reference point of globalization, whether this was viewed as an advanced stage of capitalism, the integration of financial and currency markets, supranational institutions threatening the jurisdiction of the nation state, or the exchange of aesthetic ideas and the rise of artistic collaborations across regions, states, and continents. Groups of scholars at least had a basis upon which to move forward with research and analysis—even if their own conceptualizations differed from one another. By the late 1990s, the pervasive and often inconsistent use of the term *globalization* has watered down its meaning, although there still appears widespread interest in analyzing the consequences of social life organized at larger and multiple scales.[7]

The world's youth are now associated with global movements and institutions, although they are alternatively portrayed as both the prime movers of globalization and its victims: activists coordinating their political projects around the world; suicide bombers taking their own lives in the service of a cause; underpaid laborers at the behest of multinational corporations; hackers disrupting national security systems with technological viruses; musicians and artists exchanging verse and image via the Internet; and armed children carrying weapons instead of text books. These are some of the popular and youthful faces of globalization.[8]

Although young people are at the heart of discourses on globalization, youth remains a complex social category that, depending on context, can signal chronological age, social status, political disposition, or relationship to family and community. Demographers use the term to identify a chronological period (typically 16–24 years of age). The stability of this definition may be seen in comparative research, cross-national surveys, and the many reports by the UN and other actors that monitor such patterns as shifting government expenditures and rates of educational achievement.[9] But this stable definition butts up against the work of anthropologists and historians who see "youth" as a contingent stage in life that depends ultimately on local context. What one community, society, or group sees as the beginning and end of "youth" may differ markedly, thereby rendering universal comparative demographic categories an imposition. And, outside of the academy, radical and revolutionary social movements from South Africa to the U.S. inner city have incorporated "youth" as part of their rallying cry. Many have deployed the category to challenge nation-state projects that, in a self-congratulatory way, ask young people to take responsibility, reproduce cultural values and social institutions, obey the law, and buy into the social contract, while at the same time failing to provide for their material needs.[10]

It may be worthwhile, provisionally, to understand *global dynamics* as projects and initiatives that are characterized by one or more of the following: the integration of financial and currency markets; the use of technology to overcome spatial and temporal barriers; the increasing interdependence of countries in a way that formal modern political designations such as the *nation-state* are reconstituted; and the movement of bodies, ideas, and cultural objects across bounded spaces (cities, regions, countries, etc.). But these definitional debates are not of principal concern here. It is the changing life experiences of young people that is the main focus of the book, particularly as they are being re-made by ideas of legal jurisprudence and institutions of policing and social order maintenance that operate across conventional spatial and temporal borders.

As indicated, there is no shortage of research on globalization—including volumes questioning the utility of the term itself and the present moment's uniqueness as a "global era." And there has been an upswing in interest in youth. Comparative demographers produce studies of educational attainment, youth employment, and public health outcomes; sociologists focus on migration patterns and remittances and so-called second-generation experiences of young people growing up outside the country of their parent's birthplace. There are equally illuminating anthropological discussions of youth expression,[11] including analyses of how young people make culture by sharing ideas and symbols across borders and the use of the Internet as a vehicle through which to collaborate artistically and politically.[12] And, in the fields of international relations and the sociology of global culture, there is a rich tradition of studying nongovernmental actors whose embrace of "universal rights" (e.g., human rights organizations), access to education (e.g., the United Nations), and development (e.g., the World Bank) effectively spread Western ideas and resources to the world's children—this includes case studies that show such dissemination as neither without contestation or resistance.[13] Scholars working on social justice issues have discussed the pervasive use of "law-and-order" techniques—such as "zero tolerance"—and the proliferation of "redistributive justice" social movements around the globe, both of which have realigned youth experience and the transition to adulthood and full citizenship. In other words, reflecting the current organization of academic fields, sociologists and demographers are pointing to broad comparative patterns, anthropologists are inquiring into cultural production and discursive practice in concrete settings,[14] and so on. The research on globalization or youth rarely communicates across fields. This volume reflects a common desire of participants to work beyond their disciplinary boundaries.

The discussions leading up to this volume identified the "middle range" of institutions as a critical and often overlooked approach to understanding global processes. With notable exceptions,[15] there is a tendency to study global social dynamics in highly local settings—that is, in the beliefs, ideas, and practices of people in concrete social contexts, or as they emerge in their broadest possible dimensions. From a macro perspective, economists debate the benefits of worldwide markets, some faithful to the emancipatory potential of free markets while others decry growing inequality across first and third world divides.[16] Sociologists and political scientists, at an equally broad level, critique neoliberal governance strategies, theorize the realignment of the nation-state, and examine the policies of the World Bank and the International Monetary Fund that have an impact on poverty on a global scale.[17]

From a micro perspective, social scientists illuminate the experiences of everyday people whose lives are disrupted by global forces, musicians who use the Internet to sample from diverse cultures,[18] street gangs that communicate across nations and continents,[19] and migrants who seek work in socially isolated urban ghettos and who construct their lives in two countries simultaneously.[20] Such studies are typically smaller in scale and focus on lived experience. Global dynamics such as neoliberal policies, immigration laws, and technological innovations permitting new forms of communication and resource exchange appear as context-setting factors, but the focus is on local practice.

Although the chapters in this volume engage both micro and macro levels, we highlight what lies between global structures and everyday experience: the basic institutions that organize the lives of young people, whether these are in the government, civic, or private sectors. We call attention equally to the responses of youth in and to these institutional contexts. The criminalization of youth around the world and the spread of zero tolerance as a replacement for welfare-oriented juvenile justice intervention, the interplay of multiple legal

orders—for example, secular, religious, customary, and universal—that ultimately shape normative development and transition to adulthood, the politically contested allocation of rights to young people by governments, and the
transmission of normative and juridical ideas and policies across time and
space—all these point us to the constitutive role of basic social institutions,
such as courts, media, police, schools, and the family. These institutions often
work across boundaries and borders; they are ubiquitous across societies even
if their organization frames and meanings vary widely.[21] What are seen as the
abstract workings of global dynamics are often projects that must be carried
out by concrete organizational and collective actors. The essays in this volume
bring the strengths of institutional-level analysis to the existing debates in
youth and globalization research.

Each of the chapters inquires into legal institutions and discourses that
involve young people, that shape and mediate global processes in particular settings and the responses to them. The contributors share a commitment to a
perspective that permits a study of key legal and governance institutions
that—in the context of legal structures and processes—transmit ideas, seek to
control subjects such as migrants and juveniles, carry out projects based on
notions of "universal rights," and police youth who move across national borders. All too often, globalization can appear as a "black box,"—that is, as
something that magically happens rather than a set of ideas and projects that
must be carried out with force and organized action. The essays in this volume
open up this black box by focusing on actors in real institutionalized contexts
and spaces—families, courts, prisons, gangs, public spaces, and so on.

OVERVIEW OF THE BOOK

Essays in this volume offer case studies and in-depth analyses of the impact
of globalization and institutions on young people in particular national,
regional, or local settings. The use of concrete cases, rooted in legal structures
and processes, is meant to provide the beginnings of a better empirical base
with which to analyze global structures and processes. By drawing on everyday social practices and concrete institutional forms and sites, they add clarity to our current understanding of the ways in which institutions in differ-

ent parts of the world can affect youth in one particular locale. The essays span North America, Central and South America, Europe, Australia, and Africa. The settings are diverse and include courts and prisons, inner-city streets, international human rights initiatives, shopping malls, local youth organizations, and the United Nations. Each situates the daily lives of young people within wider perspectives that engage the relationship of local and global structures, refining approaches to social phenomena that are both "here and there." Across these diverse settings, the focus is firmly on institutionalized practices within legal settings and frameworks. One of the goals of this volume is to connect cultural, institutional, and social structural features of young people's lives in concrete ways. We throw light on the institutions, actors, and social relations that make global processes possible and consequential for young people.

Examining global phenomena through legal settings enables the authors to frame the study of global/local dynamics as active social processes in which youth are central participants, not simply passive players. The chapters in this volume direct the reader to look both at the changing social structures in which young people live and the ways in which the youth themselves shape, challenge, and transform those structures through movement, representation, and protest. In this manner, the volume's contributions include both deeper understanding of critical substantive issues and creative methodological implications for addressing them.

The essays are divided into four parts. The subsequent parts of the book (parts II, III, and IV) are led off by brief introductions describing the issues that each chapter in that section addresses. Part I includes this introductory essay and a chapter by John Muncie on the complex and partial convergence of criminal justice policies and practices in advanced industrialized countries. The following three parts build on this overview. Part II (chapters by Elana Zilberg, Laurent Bonelli, and Sudhir Alladi Venkatesh and Alexandra Murphy) examines problems of criminalization and governance in urban centers, specifically San Salvador (and its nexus with Los Angeles), Paris, and U.S. ghettoes. Where the essays in this part examine policing specifically, the third part looks more broadly at problems of urban governance and efforts to manage particular youth populations (in chapters by Susan Terrio, Brenda Coughlin, and Rob White). Each author examines key institutional arenas—the streets and other public spaces (White on Australia), the courts (Terrio on France), and jails and prisons (Coughlin on the United States)—in which the voices, behaviors, and lives of young people are shaped and where they encounter a range of actors seeking to control, represent, or incarcerate them. The fourth and final part examines some of the challenges—legal, political, and cultural— embedded in efforts to enable and "empower" young people through legal and rights-based strategies (with the chapter by Elizabeth Herger Boyle, Trina Smith, and Katja Guenther on global perspective; the chapter by John Guidry on Brazil; and the chapter by Annie Bunting and Sally Engle Merry on Nigeria).

More than other social groups, youth evokes the hopes and challenges of a society. This volume offers unprecedented insight into the dramatic ways in which global structures and processes are reorganizing young people's lives in the twenty-first century. It sharpens and makes intelligible our understanding of the much-discussed era of globalization by drawing attention to a central place where aspirations become translated into daily practice—the law. Through empirically grounded and theoretically informed examinations of legal institutions and discourses, we are able to better grasp both the opportunities and challenges that societies around the world face when life for their young people is never lived only locally.

ENDNOTES

1. One of us (Venkatesh) conducted field research in Paris shortly after the riots in 2005. Among many accounts see the Web Forum "Riots in France" published by the Social Science Research Council at http://riotsfrance.ssrc.org/.

2. See Issac Balbus 1973. *The Dialectics of Legal Repression.* New York: Russell Sage.

3. See John Comaroff and Jean Comaroff 2004. "Policing Culture, Cultural Policing: Law and Social Order in Postcolonial South Africa," *Law & Social Inquiry* 29 (3): 513–545.

4. See John Muncie 2005. "The Globalization of Crime Control—the Case of Youth and Juvenile Justice: Neo-liberalism, Policy Convergence and International Conventions," *Theoretical Criminology* 9 (1): 35–64.

5. For examples from sub-Saharan Africa, the part of the world in some ways buffeted most directly by global forces, see Thomas Callaghy, Ronald Kassimir, and Robert Latham (eds.) 2001. *Intervention and Transnationalism in Africa: Global-Local Networks of Power.* Cambridge: Cambridge University Press.

6. An issue first raised in Sharon Stephens (ed.) 1995. *Children and the Politics of Culture.* Princeton: Princeton University Press. On rights talk, see Mahmood Mamdani (ed.) 2000. *Beyond Rights Talk and Culture Talk: Comparative Essays on the Politics of Rights and Culture.* London: Palgrave MacMillan. On rights activism and mobilization, see Margaret E. Keck and Kathryn Sikkink 1998. *Activists Beyond Borders: Advocacy Networks in International Politics.* Ithaca, NY: Cornell University Press.

7. See Ulrich Beck 2000. *What Is Globalization?* Cambridge, MA: Polity Press; Christopher Chase-Dunn 1999. "Globalization: A World Systems Perspective," *Journal of World Systems Research* 5(2): 187–215; and Andre Gunder Frank and Barry Gills (eds.) 1993. *The World System: Five Hundred Years or Five Thousand?* London: Routledge.

8. For recent examples from contemporary Africa, see Alcinda Honwana and Filip de Boeck (eds.) 2005. *Makers and Breakers: Children and Youth in Postcolonial Africa.* Oxford: James Currey.

9. See, for example, Cynthia Lloyd (ed.) 2005. *Growing Up Global: The Changing Transitions to Adulthood in Developing Countries.* Washington, DC: National Academies Press; and B. Bradford Brown, Reed W. Larson, and T. S. Saraswathi (eds.) 2002. *The World's Youth: Adolescence in Eight Regions of the Globe.* Cambridge: Cambridge University Press.

10. See John Comaroff and Jean Comaroff, op. cit.

11. For recent examples see Honwana and De Boeck (eds.), op. cit.; Sunaina Maira and Elisabeth Soep (eds.) 2004. *Youthscapes: The Popular, the National, the Global.* Philadelphia: University of Pennsylvania Press; and Hilary Pilkington et al. 2002. *Looking West? Cultural Globalization and Russian Youth Cultures.* University Park: Pennsylvania State University Press.

12. Seyed Masoud Mousavi Shafaee 2003. "Globalization and Contradiction between the Nation and the State in Iran: the Internet Case," *Critique: Critical Middle Eastern Studies,* 12 (2): 189–195.

13. See especially Boyle, Smith, and Guenther's chapter in this volume. Also see Elizabeth Heger Boyle, Forunata Songora, and Gail Foss 2001. "International Discourse and Local Politics: Anti-Female-Genital-Cutting Laws in Egypt, Tanzania, and the United States," *Social Problems* 48 (4): 524–544; John Boli and George M. Thomas (eds.) 1999. *Constructing Global Culture: International Nongovernmental Organizations Since 1975.* Stanford: Stanford University Press; Sue Ruddick 2003. "The Politics of Aging: Globalization and the Restructuring of Youth and Childhood," *Antipode* 35 (2); and Jens Qvortrup 1993. "Nine Theses about Childhood as a Social Phenomenon," in Jens Qvortrup (ed.) *Childhood as a Social Phenomenon.* Eurosocial Report 47. Vienna: European Centre.

14. See Arjun Appadurai 2000. "Spectral Housing and Urban Cleansing: Notes on Millenial Mumbai," *Public Culture* 12 (3): 627–651.

15. Neil Fligstein has argued for the need to take institutions seriously by linking abstract social processes with concrete developments in real historical contexts. See, for example, Neil Fligstein 1998. "Is Globalization the Cause of the Crises of Welfare States?" EUI Working Paper No. 98/5. San Domenico, Italy: European University Institute. Also, Fligstein 1996. "Markets as Politics: A Political-Cultural Approach to Market Institutions," *American Sociological Review* 61:656–673.

16. Meric S. Gertler 1996. "Between the Local and the Global: The Spatial Limits to Productive Capital," in Kevin R. Cox (ed.) *The Spaces of Globalization*. New York: Guilford.

17. David Held 1996. *Democracy and the Global Order: From the Modern State to Cosmopolitan Governance*. Stanford: Stanford University Press; David Woodward 1998. "Globalization, Uneven Development and Poverty." United Nations Development Program, Social Development and Poverty Elimination Division. Poverty Working Papers.

18. See Arun Saldanha, May 2002. "Music, Space, Identity: Geographies of Youth Culture in Bangalore," *Cultural Studies* 16 (3): 337–350.

19. See, especially, the chapter in this volume by Elana Zilberg and, for a general overview, John M. Hagedorn 2005. "The Global Impact of Gangs," *Journal of Contemporary Criminal Justice* 21 (2): 153–169.

20. Rob Smith 1997. "Transnational Migration, Assimilation, and Political Community," in Margaret Crahan and Alberto Vourvoulias-Bush (eds.). *The City and the World*. New York: Council on Foreign Relations.

21. See, for example, Boaventura de Sousa Santos and César A. Rodríguez-Garavito (eds.) 2005. *Law and Globalization from Below: Towards a Cosmopolitan Legality*. Cambridge: Cambridge University Press; and Michael Likosky (ed.) 2002. *Transnational Legal Processes: Globalisation and Power Disparities*. London: Butterworths.

2

Youth Justice and the Governance of Young People: Global, International, National, and Local Contexts

JOHN MUNCIE

THE PROBLEM OF GLOBALISATION

The concept of globalisation suggests that shifts in political economy, particularly those associated with international trade and capital mobility, are severely constraining the range of strategic political strategies and policy options that individual states can pursue (Bauman, 1998; Beck, 2000). *Globalisation* implies two inter-related transformations of particular interest to those studying the intersections of youth and the criminal law. First, criminal justice policies are converging worldwide—particularly across the Anglophone global north. The need to attract international capital compels governments to adopt similar economic, social, and criminal justice policies. Second, this homogenisation of policies, it is contended, is underpinned by a fundamental shift in the relations between the state and the market. A loss (or at least a major reconfiguration) of 'the social' is evidenced in the processes whereby neo-liberal conceptions of the 'free market' driven by multi-national corporations encourage the formulation of policies based less on principles of welfare protection and social inclusion and more on social inequality, deregulation, privatisation, penal expansionism, and welfare residualism. The privileged position of the nation and the state as the primary reference point for studying youth, law, and criminal justice policy appears increasingly subjugated to transnational configurations.

In effect, globalisation presages not only the decline of social democratic reformist politics and projects worldwide but also a widening gap between the rich and poor both within and between countries (Mishra, 1999). Such developments are likely to have a major impact on child and youth populations. It is these populations that have traditionally constituted 'the most intensively governed sector of personal existence' (Rose, 1989, p. 121); they have also endured disproportionate levels of poverty, disempowerment, vulnerability, and victimisation. Any decline in the ability of nation-states to deliver protective welfarism will have major repercussions for the state of childhood and youth.

This chapter assesses the pertinence of such issues to understanding global, international, national, and local shifts in contemporary juvenile and youth justice policy and practice. Globalisation poses some thorny questions for such an analysis. Policymaking in this area has traditionally been studied with regard to national sovereignty and the independence of the nation-state. Indeed, criminal justice remains a powerful icon of sovereign statehood and can be considered one of the last vestiges of state power that elsewhere is being eroded. Although economies are widely perceived as increasingly global, social and political institutions remain largely local or regional. As a result, the power of globalisation as an analytical concept appears both seductive and flawed. It is seductive because it seems to offer some valuable means through which sense can be made of some widely recognised shifts in juvenile policy, such as the dismantling of welfare statism and a resurgence in authoritarian responses to juvenile offending. It is flawed because it encourages the tendency to deliver reductionist and economistic readings of policy convergence.

The argument that youth justice has become a standardised global product can be sustained only at the very highest level of generality. First, globalisation is not one-dimensional. Economic globalism speaks of the import, largely United States inspired, of neo-liberal conceptions of community responsibilisation backed by an authoritarian state. However, legal globalism, largely UN inspired, unveils a contrary vision of universal human rights delivered through social democracies. Globalisation simultaneously conjures up images of both the usurpation and protection of children's rights. Second, the idea that global capital is hegemonic and capable of transforming all that it touches is both essentialist and determinist. Relying on a model of Anglo-American convergence blinds any analysis to the differentiated and differentiating impact of the global. As Clarke (2000) has argued, its effect is neither uniform nor consistent. The diversity of reform trajectories warns against any attempt to imply homogeneity. What is required in unraveling the importance of the global is a level of analysis that neither elevates nor negates globalisation but recognises that the global is realised only in specific localities, through which it will inevitably be reworked, challenged, and contested. The key issue to be addressed is how globalisation is activating diversity, not only how it is producing uniformity. The dialectic between local specificities and transnational mobilities underpins the theoretical approach adopted in this chapter.

The chapter begins by outlining three persuasive arguments—based on readings of neo-liberal governance, policy transfer, and international legal conventions—that do indeed suggest a growing homogeneity and universalism in juvenile and youth justice policy. Individual nation states are undoubtedly being challenged by such global processes. But analysis at the level of the nation-state also reveals marked diversity rather than convergence. Juvenile justice remains excessively localised through national enclaves of difference. Further, regional governments, federated states, international cities, and multiple forms of community governance all suggest alternative visions of statehood and citizenship and offer alternative routes of access to decision making on social and economic issues.

There also appear to be discrete and distinctive ways in which the neo-liberal modes of governance find expression in conservative and social democratic *rationalities* and in authoritarian, retributive human rights, or restorative *technologies*. For example, the anti-welfare neo-liberalism of the United States would seem to have little in common with other 'neo-liberal' countries such as Canada, New Zealand, Australia, and most of Western Europe (O'Malley, 2002). Globalising forces may straddle (part of) the world but also have to manifest themselves at the national and local levels, at all of which they may be subject to multiple translations or oppositions. As Robertson (1995) tried to capture in the notion of the 'glocal', global neo-liberal pressures are always mediated and can be realised only through national and local identities and sensibilities. Globalisation can only ever be one among many drivers of criminal justice and social policy, and then its influence may simultaneously pull and push in diverse ways. Above all, the global/national/local are not exclusive entities: the key issue is how they are experienced differently in different spaces and at different times. For Yeates (2002), a mutually transforming relationship among global and local processes prefigures *plurality* as a driving context for policy implementation. Youth justice reform cannot be simply reduced to global economic transformations or to universal legal treaties. All such processes are mediated by distinctive national and sub-national cultures and socio-cultural norms when they are activated on the ground.

To test these propositions, the chapter concludes by providing a more detailed immersion in the culturally *specific* national, regional, and local politics of reform. A comparison of England and Wales with Scotland reveals that the processes of convergence and transfer may not be as singular and one dimensional as might be first assumed.

GLOBALISATION 1: FROM WELFARE TO NEO-LIBERAL GOVERNANCE

It has been widely observed that, since the 1960s, penal welfarism has been undermined by the development of forms of neo-liberal or 'advanced' governance (Bell, 1993; Rose, 1996a, b; Rose, 2000; Garland, 1996). This fundamental change in criminal and youth justice has been broadly characterised as placing less emphasis on the social contexts of crime and measures of state protection and more on prescriptions of individual/family/community responsibility and accountability. The shift has been captured in the notion of 'governing at a distance'. Welfarism has been increasingly critiqued for encouraging welfare-dependent citizens, overloading the responsibilities of the state, and undermining the ability of individuals to take responsibility for their own actions. 'Old' notions of *social* engineering, *social* benefits, *social* work, and *social* welfare, it is claimed, have been transformed to create responsible and autonomous citizens (O'Malley, 2001). A 'loss of the social' thesis suggests a number of inter-related—sometimes contradictory—criminal justice processes that have occurred to varying degrees across neo-conservative and social democratic neo-liberal states. These include

- the privatising of the state sector and the commodifying of crime control;
- the widening of material inequalities between and within states, creating new insecurities and fuelling demands for centralised authoritarian law-and-order strategies;

- the devolving of responsibility for government to individuals, families, and communities (as captured in the notion of the 'the active citizen'); and

- the espousing of scientific realism and pragmatic 'what works' responses to crime and disorder in the hope that an image of an 'orderly environment' can be secured that, in turn, will help to attract 'nomadic capital'.

As global capital becomes apparently out of national control, the state reasserts its authority by creating new sets of 'criminal others' and then attempting to provide protection from such 'threatening and undesirable outsiders'. The 'asylum seeker', the 'dangerous foreigner', the 'welfare dependent', the 'work-shy', and the 'disrespectful', for example, have been typically constructed as prime targets for sustained punitive intervention. The state sets out to re-stabilise through coercion those very social relations that have been destabilised (or have been made possible) through collusion with globalised free market economics. 'Meeting needs' is subjugated to 'addressing fears'.

Numerous authors have remarked upon the impact that these processes have had in a growing homogenisation of criminal justice across Western societies, driven in particular by the spread of punitive penal policies from the United States (see, for example, Wacquant, 1999; Garland, 2001). These processes have had a marked impact on how young people are conceptualised—as vulnerable or as a threat—and on how they should be governed—through welfare-based modes of governance or various 'justice'-based responsibilisation and managerial strategies. Muncie and Hughes (2002) have identified six recurring and inter-related themes.

Diminution of welfare. The principle that children and young people should be protected from the full weight of the 'adult' criminal jurisdiction underpins the concept of welfare in youth justice, and has long been established in international conventions and in most Western jurisdictions. The 1960s and 1970s marked the high-water mark of welfare, but towards the end of the 1970s, and into the 1980s, the welfarist priorities of youth justice attracted critique on three principal fronts: First, conservative critics argued that the primary function of the youth justice system should be to *control* young offenders rather than to *care* for them. The concept of welfare was thus regarded as evidence that the youth justice system had become too lenient and 'soft on crime'. Second, academic commentators and radical youth justice practitioners questioned the legitimacy of imposing wide-ranging interventions on the basis of 'need', and challenged individualised notions of 'rehabilitation' and 'treatment'. They argued that channelling ostensibly 'welfare' interventions through a youth justice system often did more harm than good. Third, the same academics and radical practitioners, together with rights advocates and legal professionals, also argued that wide-ranging discretionary judgements in respect of 'welfare' undermined the child's *right* to 'justice'. Young people, particularly young women and girls, were considered in double jeopardy, sentenced for their 'vulnerability' and background as well as for their offence (Goldson, 2004; Muncie, 2004b).

In the wake of these criticisms a new justice-based model of corrections emerged. Its leading proponent, Von Hirsch (1976), proposed proportionality of punishment to fit the crime; determinacy of sentencing; equity and protection of rights through due process; and an end to judicial, professional, and administrative discretion be reinstated at the centre of youth and criminal justice practice. The idea of punishing the crime, not the person, had clear attractions for those seeking an end to the abuses of discretional power. Indeed the impact of this 'back to justice' model was reflected in juvenile/youth justice reform in many Western jurisdictions at the time. A focus on 'deeds' rather than 'needs' formally expunged many of the last vestiges of welfarism from many youth justice systems.

Adulteration. Such critiques of welfare, however, also coalesced with the concerns of traditional retributivists that criminals should get their 'just deserts'. Within the political climate of the 1980s a discourse of 'justice and rights' was appropriated as one of 'individual responsibility and obligation'. Accordingly, Hudson (1987) has argued that the 'just deserts' or 'back to justice' movements that emerged in many Western jurisdictions in the 1980s was evidence of a modern retributivism rather than necessarily heralding the emergence of new liberal regimes and a positive rights agenda. An adulteration of youth justice has witnessed widespread dismantling of special court procedures which had been in place for much of the twentieth century to protect young people from the stigma and formality of adult justice (Fionda, 1998; Grisso and Schwartz, 2000; Schaffner, 2002). The emphasis has become one of fighting juvenile crime rather than securing juvenile justice. This adulteration has been most marked in the United States. Since the 1980s (but beginning in Florida in 1978), most U.S. states have expanded the charges for which juvenile defendants can be tried as adults in criminal courts, lowered the age at which this can be done, changed the purpose of their juvenile codes to prioritise punishment, and resorted to more punitive training and boot camps. Accordingly, the numbers of under-18-year-olds committed to adult prisons in the United States has more than doubled since 1985, with nearly 60 per cent being of African-American origin (*CNN News*, 28 February 2000). Since 1997, four countries—the United States, Iran, Pakistan, and the Democratic Republic of Congo—have executed individuals for crimes committed before they were 18. But the use of the death penalty for juveniles committing offences when under the age of 18 is in worldwide decline because of the express provisions of the UN Convention of the Rights of the Child (see below). The five juvenile executions between 2001 and 2003 all occurred in the United States, notably in Texas, Alabama, Louisiana, and Florida (Streib, 2003). The practice was abolished only in March 2005 when the U.S. Supreme Court ruled, by a slim majority, that execution constituted a 'cruel and unusual punishment'.

The risk factor paradigm. In place of traditional attempts to isolate specific causes of crime has emerged a risk factor and crime prevention paradigm that focusses attention on the *potential* for harm, disorder, and misbehaviour (rather than crime itself). These risk factors are widely claimed to include hyperactivity, large families, poor parental supervision, low achievement, and family disharmony (Farrington, 1996). Moreover, it has been argued that these risks have a strong transatlantic replicability (Farrington, 2000). Certainly an obsession with identifying, assessing, and managing 'risk' is central to youth justice practice not only in England and the United States but also in Australia (Cunneen and White, 2006) and Canada (Smandych, 2006). Risk profiling is an imprecise science, however. Its predictive value is in doubt. *Risk* is increasingly presented as a factual reality rather than as a complex construction mediated through interpretative judgements of what is considered to be the norms of acceptable behaviour. Bio-social and psycho-social theories of risk decontextualise and depoliticise; they perpetuate a series of all-too-familiar moral judgements on the propensity of the poor to commit crime (Muncie, 2004b). Nevertheless, the paradigm has been eagerly grasped by Western governments to legitimate a wide range of pre-emptive early-intervention strategies designed to identify 'anti-social' behaviour (as established by risk profiling) and to 'nip offending in the bud'. In such legislation as England's Crime and Disorder Act of 1998 and Canada's Youth Criminal Justice Act of 2002 there is an amalgam of restorative, community, and custodial measures based on psychological risk profiling and risk management. In the process, new criminal subjects and deviant 'others' have been produced. Invariably those considered most at risk are precisely those marginalised and socially excluded (street children, the disadvantaged, the impoverished, migrant children, the destitute, and so on) who critics of neo-liberalism would claim are the first 'victims' of a widening income gap between rich and poor.

Responsibilisation. Garland (1996, p. 452) refers to a *responsibilisation strategy* involving 'central government seeking to act upon crime not in a direct fashion through state agencies (police, courts, prisons, social work, etc.) but instead by acting indirectly, seeking to activate action on the part of non-state agencies and organisations'. The clear message is that crime prevention cannot be left to the police alone but involves entire communities, from property owners and manufacturers to school authorities, families, and individuals. Each has a responsibility to reduce criminal opportunities and increase informal controls. Rose and Miller (1992) reasoned that this was not a simple case of state abrogation or of privatisation of public issues, but of a new mode of 'governing at a distance'. The state may issue directives, but responsibility for their enactment is passed down to local bodies and communities. In this climate, notions of communitarianism, 'joined up' partnerships, Communities that Care (CtC), community justice, community policing, community safety, and multi agency collaboration have proliferated, particularly in the United Kingdom, New Zealand, Australia, Canada, and the United States (Hughes and Edwards, 2002). The globalising appeal of zero tolerance policing strategies also ensures that youth crime and disorder is increasingly politicised and has come to dominate concerns about quality of life, urban renewal, and social policy in general. Social problems are defined in terms of their criminogenic potential, and criminal justice systems are taking over some of the roles that were previously undertaken by welfare and child protection agencies (Crawford, 2002).

Actuarial justice. Juvenile or youth justice has become progressively more disengaged from philosophies of welfare and justice in favour of improving internal system coherence through evidence-led policy, standardised risk assessments, technologies of actuarial justice, and the implementation of managerial performance targets. Rehabilitation and due process have been replaced by the rather less transformative rationales of processing complaints and applying punishments in an efficient and cost-effective manner. Indicators that measure 'outputs' rather than 'outcomes' have begun to take on a life of their own, so that the meeting of targets has become an end in itself (Feeley and Simon, 1992; Garland, 1996; Kempf-Leonard and Peterson, 2000).

Penal expansionism. Prison populations have been growing in many countries since the 1980s. Of the 205 countries surveyed by Walmsley (2003), 68 per cent recorded increases since the mid 1990s. An increasingly internationalised alliance of private industrial and penal interests has emerged that has a vested interest in penal expansion (Christie, 2000). This is most notable in prison-building programmes and in the technological apparatus of crime control, such as CCTV and electronic monitoring. Certain groups—particularly immigrants—are identified as a threatening and permanently excluded underclass about which little can be done but to neutralise and segregate them in 'gulags of incapacitation', a process Wacquant (2001) has referred to as the neo-liberal 'penalisation of poverty'. Vengeance and cruelty are no longer an anathema to many parts of criminal justice (Simon, 2001). Politics and culture have become saturated with images of moral breakdown, incivility, and the decline of the family (Garland, 2001). A loosely knit set of policy networks and think tanks has constructed a 'neo-liberal penal policy complex' that encourages the dissemination of punitive and exclusionary practices (Newburn, 2002).

Collectively these processes suggest an acceleration of the governance of young people through the motifs of 'crime and disorder' (Simon, 1997) in which an obsession with regulation—whether the regulation occurs through families, schools, or training programmes—encourages a generalised mistrust and fear of young people. These broad trends, recognisable in many Western juvenile and youth justice systems in the twenty-first century, lie at the heart of a neo-liberal version of the globalisation thesis.

GLOBALISATION 2: POLICY TRANSFER AND CONVERGENCE

Policy transfer can be considered as one of the pivotal mechanisms driving globalisation (Wacquant, 1999; Christie, 2000; Garland, 2001; Jones and Newburn, 2002). It has become more and more common for nation-states to look worldwide in efforts to discover 'what works' in preventing crime and to reduce re-offending. The talk then is of an emerging global youth justice (Muncie, 2005). Much of this analysis relies on tracing the export of penal policies from the United States to other advanced industrial economies. Certainly, many aspects of U.S. penal reform such as zero tolerance policing (Argentina, Australia, Brazil, England, France, Germany, Ireland), curfews (Belgium, England, France, Scotland), electronic monitoring (Australia, Canada, England, Holland, Scotland, Singapore, Sweden), mandatory sentencing (Australia; Northern Territories, Western Australia), and pre-trial detention as a 'short, sharp, shock' (France, Germany, Holland) have surfaced in many Western jurisdictions, either as rhetorical devices or as drivers of policy (Dolowitz, 2000; Dolowitz and Marsh, 2000; Garland, 2001; Newburn, 2002).

Such an argument of a United States–led global convergence appears compelling. However, as Sparks (2001, p.165) has warned, there may be inherent difficulties with this type of comparative analysis because of the 'distracting sway of the American case as a pole of attraction'. Indeed it is also clear that youth justice worldwide has been informed by potentially contra penal trajectories such as those derived from the import of restorative justice conferencing pioneered in New Zealand and Australia. Critics of United States–inspired neo-liberal globalisation would then point out the countervailing tendencies at work in numerous youth justice systems across the world.

Within restorative justice, the talk is less of formal crime control and more of informal offender/victim participation and harm minimisation. Advocates of restorative justice look to traditional forms of dispute resolution reputedly to be found in the informal customary practices of Maori, Aboriginal, and Native American indigenous populations. The prominence of faith-based ideas and communitarianism is also much in evidence. According to its proponents, restorative justice holds the potential of restoring the 'deliberative control of justice by citizens' and 'harmony based on a feeling that justice has been done' (Braithwaite, 2003, p. 57). These proponents have come to find practical expression in various forms of conferencing in Australasia, in healing circles in Canada, and in community peace committees in South Africa. Both the United Nations and the Council of Europe have given restorative justice their firm backing. The Council of Europe has recommended to all jurisdictions that mediation should be made generally available, that it should cover all stages of the criminal justice process, and, most significantly, that it should be autonomous to formal means of judicial processing. The European Forum for Victim-Offender Mediation and Restorative Justice was established in 2000. Across Africa, Stern (2001) records renewed interest in solidarity, reconciliation, and restoration as the guiding principles for resolving disputes rather than the colonial prison. The Child Justice Bill first considered by the South African government in 2002 is particularly influenced by a recognition of children's rights coupled with application of the ideals of restorative justice (Skelton, 2002; van Zyl Smit and van der Spuy, 2004). In 2002 the UN's Economic and Social Council formulated some basic universal principles of restorative justice, including non-coercive offender and victim participation, confidentiality, and procedural safeguards. It is clear that restorative justice is no longer marginal but instead has become a burgeoning worldwide industry, with local projects proliferating across much of Africa, Australasia, Canada, Europe, and the United States. The transfer of policy is clearly not one directional or one dimensional (Karstedt, 2001). Moreover, in contrast to neo-liberal repenalisation strategies, restorative justice retains the potential to offer a series of replacement discourses of 'social harm', 'social conflict', and 'redress' (De Haan, 1990; Walgrave, 1995). It opens a door to the development of a restorative *social* justice based on community building, solidarity, and empowerment (White, 2000; 2002). Nevertheless, it is probably no coincidence that restorative justice and neo-liberal ideologies have emerged simultaneously. Both proclaim an end to state monopoly and a revival of community responsibilisation.

The notion of homogenised policy transfer has also been critiqued by those concerned not only with issues of structural convergence and divergence but also with the role of 'agency' in the formulation and implementation of specific policies (Jones and Newburn, 2002; Nellis, 2000). Detailed empirical examinations of policymaking in different countries reveal important differences in substance and significant differences in the processes through which policy is reformed and implemented. Both O'Donnell and O'Sullivan (2003) and

Jones and Newburn (2002), for example, argue that the concept of zero tolerance associated with New York policing reforms in the early 1990s barely survived its import to Ireland and the United Kingdom. The strategies adopted by the NYPD were employed only by some minor experiments in mainstream British policing. Its impact has been more on the level of political rhetoric, fuelled by Fianna Fail in Ireland and by cross-party commitments in the United Kingdom to develop more punitive-sounding policies that can be widely perceived as being 'tough on crime'. Similarly, Nellis's (2000) analysis of the transatlantic transfer of electronic monitoring from the United States to England in particular (but also to Singapore, some Australian states, the Netherlands, and Sweden) makes clear that the terms 'inspiration' and 'emulation' rather than 'copying' best describe the processes involved.

These lines of enquiry suggest that policy transfer is rarely direct and complete but is partial and mediated through national and local cultures, which are themselves changing at the same time (Muncie, 2004a). The logic of assuming that we can learn 'what works' from others is certainly seductive. It implies rational planning and an uncontroversial reliance on a crime science that is free of any political interference. But it also assumes that policies can be transported and are transportable without cognisance of localised cultures, conditions, and the politics of space.

Policy transfer and international dialogue will probably become a more dominant aspect of juvenile and youth justice if only because of the possibilities opened up by the growth in international telecommunications. But at a nation-state level and at regional and local levels things may look a bit different. Individual states continue jealously to guard their own sovereignty and control over crime control and punishment. Local implementation of key reforms may also reveal a continuing adherence to some traditional values and a resistance to change (see below).

GLOBALISATION 3: INTERNATIONAL CONVENTIONS

The 1989 United Nations Convention on the Rights of the Child has established a near-global consensus that all children have a right to *protection*, to *participation*, and to basic material *provision*. It upholds children's right to life, to be free from discrimination, to be protected in armed conflicts, to be protected from degrading and cruel punishment, to receive special treatment in justice systems; and it grants freedom from discrimination, exploitation, and abuse. The only countries not to have ratified this convention are Somalia and the United States. Somalia has had no internationally recognised government since 1991, whilst the United States has claimed that this convention would undermine parental authority (Krisberg, 2006). The convention builds upon the 1985 UN Standard Minimum Rules for the Administration of Youth Justice (the Beijing Rules), which recognised the 'special needs of children' and the importance of dealing with offenders flexibly. It promoted diversion from formal court procedures and non-custodial disposals, and insisted that custody should be a last resort and for minimum periods. In addition, the Beijing Rules emphasised the need for anonymity in order to protect children from life-long stigma and labelling.

The convention cemented these themes in the fundamental right that, in all legal actions concerning those under the age of 18, the 'best interests of the child shall be a primary consideration' (Article 3.1). Further it reasserts the need to treat children differently from adults, to promote their dignity and worth with minimum use of custody, and recommends that children should participate in any proceedings relating to them (Article 12). In 1990 the UN Guidelines for the Prevention of Juvenile Delinquency (the Riyadh Guidelines) added that youth justice policy should avoid criminalising children for their minor misdemeanors. The International Covenant on Civil and Political Rights expressly outlaws capital punishment for those under 18 and promotes rehabilitative interventions. The European Convention on Human Rights, first formulated in 1953, provides for the due process of law, fairness in trial proceedings, a right to education, and a right to privacy, and declares that any deprivation of liberty (including curfews, electronic monitoring, and community supervision) should not be arbitrary or consist of any degrading treatment. Collectively these conventions and rules can be viewed as tantamount to a growing legal globalisation of juvenile justice.

Many countries have now used the UN Convention to improve protections for children and have appointed special commissioners or ombudspersons to champion children's rights. Of note has been a raft of legal reforms in Latin America during the 1990s associated with a renewed recognition of a distinctive Latin American affirmation of human rights. Venezuela and Argentina, for example, were key advocates in the formulation of the UN Convention (Carozza, 2003). A monitoring body—the UN Committee on the Rights of the Child—reports under the convention and presses governments for reform. Yet Human Rights Watch (1999) has noted that implementation has often been half-hearted and piecemeal. The convention is persuasive, but breach attracts no formal sanction. Millions of children worldwide continue to live in poverty, have no access to education, and are routinely employed in armed conflicts. Street children on every continent continue to endure harassment and physical abuse from the police, and many others work long hours in hazardous conditions in flagrant violation of the rights guaranteed to them under the UN Convention. Countries give lip service to rights simply to be granted status as a 'modern developed state' and acceptance into world monetary systems. The pressure to ratify is both moral and economic (Harris-Short, 2003). The UN Convention on the Rights of the Child may be the most ratified of all international human rights directives, but it is also the most violated. Abramson's (2000) analysis of UN observations on the implementation of juvenile justice in 141 countries notes a widespread lack of 'sympathetic understanding' necessary for compliance with the UN Convention. Describing these obligations as being largely received as 'unwanted', he notes that in many countries, torture; inhumane treatment; lack of separation from adults when incarcerated; police brutality; bad conditions in detention facilities; overcrowding; lack of rehabilitation; failure to develop alternatives to incarceration; inadequate contact between minors and their families; lack of training of judges, police, and prison authorities; lack of speedy trial; no legal assistance; disproportionate sentences; insufficient respect for the rule of law; and improper use of the juvenile justice system to tackle other social problems are rife. In addition, there is a notable lack of reliable statistics or documentation as to who is in jail and where they are.

Thirty-three countries continue to accompany their ratification with reservations. For example, Canada and the United Kingdom have issued reservations to the requirement to separate children from adults in detention. In the English case this is because of an inability to fund suitable places for young women. Many Islamic nations have filed reservations when the Convention appears to be incompatible with Islamic law and domestic legislation (Schabas, 1996). The United Kingdom has also reserved its option to deploy children in active military combat. It is the only country in Europe that extensively targets children under 18 for recruitment into the armed forces. Similarly, those jurisdictions that have introduced schemes to enforce parental responsibility, curfews, and anti-social behaviour legislation (most notably in England and Wales, France, and the United States), would again appear to be in contempt of the right to respect for private and family life and protection from arbitrary interference (Freeman, 2002). More seriously, many of the principles of restorative justice that rely on informality, flexibility, and discretion sit uneasily against legal requirements for due process and a fair and just trial.

In many countries it seems abundantly clear that it is possible to claim an adherence to the principle of universal rights whilst simultaneously pursuing policies that exacerbate structural inequalities and punitive institutional regimes. 'Cultural difference' and the absence of localised human rights cultures preclude meaningful adoption of international agreements (Harris-Short, 2003). The United States case is indicative. Violations of the UN Convention appear built in to aspects of U.S. law that allow for prosecution in adult courts and that fail to specify a minimum age of criminal responsibility (Amnesty, 1998). Moreover, relying on international statements of due process and procedural safeguards can do little to deliver justice on the ground. The development of positive rights agendas remains limited (Scraton and Haydon, 2002). Equally important is a growing recognition that securing universal children's rights depends as much (if not more) on grassroots initiatives as on 'agreements' between nation-states as epitomised by the UN Convention (Veerman and Levine, 2000). Little attention has been given to the extent to which legal globalisation itself is a concept driven by Western notions of 'civilised' human rights. Far from opening up challenges to neo-liberalism, rights agendas may simply act to bolster Western notions of individuality and freedom whilst implicitly perpetuating imperial and postcolonial notions of a barbaric and authoritarian 'global east' or 'global south'. It is indicative in itself that, of those countries where the UN Committee has identified 'tradition' and 'culture' as impeding implementation, the vast majority are 'non-Western' (Muncie, 2005).

COMPARATIVE YOUTH JUSTICE IN WESTERN SOCIETIES: NATIONAL SOVEREIGNTY AND CULTURAL DIVERSITY

Although there is a growing literature on comparative criminal justice, sentencing trends, and penal practices (see, for example, Council of Europe, 2000; Tonry and Frase, 2001; Pakes, 2004), there remain relatively few rigorous comparative analyses of youth justice that go further than describing the powers and procedures of particular jurisdictions (see, for example, Bala et al., 2002; Winterdyk, 2002; Tonry and Doob, 2004). In many respects this is not surprising. Doing comparative research is fraught with difficulties (Nelken, 1994, 2002). The classification and recording of crime differ among countries, and different countries have developed different judicial systems for defining and dealing with young offenders. What is classified as *penal custody* in one country may not be in others, though regimes may be similar. As has been noted elsewhere (Muncie, 2005), not all countries collect the same data on the same age groups and populations. None seem to do so within the same time periods. Linguistic differences in how the terms *minor, juvenile, child,* and *young person* are defined and operationalised further hinder any attempt to ensure a sound comparative base. However, even a cursory look at some of the most basic statistical data highlights national diversity rather than global similarity.

In itself, it is significant that, in most jurisdictions, the term *juvenile justice* is preferred to that of *youth justice*, whilst the UN advocates the formulation of a *child-centred criminal justice*. Ages of criminal responsibility differ markedly around the world. In the European Union these range from 8 in Scotland and 10 in England and Wales to 15 in Denmark, Finland, Norway, and Sweden and 18 in Belgium and Luxembourg. Shifting assumptions about responsibility and capacity, though, place these categories in some flux. Notable in England and Wales has been the abolition of *doli incapax* (the presumption of innocence for 10–14-year-olds) despite recurring complaints from the UN. In contrast, Ireland raised its age of criminal responsibility from 7 to 12 in its Children Act 2001, although it has yet to implement this change fully. Interestingly, too, most Central and Eastern European countries have relatively high ages of responsibility (most in accord with Russia's 16), but at least six (Estonia, Latvia, Macedonia, Moldova, Poland, Ukraine) are currently considering whether to lower this to 14 or below (Asquith, 1996). Significantly, this is exactly what occurred in Japan in 2000 (Fenwick, 2006). Similarly Canada's 2002 youth justice reforms are based on the core principle that the protection of society be uppermost. As such, the age at which the youth court is empowered to impose adult sentences has also been lowered from 16 to 14 (Smandych, 2006).

The push for 'adult justice' is, however, far from uniform. Belgium and Scotland stand out as examples where the primacy of the welfare principle remains the fundamental rationale for youth justice. In Belgium, all judicial interventions are legitimated through an educative and protective, rather than punitive and responsibilising, discourse (Put and Walgrave, 2006). Whilst in practice some welfare measures are backed by coercive powers, it remains impossible to impose legal penalties on those under age 16 (though this may be about to change through a growing emphasis on offender accountability). Equally, it is not always fully acknowledged that Scotland abolished the juvenile court in 1968 and has been operating with a welfare tribunal for the majority of offenders under the age of 16 for the past 30 years. This process has not been without its critics, not least because of the lack of legal safeguards and the apparent tendency for the adult courts to deal with those aged 16 and over with undue severity. Scotland continues to have a high percentage of its prison population dedicated to those under the age of 21. Nevertheless, the hearing system continues to ensure that child welfare considerations hold a pivotal position for younger offenders and provides a credible alternative to the punitive nature of juvenile or youth justice pursued in many other jurisdictions (McAra and Young, 1997; Whyte, 2000; Bottoms, 2002; and see below).

Restorative justice processes in New Zealand and in most Australian states are now established in statute as the fundamental rationale for youth justice. Their aim is to keep young people out of formal court processes through various types of family group conferences. Most academic and policy entrepreneur research speaks highly of such an approach in its impact both on re-offending and on ensuring that the victim as well as the offender are the *key* participants and decision-makers in determining any future action (Morris and Maxwell, 2001; Miers, 2001; Gelsthorpe and Morris, 2002). In Australasia, professional decision-making and formal court processing appear marginal to an extent not contemplated in most other Western systems, with the notable exception of Scotland. Much of this, again, is probably due to an *alliance* between neo-liberalism and social democratic politics, which produces a political willingness to hang on to vestiges of social welfarism (O'Malley, 2002).

We should be wary of thinking that restorative justice is some general panacea, however. Australian research, for example, has suggested that for indigenous populations such 'justice' may lead to a double failure: failing to be law abiding and failing to act appropriately according to an indigenous justice script rewritten by whites (Blagg, 1997; Bradley et al., 2006). South African and U.K. research has noted that whatever the communitarian ideals promoted through restoration, they generally have to work through pre-existing objectives of crime control (Skelton, 2002; Gelsthorpe and Morris, 2002). Restoration thus becomes an addition rather than an alternative. In general, the danger remains that any form of compulsory restoration may degenerate into a ceremony of public shaming and degradation, particularly when it operates within systems of justice that are driven by punitive, exclusionary, and coercive values and the primary intent of which is the infliction of further harm (as seems to be the case in most contemporary Western jurisdictions). Restoration also tends merely to reinforce notions of individual responsibility rather than to promote notions of *social* justice or *social* restoration (White, 2000, 2002).

In contrast to whatever progressive potential is sought in restorative justice, over the past decade many Western countries have reported a distinct hardening of attitudes and criminal justice responses to young offenders. Driven in particular by fears of immigration and perceptions of a 'new tidal wave of juvenile violent crime', certain groups have increasingly been identified as a threatening and permanently excluded underclass about which little can be done other than seeking their neutralisation and segregation. International research has, however, consistently found that there is no correlation between crime rates and custody rates (Council of Europe, 2000).

According to Council of Europe (2003) statistics, England and Wales, Germany, Greece, Holland, and Portugal have all reported significant increases in their daily counts of the numbers of under-18-year-olds in prison between 1995 and 2000. There has been a dramatic reversal in Dutch penal policy since the mid 1980s. Once heralded as a beacon of tolerance and humanity (Downes, 1988), Holland embarked on a substantial prison-building programme linked to a tendency to expand pre-trial detention and to deliver longer sentences on conviction (Pakes, 2000). In 2002 Dutch city councils gave the police new powers to stop and search arbitrarily, without reasonable suspicion, in designated areas of 'security risk'. The practice has amounted to the criminalisation of poor and black neighbourhoods, targeting in particular Moroccan youth (*Statewatch*, Jan–Feb, 2003, p. 8).

In Germany, the average number of over-14-year-olds in prison increased by 21 per cent during the 1990s (Suhling, 2003). In Ireland, prison building and expansion has been a notable feature of the 1990s despite falling crime rates (O'Donnell and O'Sullivan, 2003). These shifts appear, in part, to be driven by neo-liberal market reform, welfare residualism, fears of illegal migrants, changes in the labour market, and a related lowering of tolerance for crime and violence. Fear and insecurity fuel demand for a 'norm enforcing system' that is both retributive and interventionist (Junger-Tas, 2002). In France, the right-wing government of Alain Juppe from 1993 to 1997 reversed its traditional, *Bonnemaison* social crime prevention policy based on conceptions of *solidarity* (King, 1988; Pitts, 1995, 1997, 2001), instead prioritising a police-led zero tolerance and *disciplinary* approach. This is a policy that was continued by the left-wing Jospin government. The socio-economic conditions that produce youth marginalisation and estrangement are no longer given central political or academic attention (Bailleau, 1998). Rather, concern is directed to migrant children—particularly those from Africa, Asia, and Eastern Europe—who have arrived in search of political asylum and economic opportunity. Special surveillance units have been established to repress delinquency in 'sensitive neighbourhoods', penalties for recidivism have been increased, and the deportation of foreigners speeded up (Wacquant, 2001). Since the return to power of the right in 2002 in France, a new public safety law has expanded police powers of search, seizure, and arrest; instituted prison sentences for public order offences (such as being disrespectful to those in authority); lowered from 16 to 13 the age at which young offenders can be imprisoned; and introduced benefit sanctions for parents of offending children (Henley, 2002).

Such analyses clearly resonate with those who claim that the twenty-first century is witnessing a renewed *criminalisation of the undesirable and the unfortunate* coupled with the expansion of interventionist and authoritarian policies. But, although many countries may have added punitive elements to their legislation in the 1990s, repenalisation of youth offending (such as that witnessed in the United States and in England and Wales) is far from universal. A philosophy of child protection continues to hold sway, though it is increasingly tested by new discourses of responsibility. The irony is that, during the last decade, youth crime rates worldwide have generally been falling or at least remained stable.

There is, then, a quite remarkable worldwide divergence in the recourse to youth custody. The UN Survey on the Operation of Criminal Justice Systems (2002) is the only data set to provide worldwide rates of imprisonment for those under 18 years old per 100,000 of population. These statistics show the highest incarceration rates, of 38.40 per 100,000, to be in the United States; rates are 28.85 per 100,000 in South Africa and 18.26 per 100,000 in England and Wales, compared with 0.11 in Denmark, 0.07 in Norway, and 0.02 in Belgium (see Figure 2.1). (Many states, such as Australia and Canada, have no entry in the figure presumably because they either do not collect such data or declined to respond to the UN's survey).

Snapshots of European population *stocks*, derived from data held by the *World Prison Brief* (International Centre for Prison Studies, Kings College, London, 2003) and the *Penological Information Bulletin* (Council of Europe, 2002), also reveal wide disparities of the numbers in prison at specified dates. So, for example, on 1 September 2002, the following total child incarceration figures were recorded:

- 2754 in England and Wales,
- 843 in Germany (March 2001),
- 688 in France,
- 183 in Scotland,
- 114 in Austria,
- 105 in Belgium,
- 101 in the Netherlands,
- 17 in Finland,
- 13 in Norway, and
- 12 in Denmark.

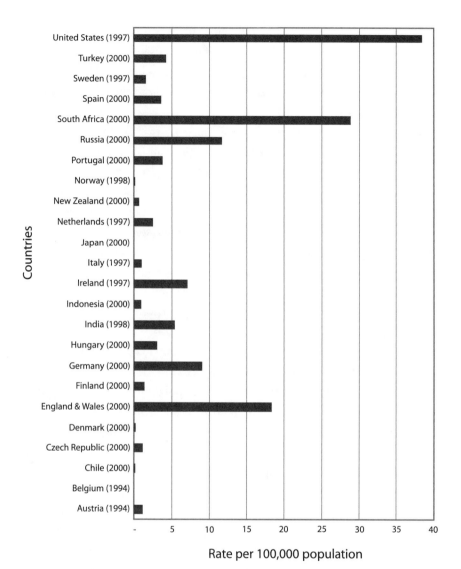

Figure 2.1. Total convicted juveniles admitted to prison: selected countries, 1994, 1997, 1998, 2000.

SOURCE: Data derived from the Seventh United Nations Survey of Crime Trends and Operations of Criminal Justice Systems (United Nations, 2002).

All such statistical data come with the usual warnings that differences in what counts as *prison* and in offender classification, as well as often haphazard modes of national data collection, preclude any absolute comparative reliability. Nevertheless, these data remain our best guide to the relative punitive climate of particular countries.

The same Council of Europe data set suggests that Spain, Italy, and the Czech Republic have witnessed *decreases* in their daily count of youth incarceration between 1995 and 2000. Canada has also reported significant decreases since the implementation of its 2002 Act because of the wider availability of community alternatives, though it has decreased from a very high base figure. (Canada, reputedly, had one of the highest rates of youth imprisonment in the world, exceeding even that of the United States.) Japan, Belgium, Finland, Norway, and Sweden stand out as countries that seem to be able to keep youth imprisonment to an absolute minimum and that have been able to maintain such a policy of miminum imprisonment throughout the 1990s.

Finland made an explicit decision some 40 years ago to abandon its Soviet-style tradition of punitive criminal justice in favour of decarceration and diversion. As a result, the young-offender prison population has been reduced by 90 per cent since 1960. There has been no associated rise in known offending. This was achieved through a long-term programme of applying suspended imprisonment for a majority of offenders on the condition that a period of probation was successfully completed. Immediate 'unconditional' sentencing into custody is now a rarity. Prison home leave, early release, and family visits are commonplace. There are no specific juvenile courts, but 15- to 21-year-olds are imprisoned only for the most exceptional reasons, and the voluntary acceptance of mediation is used as grounds for the waiving of sentence (Lappi-Seppala, 1998, 2001). The Norwegian criminologist, Nils Christie, has argued that this dramatic shift has been made possible by a conscious effort on the part of successive Finnish governments to formulate a national identity closer to that of other Scandinavian states. Finland's formulation that *good social development policy is the best criminal policy* has indeed been a remarkable success. It has shown that high incarceration rates and tough penal regimes do not control crime. They are unnecessary. Decarceration can be pursued without sacrificing public safety.

In Italy, judges have an additional power to grant a 'judicial pardon' that—together with a policy of *messa alla prova* (pre-trial probation) and a greater willingness to defer control to families—means that young people are incarcerated only for a very few serious violent offences; this may not, however, apply to non-nationals, particularly young Romanis (Nelken, 2006). Cultural difference is also a key factor. An Italian cultural tradition of soft paternal authoritarianism has been traditionally linked to low levels of penal repression. The 'cultural embeddedness' of Catholic paternalism (compared, for example, with American evangelical Protestantism) may not determine penal policy, but it does provide the parameters in which the purpose and meaning of punishment is differentially understood (Melossi, 2000).

Similarly, Japan's relative non-punitiveness has been accounted for in the context of a tradition of 'maternal protectionism' and a culture of 'amae sensitivity', which prioritises interdependence over individual accountability. The juvenile offender is deemed as much a victim as a criminal (Morita, 2002). Whether this approach can survive increases in 'heinous crimes' and moral panics over school indiscipline, *bosozoku* (high-risk car and motorcycle driving), and *enjo kosai* (teenage prostitution) is, however, open to question. Already Japan has witnessed a lowering of the age of criminal responsibility in 2000 (Fenwick, 2004, 2006).

LOCALISATION: COMPARING ENGLAND AND WALES WITH SCOTLAND

The 'catastrophic' images raised by some global neo-liberal readings of governance may help us to identify significant macro social changes, but these readings are less attuned to the simultaneous emergence of other competing transformational tendencies and to contradictions within neo-liberalism and the inherent instability of some of its strategies (Muncie and Hughes, 2002). Neo-liberalism not only has a global impact but also, under the rubric of 'governing at a distance', has encouraged the proliferation of 'local solutions' to local problems. To fully understand the workings and influences on youth justice we need to be aware of the twin and contradictory processes of *delocalisation* and *relocalisation* (Crawford, 2002). The risks and hazards of globalisation have simultaneously produced a 'retreat to the local' and nostalgia for tradition and community. For example, the local governance of crime and insecurity is evidenced in the prolific discourses of community safety in the United Kingdom and of urban security across Europe (Hughes, 2002). Both are informed by notions of community participation, proactive prevention, informalism, partnership, and multi-agency collaboration. Given that they are directed not only at crime but also at incivilities and antisocial behaviour, it is not surprising that their usual target is the (mis)behaviour of young people, particularly in 'high-risk' neighbourhoods. Yet what emerges from studies of the actual conduct of governance in particular localities is not uniformity, but diversity. In Australia and the United States there are wide divergences in custody rates from state to state. In many countries it is indeed difficult to prioritise national developments above widely divergent regional differences; this being most evident in sentencing disparities. Again, the possibility of identifying coherent and consistent patterns in (youth) governance is called into question (Hughes and Edwards, 2002).

Any basic comparative analysis cannot help but point up the atypicality and exceptional nature of England and Wales, particularly in a European context. It has come under constant criticism from the UN for its failure to raise the age of criminal responsibility. At 8 in Scotland and 10 in England, Wales, and Northern Ireland, these are the lowest ages in Europe. The UN's 2002 observations on the United Kingdom's implementation of the Convention of the Rights of the Child not only condemned such 'adulteration' but also expressed concern at the failure to incorporate the Convention into domestic legislation—specifically, the United Kingdom failed to ban corporal punishment in the home, failed to move against the current trend to incarcerate high and increasing numbers at earlier ages for lesser offences and for longer periods, showed a reluctance to provide children seeking refugee status with appropriate humanitarian assistance, and failed to reform custodial conditions that do not adequately protect children from violence, bullying, and self harm (Children's Rights Alliance, 2002).

There is no doubt that governmental responses to young people in England and Wales have become more punitive over the past decade. The notions of welfare protectionism that so dominated debates in the 1960s have been all but abandoned in favour of pre-emptive early intervention. Prior notions of universality and welfare for *all* children 'in need' have retreated into a context of classification, control, and correction, where interventions are targeted at the 'criminal', the 'near criminal', the 'possibly criminal', the 'sub-criminal', the 'anti-social', the 'disorderly' or the 'potentially problematic' in some way or another. An obsession with tackling the 'anti-social' has witnessed the expansion of police powers to remove under-16-year-olds from public places if the police 'believe' that a member of the public 'might be' 'intimidated, harassed, alarmed or distressed'. This expansion of powers also means that if two or more young people, together in a public place, fail to disperse under the instruction of a police officer, they commit a criminal offence and face the prospect of custodial detention. These powers constitute significant breaches of the UN Convention on the Rights of the Child, undermining in particular the 'best interests' principle. The numbers of children sentenced to youth custody have also almost doubled in a decade, from some 5,000 in 1993 to near 9,000 in 2002. This figure has risen to such an extent despite the fact that the recorded youth crime rate has been declining, not rising, over the period. Freeman (2002) notes that England has often adopted a half-hearted and piecemeal approach to the implementation of international directives. The UN Convention stipulates that children should be protected from custody whenever possible, and when deprived of liberty should be treated with humanity. In England a number of privately managed secure training centres for 12- to 14-year-olds have been built since 1998; there is growing evidence of inappropriate control techniques and attempted suicides in these centres. By equating 'disorder' with crime, the reach of youth justice has also been broadened to take in those below the age of criminal responsibility and the non-criminal as well as the known offender.

It is widely assumed that this punitiveness has been driven in no small measure by policy transfers from the United States. Wacquant (1999), for example, identifies how numerous American state agencies, think tanks, foundations, policy advisors, commercial enterprises, policy entrepreneurs, and academics have worked in tandem with their English counterparts, such as the Adam Smith Institute and the Institute of Economic Affairs, to forge a law-and-order consensus. In the early days of opposition, Labour persistently challenged and condemned the Conservatives' overt transatlantic policy transfers in both social and criminal justice matters. The left-of-centre preferred to look to Europe. However, after Blair's visit to the United States in 1993, which presaged the new doctrine of 'being tough on crime and tough on the causes of crime', New Labour also shifted its focus from Europe to the New Democratic policies of the United States. Since the mid 1990s, not only compulsory and conditional welfare-to-work (workfare) but also versions of zero tolerance policing, boot camps, night curfews, drug czars, electronic tagging, mandatory minimum sentences, the naming and shaming of young offenders, and strict controls over parents have all been transported to England, albeit reworked for local circumstances (Jones and Newburn, 2002).

None of this automatically applies to other parts of the United Kingdom. Although the United Kingdom is a unitary state, it contains three distinct legal jurisdictions with their own separate systems of policing and courts as well as a separate system of youth justice. In Scotland a different juvenile justice policy has been pursued since the early 1970s. The 1968 Social Work (Scotland) Act gave local authorities a general duty to promote social welfare for children in need, abolished juvenile courts, and established the children's hearing system (which came into operation in 1971). Its grounding in notions of social education appealed to a strong Scottish identification with educational processes (Whyte, 2000). Children's hearings are not a criminal court but a welfare tribunal serviced by lay people from the local community. These hearings deal with those deemed in need of care and protection as well as those involved in offending, on the grounds that their similarities far outweigh any differences (Lockyer and Stone, 1998). Cases are initially referred to a reporter from a range of bodies including education authorities, social work departments, the police, and procurators-fiscal.

When a case reaches a hearing it is deliberated upon by three lay members of a panel, the parents or guardians of the child, social work representatives, and the child himself or herself. Representation, but not necessarily legal representation, is encouraged. Victims are not present; thus strictly speaking, the process is not one of restoration. Legal aid is not available either, making the procedure at odds with the UN Convention on the Rights of the Child (Norrie, 1997). Safeguarders may be appointed but rarely are so. The hearing cannot proceed unless all parties understand *and* accept the grounds for referral. The hearing does not determine guilt or innocence (it can proceed only if guilt is admitted) and is solely concerned with deciding on future courses of action. Before reaching any decision, reports on the child from the social work department are heard, thus granting this agency a more pivotal role than it has in the English youth courts. In a review of the hearings' more positive features, Dickie (1979, p. 68) cites communication and collaboration between the relevant professions, flexibility in providing services appropriate to the child's changing needs, and a capacity to focus on the interests of the individual child with family participation as the most significant and distinctive.

A hearing has no powers to imprison or impose community penalties. Its powers are limited to one of three decisions: discharge, supervision order, or residential supervision order. However, whilst over 15,000 children are referred to a hearing each year, there are also a minority whose offences are considered so 'serious' that the hearing system is bypassed and the cases referred directly to the adult sheriff and High Court system. In 1995, 213 under-16-year-olds were charged in an adult criminal court; in 1997, 148 under-16-year-olds were so charged (Whyte, 2000). In this respect Scottish welfarism is reserved for less serious offences, and some routes into adult justice have remained unchallenged. Moreover, the hearings system deals only with those up to the age of 16. Whilst in Scotland there are almost no penal options for those under the age of 16, there remains a continuing presence of custodial institutions for older children whose regimes are far removed from the promotion of welfarism.

As in England, some of Scotland's most punitive systems still appear to be reserved for its young. Prior experience of the hearing system may lead to especially severe interventions in the adult system (Waterhouse et al., 2000). And welfarism always remains prey to shifts in the broader political climate. As McGhee et al. (1996, pp. 68–9) note, during the 1990s there was something of a shift from notions of a 'child's best interest' to that of 'public protection' and 'offender accountability' that is likely to pose a serious challenge to the philosophy behind the Children's Hearings System. Nevertheless, the Scottish hearing system is frequently evoked as a model for the reform of judicial-based systems, such as that in England and Wales. The Scottish system is said to have informed some of the aspects of restorative justice introduced to the English system in 2002 with the advent of referral orders and the establishment of youth offender panels to hear all first-time offenders.

Conversely, in 2003, Scotland—in an attempt to deal with a newly identified group of persistent offenders (but also one suspects from pressure to overcome the anomaly that Scotland is the only country in Europe to deal routinely with 16- and 17-year-olds in adult criminal courts)—decided to experiment with re-establishing youth courts for this particular age group (Audit Scotland, 2002; Scottish Executive, 2003). It has also introduced its own version of England's Anti-Social Behaviour Act. In addition, in 2003 plans were announced to give the hearings new powers to tag under-16-year-olds electronically and to force their parents to take responsibility for their offending. The Scottish communities minister clouded these authoritarian shifts in a welfarist discourse by claiming that 'we are not helping young people at all if we don't try to deal with their behaviour' (*Guardian*, 23 June 2003). As in England, Scotland too it seems is witnessing a dramatic repoliticisation of youth justice (McAra, 2006) (see Table 2.1).

Despite such convergence, the Scottish juvenile justice system continues to operate through an overtly welfare-oriented system. As such it remains distinct from the system not only of England and Wales but also those of most of Europe. Remarkably, the Scottish system has been able to maintain a degree of stability and consistency that is rarely evidenced elsewhere (Bottoms, 2002). There does, however, appear to be a growing disjuncture between the external political culture, which is becoming more punitive, and an internal institutional culture that remains resolutely welfarist (McAra, 2004).

Such comparisons underline the argument that, at a national level, some aspects of globalisation can be either reworked or ignored. At a sub-national and regional level the forces of globalisation can be further dissipated by the persistence of socially specific enclaves of difference. This dissipation is reflected in the wide disparities between courts in the custodial sentencing of young people. In England and Wales, these sentencings range from 1 custodial sentence for every 10 community sentences in the southwest to 1 in 5 in the West Midlands and the northwest. This dissipation is also reflected in the haphazard implementation of national legislation and youth justice standards in different localities (Holdaway et al., 2001). Indeed, Cross et al. (2003) have begun to find that divergence may also be growing between Wales and England. Following devolution, the Welsh Assembly decided to locate youth justice services in the portfolio of Health and Social Services rather than Crime Prevention, thus prioritising a 'children first' rather than an 'offender first' (as in England) philosophy.

There is also always a space to be exploited between written and imple-

Table 2.1 Comparing Scotland with England and Wales

Characteristic	Scotland	England and Wales
Philosophy	Welfare Need Offender	Retributive justice Just deserts Offence
Age of criminal responsiblity	8 years old	10 years old
Institutions	Children's Hearings (for under-16-year-olds); experimenting with youth courts for 16- and 17-year-olds	Youth Court (for under-18-year-olds)
Penal options	None Residential supervision	Secure training Prison
Compliance with UN Convention	16- and 17-year-olds treated as adults No legal representation Low age of responsibility	12-year-olds in custody Low age of responsibility Adult trials
Restoration	None (no victim involvement)	Youth Offender Panels (victim involvement)
Prevention	Targeting anti-social behaviour Curfews Zero tolerance policing	Targeting anti-social behaviour Punishing parents Curfews Zero tolerance policing Early intervention

mented policy. The translation of policy into practice depends on how it is visioned and reworked (or made to work) by those empowered to put it into practice. Whatever the rhetoric of government intention, the history of youth justice in England and Wales is also a history of active and passive resistance from pressure groups and from the magistracy, the police, and the youth justice workers through which such reform is to be effected. As a result, youth justice practice is likely to continue to be dominated by a complex of both rehabilitative 'needs' and responsibilised 'deeds' programmes. Joined up strategic co-operation will often coexist with sceptical and acrimonious relations at a practitioner level (Liddle and Gelsthorpe, 1994). A social work ethic of 'supporting young people' may well subvert any national and global neo-liberal pressure simply to responsibilise the young. This is also because many of the 'new' global, neo-liberal targets for intervention—inadequate parenting, low self esteem, poor social skills, poor cognitive skills—are remarkably similar to those targets identified by a welfare mode of governance. The incongruity between such latent welfarism and the retributive nature of penal expansionism may well create some space, even in such countries as England, in which the complex welfare needs of children in trouble can be re-expressed (Goldson, 2000). The renewed emphasis on local governance will usually open up spaces for resistance, re-interpretation, and avoidance. The cultural dynamics and institutional constraints of particular localities can empower or disempower key professions and enable external policy imperatives to be mediated or resisted (McAra, 2004). All of this affords a continuing centrality to local agencies and actors in the precise ways in which the global, the national, and the sub-national are activated on the ground (Stenson and Edwards, 2004).

CONCLUSION: RETHINKING GLOBALISATION

Global communication networks, the free flow of economic capital, the prevalence of international agreements and the predominance of fears for public safety (particularly since September 11, 2001)—all have encouraged a view of a 'smaller', more interconnected world. Local contexts that have traditionally been the focus of juvenile or youth justice analysis are clearly no longer entirely autonomous in their cultural, economic, and political relationships. But this should not be read as an automatically leveling process. Globalisation is a differentiating and polarising process (Bauman, 1998). The language and concepts of *youth, adulthood, criminal law, justice,* and *rights* appear to be uncontroversial in their concern to deal with universal human conditions, but in practice they are defined and limited by the nation-state. In this sense they are all social constructions of specific political and historical configurations. Globalisation has to work through these specific contingencies. If there is such a thing as an emergent global penality, then it will be shaped and radically reworked through local culture, history, and politics, in which particular notions of *justice, youth,* and *rights* come to take on their concrete meaning.

Understanding global transformations and assessing their local impact provides the contemporary analyst with some fundamental methodological problems. Firstly, as Yeates (2001) has noted, there is a problem of definition. The concept of *globalisation* seems to come with a wide diversity of definition and use; not least an uneasy positioning alongside such competing terms as:

- *transnationalisation* (the dissolving of national boundaries)
- *supranationalisation* (transcending national limits)
- *internationalisation* (exchanges of capital and labour)
- *universalisation* (spread of information and cultural phenomena worldwide)
- *neo-liberalisation* (removal of regulatory barriers to international exchange/transfer)
- *Westernisation* (homogenisation, driven by advanced industrial economies)
- *anglo-americanisation* (homogenisation, driven by USA/UK alliance), and
- *modernisation* (the diffusion of managerial economics).

However it is framed, there is clearly a need to recognise *globalisation* as a series of specific and contingent *globalisations* rather than always to assume it will have some unitary character. It should also be viewed as something continually 'on the move': an ongoing, unfinished, and negotiated *process* in a continual state of 'becoming' rather than 'completed'. Second is the issue of how adequately to assess the impact of the global on the local when most research continues to be parochially based in local contexts. Third, how do we recognise and understand the significance of local difference and diversity when the tools are not available for us to even have access to some rudimentary but reliable comparative data, let alone for any single person to be able ever to claim to be an 'expert' on institutions of youth and criminal justice worldwide? Fourth, the entire terrain of global governance and global human rights has, to date, tended to proceed from a Western perspective. An inability to even 'recognise' non-Western sites is all pervasive, as is an inability to 'read' and 'hear' diverse institutional frameworks and lived experiences. These problems are compounded by the fact that globalisation has been applied predominantly to transformations in Western and Anglophone countries. Our understanding of global processes so far might itself be rightly considered as peculiarly ethnocentric.

The empirical 'evidence' of juvenile or youth justice reform considered in this chapter does more to deny than to confirm any flattening of national or local political and cultural differences. In every country and in every locality, youth justice appears to be 'made up' through unstable and constantly shifting alliances among neo-liberal, conservative, and social democratic mentalities. Once it is recognised that differences *within* nation-state territories may also be greater than some differences *between* them, then taking the national (let alone the international and the global) as the basic unit for understanding policy shifts and implementation becomes unsustainable (Stenson and Edwards, 2004). In terms of policy, the authoritarian, the retributive, the restorative, and the protective continually jostle with each other to construct a multi-modal landscape of youth governance in many jurisdictions (Muncie, 2004a). Further analysis needs to be carefully attuned to ongoing processes of multiplicity (as well as uniformity), divergence (as well as convergence), and contingency (as well as determinism) and to how this hybridity activates multiple lines of invention, contestation, and contradiction in policymaking and implementation. Certainly such analysis would also need to be more attuned to the racialised and gendered aspects of globalisation and localisation than has been possible here.

Globalisation does not simply produce uniform or homogenising outcomes. It also produces social differentiation, segmentation, and contestation. Economic globalisation suggests the unfettered freedom of the market; legal globalisation suggests universal regulation through the instruments of human rights. Similarly, whilst some nation-states may well be in a process of being reconstituted by global (neo-liberal economics), international (e.g., UN conventions; European integration), and national (e.g., privatisation) pressures, criminal justice tends to be held onto as a powerful symbolic display of local sovereignty. The nation-state typically attempts to 'resolve' the insecurities and uncertainties brought about by (economic) globalisation by prioritising its role as provider of public safety and elevating its credentials of fighting crime and disorder in order to convince the 'global economy' that this is a 'safe place' in which to operate (Bauman, 1998). The epitome of the defence of local sovereignty, of course, is the United States and its belligerent opposition to the authority of any international courts and human rights conventions.

Questions of who constitutes the youth of a population, what rights and responsibilities they are to be given, who is criminalised, and how they are to be dealt with are nationally and locally specific political and cultural decisions. The forces of globalisation, such as neo-liberal economics and international human rights conventions, cannot be ignored, but neither should the processes through which these forces have come to be reinterpreted and negotiated in different localities and communities. Essentialist conceptions of globalisation imply homogeneity and hegemonic dominance, but globalisation is merely one element in a series of complex processes and political strategies that make up the multi-modal landscape of juvenile or youth justice that is being continually pushed and pulled in different directions at the same time (Muncie, 2005). As a result, it will be impossible and fruitless to try and construct any future globalised or comparative analysis that depends on the prior identification of distinct and pure models of juvenile or youth policy and practice.

The problem with the concept of globalisation is that it inevitably draws our attention to macro political and economic determinants. Dangers of over-generalisation and neglect of local variance abound. What is required is an analysis of how global pressures work themselves out differentially in individual jurisdictions. But to do so also requires a detailed knowledge of how youth, law, and justice are not in themselves universally framed but are the product of historically specific and continually reconstituting local settings.

REFERENCES

Abramson, B. (2000) *Juvenile Justice: The 'Unwanted Child' of State Responsibilities. An Analysis of the Concluding Observations of the UN Committee on the Rights of the Child, in Regard to Juvenile Justice from 1993 to 2000*, International Network on Juvenile Justice/Defence for Children International, www.defence-for-children.org.

Amnesty International (1998) *Betraying the Young: Children in the US Justice System*, AI Index AMR 51/60/98, www.web.amnesty.org.

Asquith, S. (1996) *Juvenile Justice and Juvenile Delinquency in Central and Eastern Europe*, University of Glasgow, Centre for the Child and Society, www.eurochild.gla.ac.uk.

Audit Scotland (2002) *Dealing with Offending by Young People*, Edinburgh, Auditor General.

Bailleau, F. (1998) 'A crisis of youth or of juridical response?' in Ruggiero, V., South, N., and Taylor, I. (eds.) *The New European Criminology*, London, Routledge.

Bala, N., Hornick, J., Snyder, H., and Paetsch, J. (eds.) (2002) *Juvenile Justice Systems: An International Comparison of Problems and Solutions*, Toronto, Thompson.

Bauman, Z. (1998) *Globalisation: The Human Consequences*, Cambridge, Polity.

Bazemore, G., and Walgrave, L. (eds.) (1999) *Restorative Juvenile Justice: Repairing the Harm of Youth Crime*, New York, Criminal Justice Press.

Beck, U. (2000) *What Is Globalisation?* Cambridge, Polity.

Bell, V. (1993) 'Governing childhood: Neo-liberalism and the law', *Economy and Society*, vol. 22, no. 3 pp. 390–403.

Blagg, H. (1997) 'A just measure of shame? Aboriginal youth and conferencing in Australia', *British Journal of Criminology*, vol. 37, no. 4 pp. 481–501.

Bottoms, A. (2002) 'The divergent development of juvenile justice policy and practice in England and Scotland' in Rosenheim, M., et al. (eds.) *A Century of Juvenile Justice*, Chicago, University of Chicago Press.

Bradley, T., Tauri, J., and Walters, R., (2006) 'Demythologising youth justice in Aotearoa/ New Zealand' in Muncie, J., and Goldson, B. (eds.) *Comparative Youth Justice*, London, Sage.

Braithwaite, J. (2003) 'Restorative justice and a better future' in McLaughlin, E., et al. (eds.) *Restorative Justice: Critical Issues*, London, Sage.

Carozza, P. (2003) 'From conquest to constitutions: Retrieving a Latin American tradition of the idea of human rights', *Human Rights Quarterly*, vol. 25, no. 2 pp. 281–313.

Children's Rights Alliance (2002) *State of Children's Rights in England*, London, CRA for England.

Christie, N. (2000) *Crime Control as Industry*, London, Routledge.

Clarke, J. (2000) 'A world of difference? Globalisation and the study of social policy' in Lewis, G., Gewirtz, S., and Clarke, J. (eds.) *Rethinking Social Policy*, London, Sage.

Council of Europe (2000) *Crime and Criminal Justice in Europe*, Strasbourg, Council of Europe.

Council of Europe (2002) *Penological Information Bulletin*, nos. 23 and 24, Strasbourg, Council of Europe.

Council of Europe (2003) *European Sourcebook of Crime and Criminal Justice Statistics*, 2nd edition, Strasbourg, Council of Europe.

Crawford, A. (1997) *The Local Governance of Crime: Appeals to Community and Partnership*, Oxford, Clarendon Press.

Crawford, A. (2001) 'The growth of crime prevention in France as contrasted with the English experience' in Hughes, G., McLaughlin, E., and Muncie, J. (eds.) *Crime Prevention and Community Safety: New Directions*, London, Sage.

Crawford, A. (2002) 'The governance of crime and insecurity in an anxious age: The trans-European and the local' in Crawford, A. (ed.) *Crime and Insecurity: The Governance of Safety in Europe*, Cullompton, Willan.

Cross, N., Evans, P., and Minkes, J. (2003) 'Still children first? Developments in youth justice in Wales', *Youth Justice*, vol. 2, no. 3 pp. 151–62.

Cunneen, C., and White, R. (2002) *Juvenile Justice: Youth and Crime in Australia*, Melbourne, Oxford University Press.

Cunneen, C., and White, R. (2006) 'Australia: Control, containment or empowerment?' in Muncie, J., and Goldson, B. (eds.) *Comparative Youth Justice*, London, Sage.

De Haan, W. (1990) *The Politics of Redress*, London, Unwin Hyman.

Dickie, D. (1979) 'The social work role in Scottish juvenile justice' in Parker, M. (ed) *Social Work and the Courts*, London, Edward Arnold.

Dolowitz, D., (ed.) (2000) *Policy Transfer and British Social Policy: Learning from the USA?* Buckingham, Open University.

Dolowitz, D., and Marsh, D. (2000) 'Learning from abroad: The role of policy transfer in contemporary policy making', *Governance*, vol. 13, no. 1 pp. 5–24.

Downes, D. (1988) *Contrasts in Tolerance*, Oxford, Oxford University Press.

Dunkel, F. (1991) 'Legal differences in juvenile criminology in Europe' in Booth, T. (ed.) *Juvenile Justice in the New Europe*, Social Services Monographs, University of Sheffield.

Farrington, D. (1996) *Understanding and Preventing Youth Crime*, Social Policy Research Findings, no. 93, York, Joseph Rowntree Foundation.

Farrington, D. (2000) 'Explaining and preventing crime: The globalisation of knowledge', *Criminology*, vol. 38, no. 1 pp. 1–24.

Feeley, M., and Simon, J. (1992) 'The new penology: notes on the emerging strategy of corrections and its implications', *Criminology*, vol. 30, no. 4 pp. 449–74.

Fenwick, M. (2004) 'Youth crime and crime control in contemporary Japan' in Sumner, C. (ed.) *The Blackwell Companion to Criminology*, Oxford, Blackwell.

Fenwick, M. (2006) 'Japan: From child protection to penal populism' in Muncie, J., and Goldson, B. (eds.) *Comparative Youth Justice*, London, Sage.

Fionda, J. (1998) 'The age of innocence?—The concept of childhood in the punishment of young offenders', *Child and Family Law Quarterly*, vol. 10, no. 1 pp. 77–87.

Freeman, M. (2002) 'Children's rights ten years after ratification' in Franklin, B. (ed.) *The New Handbook of Children's Rights*, London, Routledge.

Garland, D. (1996) 'The limits of the sovereign state', *British Journal of Criminology*, vol. 36 no. 4 pp. 445–71.

Garland, D. (2001) *The Culture of Control*, Oxford, Oxford University Press.

Gelsthorpe, L., and Morris, A. (2002) 'Restorative youth justice: the last vestiges of welfare?' in Muncie, J., Hughes, G., and McLaughlin, E. (eds.) *Youth Justice: Critical Readings*, London, Sage.

Goldson, B. (2000) 'Children in need or young offenders?', *Child and Family Social Work*, vol. 5 pp. 255–65.

Goldson, B. (2004) 'Youth crime and youth justice' in Muncie, J., and Wilson, D. (eds.) *The Student Handbook of Criminal Justice and Criminology*, London, Cavendish.

Grisso, T., and Schwartz, R. G. (eds.) (2000) *Youth on Trial*, Chicago, University of Chicago Press.

Harris-Short, S. (2003) 'International human rights law: Imperialist, inept and ineffective? Cultural relativism and the UN Convention on the Rights of the Child', *Human Rights Quarterly*, vol. 25, no. 1 pp. 130–81.

Henley, J. (2002) 'A harsh lesson for les miserables', *Guardian Unlimited* 8 August, www.guardian.co.uk.

Holdaway, S., Davidson, N., Dignan, J., Hammersley, R., Hine, J., and Marsh, P. (2001) *New Strategies to Address Youth Offending: The National Evaluation of the Pilot Youth Offending Teams*, Research Directorate Occasional Paper No. 69, London, Home Office.

Hudson, B. (1987) *Justice through Punishment*, Basingstoke, Macmillan.

Hughes, G. (2002) 'Plotting the rise of community safety' in Hughes, G., and Edwards, A. (eds.) *Crime Control and Community*, Cullompton, Willan.

Hughes, G., and Edwards, A. (eds.) (2002) *Crime Control and Community: The New Politics of Public Safety*, Cullompton, Willan.

Human Rights Watch (1999) *Promises broken: An assessment of children's rights on the 10th anniversary of the convention of the rights of the child*, www.hrw.org/campaigns/crp/promises.

International Centre for Prison Studies (2003) *World Prison Brief* www.kcl.ac.uk/depsta/rel/0icps/worldbrief.

Jones, J., and Newburn, T. (2002) 'Policy convergence and crime control in the USA and the UK', *Criminal Justice*, vol. 2, no. 2 pp. 173–203.

Junger-Tas, J. (2002) 'The juvenile justice system: Past and present trends in Western society' in Weijers, I., and Duff, A. (eds.) *Punishing Juveniles*, Oxford, Hart.

Justice (2000) *Restoring Youth Justice: New Directions in Domestic and International Law and Practice*, London, Justice.

Karstedt, S. (2001) 'Comparing cultures, comparing crime: Challenges, prospects and problems for a global criminology', *Crime, Law and Social Change*, vol. 36, no. 3 pp. 285–308.

Kempf-Leonard, K., and Peterson, E. (2000) 'Expanding realms of the new penology: The advent of actuarial justice for juveniles', *Punishment and Society* vol. 2, no. 1 pp. 66–97.

King, M. (1988) *How to make social crime prevention work: The French experience*, London, NACRO.

King, M. (1991) 'The political construction of crime prevention: A contrast between the French and British experiences' in Stenson, K., and Cowell, D. (eds.) *The Politics of Crime Control*, London, Sage.

King, M., and Petit, M.-A. (1985) 'Thin stick and fat carrot—the French juvenile system', *Youth and Policy*, no. 15, pp. 26–31.

Komen, M. (2002) 'Dangerous children: Juvenile delinquency and judicial intervention in the Netherlands, 1960–1995', *Crime, Law and Social Change*, vol. 37, pp. 379–401.

Krisberg B. (2006) 'Rediscovering the juvenile justice ideal in the United States' in Muncie, J., and Goldson, B. (eds.) *Comparative Youth Justice*, London, Sage.

Lacey, N., and Zedner L. (2000) 'Community and governance: A cultural comparison' in Karstedt, S., and Bussman, K-D. (eds) *Social Dynamics of Crime and Control*, Oxford, Hart.

Lappi-Seppala, T. (1998) *Regulating the Prison Population*, Research Communications no. 38 Helsinki, National Research Institute of Legal Policy.

Lappi-Seppala, T. (2001) 'Sentencing and punishment in Finland' in Tonry, M., and Frase, R. (eds.) *Sentencing and Sanctions in Western Countries*, Oxford, Oxford University Press.

Liddle, M., and Gelsthorpe, L. (1994) *Crime Prevention and Inter-Agency Co-operation*, Crime Prevention Unit, Paper no. 53. London. Home Office.

Lockyer, A., and Stone, F. (eds.) (1998) *Juvenile Justice in Scotland: Twenty Five Years of the Welfare Approach*, Edinburgh, T. and T. Clark.

McAra, L. (2004) 'The cultural and institutional dynamics of transformation: Youth justice in Scotland, England and Wales', *Cambrian Law Review*, vol. 35, pp. 23–54.

McAra, L. (2006) 'Welfare in crisis? Key developments in Scottish youth justice' in Muncie, J., and Goldson, B. (eds.) *Comparative Youth Justice*, London, Sage.

McAra, L., and Young, P. (1997) 'Juvenile Justice in Scotland', *Criminal Justice*, vol. 15, no. 3 pp. 8–10.

McGhee, J., Waterhouse, L., and Whyte, B. (1996) 'Children's hearings and children in trouble' in Asquith, S. (ed) *Children and Young People in Conflict with the Law*, London, Jessica Langley.

Mears, D. (2002) 'Sentencing guidelines and the transformation of juvenile justice in the 21st century', *Journal of Contemporary Criminal Justice*, vol. 18, no. 1 pp. 6–19.

Melossi, D. (2000) 'Translating social control: Reflections on the comparison of Italian and North American cultures' in Karstedt, S., and Bussman, K-D. (eds.) *Social Dynamics of Crime and Control*, Oxford, Hart.

Mérigeau, M. (1996) 'Legal Frameworks and Interventions' in McCarney, W. (ed) *Juvenile Delinquents and Young People in Danger in an Open Environment*, Winchester, Waterside Press.

Miers, D. (2001) *An International Review of Restorative Justice*, Crime Reduction Research Series Paper no. 10, London, Home Office.

Mishra, R. (1999) *Globalisation and the Welfare State*, Cheltenham, Edward Elgar.

Morita, A. (2002) 'Juvenile justice in Japan: A historical and cross-cultural perspective' in Rosenheim, M, Zimring, F., Tanenhaus, D., and Dohrn, B. (eds.) *A Century of Juvenile Justice*, Chicago, University of Chicago Press.

Morris, A., and Maxwell, G. (eds.) (2001) *Restorative Justice for Juveniles*, Oxford, Hart.

Morris, A., and McIsaac, M. (1978) *Juvenile Justice?* London, Heinemann.

Muncie, J. (2001) 'A new deal for youth? Early intervention and correctionalism' in Hughes, G., McLaughlin, E., and Muncie, J. (eds.) *Crime Prevention and Community Safety: New Directions*, London, Sage.

Muncie, J. (2002) 'Policy transfers and what works: Some reflections on comparative youth justice', *Youth Justice,* vol. 1, no. 3 pp. 27–35.

Muncie, J. (2003) 'Juvenile justice in Europe: Some conceptual, analytical and statistical comparisons', *ChildRight*, no. 202 pp. 14–17.

Muncie, J. (2004a) 'Youth justice: Globalisation and multi-modal governance' in Newburn, T., and Sparks, R. (eds.) *Criminal Justice and Political Cultures*, Cullompton, Willan.

Muncie, J. (2004b) *Youth and Crime*, 2nd edition, London, Sage.

Muncie, J. (2005) 'The globalisation of crime control: The case of youth and juvenile justice', *Theoretical Criminology*, vol. 9, no. 1 pp. 35–64.

Muncie, J., and Hughes, G. (2002) 'Modes of youth governance: Political rationalities, criminalisation and resistance' in Muncie, J., Hughes, G., and McLaughlin, E. (eds.) *Youth Justice: Critical Readings,* London, Sage.

Nelken, D. (1994) 'Whom can you trust? The future of comparative criminology' in Nelken, D. (ed.) *The Futures of Criminology,* London, Sage.

Nelken, D. (2002) 'Comparing criminal justice' in M. Maguire et al. (eds.) *The Oxford Handbook of Criminology*, 3rd edition, Oxford, Oxford University Press.

Nelken, D. (2006) 'Italy: A lesson in tolerance?' in Muncie, J., and Goldson, B. (eds.) *Comparative Youth Justice*, London, Sage.

Nellis, M. (2000) 'Law and order: The electronic monitoring of offenders' in Dolowitz, D. (ed.) *Policy Transfer and British Social Policy*, Buckingham, Open University.

Newburn, T. (2002) 'Atlantic crossings: Policy transfer and crime control in the USA and Britain', *Punishment and Society*, vol. 4, no. 2 pp. 165–94.

Newburn, T., and Sparks, R. (eds.) (2004) *Criminal Justice and Political Cultures: National and International Dimensions of Crime Control*, Cullompton, Willan.

Norrie, K. (1997) *Children's Hearings in Scotland*, Edinburgh, Sweet and Maxwell.

O'Donnell, I., and O'Sullivan, E. (2003) 'The politics of intolerance—Irish style', *British Journal of Criminology*, vol. 43, no. 1 pp. 41–62.

O'Mahony, D., and Deazley R. (2000) *Juvenile Crime and Justice: Review of the Criminal Justice System in Northern Ireland*, Research Report No. 17, Belfast, Northern Ireland Office.

O'Malley, P. (2001) 'Criminologies of catastrophe? Understanding criminal justice on the edge of the new millennium', *Australian and New Zealand Journal of Criminology*, vol. 33, no. 2 pp. 153–67.

O'Malley, P. (2002) 'Globalising risk? Distinguishing styles of neo liberal criminal justice in Australia and the USA', *Criminal Justice*, vol. 2, no. 2 pp. 205–22.

Pakes, F. (2000) 'League champions in mid table: On the major changes in Dutch prison policy', *Howard Journal*, vol. 39, no. 1 pp. 30–39.

Pakes, P. (2004) *Comparative Criminal Justice*, Cullompton, Willan.

Pitts, J. (1995) 'Public issues and private troubles: A tale of two cities', *Social Work in Europe*, vol. 2, no. 1 pp. 3–11.

Pitts, J. (1997) 'Youth crime, social change and crime control in Britain and France in the 1980s and 1990s' in Jones, H. (ed.) *Towards a Classless Society*, London, Routledge.

Pitts, J. (2001) *The New Politics of Youth Crime: Discipline or Solidarity?* Basingstoke, Palgrave.

Put, J., and Walgrave, L. (2006) 'Belgium: From protection towards accountability?' in Muncie, J., and Goldson, B. (eds.) *Comparative Youth Justice*, London, Sage.

Robertson, R. (1995) 'Globalisation: Time-space and homogeneity-heterogeneity' in Featherstone, M., Lash, S., and Robertson, R. (eds.) *Global Modernities*, London, Sage.

Roche, S. (2002) 'Toward a new governance of crime and insecurity in France' in A. Crawford (ed.) *Crime and Insecurity: The Governance of Safety in Europe*, Cullompton, Willan.

Rose, N. (1989) *Governing the Soul*, London, Routledge.

Rose, N. (1996a) 'The death of the social? Refiguring the territory of government', *Economy and Society*, vol. 25, no. 3 pp. 327–46.

Rose, N. (1996b) 'Governing 'advanced' liberal democracies' in Barry, A., Osborne, T., and Rose, N. (eds.) *Foucault and Political Reason*, London, UCL Press.

Rose, N. (2000) 'Government and Control', *British Journal of Criminology*, vol. 40 pp. 321–39.

Rose, N., and Miller, P. (1992) 'Political power beyond the state: Problematics of government', *British Journal of Sociology*, vol.43 no.2 pp.173–205.

Ruxton, S. (1996) *Children in Europe*, London, NCH Action for Children.

Schabas, W. (1996) 'Reservations to the Convention on the Rights of the Child', *Human Rights Quarterly*, vol. 18, no. 4 pp. 472–91.

Schaffner, L. (2002) 'An age of reason: Paradoxes in the US legal construction of adulthood', *International Journal of Children's Rights*, vol.10 pp. 201–32.

Scottish Consortium on Crime and Criminal Justice (2000) *Rethinking Criminal Justice in Scotland*, Edinburgh, Scottish Consortium.

Scottish Executive (2003) *Youth Court Feasibility Project Group Report*, Edinburgh, Scottish Executive.

Scraton, P. and Haydon, D. (2002) 'Challenging the criminalisation of children and young people: Securing a rights based agenda' in Muncie, J., Hughes, G., and McLaughlin, E. (eds.) *Youth Justice: Critical Readings*, London, Sage.

Simon, J. (1997) 'Governing through Crime' in Friedman, L., and Fisher, G. (eds.) *The Crime Conundrum*, Boulder, Col., Westview.

Simon, J. (2001) 'Entitlement to cruelty: Neo-liberalism and the punitive mentality in the United States' in Stenson, K., and Sullivan, R. R. (eds.) *Crime, Risk and Justice*, Cullompton, Willan.

Skelton, A. (2002) 'Restorative justice as a framework for juvenile justice reform: A South African perspective', *British Journal of Criminology*, vol. 42, no. 3 pp. 496–513.

Smandych, R. (ed.) (2001) *Youth Justice: History, Legislation and Reform*, Toronto, Harcourt.

Smandych, R. (2006) 'Canada: Repenalisation and young offenders' rights' in Muncie, J., and Goldson, B. (eds.) *Comparative Youth Justice*, London, Sage.

Smith, D. (2000) 'Learning from the Scottish Juvenile Justice System' *Probation Journal*, vol. 47, no. 1 pp. 12–17.

Sparks, R. (2001) 'Degrees of estrangement: The cultural theory of risk and comparative penology', *Theoretical Criminology*, vol. 5, no. 2 pp. 159–76.

Stenson, K., and Edwards, A. (2004) 'Policy transfer in local crime control: Beyond naïve emulation' in Newburn, T., and Sparks, R. (eds.) *Criminal Justice and Political Cultures: National and International Dimensions of Crime Control*, Cullompton, Willan.

Stern, V. (2001) 'An alternative vision: Criminal justice developments in non-Western societies', *Social Justice*, vol. 28, no. 3 pp. 88–104.

Streib, V. (2003) *The Juvenile Death Penalty Today*, www.law.onu.edu/faculty/streib.

Suhling, S. (2003) 'Factors contributing to rising imprisonment figures in Germany', *The Howard Journal*, vol. 42, no. 1 pp. 55–68

Tham, H. (2002) 'Law and order as a leftist project? The case of Sweden', *Punishment and Society*, vol. 3, no. 3 pp. 409–26.

Tonry, M. (2001) 'Symbol, substance and severity in western penal policies', *Punishment and Society*, vol. 3, no. 4 pp. 517–36.

Tonry, M., and Doob, A. (eds.) (2004) *Youth Crime and Youth Justice: Comparative and Cross-national Perspectives: Crime and Justice* vol. 31, Chicago, Chicago University Press.

Tonry, M., and Frase, R. (eds.) (2001) *Sentencing and Sanctions in Western Countries*, Oxford, Oxford University Press.

United Nations Office for Drug Control and Crime Prevention (2002) *The Seventh Survey on Crime Trends and the Operations of Criminal Justice Systems,* www.odccp.org/odccp/crime-cicp-survey-seventh.html.

van Zyl Smit, D., and van der Spuy, E. (2004) 'Importing criminological ideas in a new democracy: Recent South African experiences' in Newburn, T., and Sparks, R. (eds.)

Criminal Justice and Political Cultures: National and International Dimensions of Crime Control, Cullompton, Willan.

Veerman, P., and Levine, H. (2000) 'Implementing children's rights on a local level', *International Journal of Children's Rights*, vol. 8, pp. 373–84.

Von Hirsch, A. (1976) *Doing Justice*, New York, Hill and Wang.

Wacquant, L. (1999) 'How penal common sense comes to Europeans: Notes on the transatlantic diffusion of the neo-liberal doxa', *European Societies*, vol. 1, no. 3 pp. 319–52.

Wacquant, L. (2001) 'The penalization of poverty and the rise of neo-liberalism', *European Journal on Criminal Policy and Research*, vol. 9, pp. 401–12.

Walgrave, L. (1995) 'Restorative justice for juveniles: Just a technique or a fully fledged alternative?' *Howard Journal*, vol. 34, no. 3 pp. 228–49.

Walgrave, L., and Mehlbye, J. (eds.) (1998) *Confronting Youth in Europe—Juvenile Crime and Juvenile Justice*, Copenhagen, Denmark, Institute of Local Government Studies.

Walmsley, R. (2003) *World Prison Population List*, 4th edition, Research Findings No. 188, London, Home Office.

Waterhouse, L., McGhee, J., Whyte, B., Loucks, N., Kay, H., and Stewart, R. (2000) *The Evaluation of Children's Hearings in Scotland*, vol. 3, *Children in Focus*, Edinburgh, Scottish Executive.

White, R. (2000) 'Social justice, community building and restorative strategies', *Contemporary Justice Review*, vol. 3, no. 1 pp. 55–72.

White, R. (2002) 'Communities, conferences and restorative social justice', *Criminal Justice*, vol. 3, no. 2 pp. 139–60.

Whyte, B. (2000) 'Youth justice in Scotland' in Pickford, J. (ed.) *Youth Justice: Theory and Practice*, London, Cavendish.

Winterdyk, J. (ed.) (2002) *Juvenile Justice Systems: International Perspectives*, 2nd edition, Toronto, Canadian Scholars' Press.

Yeates, N. (2001) *Globalisation and Social Policy*, London, Sage.

Yeates, N. (2002) 'Globalisation and social policy: From global neo-liberal hegemony to global political pluralism' *Global Social Policy*, vol. 2, no. 1 pp. 69–91.

II

Criminalization and Urban Governance

States are responsible for maintaining social order, whether they do so by themselves or in conjunction with actors in civil society. In their respective essays in the preceding section, Venkatesh and Kassimir and Muncie addressed the ways in which global social dynamics have altered the capacity of states—and those working alongside state actors—to realize this objective. In this section, the view is from the bottom up—that is, from the vantage point of young people whose activities challenge the state and make problematic its capacity to govern.

In conventional discourse—such as the media and everyday talk—social practices that challenge states are labeled "criminality" and the young people who are involved are labeled "criminal." Yet, in reality, these activities may have aspects that either do not justify the label or, seen through a social or cultural rather than legal lens, escape this designation. Should one view young people who move illegally across national borders to find work as migrant laborers or criminal trespassers? When minority youth challenge police harassment by refusing to adhere to state codes of conduct, are they breaking the law or exercising their right to protest? When youth and residents of the ghetto respond to inadequate policing by resolving conflicts on their own, are they taking the law into their own hands or creating civil society? The essays in part II argue that such ostensibly "criminal" actions are, in practice, much more complex and revealing than the conventional readings may suggest.

Migration, the creation of ghettoized ethnic enclaves, and the reproduction of gang activity are examined in the three chapters in this section. The authors situate their respective case studies in the context of an increasingly interconnected world—a world in which states communicate with each other to develop common modes of policing and social control, but also one in which young people themselves share ideas, develop social relations, and physically move across regional and national borders. In their chapters, the authors look closely at these practices from the vantage point of youth themselves—from the perspective of those who are migrating across countries and continents, confronting the state, participating in gangs, being deported, and so on.

Elana Zilberg examines how the U.S. state manages migration and border traffic as it carries out its project of maintaining law and order. In her multi-site ethnographic study, Salvadoran youth move between Los Angeles and San Salvador, sometimes because of voluntary migration and other times because they are deported by the U.S. government. As young people move between the two cities, they grow and mature in two different social contexts. Their lives—as "refugees," Zilberg writes—emerge in a transnational social space, which poses challenges for states as well as for nongovernmental organizations and advocates.

Laurent Bonelli focuses on the young people who have migrated from North Africa and ended up in urban France. The relatively recent media attention given to the rioting in French suburbs failed to capture the complex, everyday ways in which the French state interacts with migrant youth in these spaces. Bonelli fills this void by looking at police and youth as they confront one another in a working-class neighborhood.

Finally, Sudhir Alladi Venkatesh and Alexandra Murphy describe the ways in which youth and residents of the ghetto resolve conflicts when the state does not respond in a timely and effective manner. They argue that a structure of "indigenous justice" has supplanted the state-sanctioned mode of juridical practice: low-income African-American residents, unable to rely on police and the courts, develop innovative ways to address problems and create resolutions that are outside the formal system of jurisprudence. What appears to be taking the law into their own hands is actually a complicated and efficacious response by residents of low-income neighborhoods to find solutions when the state is not responsive. With its rich ethnographic detail, the chapter helps us to move beyond the tropes of disorganization and dysfunctionality that have saturated both popular and scholarly discourse.

3

Refugee Gang Youth: Zero Tolerance and the Security State in Contemporary U.S.-Salvadoran Relations

ELANA ZILBERG

In contemporary U.S.-Salvadoran relations the terms *youth, the law,* and *globalization* have come to be linked through the emergence of a curious new class of Salvadoran refugee: gang-affiliated, -alleged, and -impacted youth.[1] These "refugee gang youth" are produced by the collision of traveling bodies and policies—the deportation of Salvadoran immigrant youth and young adults from Los Angeles and the importation of U.S. zero tolerance gang-abatement strategies in El Salvador.

The policing, incarceration, and deportation of Salvadoran gang-affiliated immigrant youth from Los Angeles to El Salvador reveal how the relationship of young people to the law is changing in light of globalization. Deportation in particular demonstrates that the relationship of youth to the legal realm cannot be understood in purely local or national terms. Indeed, Salvadoran immigrant gang youth travel through and are interpolated by multiple legal regimes (criminal, immigration, refugee, and human rights law) within and between nation-states (the United States and El Salvador) and multilateral entities (the

My thanks go to the following people for their thoughtful commentary on various versions of this essay: Sudhir Alladi Venkatesh, Ron Kassimir, John and Jean Comaroff, Sasha Abramsky, Robert Horwitz, José Miguel Cruz, Sonia Baires, Silvia Beltrán, Susan Bibler Coutin, Esra Özyürek, Nancy Postero, and Liz Lilliott, and the anonymous reviewers of this volume. I would also like gratefully to acknowledge the support of the Global Security and Cooperation Project of the Social Science Research Council, which funded the second phase of the research conducted for this essay. Finally, my heartfelt thanks go to Homies Unidos for the privilege of access to its members and programs.

United Nations, its affiliates, and internationally funded nongovernmental organizations [NGOs]).

This chapter offers an ethnographic examination of how these legal regimes are reorganizing across national boundaries both in reaction to and in the service of the globalization of Latino youth gangs. Indeed, in an effort to reassert the sovereignty of the nation-state, the law actually spawns and reproduces transnational formations such as La Mara Salvatrucha and the 18th Street Gang, as well as Central American adaptations of U.S. zero tolerance gang-abatement projects such as those of William Bratton and Rudolf Guiliani.[2] In so doing, the law effectively undermines the very sovereignty it sets out to defend. Most ironically, the exportation of zero tolerance policing strategies alongside the deportation of gang youth only fuels undocumented migration from El Salvador to the United States further. Indeed, the United States and El Salvador appear to be locked in a repeating history. Salvadorans were forced out of El Salvador as civil war refugees in the 1980s, only to be forced out of the United States in the 1990s as criminal deportees. Today, Salvadoran youth and young adults are fleeing El Salvador once again, this time as a result of the combined pressures of both gang and state violence. They do so even though many risk re-imprisonment upon re-entry into the United States followed by deportation. The lesson is a simple one: What goes around comes around.

In what follows, I explore the boomerang effects of these changing relationships of youth, the law, and globalization in contemporary U.S.-Salvadoran relations through an ethnographic engagement with a transnational youth violence prevention organization, Homies Unidos (Homies). Homies functions as a liaison between gangs, civil society, and the state, and is one of the only alternative spaces of representation available to gang and deported gang youth. While the organization works with gang-affiliated, -alleged, and -impacted youth in general to redirect the gang structure, its disciplines, and its solidarities into tools for stopping the violence committed by gangs and against gangs, it also functions as a support group for gang members deported from the United States who are seeking an alternative to violence.

I focus on Homies Unidos precisely because its mandate brings together multiple legal regimes (immigration, criminal, and refugee) across national boundaries (U.S. and Salvadoran). Homies may be the only organization working both on the immigration consequences of the criminal justice system for youth and on the transnational implications of the globalization of zero tolerance gang-abatement strategies between the United States and Central America. Indeed, this organization was the first to articulate a critical counter discourse to the cultural politics of deportation. The organization has offices in both San Salvador and Los Angeles. Although it is impossible to engage one side of this transnational field without the other, for the purposes of this chapter I will focus primarily on its operations in San Salvador between 1996 and 2003.

Homies Unidos in San Salvador is, from start to finish, an organization forced into being and enabled by transnational forces. On the one hand, it was established to meet the needs created by the immigration consequences and transnational implications of U.S. zero tolerance crime-prevention strategies: the globalization of youth gangs. On the other hand, Homies Unidos was enabled by the post-war flourishing of, some might say, the "infatuation with civil society" (Comaroff and Comaroff 2000: 292) and the corresponding proliferation of NGOs. The project emerged in a heady moment in El Salvador when the opening up of political spaces to the opposition coincided with the globalization of human rights discourses in general and of children and youth rights discourses in particular. Homies also relies on solidarity networks established between the Salvadoran and United States left during the civil war. As a marriage of Latin American and U.S. social movements, it interpolates Salvadoran revolutionary politics with the nonviolent civil rights movements of Martin Luther King and César Chávez. It was within this constellation of post–civil war transnational and global forces that Homies Unidos was born, began to flourish, and—as I will argue—is now floundering.

Indeed, 1996 to 2003 marks both the founding and, ostensibly temporary, shutting down of Homies Unidos–San Salvador program. The fortunes of the organization correspond to a particular historical course within El Salvador: the rise and wane of a human rights and police reform agenda, and its succession by the rise—one could say return—of the security state through the globalization of U.S. zero tolerance strategies. This chapter offers an analysis of Homies Unidos's struggle with this complex transnational force field as it coheres around the topics of youth, globalization, and the law.

A TRANSNATIONAL HISTORICAL CONTEXT

The contemporary transnational flows of gangs and governance between the United States and El Salvador have a powerful prehistory in the twelve-year U.S.-funded Salvadoran civil war. Between 1979 and 1992 an estimated one million Salvadorans fled war-induced physical and economic insecurity to seek refuge in the United States. Nearly half of this population settled in the Los Angeles area. During this same period, the United States not only funded, but also advised and trained the Salvadoran military and police.

By the war's end, the United States and El Salvador had become deeply interconnected "from above" and "from below"[3]—that is, through formal state relations as well as through informal and grassroots transnational ties. The circulation of Salvadoran immigrant youth gangs and of U.S. policing models must therefore be understood first within the longer history of U.S.-Salvadoran security policy relations and, second, within the contemporary dense transnational networks of communication and the uneven flows of labor, goods, money, information, and ideas between the United States and El Salvador.[4]

U.S. immigration law has played a formative role in the lives of the Salvadoran diaspora. Most Salvadorans arrived in the United States without documentation and, therefore, fell outside the law. As legal remedies became available to adjust their undocumented or "illegal" status, Salvadoran immigrants learned to construct their migration narratives within the discursive frames of immigration, refugee, and asylum law. As a result, Salvadorans have become skilled in positioning their experiences within the legal identities imposed upon them by the constraints of the law (Coutin 2000). The law has in turn shaped Salvadoran subjectivities and notions of selfhood.

Ironically, it was only in November 1990, as the 12-year civil war was drawing to an end that Salvadorans were granted formal and legal Temporary Protective Status (TPS) as refugees in the United States.[5] Yet during this same period, recognition grew that the majority of Salvadorans living in the United States, irrespective of the conditions behind their flight—political and/or economic—were in the United States to stay. Thus while Central American community organizations devoted their resources and energies to the available legal remedies, all in one way or another invested in the identity of the refugee, they did so with their eyes firmly on this prize: permanent residency and citizenship. As Susan Coutin notes, the "language of settlement" (in the U.S.) grew in importance in the 1990s, when Salvadoran community leaders disparaged the term "refugee," opting for "immigrant" as a more self-empowering term (2000). This language of settlement or permanency belied conditions on the ground in cities such as Los Angeles. Salvadoran settlement coincided with a vicious anti-immigrant politics. These politics gained momentum with the 1992 Rodney King riots and culminated in 1994 with California's Proposition 187. The state's initiative attacked undocumented immigrant access to healthcare, education, and welfare, and would combine with a virulent anti-crime agenda directed at youth of color. Indeed, while the immigrant rights movement fought this attack on legal immigrants' rights to entitlement programs and other services, something else was going on. In 1994, when Latinos organized against Proposition 187, another ballot emerged on the agenda—Proposition 184, or the "Three Strikes and You're Out" initiative. Latinos were strangely silent about this draconian anti-crime measure, which was generally understood as an African-American issue (Zilberg 1994).

The terrible irony is that the Three Strikes initiative was more than a black concern. Latino immigrant youth, alongside African Americans, became fodder for the flourishing prison industrial complex, fed as it was by the war on drugs playing out on the streets of inner-city neighborhoods (Zilberg 2002b, 2004). This growing relationship between criminal and immigration law culminated in 1996 with the passage of the Illegal Immigration Reform and Immigrant Responsibility Act of 1996 (IIRAIRA), which mandated the deportation of immigrants—documented or undocumented—with criminal records at the end of their jail sentences.

The siphoning off of immigrant gang youth through deportation has since come to serve as a key management strategy for the North. Zero tolerance gang-abatement strategies and anti-gang legislation, combined with changes in immigration law, have resulted in the deportation to El Salvador of thousands of Salvadoran immigrant gang youth. They include legal permanent residents, many of whom have lived the better part of their lives in the United States, and some of whom are deported for nonviolent crimes. Prior to 1996, approximately 1,000 Salvadorans with criminal records were deported annually. By 2003 that number had risen to approximately 2,000 (Department of

Homeland Security Yearbook of Immigration Statistics).[6] The result for many Salvadoran immigrants is a tragic reversal and indeed repetition of family dislocation and separation of the civil war era. The results in El Salvador have been disastrous.

THE TRANSNATIONAL IMPLICATIONS
OF U.S. CRIMINAL AND IMMIGRATION LAW

As a result of the immigration consequences of U.S. criminal law, El Salvador has become host to the Latino immigrant youth gangs La Mara Salvatrucha and the 18th Street Gang as well as other smaller Chicano gangs. Upon their arrival, deported youth and young adults[7] walk into and contribute to a complex force field of violence, not to mention social discrimination. Indeed, the deportation of gang youth has only served to intensify already high levels of violence in El Salvador. Gang violence combines with the incomplete disarmament of a highly militarized society, the re-emergence of the paramilitary social cleansing practices of the 1980s death squads, organized crime, and the uneven progress of police (Call 1999, 1996; Call and Stanley 2001; Costa 1999; Stanley 1996) and of judicial reforms (Popkin 2000). Together these provide for the reproduction and articulation of both Salvadoran and U.S. patterns of violence—both of which have a complex transnational history.

The globalization of these youth gangs unfolded in the context of the internationally sponsored and monitored post–civil war police and human rights reforms in El Salvador negotiated into the UN-brokered 1992 Salvadoran peace accords. During this period, one of the United States' primary tasks was to aid in the construction of a new National Civil Police (PNC) force in collaboration with other countries such as Spain and France. The United States' technical assistance was provided through the International Criminal Investigation Technical Assistance Program (ICITAP).[8] The establishment of the PNC was a pivotal issue in the peace negotiations, and involved de-linking police from military and intelligence functions as well as promoting the "modernization" and "professionalization" of a new civilian police force. At the same time, the Salvadoran penal code was substantially rewritten in accordance with the post-war judicial and human rights reforms. These changes, which included new protections for juvenile offenders and assurance of due process, and which banned the use of forced confessions, culminated the 1998 Penal Code Reform.

Twelve years after the signing of the peace accords, El Salvador is at a new juncture. Most of the international entities charged with oversight of the implementation of the peace accords have withdrawn from El Salvador. ICITAP, for instance, was due to end its monitoring the implementation of this aspect of the peace accords in 2003. Strangely, this retreat coincided with the successful transfer of U.S. zero tolerance gang-abatement strategies in the form of *El Plan Mano Dura* (literally the Firm Hand Plan but, more appropriately, the Iron Fist Plan) and now *Mano Súper Dura* (Super Hard or Firm), as well as new supporting anti-gang legislation. Both undermine post-war human rights reforms in general and in juvenile justice in particular.

THE WANE OF HUMAN RIGHTS
AND THE RISE OF THE SECURITY STATE

The contemporary Salvadoran politics surrounding youth, the law, and globalization is thus marked by the wane of an international human rights agenda, on the one hand, and the rise a U.S. law enforcement model on the other. In this next section, I explore how the preceding complex force field of global flows register on the ground in post–civil war El Salvador. I do so through a close examination of Homies Unidos and its always awkward, now untenable relations with civil society, the gangs, and the state.

The public forum in posh San Salvador hotels has become a primary stage for the performance of civil society and democratic debate in post-war El Salvador. I want here to examine two such forums, with vastly distinct agendas, but where the themes of migration, violence, and youth become integrally intertwined. My intention here is not simply to settle with an analysis of these ideologically saturated discourses and their conflation in the contemporary Salvadoran "folk devil" (Cohen 1972; Hall et al. 1978) of the deported gang youth. Above and beyond discourse analysis, I want here to think through Homies Unidos's silent, visibly uncomfortable, but ubiquitous presence in this Habermasian public sphere and its idealized speech community where formerly suspect, banned, and exiled political forces now sit at the table with the state. In the following section I move back and forth between two events where the themes of youth, violence, and migration become linked: a forum on youth violence sponsored in 2002 by the Salvadoran legislative assembly, and a presidential debate on the topic of Salvadoran migration sponsored in 1998 by the Permanent Forum on Migrants.

I have arrived late to a forum for seeking solutions to the phenomenon of student youth violence. The event is being held at the Hotel Transcontinental and sponsored by the Salvadoran legislative assembly with the University of Texas at Austin. The latter has been providing technical assistance to the assembly through its "Modernization of the State" project. The Salvadoran Attorney General is speaking very broadly about the causes behind youth violence. I survey the room to find a seat. Luis Ernesto Romero (AKA Pansa Loca)[9] of Homies Unidos sees me and signals to me to come over to sit with him and his "homies." This is in August 2002.

The first and last time I saw Homies Unidos members in a setting like this was in November 1998, in the exclusive Hotel El Salvador. It was at a presidential candidates' debate on migration sponsored by the Permanent Forum on Migrants.[10] I remember then being taken aback by the contrasts at play there. In the back row of the elegant, plush salon were eight or so gang members—most deportees from the United States, the men with shaved heads, all with tattoos designating their affiliations with U.S. Latino immigrant gangs. Some wore the expected baggy attire. Needless to say, the entrance of these young people against the sea of tailored suits was enough to turn the heads of the crowd. These unlikely members of Salvadoran civil society had come to the debate as members of Homies Unidos in San Salvador and as loosely affiliated participants in this social movement for migrants' rights. That was four years ago. Homies has since become a fixture at these sorts of events, and they are here today as members of a social movement for youth rights. Some of the same faces from 1998 are here today. Some have since been lost, killed on the streets of San Salvador. Some are new faces, recently arrived courtesy of U.S. Marshall planes.

Although the ostensible theme of the 1998 forum was migration, crime and youth gang violence surfaced as a powerful interpretive thread through the candidates' presentations. The topic of the 2002 forum is youth violence. Nonetheless, migration and the subsequent deportation of gang youth surface as a key explanatory concept. In each case, youth, violence, and migration have become integrally linked terms.

The 1998 debate was kicked off by the *Farabundo Marti National Liberation Front* (FMLN) presidential candidate and former guerilla commander, Facundo Guardado. Guardado chose insecurity as the theme of his speech and used it as an analytical blade to dissect the history of Salvadoran migration into three historical waves: pre–, during, and post–civil war periods. According to his schema, prior to the civil war Salvadoran insecurity was—as were the reasons for migration—economic: the inability to earn a living. Leading up to and during the civil war, Salvadoran insecurity was—as again were the reasons for migration—political: the inability to exercise your political rights or to enjoy your human rights. In the post–civil war period, Salvadoran insecurity is—as are the reasons for contemporary migration—crime.

Guardado was followed by the candidate for the right-wing party, the League for Democratic Reform (LIDER), who offered his own theory about the relationship of migration and violence. He warned against the dark side of El Salvador's migration story, explaining the phenomena of wanton sexuality, drugs, gang violence, and AIDS in terms of migration and *Americanization.* These, he concluded, were all cultural contaminants Salvadorans had brought back with them from the United States. The direction and object of his scorn couldn't have been clearer—those young people sitting in the back of the room. What, I wondered were *they* thinking? Indeed, I had returned to El Salvador in 2002 precisely to investigate how deported gang youth had become agents in and foils for the fearful practices and imaginaries that surround post–civil war violence in El Salvador.

It is with these things in mind that I make my way across the hotel ballroom to Homies Unidos, who greet me with both the formal Latin American kiss on the cheek and gang-style handshake. I take my place between Chamaco and Travieso (both deportees from the United States) on one side, and La Huera (a native veteran of the 18th Street Gang) on the other. I say "native," because, although Huera has traveled to the United States, she has never resided there. Unlike the other Homies present at today's forum, she was "jumped" or initiated into her gang in El Salvador, albeit into a *clika* (cell) of the 18th Street Gang that had been started in El Salvador by deportees from Los Angeles.

By the time I sit down, the attorney general has relinquished the floor to the next speaker, Mauricio Sandoval, the then-director of the National Civil Police. Gangs are not new to El Salvador, he explains, but appeared in the 1970s. Back then, however, they were not considered violent, but were even thought to be of service to and working in the defense of their communities. But, says Sandoval, in the 1990s these groups turned violent, a condition aggravated by the deportation of delinquent youth from the United States and the associated process of "transculturalization."

Although Sandoval suggests that the responses to youth violence must include all sectors of the state (the police, the attorney general, and the prisons as well as broader sociocultural conditions), he narrows in on the judicial system. First, he calls for a revision of the law governing juvenile offenders. Then he decries the use of "human rights as a defensive strategy" on behalf of these juvenile offenders. And herein lies the crux of what is at stake in El Salvador, the *reform* (some would say dismantling) of post–civil war *reforms*. The latter, enshrined in the 1998 Penal Code, emerged as a result of the 1992 Peace Accords signed between the Salvadoran government and the opposition, the FMLN. Chamaco leans over to me, "Man, that guy just wants to put us all away."

Up next is Salvador Samayoa, president of the National Council for Public Security. Samayoa offers very different solutions from Sandoval's: "I don't believe that this problem will be solved by the police, but rather by social prevention." Chamaco likes this last comment: "That's cool. What this guy is saying is *good.*" Samayoa then begins to talk about the programs he has seen in operation in New York. He lists them off one after the other as models to emulate, painting a rosy picture of success stories in Latino immigrant communities. Yet, here I am sitting in the midst of a group of young men who are a product of the failure of U.S. institutions with Latino immigrant youth, and of the least progressive of prevention strategies: deportation.

The last speaker of the morning is Padre José Pepe Morataya, a Spanish priest of the Silesian order. He is speaking in his capacity as general manager of the *El Poligono Don Bosco*, a Catholic program that operates a very impressive complex of cooperative bakeries, carpentry workshops, and alternative schools. Don Bosco is invariably the example cited alongside Homies Unidos as the only program focused on the needs of gang youth in the country. Yet Don Bosco and Homies Unidos have a mutual disregard for each other's programs. Is this, I wonder, because of their distinct organizing strategies, or something else?

Padre Pepe's charismatic and inflammatory speech brings into sharp relief the points of contention between the organizations. Organized violence, he asserts, comes from migration. The priest continues in this vein: El Salvador receives 500 deportees from the United States a month. On their arrival, with the help of other deportees, they tour the country to survey the terrain and to assess existing networks of crime in order to set up their base of operations. They successfully create networks throughout Central America. Salvadorans have become well known as the regional leaders of these transnational gangs.

His discourse creates a stir around me. Up till now, Chamaco, seemingly bored by the drone of talking heads, has been doodling the name of his gang, "CV Amigos Westside Los Angeles," under the legislative assembly's logo on the notepaper provided in the event packet. (Sometimes the poetics just scream out at you.) But Padre Pepe has caught his attention: "*Solo pajá*" (total bullshit) say Chamaco and Travieso to each other, shaking their heads and laughing.

The picture of the deportees' privileged tour through El Salvador is much different from the experience and geographical disorientation of those who come through the doors of Homies Unidos. Homies guides deportees through the shock and alienation they experience upon their return to what for many of them is an unknown "homeland." Deportees often express fear at having to go as far as the corner store. Just getting on a bus can be a traumatic and dangerous experience. They rely on Homies to teach them how to navigate hostile and foreign terrain, or to derive a sense of place (Zilberg 2004).

Pepe Morataya comes to the end of his speech, and the question-and-answer period begins. The master of ceremonies (MC) reads from a long list of questions from the audience written on index cards. How is it that the PNC can be struggling to diminish organized crime and drug trafficking, if there are police involved in these problems? Would you define a gang member as a delinquent? Is being a youth becoming a crime in itself? Is the PNC saying that youth should be punished as adults? Why hasn't the legislative assembly approved the *Ley de Juventud* (Law of the Youth)? Is there a problem providing alternative education to gang members? Why are there no educational opportunities for deportees who have completed 9th grade in the United States? The last is Travieso's question.

As the first respondent begins there is movement across the room and Huera stands, signaling to the Homies to join her. She joins a group of youth unfolding banners. "Youth is not synonymous with violence nor drugs"; "Youth is not a crime." The leader of the group is trying to get the attention of the MC, who responds by asking them to respect the established order. This is not the time, nor the place. The audience intervenes, admonishing the MC to let the group speak. He concedes.

> We are trying to build a youth culture with the object of contributing to our community. So far all we have heard are the negatives. We have not heard you say anything positive about us. Here we are conducting national consultations working to develop *La Ley de Juventud.* We have heard you speak, but the needs of Salvadoran youth have still not been fulfilled. You want to silence us, but why should we let adults speak for us?

"Yes, yes," from the audience. Applause.

> We don't use any violence or drugs. What we want is for you to listen to us truthfully. Not to leave us on the sidelines, nor as a question on a little piece of paper [the index card]. We want answers.

With that, the youth return the floor to the panelists. Sandoval resumes from where he left off when interrupted by *la juventud.*

EL PLAN MANO DURA

El Salvador's contemporary politics surrounding youth, globalization, and the law are situated between then police director Sandoval's call for reforms to the juvenile offender law on the one hand, and La Huera's call for *La Ley de Juventud* on the other. The former is linked to a post–human rights agenda and to U.S. zero tolerance and gang-abatement strategies. The latter is linked to an international movement for human and youth rights.

In the months following the forum on youth violence, *La Ley de Juventud* would flounder in committee with post-electoral changes in the legislature and with the end of the University of Texas's Modernization of the State program. The university had funded a consultant to oversee the development and passage of the law. Sandoval's agenda, on the other hand, would gain considerable momentum, culminating in his successor's implementation of *El Plan Mano Dura*. Chamaco's disconcerted commentary during Sandoval's address, "Man, this guy just wants to put us all away," would prove correct.[11]

The plan's implementation represents a victory for the post–human rights agenda of the right. Interestingly, this post–human rights agenda is intellectually grounded in former leftist FMLN commander Joaquin Villalobos's writings. Villalobos, who now advises the Salvadoran government on security issues, argued that human rights–inspired legislation in post–civil war El Salvador is more appropriate for European countries such as Switzerland, where crime is low and its citizens are educated in their responsibilities in a functioning democracy. El Salvador, however, is in need of a firmer hand until its population has been disciplined (in the Foucauldian sense) as governable democratic citizens.[12] Human rights as enshrined in the 1998 Penal Code are *leyes para los suizos* (laws for the Swiss), not for Salvadorans (Villalobos 2001: 184). More interestingly yet, the reforms of the reforms deemed more suitable to this "weak" and "immature" democracy are derived from laws that purportedly have worked for the *gringos* (which is to say for the United States). Indeed, *El Plan Mano Dura* represents the successful transnationalization of U.S. zero tolerance strategies in El Salvador.[13]

This is not to say that the United States and its policing models did not already have considerable influence over the PNC. But U.S. technical assistance and funding was structured, at least initially, around the implementation of the peace accords and political violence rather than post–civil war criminal or social violence.[14] Still, under U.S. embassy sponsorship, most senior police officers had already been introduced to U.S. zero tolerance models through their visits to police departments in New York, Boston, Chicago, Los Angeles, and Houston. The walls of Salvadoran police offices are invariably lined with certificates from the U.S. Justice Department to commemorate these trainings and exchanges. Moreover, a number of U.S. crime prevention models including 911, DARE, Bratton's CompStat crime mapping computer sys-

tems, the Field Interview Card, and the San Jose version of community policing in the form of Community Police Intervention Patrols (PIPCOM) had
been introduced into El Salvador directly by the U.S. ICITAP, which main-
tains offices in both the U.S. embassy and the PNC headquarters. This U.S.
involvement in the construction of the PNC was based on the need to address
the militarization of the police force and the culmination of 12 years of civil
war, rather than an anticipation of post–civil war violent crime. Ten years after
the signing of the peace accords, El Salvador is now at a crucial juncture. International cooperation—U.S. and European—in the implementation of those
accords has all but come to an end.

El Plan Mano Dura is by no means the first attempt to introduce zero tolerance crime prevention strategies in El Salvador. Indeed, in 1998, just days
after the aforementioned presidential debate on migration, FMLN candidate
Facundo Guardado made "crime" his key campaign issue with his *Tarjeta
Roja* (Red Card) proposal. The *Tarjeta Roja* proposal was the flip side of California's Three Strikes and You're Out proposition-turned-state-law. Guardado's
anti-crime platform mirrored those U.S. cultural politics, the very sort that
feeds into the criminalization and subsequent deportation of a key sector of
Homies Unidos's membership sitting in the back row of that conference salon
where he presented his thesis about migration and crime.[15] Unlike *El Plan
Mano Dura, La Tarjeta Roja,* as it was proposed by Guardado, was not targeted
at gang members or deportees per se, but rather, like Three Strikes, promised
to reduce violent crime. Repeat offenders would receive a red card signifying
life sentences.[16]

Guardado's proposal was only one of many draconian measures introduced.
The Nationalist Republican Alliance (ARENA) government had already
explored the possibility of instituting a quasi-transnational probation system for
criminal deportees and had twice introduced emergency crime legislation—in
1996 and again in 1999—in the form of the Social Defense Law, which if it
had passed, would have jailed Salvadorans deported from the United States for
criminal offenses upon their arrival. Under this proposal, these deportees would
receive triple punishment for their offense: jail time in the United States, deportation to El Salvador, and reimprisonment in El Salvador.

As Vice-minister of Citizen Security Renee Dominguez put it when I met
with him in May 2003, "the project [to introduce gang-abatement legislation]

was already developed but was put on hold, because it did not have the necessary resonance in society." We were leafing through a booklet of U.S. gang-abatement legislation (curfews, injunctions, limits on free association, criminalization of gang membership, grafitti, limits on the use of cell phones by alleged gang members, and so on) compiled from the United States' National Youth Gang Center's website for the ministry by the aforementioned National Council on Public Security.

Certainly there was sufficient "resonance in society" by 1998. That year, the Institute of Public Opinion at the Jesuit-run University of Central America (IUDOP) released a study that revealed that 45 percent of the country supported "social cleansing" of those elements deemed responsible for the violence—even if that meant the recurrence of paramilitary death squad activity (IUDOP 1998). Some speculate that the mayor of San Miguel, the third largest city in El Salvador, was elected *for* rather than despite his alleged associations with *La Sombra Negra* (the Black Shadow), the post–civil war death squad that had targeted gang youth. The study also revealed that 80 percent of the population wanted to see the military step in to suppress delinquency. In a country that had only recently demilitarized its police forces—a hard won post–civil war reform—these sentiments were more than disturbing.

Perhaps what Dominguez meant by "resonance in society" was resonance in *civil society*. Indeed, it is the human rights agenda of post–civil war Salvadoran civil society, more than anything else, that has put the brakes on zero tolerance strategies—a point stressed by Sandoval in his address to that forum on youth violence. As director of IUDOP, Miguel Cruz, explained to me in 2002, the post–civil war era consists of "*una ensalada*" (a salad), an incoherent and contradictory set of progressive and regressive laws. He noted:

> Over the last three years, since the passage of the 1998 [progressive] penal reforms, we have seen a back-sliding of those reforms with various amendments. After the war, there was a huge effort to reform. Then came the discourse that behind the level of violence is the liberty that comes with human rights discourse. So the progressive spirit is in danger. [This backlash had] not yet actually affected youth. Despite the attempts to reform the juvenile offender laws, there has been strong support for it [those laws] especially from the family courts, even though there has been pressure to criminalize all sorts of activities. This could change, of course. (Taken from an interview with Cruz conducted in August 2002)

The introduction of *El Plan Mano Dura* has done precisely that—changed juvenile offender laws to criminalize a whole category of youth between the ages of 12 and 18. As Silvia Beltrán, director of Homies Unidos in Los Angeles, explains, the implementation of *El Plan Mano Dura* "practically makes being young and poor a crime. The police and army are targeting youth who congregate in poor communities."

LET'S LEAVE IT TENTATIVE

Let's return now to my earlier discussion of the forum on youth violence. I did not mention then that the members of Homies Unidos present at the forum that day did not in fact join their homegirl Huera and the group of youth in their public petition to be seen and heard through *La Ley de Juventud.* I asked them why. "Na," they shook their heads. "We don't like to do that kind of stuff." "We're already visible enough. As it is, every time we walk into places like that, people always turn and stare." Huera was not appeased by this response. She felt very let down by her homies and by their refusal to stand up and to be counted in this movement. But I discerned from this that although Homies Unidos may have become a fixture at these events, its members were still uncomfortable and uneasy participants in civil society. They felt marginalized within, not yet legitimately of, and yet uncomfortably visible within it.

Homies Unidos's uneasy place in Salvadoran civil society would become all the more apparent the next day, when my own positionality at the forum— in "*el mero centro de Homies Unidos*" (smack in the middle of Homies Unidos)—was duly noted by the director of the National Council for Public Security, Oscar Bonilla—right-hand man to the Council's president, Samayoa. Laughing off his remark, which was delivered to me with eyebrows raised, but feeling marked, I asked if the Council had worked with the organization: "No, I don't look upon them with much credibility."

Some social movement theorists argue that "models that succeed are [in fact] rooted in subterranean and social patterns [that] don't quite fit existing institutional and cultural norms" (Clemens in Lucero 2000: 18). But within Salvadoran civil society, Homies Unidos is ultimately a disconcerting and untenable blend of what the literature would dub "distasteful" movements with those sanctioned as progressive social movements (Esseveld and Eyerman in Lucero 2000: 245). These tattooed young men and women—many with criminal records—are unlikely contenders alongside the "candidates of choice" in "approved" marginalized groups: indigenous, ethnic, ecological, women, gay, and human rights movements (Alvarez et al. 1998: 6).

A week after that forum on youth violence, Homies Unidos meets to discuss, among other things, an invitation by the PNC to present their gang violence prevention program at Homies Unidos's office. The discussion is heated. Someone recalls that in the past the PNC had invited gang members to a meeting, ostensibly to talk about their programs, but arrested them all instead. "I don't want them to know where our offices are so they can come and spy on us." "We already have problems working in the communities as it is. I don't want to be seen as no snitch. What they want from us is information." One Homie is adamant, "With so many homies in Mariona [prison] right now, why work with the police?"[17] The two Homies who had introduced the PNC proposal are defensive. "I'm no snitch. I'm not working for the police." They bring the discussion to a close, "We'll leave it tentative then?" "Okay, we'll put it down as tentative."

This tentative relationship with the police marked a shift in Homies Unidos. In contrast to its LA operations, early on in its formation, the San Salvador program had succeeded in building working relations with both the PNC and CAM (San Salvador's metropolitan police force). Relations between Homies Unidos and the police were possible in El Salvador, and not Los Angeles, precisely because of the police reform agendas that did or did not attach to those conjunctural events: 1992 Salvadoran peace accords versus the 1992 Rodney King riots.[18] The peace accords instigated the construction of an entirely new police force that—successful or not—was to be grounded in a culture of human rights. Ironically, the LA riots overshadowed the police reforms called for by the Christopher Commission resulting from the Rodney King beating, and unleashed instead the full ire of zero tolerance strategies, which would combine with anti-immigrant policies to contribute to the conditions for gang violence in El Salvador.

Over the following months, with the explosion of a very public and gruesome murder attributed to deported gang members, Homies Unidos's relationship to the PNC would become even more "tentative." That case, dubbed the "Case of Rosa N.," was just the first in a series of macabre mutilations and decapitations attributed to members of the 18th Street Gang. Between December 2002 and March 2003, Sandoval launched a major media campaign around these "*descabezamientos*" (beheadings or decapitations), conducted mass arrests of gang members, and called for the passage of special anti-gang laws.

The Homies Unidos office is abuzz with news on the media coverage and police reaction to the recent mutilations attributed to 18th Street. There is a mixture of fury and fright in the air. Some of the accused are among those who have passed through Homies Unidos's doors and are known to its members. Most of the gang members had actually been picked up for the vague and all encompassing infraction of "*asociaciones ilícitas*" (illicit associations) and not for any direct evidential links to the crimes. The alleged ringleaders of the Rosa N. case are released after documentation is produced corroborating their claims that they were being held by the PNC under the 72 hour rule during the period in which the crime was said to have taken place. Even so, fear arises around the inevitable guilt by association that will be made between the organization, the gangs, and the scandal.

There is some discussion as to whether Homies will express public indignation at the mass arrests of gang members and Sandoval's proposed new law targeting gang violence, but some members want the organization to lay low and to avoid press coverage altogether. They do not want to be associated with the current events. Still other members are concerned as much about the reaction of the gangs as they are about those of the public and the police.

Homies Unidos has long been the place where journalists—Salvadoran and international—make contact with active gang members in the field. But, in the context of the Rosa N. case, this was having repercussions for the organization. Gang members, often quite willing to perform their gangster identities before the camera, were becoming more camera-shy as the media and police mounted campaigns against them, and Homies were struggling with their mediating role therein. "We must ask in advance and get the permission of the *clika*. Please Homies, let's respect the law of the street." But the problem had already gone beyond the organization's control. Journalists from the major national newspaper were entering gang territory and misappropriating Homies Unidos's name to secure interviews with the gang members. As a result, some of Homies's bridges with the gangs had been damaged if not broken. Outreach coordinators were becoming more reluctant to take people out into the field or even to go themselves. The neighbors in the complex where the office is located are growing suspicious of and hostile toward the organization. Everybody feels that it's time to move the office to neutral ground. As one Homie puts it, "Getting a new office is like starting over, a fresh start." This would be the organization's fifth move in its six-year history.

Not long after their latest move, the office is burglarized. All the equipment is stolen: TVs, computers, videos, and the weight equipment. Word is that it's an "inside" job—disgruntled program participants perhaps? Who knows. But the staff members feel that they can't return. They recover what they can and abandon the location. It's only four months since they felt compelled to move from the last location to start anew. The mood is heavy and spirits very low. "Imagine that this would happen to *us*. We who used to do such things ourselves!" Shut out of the *barrios*—the ground of the organization's field operations—by the combined heat of gang politics and the heavy police presence, Homies Unidos is now also without an office. This organization, first conceived of as an alternative space of representation for gang youth, and as a safe and neutral space for those willing to try to give up *la vida loca* (the crazy life), had turned first into an impossible space; now it had become a non-space.

One month later, the ruling right-wing party, ARENA, in concert with the PNC, unleashed its zero tolerance strategy, *El Plan Mano Dura*. In July 2003, Paco Flores, the Salvadoran president at the time, stood in front of television cameras at night in the neighborhood of La Dina. Posing in front of a wall graffitied with the insignia of the 18th Street Gang, wearing a black leather jacket and flanked by the new chief of police and the head of the Salvadoran armed forces, Flores declared a state of emergency and unleashed the police campaign, *El Plan Mano Dura*, and legislative proposal, *La Ley Anti-Mara* (the Anti-Gang Law).

Like U.S. anti-gang legislation, in the name of prevention, *El Plan Mano Dura* works actively to build a criminal record against youth through petty infractions and channels young people into the criminal justice system before serious crimes are committed. The goal is to get the young person into the system by giving law enforcement probable cause to arrest them. Although many of these practices are already in effect under the catchall category of "illicit association," the supporting legislation increases fines and prison sentences for minors, and makes illicit a whole range of additional activities, heretofore legal. The plan makes gang membership illegal and prohibits the association of two or more gang members. It has a very loose interpretation of what constitutes gang affiliation and thus probable cause for detaining alleged gang members.

For instance, the plan outlaws and criminalizes the wearing of tattoos that designate gang or criminal affiliation and any that appear on the face, head, neck, or genital region. In the initial plan, tattoo artists were to keep a registry of each of their tattoos, a description of the tattoo and the name, address, age, and signature of the client. These tattoo regulation laws mirror gun regulation laws. The tattoo has become encoded as a dangerous weapon—but with this difference: guns, in the right hands, are considered legitimate weapons. These tattoo registries were to be subject to inspection by the ministry of health.

Mano Dura and the anti-gang laws draw upon U.S. legislation such as the Street Terrorism Enforcement Prevention Act (STEP)[19] and anti-loitering laws, which were designed to retake command of the politically marked space of the street and to prohibit or make "illicit" all forms of association and communication between two or more presumed "gang members"—be they standing, sitting, walking, driving, gathering, appearing, whistling, or gesturing—anywhere in public view, which is to say, *in* the streets of the *barrio* (Zilberg 2002b).

El Plan Mano Dura was the last straw for Homies Unidos. If the organization was weakened before Flores's announcement, its tattooed peace workers were completely immobilized and their already-fraught association with and community outreach to their constituency—gang and poor youth—was now "illicit." Indeed, like its U.S. counterparts, *El Plan Mano Dura* makes no distinction between gang peace activists, nonactive gang members and active ones. It categorizes all youth and young adults in targeted neighborhoods as at-risk.[20]

Shut out of the *barrios* and "evicted" from their offices, Homies Unidos refocused its energies on its cultural and arts programs. The latter involved leveraging the expressive cultural practices associated with gang and hip-hop culture—graffiti, tattoos, break dancing, rap, and spoken word—as points of intervention for social change. The program aimed to direct the cultural agency of youth into nonviolent pursuits and to destigmatize these practices—and thus the youth attached to them—in the eyes of society at large. But under *El Plan Mano Dura*, such practices were all now probable cause for determining gang membership and thus for incarceration. The organization's original plan to hold these events in public squares and parks had to be scrapped; private galleries, studios, and university halls were substituted.

Indeed, William Huezo Soriano (AKA Weasel), the former director of this arts program and successful tattoo artist in his own right—suffering under the combined pressures of gang violence and police harassment alongside declining revenue from his tattoo business—subsequently fled El Salvador to seek refuge with his family in the United States. After three attempts to cross into the United States, he was caught at the Tijuana–San Ysidro border and placed in an INS detention facility. What goes around does, indeed, come around.

REFUGEE GANG YOUTH?

How then do zero-tolerance gang-abatement strategies work out when deportation is not a viable arena for Salvadoran state action? I would argue that the importation of these strategies alongside the deportation of immigrant gang youth only fuels the undocumented migration and the illegal reentry of gang-affiliated, -alleged, and -impacted youth further, thereby reproducing and exacerbating the ongoing circulation of violence between the United States and El Salvador. For instance, in the months leading up to the introduction of *Mano Dura*, Salvadoran migration police on the Salvadoran-Honduran border had been placed on high alert. Honduran youth were apparently fleeing to El Salvador to escape the effects of similar zero tolerance strategies, put into effect through Honduran legislation a year before their introduction in El Salvador. Thus, although deportation is not an option for the Salvadoran state, undocumented migration is still a possibility, albeit a perilous one, for the gang member.

Many deportees—who, like William, have attempted to build new lives for themselves in their unfamiliar but native countries—have also attempted illegal reentry into the United States as their best available option despite the risk of re-imprisonment if caught. Might these gang-affiliated, -alleged, and -impacted youth, pushed out of El Salvador by the combined pressures of gangs and police, constitute a new class of refugee—many themselves children of civil war refugees?

It is first and foremost in the legal arena where the immigration consequences and transnational implications of criminal law and zero tolerance strategies are being played out. Immigration and criminal attorneys and public defenders are on the frontlines of this work. Yet these attorneys have only very recently become aware of each other and the consequences of one set of laws for the other. In recognition of this need, the Los Angeles public defender's office now contracts an immigration attorney to consult with its criminal attorneys over the complex articulation of criminal and immigration law as it affects immigrant youth. These initiatives, however, are incipient. By and large, attorneys have very few resources to which they can turn in their work to defend immigrant youth and young adults in criminal reentry and deportation proceedings. This is particularly true for immigration attorneys who find themselves in the curious position of applying for withholding from deportation and, where possible, political asylum on the premise that these youth and young adults have a well-founded fear of persecution and for their physical integrity from the state and the gangs upon return to El Salvador. This ironic twist at work in the emergence of deported gang members as a new, albeit unlikely, class of refugees makes for a very curious merging of quite distinct legal fields. There is important work to be done in understanding the implications of this growing articulation between them.

Certainly, there are direct historic lessons to draw from the 1980s, and from the criminalized church-based Sanctuary Movement's work with "deserving refugees" fleeing human rights abuses and the civil war violence within the context of a Salvadoran guerilla movement labeled "terrorist." How will this legal political history converge with or diverge from today's "undeserving" refugee? If the comparison drawn here between civil war and gang youth refugees comes across as a flippant or irresponsible blurring of boundaries between the domains of the political and criminal, consider this equally disconcerting fact: *El Plan Mano Dura* takes U.S. zero tolerance strategies one step further by reintroducing the collaboration of the Salvadoran military with its National Civil Police. This threatens to undermine the demilitarization of the police forces—an important and key post–civil war reform, and a fundamental human rights issue over which the 12-year civil war was fought.

CONCLUSION: MAKING THE CASE
FOR TRANSNATIONAL YOUTH STUDIES

I have focused here on the transnational youth violence intervention and prevention organization, Homies Unidos, precisely because it works on the immigration consequences of the criminal justice system for youth and on the transnational implications of the globalization of zero tolerance gang-abatement strategies between the United States and Central America. Its work reveals how the multiple legal regimes (immigration, criminal, and refugee) come together across national boundaries (U.S. and Salvadoran). Shut down in San Salvador, the Los Angeles office, which was itself started by a return deportee, is similarly embattled from all sides. In addition to grappling with the boomerang effects of the globalization of zero tolerance policing strategies, the conditions on the ground in Los Angeles make for an exceedingly large mandate for this very small and very grassroots community-based organization.

On the local level, the organization works to contest the impact of gang injunctions on neighborhood youth and on their own capacity to conduct violence prevention work with those youth. They do so in the context of William Bratton's installation as police chief there and his post–9/11 call for an "all out assault" against "homeland terrorism" (gang crime) and "street terrorists" (gang youth). Indeed, Bratton began his term by drawing explicit links between juvenile crime and terrorism. The convergence of the now slippery domains of crime, terrorism, and immigration has disturbing ramifications for immigrant youth, particularly given that there is federal funding to be gained in making this link between gangs and terrorists explicit.

The association of the criminal with the terrorist has more recently taken on a most threatening specter. Since November 2004 a spate of unsubstantiated articles—published on the Internet, in the *Boston Herald, Washington Times,* and the *LA Times*—have insinuated links between La Mara Salvatrucha and Al Queda.[21] Police and intelligence officials have since denied any evidence of such links, but the implicit has been made explicit, if only through rumor and innuendo—and Homies Unidos is on nervous alert. Meanwhile, on the national level, the organization is struggling to put immigration on the agenda of youth criminal justice coalitions.

The work of Homies Unidos demonstrates that the policing of immigrant gang-affiliated, -alleged, and -impacted youth calls for transnational youth studies. The globalization of Latino immigrant youth gangs and of U.S. gang-abatement strategies points to the global reach of these research concerns that were traditionally confined to local and national domains. It problematizes the position taken in this volume that all empirical studies of globalization are ultimately local (Muncie 2006, chapter 2 this volume). Indeed, the deportation of immigrant gang youth suggests that what happens in U.S. cities such as Los Angeles affects and is affected by what happens in Latin American cities such as San Salvador. In this instance, a scale of analysis that can account for the law both within and between localities of more than one nation-state becomes essential in our work to unravel the human consequences and lived experiences of globalization for youth today.

ENDNOTES

1. I use the terms *affiliated, alleged,* and *impacted* in order to suggest that active gang membership is not as readily apparent as zero tolerance policing strategies would imply, to acknowledge that youth can be simultaneously villains and victims in gang warfare, and that unaffiliated youth are targets of both gangs and police.

2. After their respective terms as the New York City Police Department's chief of police and New York City's mayor, William Bratton and Rudolf Guiliani both became private sector consultants to countries such as Mexico, Venezuela, and South Africa, offering technical expertise in their applications of the Broken Windows zero tolerance policing philosophy.

3. For a discussion of transnationalism "from above" and "from below" see Smith and Guarnizo 1999: 3–34.

4. I address these other flows in my book-in-progress, *The Courier and the Deportee: The Production of Transnational Space at the Nexus of Migration, Trade and Security.*

5. This belated recognition of Salvadorans' *refugeeness* was further bolstered by the settlement of the American Baptist Church (ABC) case in January 1991, which reopened 150,000 political asylum cases that formerly had been denied and which was to extend the asylum process to Salvadorans and Guatemalans as a class.

6. The vast majority of Salvadoran gang youth opt for "voluntary departure" under the misguided understanding that they will be allowed to return to the United States after a set period, and that their passports will not be marked "deported."

7. I use the terms *youth* and *young adults* interchangeably here. I do so because gang-affiliated Salvadoran immigrants are deported for criminal offenses committed as adults, that is to say at age 18 or above. However, the United Nations General Assembly has defined *youth*

as those persons falling between the ages of 15 and 24 years inclusively. Within the category of *youth* they distinguish between *teenagers* (13–19) and *young adults* (20–24). Individual countries use slightly different variations of this age range. For instance, in El Salvador the planning group for the Youth Law (discussed later in this chapter) was age 30.

8. ICITAP was created by the U.S. Justice Department in 1986 to respond to a request from the U.S. State Department for assistance in training police forces in Latin America. Since then its activities have expanded to encompass two principle types of assistance projects: (1) the development of police forces in the context of international peacekeeping operations, and (2) the enhancement of capabilities of existing police forces in emerging democracies (http://www.usdoj .gov/criminal/icitap/).

9. *Pansa Loca* means *Crazy Belly*. While the Spanish spelling would be *panza* with a "z," the use of the "s" here denotes the influence of Spanglish on the spelling of Latino gang pseudonyms in the United States.

10. With 20 percent of their population living abroad, primarily in the United States, the Salvadoran economy is heavily subsidized by migrant remittances. There are, as a result, tremendous anxieties and expectations surrounding migration, including how to leverage remittances productively, to ensure the diaspora's attachment to the homeland, and to cope with family disintegration and other social stresses associated with migration (Zilberg and Lungo 1999).

11. *La Ley de Juventud* would regain momentum with the creation of the *La Secretaría de la Juventud* (Secretariat of Youth) in 2004. The Secretariat offers an alternative to *Mano Dura* with its *Mano Amiga* (Friendly Hand) program for violence prevention. However, as Miguel Cruz and Marlon Carranza note, the Secretariat has no autonomy from the president, and it is focused only on violence prevention. Moreover, despite the addition of *Mano Extendida* (Extended Hand)—an initiative included in the followup to *Mano Dura, Mano Súper Dura* for the rehabilitation rather than the repression of gang members—it is evident that there is much more effort and money being devoted to repressive measures. Whereas *Mano Extendida* has so far been extended to twenty gang members, between *Mano Dura* and *Mano Súper Dura*, 30,000 youth accused of being gang members were arrested between July 2003 and July 2005 (Cruz and Carranza 2005: 25).

12. Interestingly, Villalobos has since come out against the *Mano Dura* policy (2005).

13. As I mentioned previously, the transnationalization of zero tolerance crime prevention strategies between the United States and El Salvador originated in the Cold War and with counter-insurgency tactics, which circulated between the United States and El Salvador during the 1980s. Both strategies draw on emergency anti-terrorist legislation to seize their respective targets—the gang member and the guerilla.

14. The exception here was the successful campaign against kidnappings of the family members of prominent businessmen. For a discussion, which complicates the distinction between political and criminal or social violence, see Zilberg 2006.

15. It was the linguistic resonance between *Three Strikes* and *La Tarjeta Roja* that first drew me to look at the traveling of crime prevention strategies as one more component of the transnational networks between the United States and El Salvador.

16. The symbolism in each case is drawn from sports—baseball in the United States and soccer in El Salvador. The intimate relationship between sports and nationalism resonates in

both U.S. and Salvadoran policy initiatives. Following Three Strikes as it does by four years, *La Tarjeta Roja* reads like an attempt to translate the same principle into Salvadoran cultural terms. In El Salvador, this relationship between sports and nationalism has a powerful precedent in the infamous Soccer War over border skirmishes with Honduras.

17. He was referring to, among others, the three deported gang members who had been arrested in the much-publicized case *La Tormenta Toxica* (The Toxic Storm). That case revolved around a private beach-side party that the police attempted to turn into a major drug bust around the time of President George Bush's visit to El Salvador. Fifteen people, mostly middle- and upper-middle-class youth, one the son of a state assembly member, were arrested. All were released except for the three deportees, who—over a year later—were still in prison awaiting trial.

18. As Miguel Cruz of IUDOP notes, given that El Salvador's PNC was intended to be an entirely new institution, "reform" may not even be the appropriate term for the Salvadoran context (Latin American Studies Association panel discussion, Dallas, Texas, March, 2003).

19. See California Penal Code Section 186.2.

20. My previous research with Homies Unidos in Los Angeles showed that gang peace activists were subject to the same zero tolerance gang-abatement strategies as active gang members. Indeed, the LAPD actively undermined the efforts of Homies Unidos youth peace activists. Program director Alex Sanchez was arrested by the Rampart CRASH unit, who turned him over to the INS. In LA, STEP and its microphysics of constraining everyday movement on the streets of the *barrio* was effectively used to criminalize Homies Unidos's outreach and organizing in the *barrios* (Zilberg 2002a).

21. Take for instance the language of this Internet intelligence news source article entitled "Criminals, jihadists threaten U.S. border: Unholy alliance of terrorists, gang, revolutionaries pose new security threat." The article begins thus: "What would happen if criminal gangsters, revolutionaries and Islamic terrorists all got together in a common goal of overthrowing governments of America's neighbors and smuggling operatives into and out of the U.S.? Some senior police and intelligence sources [say] . . . that is just what is happening in Central America today" (Farah 2005). Similarly, Newt Gingrich hosted an hour-long special on the Fox News Channel entitled "American Gangs: Ties to Terror?" in which he considers hypothetical links between gangs and terrorists (June 25, 2005).

SELECTED REFERENCES

Alvarez, Sonia E., Evelina Dagnino, and Arturo Escobar. 1998. *Cultures of Politics, Politics of Cultures: Re-Visioning Latin American Social Movements.* Boulder, Colorado: Westview Press.

Bran, Sergio. 1998. "Violencia, Cultura, Inseguridad Pública en El Salvador." *REALIDAD: Revista de Ciencias Sociales y Humanidades.* P. 100, Vol. 64.

Call, Charles. 1996. "Policing the New World Order." *Strategic Forum* 84: 1–4.

———. 1999. "From Soldiers to Cops: 'War Transitions' and the Demilitarization of Policing in Latin Ameria and the Caribbean," PhD dissertation, Stanford University.

———. 2003. "Democratization, War and State-Building: Constructing the Rule of Law in El Salvador." *Journal of Latin American Studies*, November, 35(04): 827–862.

Call, Charles, and William Stanley. 2001. "Protecting the People: Public Security Choices After Civil Wars." *Global Governance* 7 (2): 151–71.

Cohen, Stanley. 1972. *Folk Devils and Moral Panics: The Creation of the Mods and Rockers*. New York: St. Martin's Press.

Comaroff, John, and Jean Comaroff. 2000. "Millennial Capitalism: First Thoughts in a Second Coming." *Public Culture: Millennial Capitalism and the Culture of Neoliberalism*. Special Issue, 12 (2): 291–343.

Coutin, Susan Bibler. 2000. *Legalizing Moves: Salvadoran Immigrants' Struggle for U.S. Residency*. Ann Arbor: University of Michigan Press.

Costa, Gino. 1999. *La Policía Nacional Civil de El Salvador (1990–1997)*. San Salvador: Universidad Centroamericana José Simeón Cañas.

Cruz, José Miguel. 1997. "Los Factores Posibilitadores y Las Expresiones de la Violencia en los Noventa." *ECA-Estudios Centroamericanos* 52: 978–92.

———. 2000. "Violencia, Democracia y Cultura en America Latina." *ECA-Estudios Centroamericanos* 55: 511–25.

Cruz, José Miguel, and Marlon Carranza. 2005. "Pandillas u politícas públicas: el caso de El Salvador." Paper prepared for the "Seminario sobre Juventudes, Violencia y Exclusión. Desafíos para las Políticas Públicas." Organized by INDES-Guatemala, October 10–14, 2005.

Cruz, José M., and Luis A. González. 1997. "Magnitud de la Violencia en El Salvador." *ECA-Estudios Centroamericanos* 52: 953–66.

Cruz, José M., and Portillo Peña. 1998. *Solidarid y Violencia en las Pandillas del Gran San Salvador: Más alla de la vida Loca*. San Salvador: UCA.

DeCesare, Donna. 1998. "The Children of War: Street Gangs in El Salvador." *NACLA Report on the Americas* 32 (1): 21–9.

DeCesare, Donna, and Fen Montaigne. 1999. "Deporting America's Gang Culture." *Mother Jones* July 1: 44–51.

Farah, Joseph. 2005. "Criminals, Jihadists Threaten U.S. Border: Unholy Alliance of Terrorists, Gangs, Revolutionaries Pose New Security Risk." *Joseph Farah's G2 Bulletin, Worldnetnews.com*. Posted January 17, 2005.

Freemon, Celeste. 2003. "View from Parker Center: A One-on-One with Police Chief Bill Bratton." *LA Weekly*, January 10–16. www.laweekly.com

Freire, Paulo. 1993[70]. *Pedagogy of the Oppressed*. Myra Bergman Ramos, trans. New York: Continuum.

Gingrich, Newt. 2005. "American Gangs: Ties to Terror?" *Fox News Channel*, June 5.

Hall, Stuart, Chas Critcher, Tony Jefferson, John Clarke, and Brian Roberts. 1978. *Policing the Crisis: Mugging, the State, and Law and Order*. New York: Holmes & Meier.

IUDOP. (Instituto Universitarío de Opinión Pública). "Delincuencia y Opinion Pública." *ECA-Estudios Centroamericanos* 53: 785–802.

Krauskopf, DINA. 2002. "Juventud en Riesgo y Violencia." Paper presented to Permanent

Seminar of the Program Towards a Society without Violence, United Nations Development Programme, San Salvador: El Salvador.

Lucero, Jose Antonio. 2000. "On Feuds, Tumults, and Turns: Politics and Culture in Social Movement Theory." *Comparative Politics* 32 (January 2): 231–49.

McPhee, Michele. 2005. "Eastie Gang Linked to al-Qaeda." *Boston Herald,* January 5.

Muncie, John. 2006. "Youth Justice and the Governance of Young People: Global, International, National, and Local Contexts." Chapter 2, this volume.

Papadopoulos, Renos et al. 1998. *Violencia en una Sociedad en Transición.* San Salvador: Programa de las Naciones Unidas para el Desarollo.

Popkin, Margaret. 2000. *Peace without Justice: Obstacles to Building the Rule of Law in El Salvador.* University Park, PA: Pennsylvania State University Press.

Ramos, Carlos Guillermo, ed. 1998. *America Central en Los Noventa: Problemas de Juventud.* San Salvador: FLACSO.

Ramos, Carlos Guillermo, et al. 2000. *Violencia en una Sociedad en Transicion: Ensayos.* San Salvador: Programa de las Naciones Unidas para el Desarollo.

Seper, Jerry. 2004. "Al Qaeda Seeks Ties to Local Gangs." *The Washington Times,* September 28.

Smith, Michael Peter, and Luis Guarnizo.1998. *Transnationalism from Below.* New Brunswick: Transaction Publishers.

Smutt, Marcela, and Jenny Lissette E. Miranda. 1998. *El Fenómeno de las Pandillas de El Salvador.* San Salvador: FLACSO and UNICEF.

Stanley, William. 1996. *Protectors or Perpetrators? The Institutional Crisis of the Salvadoran Civilian Police.* Washington DC: Office on Latin America and Hemisphere Initiatives.

Villalobos, Joaquin. 2001. *De La Tortura a La Protección Ciudadana: La Policia Nacional Civil de El Salvador Como Instrumento de al Pacificacion y Democratizacion.* San Salvador: INELSA.

———. 2005 "El Salvador, lo que no debe hacerse con las pandillas." *El Diario de Hoy* (El Salvador), June 22.

Ziegler, Melissa, and Rachel Nield. 2002. "From Peace to Governance: Police Reform and the International Community." Report from Conference *Police Reform and the International Community: From Peace Processes to Democratic Governance,* November 16, 2001. Washington DC: Washington Office on Latin America.

Zilberg, Elana. 1994. "From the Rodney King Beating to Immigrant Bashing." *(sub)Text* 1 (4): 9.

———. 2002a. "From Riots to Rampart: A Spatial Cultural Politics of Salvadoran Migration to and from Los Angeles." PhD dissertation, Department of Anthropology, University of Texas at Austin.

———. 2002b. "A Troubled Corner: The Ruined and Rebuilt Environment of a Central American Barrio in Post–Rodney King Riot Los Angeles." *City and Society* XIV (2): 31–55.

———. 2004. "Fools Banished from the Kingdom: Remapping Geographies of Gang Violence between the Americas (Los Angeles and San Salvador)." *American Quarterly* 56 (3): 759–779; Special Issue: *Los Angeles and the Future of Urban Cultures,* Guest Editors Raúl Homero Villa and George J. Sánchez.

———. 2006. "Gangster in Guerilla Face: The Political Folklore of '*Doble Cara*' in Post–Civil War El Salvador." *Anthropological Theory* (forthcoming).

Zilberg, Elana, and Mario Úcles Lungo. 1999. "Se han Vuelto Haraganes? Jóvenes, Migración y Identidades Laborales." *Transformando El Salvador Migraciòn Sociedad y Cultura*. Susan Kandel Mario Lungo, ed. San Salvador: FUNDE.

4

Policing the Youth: Toward a Redefinition of Discipline and Social Control in French Working-Class Neighborhoods

LAURENT BONELLI

Repression, as cruel as recession
—La Rumeur, *L'ombre dans la mesure*
(EMI music France 2002)

Even before the disorders of November 2005, the "explosion of insecurity" in French working-class suburbs (*banlieues*) had become an unavoidable subject of political, electoral, and media debate. Anxious or alarmist talk, special essay collections, and spectacular reports are appearing and becoming more and more common, pushing into the background whole areas of the country's social and political affairs. Analysts, "experts" and essayists dealing with security are predicting an exponential growth in crime, the emergence of no-go areas controlled by lawless criminals who are getting younger, more recidivist, and more violent. At the same moment, the various political parties, taken as a whole, refer to their constituencies' "demand for security" and ask for more energetic action by the police and the courts. Since the mid-1990s, urban security has thus become one of the main priorities of successive governments, which have devoted to it major resources, both economic and legislative.

To understand this extraordinary inflation of the subject of security in our society, it is important to analyze the *configuration*—as defined by Norbert Elias[1]—in which security acquires meaning; that is, we must reconstitute all the chains of interdependency that link together numerous social agents belonging to spheres as different as the police, politics, the media, academia, business, and so on. This suggests that we should bring out the fluctuating balances of tensions and power relationships among these different actors by emphasizing their historicity and the mindsets they convey. In reality, a social problem does not exist in and of itself: attaining the status of a "problem" presupposes a genuine social action. Not every social transformation becomes a social problem, and making a particular situation visible "presupposes the action of social groups interested in producing a new way of seeing the world in order to act on it."[2] This amounts to saying that, in addition to objective changes—without which the problem would not arise—there is also a specific activity of public formulation, a mobilization effort that must in each case be questioned and made clear. That is what I propose to do here by relating the morphological and social transformations of working-class neighborhoods in France to developments in ways of perceiving the "violence" of the adolescents living in these neighborhoods and the effects of the increasing efforts of the police to deal with these "urban disorders."

SOCIAL DETERIORATION AND DISAFFILIATION

The expression *working-class neighborhoods* (*quartiers populaires*) refers essentially to large areas on the outskirts of cities, which in France are called *les banlieues* (the suburbs), and, to a lesser extent, to the inner-city neighborhoods. All these zones are characterized by a concentration of low-skilled workers, a high level of public housing, and important rates of unemployment, youth, and migrants.

During the period between the 1960s and today, *les banlieues* have undergone major changes. Built between the 1950s and the 1970s, these areas, with such eloquent names as "City of 4000" (for 4,000 apartments) in La Courneuve, "City of 3000" in Aulnay-sous-bois, and so on, sought to provide a rational, planned response to the issue of housing and to urban development in general. They were intended to replace the hovels, still numerous at that time; to improve the condition of modest families; and to bring workers closer to their factories.[3] These efforts to create social housing should be connected with the increase in the numbers of blue-collar workers, which rose from

6,485,000 in 1954 (33.2 percent of the economically active population) to 8,191,000 (37.2 percent) in 1975, with a 1 percent rate of annual growth between 1954 and 1978. In 1974, the concentration of the labor force in factories reached its apex, with unskilled industrial workers in 2,600,000 jobs.[4] Although retrospective examination of this period tends to make it look like a golden age, which it probably was not,[5] it nonetheless represents a period of social progress for many French working-class families that were finally able to have access to running water, electricity, and other conveniences, and for whom the future at last seemed to be open.

The gradual departure of families who were more well off and able to buy homes, the arrival of immigrant families, and the increasingly precarious condition of those who were still experiencing the effects of the economic crisis were to change profoundly the social morphology of these neighborhoods.

First of all, as a result of the liberal housing policies promoted during the 1970s (aid for investment in real estate), the better-off strata in these neighborhoods (chiefly skilled workers) gradually left them and bought or built houses in the many new cities that were flourishing in France at that time.[6] This shift, which took place in the context of these groups' social and residential rise, was at the same time a cause and a result of the evolution of the low-cost housing projects (*habitations à loyer modéré*, or HLM). On one hand, this desertion of the working-class areas was motivated in part by the arrival of migrant families (especially from Algeria and Morocco), who had been rehoused by the state authorities.[7] In reality, despite their precarious living conditions, during the 1970s and 1980s these groups were kept largely outside public housing. It was only through a deliberate policy instituted by the state authorities that they were able to gain access to this housing, thereby accelerating the departure of skilled workers and the middle classes: the first buildings vacated were the ones in which the immigrants were housed. In another way, the consequences—especially the economic ones—of vacating these buildings forced lenders (whether private or municipal) to open the projects to families they had previously rejected. They thereby transformed the social and ethnic composition of these neighborhoods, and by doing so hastened other groups' departure from them and increased the concentration of new groups in them.[8]

At the same period, industrial jobs (especially unskilled jobs) held by people living in these zones were hard hit by the economic crisis. Businesses made major efforts to automate their operations, and the labor-intensive manufacturing done by low-skilled workers was replaced by imports from southern hemisphere countries. Between 1975 and 1999, the number of unskilled workers nationwide fell from 3,840,000 to 2,163,000, for a decrease of 44 percent. The unskilled jobs that disappeared were concentrated in industrial production. In textiles, clothing, wood-working, and leather-working, three-quarters of the jobs for unskilled labor disappeared over 20 years.[9] This situation concerned especially immigrants. In 1999, there were 2,100,000 active immigrants (8.1 percent of the economically active population). Whereas blue-collar workers represent 26.3 percent of the economically active population as a whole, they represent 48.7 percent of immigrants. Among Moroccans and Algerians, the rates rise to 58.2 percent and 48.7 percent, respectively. The proportions are even higher at the level of unskilled work (9.2 percent of the economically active population), which occupies 19.1 percent of immigrants as a whole, 31 percent of Moroccans, and 21.5 percent of Algerians.[10]

The transformations accompanying passage to a post-Fordist model of production largely destroyed the traditional worker's world. Large-scale unemployment and the precariousness of unskilled jobs reintroduced an insecurity and unpredictability that the advent of a wage-earning society (based on economic growth and a strong welfare state) had significantly reduced. At the same time, this deobjectivization of wage earners destabilized elements that had been stable and led to disaffiliation (*désaffiliation*).

Even before 1975, unemployment among blue-collar workers was higher than that in other social categories. Blue-collar workers were affected, more directly than the others, by the consequences of changes in the means of production. When the economic crisis came, unemployment increased sharply, especially among the oldest workers. Employees and workers were the socioprofessional categories most affected. In 1999, rates of unemployment in these categories were above 14 percent; for immigrants, these rates were above 21 percent. Next, industrial transformations—especially rapidly changing rates of production (*production à flux tendu*)—tended to make recourse to temporary and part-time workers a general practice. In 1995, 14 percent of all workers and 25 percent of unskilled workers had limited-term contracts: temporary, apprentice, fixed-term, or trainee. The proportion of such jobs was only 9 percent among wage earners.[11] In March 2001, 17 percent of unskilled wage earners were in fixed-term, temporary, or trainee positions, as contrasted with 7 percent of more skilled wage earners. In 1982, special forms of employment consisted mainly of fixed-term positions and involved only 4 percent of unskilled jobs. Although fixed-term jobs and trainee positions increased in a fairly uniform way across all kinds of unskilled labor, temporary contracts are specific to the world of workers. In March 2001, the rate of temporary workers often rose above 10 percent in areas employing unskilled workers.[12] Thus in working-class neighborhoods we see a decrease in the level of activity (the number of people with jobs) at the same time that job insecurity is increasing.

These phenomena, which radically modify the social structure of the working classes, also have symbolic consequences: they destroy the cognitive and normative structures of working-class members. Thus one cannot understand the development of these milieus without at the same time taking these two dimensions into account. This is particularly necessary when thinking about the question of "deviance" among the young. On one hand, this deviance is redefined under the impact of changes in access to unskilled jobs and to earlier modes of reproduction and discipline; on the other, it is the web of meanings in which deviance is caught (and especially the idea that "boys will be boys") that is collapsing.

The violence of certain groups of working-class young people is not a new phenomenon: remember the acts of aggression committed by the juvenile gangs of the 1960s or the 1970s.[13] But for all that, the ways of regulating their violence and perceiving it have greatly changed. The teenagers' characteristic tendency to hang out in public areas, which led to a series of deviant behaviors (verbal and physical aggression, minor theft, vandalism, etc.) usually ended in the absorption of the most unskilled groups into the industrial proletariat. Far from being incompatible with the culture of the workshop, the values to which these youths adhered (masculinity, violence, anti-authoritarianism, etc.) found acceptance there. One has only to think of the maleness of workshops[14] and the struggle against the "little boss," the foreman, to see this acceptance. These values sometimes even fed labor union and political action. Over the years, assimilation into a vocation was accompanied by a more conformist way of life (settling down), but without any real normative break.

Today, these same young people can no longer enter a world that has largely declined[15] any more than they can get the new unskilled jobs to which their absence of diplomas objectively dooms them. These jobs are created exclusively in the service sector.[16] And while it is true that the work of a supermarket cashier is assembly-line work, it nonetheless differs profoundly from the latter in that it involves the customer, who imposes forms of civility and "normalized" behavior (docility, politeness, even deference)[17] that are opposed to the street culture values. Moreover, gender difference is particularly clear in this market. Girls, who have been socialized in a different way and urged by their extended families to leave home as soon as possible,[18] adopt these modes of life much more willingly, allowing them to do better in school and on the job market than their male counterparts. In this context of competition for unskilled jobs, young men with values that function as a social stigma are at a particular disadvantage.

At the same time that the world of unskilled jobs has been transformed, the expansion of education in France has kept within the school system social groups that would earlier have been excluded from it. By temporarily removing them from productive activities and cutting them off from the world of work, school destroys the natural process of working-class reproduction based on an anticipated adaptation to subordinate positions, and inclines children of the working class to refuse manual labor and the working-class condition.[19] Thus teenagers from working-class neighborhoods are kept in school, while at the same time they are doomed, by their lack of cultural capital, to almost certain academic failure. The hiatus between the possible future (maintained by the discourse on academic "democratization") and the probable future (which these teenagers experience directly or indirectly) saps the foundation of the teacher's authority. The discourse seeking to make hopes of social advancement hinge on the schools succeeds only in turning against school those who expect from it what it cannot give them (or if it does, it does so at low wages). The relative autonomy of the educational system does not mean that it can eradicate inequalities, since it only retranslates them into academic terms.[20] This disillusionment results in a banalizing of concrete, everyday violence—especially in middle schools—that explains why social actors genuinely overwhelmed by their work are receptive to forms of support, particularly support by the police, to which they formerly rejected.

Still in school or already expelled from it, unneeded in a job market in which they participate only intermittently, a considerable number of these teenagers constitute what Robert Castel calls "the disaffiliated," the "useless people in the world, who spend time in it without really belonging to it. They occupy the position of supernumeraries, floating in a kind of social no man's land, unintegrated and probably unintegratable [. . .] They are not connected with networks of productive exchange, they have missed the train of modernization and are left on the platform with very little baggage."[21]

These teenagers tend to remain—for varying amounts of time and according to differing modalities—within a group of peers with whom they share the same social, cultural, and vocational lack of dignity. The group protects them from the calls to shape up issued by various institutions (schools, local social workers, etc.), other teenagers (those who have jobs or are succeeding in school), or girls (who spend a longer time in school, which makes them "more susceptible to the seduction of those who have cultural capital and/or economic capital, and makes them shun the 'natural' attractions of physical strength and masculinity").[22] Here we see being cobbled together an identity composed of common values and norms (concerning music, clothing, language, culture)[23] that emphasizes the importance of spatial (more than communitarian or ethnic) solidarities centered on a neighborhood, and even on a particular stairway. These fluctuant forms of sociability shape a world of immobile hanging out around apartment towers, boredom (omnipresent in rap music), anger, stories told over and over, deformed and amplified, and rumors. But this is also a world aware of the injustice fed by racism, repeated security checks made by the police, the humiliation of their fathers, and so on. Like the Algerian sub-proletarians described by Pierre Bourdieu, these young people's relationship to time is characterized by immediacy and everyday survival: temporary contracts (in construction, maintenance, security, etc.), black market labor, and what the French call *le business*, a sufficiently vague term designating a set of activities that range from bartering goods for services to petty dealing and receiving stolen property.[24] These activities can be understood through the Foucauldian concept of *illegalisms*.[25] This concept describes not only the transgression of the norms but also the whole of activities of definition, categorization, and management of the behaviors defined as undisciplined. It allows the analysis to break with the false neutrality of legal categories, presenting order and disorder as stable and universal historical categories, without moral judgment. In this sense, the concept of *illegalisms* shows the power relationship in the definition of norms, and how the weak resist the dominant order or accommodate it. In the case of the *banlieues'* young people, a way of life and shared subjectivity are made of practices both dominated (particularly because they are negatively defined and tend to function by inverting the stigma) and partly autonomous (in the sense that they constitute constantly renewed efforts to save one's honor symbolically or to win respect).[26]

In the working-class milieus that are now affected by a competition for access to rare resources—unskilled jobs, housing, social benefits, and so on—that exacerbates tensions within them, these behaviors collide with the normative systems of "old" workers who are in precarious situations and are prisoners of housing projects the collective decline of which is embodied in a particularly visible—and noisy—way by these young people.[27] The permanent occupation of the public sphere by those whom Norbert Elias and John L. Scotson call "the minority of the worst"[28] constantly reminds the "old" workers of the loss of social status and workers' pride associated with it, vestiges of an industrial world in decline. This loss leads these groups to fall back on the domestic space and generates a deep malaise that pollsters record in a truncated manner as "the fear of crime." This malaise is made even stronger by the symbolic disappearance of the workers' group as a more or less unified group with its own spokesmen. In fact, the individualization of the wage-earning condition, by structurally breaking up this group, has destroyed the collective dynamics at the origin of its political existence.[29]

WORKING-CLASS (DE)POLITICIZATIONS

Examination of the electoral results in French working-class neighborhoods reveals an increasingly marked lack of interest in political competitions. This is shown by the high rates of abstention seen in elections, which differ significantly from local and national averages. Thus Henri Rey shows, in a study he carried out in 32 neighborhoods benefiting from urban policies, that the average abstention rate is 52.1 percent, or 20 percent greater than the general average.[30] Abstention in some neighborhoods in Seine Saint-Denis reached 70 percent, to which must be added 20 percent to 30 percent of foreign residents who do not have the right to vote, as well as a considerable number of residents who are not registered voters.

It would be overly ambitious to try to draw up here an exhaustive analysis of working-class politicization, which would raise epistemological problems (what constitutes "political" behavior?) and require a separate study.[31] Therefore I will limit myself to suggesting a few approaches to the question, connecting these approaches to the morphological and social transformations I have described. I will take up in succession communist activism, first-generation immigrants' participation in politics, and the way urban unqualified young people relate to the political stakes.

The French Communist Party (PCF) long drew its strength from the series of structures of party supervision starting with the most everyday life of working-class milieus (in apartment buildings, neighborhoods, factories, etc.) reaching the centers of local (municipal) or national (parliamentary) power. This ensured that social facts connected with everyday experience would be transformed into political facts. Moreover, by promoting in the party officials from the working-class, it was long seen as uniting representatives and the represented. This allowed it to claim with a certain success the status of "the party of the working class," particularly well established in the country's industrial bastions.[32] Massive unemployment on one hand, and on the other the individualization and the increasing precariousness of status, had serious negative effects on the PCF at the very time when its main clientele (skilled workers) were leaving the public housing projects and moving into private homes. Weakened in their traditional strongholds, while in the meantime urban disorders were increasing (in Vaulx en Velin, for example), the communists became fixated on defending those who were closest to the identity of the class they were defending—that is, workers with fixed status (often French), as opposed to young people with no vocational future (often of foreign origin). This hiatus blocked the integration of young recruits from the projects (and particularly from the world of associations) into the party.[33] The result was a break between the communists and the young people in the neighborhoods, manifested at best by indifference and at worst by hostility. As one member of the PCF's national direction emphasized,

Before, we didn't understand the hooligans either, but since there were always a couple of them who put up posters for us, they were at least aware that we were on their side. Today, this is no longer the case. We no longer represent anything for these young people. (interview with author, March 12, 2002)

Although the PCF long functioned as a leader in the political socialization of working-class milieus, it no longer plays this role in the housing projects surrounding French cities.

North African immigrants' relationships to politics have also been profoundly transformed as a result of industrial restructuring and permanent residence in France. For the first generations of immigrants, who were excluded from participating in the French political game, this relationship remained schematically structured around two poles: the politics of their home countries and the social struggles in factories or households. Immigrant workers' interest in politics in their home countries was connected with battles for independence (waged by the Algerian FLN, for instance) and at the same time was bound up with the prospect of returning to their countries of origin. As the likelihood of a return home diminished[34] and burning issues connected with decolonization died down, this interest gradually faded away, as did the power of the organizations that supported it.

The second pole of the politicization of immigrant workers in France was organized during social and labor union conflicts. The concentration of the immigrants at the bottom of the social ladder (as workers) weakened them. The first to lose their jobs as a result of restructuring, they also witnessed the collapse of the fragile solidarity with the French workers with whom they became competitors during this period of decreasing jobs. The problem is well illustrated by the great workers' strikes in the Peugeot and Citroën automobile factories in 1982 and 1984, as well as by the more than ambiguous attitude of the labor unions (as Confédération Générale du Travail or CGT) at this time.

The political socialization of their children followed paths different from those of labor unionism, communist activism, or struggles for liberation. Lacking a fixed status in the world of work (they are young people who are lifelong temporary workers, have never held a job, etc.), in a precarious situation in the industrial world (they are fixed-term contract workers, experiencing rapid rotation from one job to another and shifting work schedules), these youths could hardly experience union membership of a traditional kind. It took very special situations (such as the strike of workers at the McDonald's in Paris in 2002) for them to gain access to that universe of protest, with its rules and its codes. The same is true for the institutional political universe. Cut off, as we have seen, from the Communist Party, they did not join its competitors, either. The distant and abstract nature of the stakes involved and the absence of activists they knew and recognized in their own neighborhoods prevented them from throwing off their feeling of collective political incompetence, and resulted in most cases in withdrawal, indifference, or even mistrust. The invective a young man from Dammarie les Lys addressed to an audience of association, labor union, and political activists during a forum on police brutality a few weeks after the 2002 presidential election sums up this gap:[35]

> You all voted for Chirac in the second round! You're happy, that's democracy! But I don't give a damn about Le Pen. Le Pen never did anything to me! He's not the one who's killing our brothers! He has never been Home Office minister! In Dammarie, since 1997, we have had three guys shot down by the police. In 1997, that was the left. Today it's Sarkozy [right wing Home Office minister]. For us, it doesn't change anything!!! First, we need to organize ourselves in our 'hoods, and later we will talk with the politicians!

Moreover, many of these youths are not registered voters.

Finally, few second-generation teenagers are informed about the political struggles that are shaking their parents' country. That explains why the opposition groups existing in France, and especially the radical groups, have little attraction for them.[36] For example, the difficulty these teenagers experience in talking about the situation in Algeria in part explains the displacement of their commitment—especially among the girls—to the Palestinian question. Their solidarity with the Palestinians—which takes the form of creating committees, organizing debates, exhibitions, protests—is explained not only by the work of professional activists but also by a vague feeling that the situation of the Palestinians resembles that of young immigrants in France: discrimination, racism, repeated contacts with the police, and so on. The latter elements are fundamental for understanding the activism seen in these neighborhoods over the past 20 years. It is around various questions concerning the police and the judicial system that these groups' biggest political protests have been organized.

From the march for equality and against racism (1983) to the creation of the group Young Arabs of Lyon and the Banlieues (JALB) and the Immigration and Banlieues Movement (MIB), police abuses, racist crimes, double jeopardy, and suicides in prison have been the common denominator of political engagement.[37] This is not surprising, since in working-class milieus activism is based on everyday experience rather than on abstract frameworks. However, adolescents' or young adults' relationship to *political action* only rarely finds outlets in the arenas of *politics*, whose language and principles of vision and division of the world are alien to them. The relationship formed between professionals and outsiders is thus based simultaneously on a denial of the political for the protests that most radically challenge the rules of the game or legitimate distinctions, and on supporting the most conformist initiatives. That is why protests against police brutality, for instance, are usually explained in terms of emotion or instrumentality,[38] whereas protests against violence in general get a favorable response at the institutional level.[39]

This denial of the political goes far beyond the sphere of local authorities, and is just as acute within groups or parties that would seem objectively to be the closest to these populations. Borrowing neither the extreme left's vocabulary, its topics, nor its registers of action, not even sharing the same history of struggle, the protests in these neighborhoods are consigned to the category of the infra-political, the spontaneous, or worse yet, to "communitarianism." The repeated failures of the extreme left to lead autonomous actions in these neighborhoods, like their reluctance to commit themselves to fighting alongside religious associations, shows how different the symbolic economies structuring these forms of militant action are, and how difficult communication between them is. The debates over participation in the European social forum at Saint-Denis (November 2003) by associations such as the Young Muslims of France, or the quarrels over support for girls who have been expelled from schools for wearing "Islamic scarfs," clearly underline this uneasiness.

The collapse of the structures of representation in working-class milieus, the latter's increasing lack of interest in political competitions, and the way their protests have been disqualified in the legitimate political arena all constitute key factors for understanding the development of the categories through which everyday life in the projects is perceived. They also explain the shift toward a security-oriented conception of social relationships. In fact, they make these universes into object-universes, that is, they are universes that are no longer able to produce—with even a minimal chance of success—a representation of themselves in the symbolic struggle for the description of the world. This leaves the field open for representations (whether political, media, institutional, or even academic) that are strongly marked by an unconscious social ethnocentrism.[40] Perceiving working-class milieus alternatively from the point of view of lack and deficit or that of immorality and dangerousness, these representations ignore the power relationships structuring the production of norms. These perceptions can thus claim to impose norms by strengthening discipline and the structures of normalization.

FROM THE SOCIAL CAUSES OF CRIME TO THE DELINQUENT'S INDIVIDUAL RESPONSIBILITY

Contrary to what spontaneous ways of seeing things might suggest, the morphological and social transformations of working-class neighborhoods do not suffice to explain in a mechanical way the growing interest one segment of the political class takes in the problems of the *banlieues*, any more than they allow us to understand the developments in the ways these problems are dealt with by public authorities. For that, we must look into the endogenous logics of the field of politics and the relationships these logics entertain with the media and with security professionals.

The attention given by politicians to questions of crime is recent. It dates from the end of the 1970s, when for the first time—with the Peyrefitte report in particular[41]—a distinction was drawn, under the label of *insecurity*, between crime and the fear of crime. This shift is crucial to the extent that politicians, if they cannot do anything to stop delinquency (which remains the exclusive responsibility of the police and the courts), can act on the feeling of insecurity among their constituents. That was the starting point for certain elected officials' specialization in this theme and its constitution as a political property.

Joyriding and confrontations between the police and groups of young people in Minguettes and Vénissieux during the summer of 1981 are thus often presented as the first important occasion on which public authorities showed an interest in the problems of the suburban projects. The chief measures taken on that occasion acquire their full meaning in the context of political change (the victory of François Mitterrand and the left) and the consequent replacement of political officials. Agreeing that these disorders were the result of social causes such as precariousness, unemployment, and the physical deterioration of working-class housing, the policies pursued by the government bore on the social development of the neighborhoods, the prevention of crime, the improvement of the buildings, and the social integration of young people. These measures were for the most part grouped under the generic label of *politiques de la Ville* (urban policies) and led, at the end of the decade, to the creation of an inter-ministerial Delegation to the City (DIV) and a *ministère de la Ville* (ministry of urban affairs). In this, they reflect the sensibilities of a left wing that sees itself as the guarantor of freedom, as opposed to a right wing that has historically been the party of security.

Nonetheless, at that time the urban question was not a priority for governmental action, so it was assigned to relatively low-level actors within the state's new elites. The various institutions of the *politiques de la Ville*, their financiers (such as the *Caisse des dépôts et consignations*), and the expert studies they commissioned attracted actors from the modernizing group.[42] Broadly involved in the transformations of the state in the postwar period, these politico-administrative elites, whose eponymous political figures were Pierre Mendès-France and Michel Rocard, successively, came to power in the Socialist Party by a much closer margin than other groups such as the CERES, for instance.[43] They therefore fell back on peripheral projects of governmental action, especially *la Ville*. Importing onto this terrain their principles of rationality and the rationalization of the state (logics of projects, territories, partnerships, etc.), they played an important role in constructing the cognitive categories of the problem that were to structure in large measure its public perception.[44] These approaches, which contradict analyses in terms of domination and put the emphasis on the individual "handicaps" of territories and populations, largely *depoliticized* this subject and laid the foundations of the later political consensus. These analyses achieved their full scope at the beginning of the 1990s, thanks to the increasing attention given by the media to sporadic flare-ups in the *banlieues*;[45] and thanks also to transformations in the relationships between politicians and the media, in the process of producing a symbolic definition of social problems.[46] It was then that urban disorders acquired the status of a political property over which professional politicians fought. Paradoxically, the symbolic profits attached to this theme eluded those who had contributed to its emergence.

The victory of the right-wing parties in 1993 marked a first shift: the problems of the *banlieues* became a question of policing and economic development. As is indicated by the first parliamentary report on the *politique de la Ville*, presented by Gérard Larcher, who had been a right-wing senator before the political change,

> it is not surprising [. . .] that the urban policy known as *de la Ville*, incriminating the errors of urban planning and development, still too reluctant to condemn unacceptable social deviance, drowned in bureaucracy, and primarily preoccupied with the consequences of media coverage, has now resulted in an obvious failure. By accusing concrete of being the source of all evils, we have forgotten the people themselves. Now, without making individuals responsible [. . .] it will not be possible to restore balance—with its assumed difference—in our cities.[47]

Making the individual responsible—which is connected with the conservative *doxa*—is at the heart of the measures taken by the government. The law providing guidelines and programming for internal security (LOPS), adopted in 1995, seeks to strengthen and harden the repression of petty crime, whereas the various measures taken in connection with the *politique de la Ville* emphasized economic development such as free tax zones, subsidized jobs, and so on.

The Socialist Party's return to power in June 1997 confirms this development. In the internal competitions within the party, the modernizers lost all the political influence they had won during the 1980s and 1990s. It was other groups that took up the urban question, which had become a central issue. Since political struggles are inseparable from struggles to define the social world, the weakening of the role of these elites in the state was accompanied by the decline in the prominence of their ideas. The overall approach to urban problems they defended gave way to a view more directly centered on urban security, which was raised to the rank of the government's second priority after employment. There was, moreover, no minister *de la Ville* in the first Jospin government. A minister was named only a year later, in March 1998, and remained condemned to a virtual nonexistence both symbolic and material compared with his colleagues at the home office and the justice ministry. Socialist officials henceforth stressed that "the primary cause of crime is the criminal himself."

For the left-wing parties, that was the end of the idea that crime has social causes: "we know that crime is not social in nature and is in each case a matter of individual responsibility," reported Christophe Caresche, a socialist congressman from Paris.[48] These schemas presuppose that teenagers in working-class neighborhoods have made an easy, rational, and lasting choice of a system of "delinquent" values, as opposed to "conventional" values in which work remains central. It therefore becomes important to raise the cost of a delinquent act by increasing the punishment. As Julien Dray, the national secretary of the Socialist Party in charge of security, said at a national meeting on security held in Evry on October 27, 2001, "let us refer, for once, to the precepts of neo-classical economists: for the rational *homo economicus*, the price of the possible punishment must exceed the benefits expected from the crime." These conceptions thus emphasize the systematic pursuit of all crimes and infractions. Jacques Chirac, the president of the republic, declared: "we have many criminals, especially young criminals, who don't even feel they are doing something wrong and who attack people [and] nothing is done about it. We must therefore accept the principle that any aggression, any crime, must be punished on the first offense."[49]

The erasure of the opposition between left and right in the mode of perceiving working-class *illegalisms* and the emphasis put on individual responsibility transform the economy of punishment. These developments are the result of a restructuring of earlier disciplinary processes, and they validate and authorize specific systems of knowledge.

These systems of knowledge, which are essentially behaviorist in type, put the accent on deviant or antisocial behaviors and on the incivility of young people in working-class neighborhoods. These systems see such behaviors and attitudes as the cause of insecurity and the point of departure for "careers" in crime.[50] Strongly influenced by the works of J. Q. Wilson and G. Kelling in the United States, and particularly by their theory of "broken windows,"[51] these systems of knowledge emphasize a delinquent *continuum* that begins with insignificant acts and leads to the commission of much more serious acts if not promptly repressed. After serving as the basis for Rudolph Giuliani's reforms in New York and becoming acclimated in the United Kingdom with Tony Blair's law-and-order legislation, these ideas are being used in France in a particularly radical way, in a conception of urban violence as gradually leading to acts as heterogeneous as stealing a car, vandalizing a mailbox, impoliteness, organized crime, and Islamic terrorism.[52]

The many scientific and empirical refutations of these approaches have not prevented them from becoming established in the world of politics.[53] This success has to do with the configuration in which they are placed, with the position of those who express them, and with the implicit philosophy they convey.

First, these theories operate in the context of the decline of alternative expert analysis, whether those experts are political (the PCF, neighborhood and/or immigrant organizations) or proceed from other institutions, such as the agencies involved in social prevention (which have been hard hit by the consequences of disaffiliation). This weakening authorized a renewal of the cognitive frameworks for dealing with the social question, under the influence of actors interested in producing new categories that conform more closely to their points of view and interests.

Next, these theories benefited from the legitimacy and the positions of authority held by their spokesmen. Occupying *simultaneously* or *successively* positions in academia (through university teaching, notably in programs specializing in security; through publication, etc.), politics (as activists, members of ministerial cabinets, technical advisers, etc.), administration (through participation in training programs, technical teams, reports, etc.), and the media (as experts brought in to give sense to a series of unconnected minor events), these multi-positioned actors benefit from the intersecting legitimacies of these different social universes, which tend to function as *multipliers of symbolic capital*. These actors thus help put into circulation and diffuse new analytical frameworks far beyond the area in which they were elaborated.[54]

Finally, by enclosing the causes of crime within the observation of criminal behaviors, these systems of knowledge provide theoretical frameworks that seem immediately transposable into theories of practice for politicians concerned with reforms or with improving the everyday operations of institutions.

Focusing the analysis on the consequences of working-class *illegalisms* also results in a reduction of social complexity that encourages people to forget the extent to which politicians are responsible for the structural transformations in the wage-earning sector. In other words, the talk about "urban violence" or "violence in the schools" creates a politics of forgetting and remaining silent about disaffiliation that allows successive governments to castigate the "bad poor" and the "failure of working-class families to be responsible," and also allows them to emphasize the need to use the police to solve these issues.

CAN DISAFFILIATION BE MANAGED BY POLICE METHODS?

Police agencies play a special role in the process of elaborating, disseminating, and naturalizing these systems of knowledge. The police are characterized by their ability to produce statements concerning violations of the law, risks, and threats. Their success depends on a system of exchanges among social agents occupying different positions within the state and outside it: government, politicians, judges, social institutions, social control institutions, groups of concerned citizens, criminal groups, and so on. The definitions of order (and disorder) and their modes of regulation are therefore constantly changing, depending on the development of the relationships between each of them.[55] Transformations in the way most professional politicians see working-class *illegalisms*—such as the genuine difficulties the various institutions (schools, housing projects, public transportation, etc.) present in these neighborhoods encounter in dealing with these populations and their behaviors—necessarily strengthen certain kinds of evaluations that emphasize policing. This reformulation of the social question as primarily a question of policing gives the institution a central role in shaping the problem. This reformulation modifies earlier balances, both internal and with other social spaces: the courts, the schools, social services, and so on.[56]

This modification is not without difficulties. Although the police force is given precedence, symbolically or in terms of funding, the responses it can provide remain ambivalent. Campaigns of social pacification do not interest many policemen; in the police, the hierarchy of norms is different, placing at the top of the ladder detective work or even intelligence work. The police force is *de facto* an institution that may be characterized more than others by the choice of its assignments and the way in which it will carry them out. This is particularly the case for "generalist" branches of the police, such as urban police. The latter's officers almost become the "street corner politicians" described by W. K. Muir;[57] that is, agents that select among the spectrum of violations of the law, which the multiplication of rules and regulations make daily more numerous, those they will consider and those they will not. This hierarchy of norms, never codified as such, ultimately determines what will be pursued and what will not in the daily activity of police officers.

This latitude of action is not necessarily in accord with external demands. In this way, the question of groups of teenagers hanging around in the lobbies of apartment buildings until all hours is interesting, since it is the point of convergence for numerous complaints from both individuals and institutional agents. The gap between these relatively anodyne but repeated requests for police action and the pursuit of criminals limits police officers' enthusiasm for intervention. In fact, requests for the settlement of petty disorders greatly exceeds the capacities of the police and its *savoir-faire* (or its *savoir-être*). As a police superintendent in a large city in southwestern France noted,

> The specialty in this area is rugby, that is, you pass the ball to the next guy. The problem is that the police force is on the wing, right near the sideline, and we can't pass the ball to anybody! (Superintendent of urban police, 44 years old. Interview with the author, March 28, 2001.)

Moreover, these kinds of missions, which often amount to repression without crimes and security checks without infractions, remain very difficult. This is the way a police chief in the Paris region summed up the activity of his anti-crime brigades (BAC) in the lobbies of apartment buildings:

> If they find something—a weapon, hashish, whatever—they take the people in for questioning, but if not, they just check their papers and tell them to move on, saying that they're annoying everybody. (Chief superintendent of urban police, 53 years old. Interview with the author, March 22, 2001.)

In every case, these assignments are not very gratifying judicially, and their repetition establishes a strong atmosphere of distrust between the police forces and the juvenile groups they are keeping an eye on. This distrust is immediately reflected in an increase in insults, and even rebellions, which rose from 11,687 in 1974 to 52,398 in 2004.[58] Moreover, these two kinds of offenses usually become the only charge that can be brought in these situations.[59] As a magistrate emphasized:

> You end up realizing that it is the security check itself—supervised and ordered by the judicial authority—that provokes the offenses. At the outset, you've got a person who hasn't done anything, whom there is no reason to check, and who ultimately finds himself in court for an offense that was directly provoked by the check itself. That is in fact the outrage, because it is completely humiliating to be subjected to a security check when there is no reason for it, and it is particularly humiliating to be handcuffed or taken to the police station because you don't have your identity card in your pocket. Thus in such cases, the result is quite often and quite legitimately the arrest of people who don't want to show their identity card because they've done nothing wrong or who show it but contest the legitimacy of the officer's action. And in such cases, without supervision and without the will of the judicial institution, the person is systematically convicted in accord with fast-track procedures in which he is not able to exercise his right to defend himself. (High Court judge. Interview with the author, May 26, 2002.)

Judicial authority is thus put in the service of a logic of public order very different from its ordinary modes of functioning, and it is called upon to complete the police's action by imposing sanctions. For the past decade, French ministers of justice have issued repeated circulars calling for fast-track procedures, systematically prosecuting all offenses, and prosecuting them with greater severity.

We are witnessing a decrease in the time required for dealing with petty crimes. This is the point of the so-called *traitement en temps réel de la délinquance* (TTR, real-time processing of delinquency), experimentally introduced in the early 1990s by the court at Bobigny and generalized by Elizabeth Guigou when she became minister of justice in 1997. TTR constitutes a major transformation of the French penal system. Its principle is simple: "every case investigated, whether a felony, a misdemeanor, or a fifth class offense, must immediately be reported by telephone to the prosecutor by the investigating agency; every case thus reported must be immediately processed by the prosecutor."[60] At first limited in scope, this principle was extended to all prosecutors, increasing the workload of some of them by 90 percent. It seeks to make the time taken to judge the offense approximate the time taken to commit the act: "if the slowness of the judicial institution is stigmatized, that is not so much because it is intrinsically bad as because it no longer corresponds to the reality of a society whose tempos are quite different."[61] What is at stake here is in fact a change in the ways judicial activity is evaluated, which in turn leads to a transformation of its meaning. Speaking of TTR, Philippe Mary explained that "these systems of telescoped and accelerated justice look like the spearheads of the mangerialism that is beginning to impregnate the administration of criminal justice as a whole, and is among the clearest indicators of the systemic logic in which justice is understood not as a rational system, but through the rationality of the system."[62]

At the same time, we see an *extension* of the penal sphere to cover behaviors that were previously not prosecuted by the penal system (petty violence in the schools, using public transportation without a ticket, and more generally "incivilities"). This is the point of the judicial third way, whose stated goal is to reduce dismissals. This penal inflation results in the creation, further up the chain of criminal justice, of all the procedures of penal mediation, conciliation, and reparation carried outside the courts.

Finally, we see an increasing severity in the punishments imposed for petty offenses. The severity of *chambres de comparution immédiate* (courts in which the accused appear immediately) in comparison with ordinary jurisdictions is particularly emblematic in this regard. The changes in juvenile courts, where we see a massive increase in penal judgments to the detriment of educative judgments, which take longer to put in place, are a significant example of this shift. The penal judgments represent 75 percent in 2002; they were 30 percent in 1990.[63]

This increase in severity observable in the judiciary is also manifest in police methods. Some policemen do not hesitate to refer to a *militarization of relationships* illustrated by the attitudes ("jumping on" offenders, "stop and frisk" operations) and the clothes worn by the specialized units working in these neighborhoods: black jumpsuits, accompanied by numerous accessories (*tonfas*,[64] large tear-gas bombs, etc.), helmets, weapons (flash balls, pump guns, tasers). The vocabulary borrows increasingly from the military register. Policemen such as Richard Bousquet, a chief superintendent responsible to the union of superintendents and superior officers of the national police (SCHFPN), speaks of a "logic of war," "security zones" surrounding stairways, "drug infantrymen,"[65] and so on.

The logics of action are in accord. Justifying the use of specialized mobile units (UMS), the prefect of a department on the outskirts of Paris explained:

> They're a major tool for containing urban violence in the department. As soon as a fight between gangs erupts and a (police) team is in trouble, I have thirty husky guys who can be on the scene in 10 to 15 minutes. That calms 'em down . . . and it's more effective than a CRS (Anti Riot Units) that is unfamiliar with the terrain and is deployed blind [. . .] Community policing does no good if it's not supported by the cavalry. The community policeman doesn't arrest anyone, and if he thinks he's got no backup, he tends to keep out of sight. So it's out of the question for me to give up my cavalry. (Prefect, former interministerial delegate for Urban Social Development, 53 years old. Interview with the author, January 25, 1999.)

The head of urban police in a district in one of the 30 departments classified as "very sensitive" described his everyday work in "his" housing projects in the following statement:

> It's Kosovo down there. We're on a pacification mission. We have to hold the high ground, the way soldiers hold the ridge tops. We're seeing an escalation in the equipment used. We're no longer using flash balls, which was the thing you had to have five years ago. Policemen have powerful grenades for use when they're surrounded, and they use riot guns. The bullets are only rubber, of course, but for the policeman, the main thing is to be able to point a riot gun at someone. Before, these riot-control weapons weren't let out of the armories, or else, only for very specific and limited missions [. . .] That comes from assignments to hold the ground at any price, even if you don't have enough men. And it has to be held, somehow. (Chief superintendent of urban police, 51 years old. Interview with the author, April 27, 1999.)

That said, these assignments are not enough to justify this increase in severity, which also results from more structural motives, the most important of which is the youth of these specialized units. This is due not only to the physical tests that have to be passed to get into them, but also to fast turnover. The most experienced police officers leave these assignments; their seniority allows them to ask for transfers to "quieter" units or ones closer to the regions from which they come. The specialized units are thus usually deprived of veterans who could teach recruits the ropes and give them a few tips on how to read a situation many of them find incomprehensible, especially in the absence of adequate training. These young officers, who are not very sure of themselves professionally and who often come from small provincial towns, are socially very distant from the projects and their inhabitants, whether or not the latter are of immigrant origin. Whence their persistent uneasiness about operating among these projects with whose codes and functioning they are not familiar. This uneasiness is often manifested in a reluctance to intervene; it is especially manifested in a limited application of police work and an absence of the detachment characteristic of more experienced officers familiar with their terrain.

Everyday interactions with groups of young people take the form of ritualized confrontations in which what matters is saving the group's honor, or even avenging affronts in a macho way. This *mimetic rivalry* is perhaps most clearly put in this remark addressed by an officer to a teenager: "your shirt says *Lacoste*, mine says *Police*."[66] In this relationship, every symbolic or physical defeat for one side is seen as a victory for the other. This explains the crowds that regularly gather during security checks, and even the stone-throwing that elicits useless, repeated identity card checks, intimidations, humiliations, and even beatings. For groups of young people, it's a matter of "putting pressure" (*mettre la pression*)—to use an expression often heard during interviews with young "offenders—on police officers to show them that they are outnumbered and hence that the balance of power is unfavorable to them. For police officers, conversely, what is at stake is to show that they have control of the public space, even if they have to make illegitimate use of their monopoly on the use of force or of the authority—moral and legal, especially—conferred on them by their status.[67]

Hardening the modes of action and of relationships, as well as the increase in the number of prosecutions for insults, have not solved the initial problem—that of the petty offenses that led to this kind of police intervention in the first place.

THE USE OF SOCIAL AND EDUCATIVE SERVICES
TO ACHIEVE POLICING GOALS

Police officers who have to deal every day with these kinds of contradictions are all the more inclined to enter into partnership structures such as Local Security Contracts (CLS) because they have everything to gain from such partnerships in a practical sense as well as a symbolic one.[68] Involving other social actors in controlling and normalizing these deviant behaviors is one of the less expensive and most effective ways of responding to problems they are incapable of resolving, for reasons that are both internal (police priorities and hierarchical inversion) and connected with their prerogatives (the necessity of observing an offense and the shifting of the location of the problems, a move of sometimes only a few meters in cases of intensive police operations).

Thus we see in France an effort to involve other institutions in police work, either directly—as in the cases of public housing authorities, public transportation, and even municipalities, which develop their own security forces—or indirectly, as in the cases of the schools, the ANPE (National Employment Agency), local social work offices, and so on, which are called upon to provide information about the teenagers they are supervising or meet. This collaboration is based on breaking down barriers to exchanging information among "partners." This exchange, "in accord with the respective ethical codes" of detailed personal data on individuals who "are problems" is seen as one of the keys to successful public action on the local level. In the arenas where this exchange is deployed it is known as *shared secrecy.* The example of the local security contract in Chalon sur Saône—whose current mayor is former minister of justice—is particularly emblematic, though far from unique:

> We have to talk about traceability here. This is a serious matter. Everyone involved more or less knows the first and last names that keep coming up, in case after case, in working group after working group, in the everyday work of our CLS. Except these "descriptions" are not brought together in any one place. [. . .] With the authorization of the co-signatories, [we must] draw up a list of the family and phratry names that have regularly recurred in 2001 and 2002 in the day-to-day activities and in the follow-up by the main agents of the CLS. Whether there are ten, twenty, or fifty families, this list has to be drawn up by combining the data collected by the national police, the municipal police, the

family assistance fund (CAF), national education, public housing authorities, the city, and the sub-prefecture. [. . .] Then we have to draw up, by families, a "report of activities." Who's working? Where? Who's not working? Who's responsible to whom? What have the institutions already asked for? This report is necessary, it will give us a picture of the situation, and from then on this family or that phratry will be convinced that something is going on and that henceforth, they'll no longer be able to "play" between the lines and play this or that office off against this or that decision-maker.[69]

This information-sharing is a process of disclosure the goal of which is to destroy the different personalities or facets that an individual might present to different institutions. It refers to the mechanisms of secrecy described by Erving Goffman: "the different images of himself that are commonly reflected back to him at every level of his entourage here end up being reduced, behind his back, to a single one."[70]

This exchange remains profoundly unequal, since the police retain to a large extent the leadership role in the exchange itself and also with regard to the judicial system. As one police superintendent put it,

In the GLTD [local group for dealing with delinquency], we come in with a list of kids who are raising hell in the neighborhood, and the judge says, "Ah! We can't do anything unless we have names, etc." I answered that we weren't there to waste our time, and if they didn't want to do anything, we'd leave. (Superintendent of urban police, 44 years old. Interview with the author, March 28, 2001.)

This "partnership" gives police officers a central position that is fairly new in the regulation of behaviors publicly described as deviant, which used to be dealt with by other social institutions or in other ways.[71] This new approach prompted a teenager who had had regular confrontations with the police to say, not without a certain humor:

Now, when the BAC [anti-criminality brigade] beats us up they call us by our first names. (Interview with the author, March 22, 2001.)

The power implicit in police reports transfigures the ways these phenomena are dealt with. Murray Edelman points out that bureaucracies tend "to construct problems as justifications for the solutions they are proposing."[72] The police officers' professional *habitus*, which places criminal justice at the top of the hierarchy of norms—shown by that old saw "we're not social workers"—emphasizes coercion. Arrests and prosecutions are the cornerstone of their professional practices. And even if many police officers are aware that prison terms and fines do not suffice to get rid of the criminals they meet, they remain the prisoners of a highly solidified way of understanding the world: that of their institution and its social functions. This limited understanding results in a naturalization of crime—to which terms such as *juvenile delinquent*, *hoodlum*, and *hooligan* attest—to the detriment of views that situate the criminal act in a more complex life history where it co-exists with many other forms of integration (academic, familial, affective, vocational, etc.).

These cognitive conflicts weigh heavily on the kinds of public solutions that will be considered. Disaffiliation and the evils that flow from it are thus transformed into "juvenile delinquency," "urban violence," or "violence in the schools"—problems that have been constituted administratively and call for responses in which the police play a privileged role. The standards and the police formats—even if they sometimes provoke resistance—thus tend to become the pertinent lens through which certain populations are viewed. They are gradually establishing themselves in social spaces where they were not previously used. As Richard V. Ericson and Kevin D. Haggerty have noted, "there is no limit to police participation in the construction and management of social problems. [The police are] shaping the knowledge requirements of other institutions in order to assist those institutions in the risk management of the special populations for whom they are responsible."[73] This is sometimes the case in the schools. A high school principal in the Paris region explained:

> Things are also going well with the police. Schools no longer hesitate to call on them when there's an incident. Conversely, the police need the schools' help when they want to question someone: we give them the address, show them photos, etc. It's an ongoing collaboration that has been established. Principals are becoming less reluctant; a mentality is spreading that says: if my colleagues are doing it, there's no reason I shouldn't do it too. In other places, where there has been no local security contract, it's a surprise. One of my colleagues was amazed to see the police coming into my school—in uniform, moreover. He told me that at his school that would cause a riot and the teachers would go on

strike. They remain very marked by a 1968 mentality, and for them, the police are the CRS [anti-riot units]. (Interview with the author, March 22, 2001.)

The sources of this ongoing collaboration—which we also find in other institutions such as social workers, sociocultural agents, and so on—are to be sought in the awkward position in which the subaltern agents of the state (or of local collectivities) find themselves, particularly those who are supposed to fulfill the functions called "social." Without having the resources to do so, these agents have to compensate for the most intolerable effects and deficiencies of the logic of the market and of the economic changes that have taken place over the past 20 years. The contradiction between these overly ambitious goals and their actual interactions with the most economically and culturally deprived populations can be resolved only by sacrificing—and excluding—the disturbing elements, who endanger the slight chance of improving the collective social destiny. Thus it is the police—and the judicial system—that will be asked to resolve the central question asked by Robert Castel: "what should we do with individuals who raise inextricable problems because they are not where they should be, but who have no place anywhere in the social structure?"[74]

Systematic prosecution, incarceration, or isolation in specialized educational structures that provide close supervision (UEER, CER) are thus becoming the natural mode of regulating these supernumeraries.

These measures are very functional politically, especially during election campaigns. They allow successive governments to escape the consequences of their policies and lend new force to the myth of the sovereignty of the political, which has recently been given a pounding, especially in economic and financial affairs.[75] But these same measures pose a problem over the middle and long terms.

In fact, the police do not have the means to put an end to petty crime, which often constitutes—along with temporary work, welfare payments, and black market labor—one of the only ways that small groups permanently excluded from the circuit of productive exchanges can live and survive. The police can arrest as many drug dealers as they want, but there is a genuine *reserve army* of young people ready to replace them.[76] That is, moreover, what explains the feeling of a "bottomless well" referred to by several urban police officers during an interview. As studies conducted in the United States emphasize, nothing demonstrates that the decline in crime in the United States is the result of an increase in the number of police officers on the ground or intensive policing strategies.[77]

Next, incarceration—which has just reached record levels in France, with 63,449 prisoners in April 2004—remains marked by very high rates of recidivism. Imprisonment increases the stigma initially incurred on the academic, job, and even sexual markets. This makes integration of the offender into life that complies with the dominant norms even more difficult, and the pursuit of illicit activities more likely. By an effect of inversion, incarceration also tends to become a mark of honor among members of a peer group, confirming the individual in the social role of a delinquent. In the same way, the saturation of the police presence in some neighborhoods creates a wall of incomprehension between their populations—especially the youth—and institutions. Such saturation radicalizes and hardens everyone's positions, as is shown by the increase of illegitimate police violence seen in recent months in Poissy, Saint-Denis, Dammarie les Lys, Nîmes, and elsewhere.[78]

The headlong rush into this securitarian maelstrom generates representations of the world in which everything becomes threatening and each uncertainty turns into a fear.[79] This movement increases racism and distrust in dealing with those who tend to become new dangerous classes, thus deepening their marginalization. It is a movement that clearly constitutes a dead end, unless we admit that increasing inequalities and excluding certain social groups is a matter to be dealt with only by the police. That is, it is a dead end unless we accept the conservative *doxa* that limits the kingly functions of the state to maintaining the social order and subordinates the whole of the state's intellectual, administrative, and political activities to that end.

ENDNOTES

1. N. Elias, *Qu'est-ce que la sociologie?* Paris, Ed. de l'aube, 1991, pp. 154 ff.

2. R. Lenoir, "Objet sociologique et problème social," in P. Champagne, R. Lenoir, D. Merllié, and L. Pinto, *Initiation à la pratique sociologique*, Paris, Dunod, 1996, p. 77.

3. Between 1955 and 1975, two million low-cost housing units were constructed in France. On the development of the housing issue after World War II, see J.-P Flamand, *Loger le peuple: essai sur l'histoire du logement social en France*, La Découverte, Paris 1989; and C. Bachmann and

N. Le Guennec, *Violences urbaines. Ascension et chute des classes moyennes à travers cinquante ans de politique de la ville*, Paris, Albin Michel, 1996, especially part III, pp. 105 ff.

4. B. Seys, "L'évolution de la population active," *INSEE Première* no. 434, March 1996.

5. On the basis of a study carried out in the suburbs of Paris, Olivier Masclet shows both the reticence of working-class families to move into these large housing projects and the exclusion of immigrant families who have been able to get access to them only because they are being gradually deserted and are decaying. See O. Masclet, *La gauche et les cités. Enquête sur un rendez-vous manqué*, Paris, La dispute, 2003.

6. P. Bourdieu, *Les structures sociales de l'Economie*, Paris, Seuil, 2000, especially pp. 113 ff.

7. The categories "French" and "immigrant" need to be handled prudently. In fact, they are not based on objective categories designating a social group, but on the contrary are a perpetual stake in struggles inside and outside the group. Moreover, they tend to conflate under a single label those heterogeneous social situations, statuses, and conditions that oppose individuals to one another more than they unite them. The same goes for the government's statistical representations, which, far from being neutral, involve presuppositions that cannot be neglected when distinguishing statistically who belongs to the national community and who does not. However, in the absence of alternative indicators, it is on these taxonomies that are based the various socio-morphological data on "immigrants" that are used below. For the French National Institute of Statistics and Economic Studies (INSEE), "any person residing in France who was born in a foreign country and who declares foreign citizenship or acquired French citizenship is considered an immigrant." In 1999, the immigrant population 15 years of age or older living in households was said to be 3,800,000 persons. Almost 30 percent of them had acquired French citizenship. (S. Thave, "L'emploi des immigrés en 1999," *INSEE Première* no. 717, May 2000).

8. In 1996, more than a third of immigrant households (and half of the families from North Africa) were living in public housing; for other groups, the rate was less than one out of six. J. Boëldieu et S. Thave, "Le logement des immigrés en 1996," *INSEE Première* no. 730, August 2000.

9. O. Chardon, "Les transformations de l'emploi non qualifié depuis vingt ans," *INSEE Première* no. 796, July 2001.

10. S. Thave, "L'emploi des immigrés en 1999," *op. cit.*

11. M. Cézard, "Les ouvriers," *INSEE Première* no. 455, May 1996.

12. O. Chardon, "Les transformations de l'emploi non qualifié depuis vingt ans," *op. cit.*

13. On the behavior of these groups, see G. Mauger and C. Fossé-Poliak, "Les loubards," *Actes de la recherche en sciences sociales* no. 50, November 1983.

14. See especially P. Willis, "L'école des ouvriers," *Actes de la recherche en sciences sociales* no. 24, November 1978.

15. On changes in the structure of industrial employment and its effects on adolescents in working-class neighborhoods, see M. Pialoux, "Jeunesse sans avenir et travail intérimaire," *Actes de la recherche en sciences sociales* no. 26–27, March–April 1979, pp. 19–47.

16. "In commerce, unskilled or semiskilled jobs have accompanied the rise of large-scale retailing: there are 273,000 more cashiers, salespeople in groceries, and employees in convience stores than there were twenty years ago. [. . .] In the area of maintenance, there are 117,000 more people working in the area of office and industrial cleaning than in 1982. Similarly, there are more jobs in security and surveillance. [. . .] The increase in restaurants and espe-

cially fast-food outlets has provided jobs for waiters, assistant cooks, and dishwashers, whose numbers have grown by more than 25 percent. As a whole, there are a million more unskilled jobs than there were twenty years ago. In 2001, these jobs represented half of unskilled employment, as opposed to less than a third in 1982." O. Chardon, "Les transformations de l'emploi non qualifié depuis vingt ans," *op. cit.*: p. 1.

17. Philippe Bourgois's work on New York crack dealers is very helpful in understanding how these norms and values oppose point-for-point those current in new unskilled jobs. See P. Bourgois, *In Search of Respect. Selling Crack in El Barrio,* Cambridge University Press 1995, especially chapters 4 and 5.

18. Children from immigrant households living in public housing projects left the parental home late: 48 percent of young people aged between 20 and 34 are still living with their parents, or twice as often as the average. J. Boëldieu and S. Thave, "Le logement des immigrés en 1996," *op. cit.*

19. On this subject, see S. Beaud and M. Pialoux, *Retour sur la condition ouvrière,* Paris, Fayard, 1999, especially Part 2, "Le salut par l'école"; and C. Grignon, *L'ordre des choses. Les fonctions sociales de l'enseignement technique,* Paris, Editions de Minuit, 1971.

20. F. Poupeau, *Contestations scolaires et ordre social,* Paris, Syllepse, 2004.

21. R. Castel, *Les métamorphoses de la question sociale. Une chronique du salariat,* Paris, Gallimard, 1999, pp. 665–66.

22. G. Mauger, "La reproduction des milieux populaires en 'crise'," *Ville– Ecole–Intégration* no. 113, 1998.

23. D. Lepoutre, *Cúur de banlieue. Codes rites et langages,* Paris, Odile Jacob, 1997.

24. "Because they cannot provide the minimum security and assurance regarding the present and the immediate future that are provided by permanent employment and a regular salary, unemployment, temporary employment, and work as a simple occupation prevent any effort to rationalize economic behavior with reference to a future end, and imprison existence in a dread of tomorrow, that is, in a fascination with the immediate." P. Bourdieu, "Les sous prolétaires algériens," *Agone* no. 26/27, 2002, p. 205 [*Les temps modernes,* December 1962].

25. M. Foucault, *Surveiller et punir. Naissance de la prison,* Paris, Gallimard, 1975, pp. 98 ff.

26. P. Bourgois, *In Search of Respect, op. cit.*

27. S. Beaud , "L'école et le quartier," *Critiques sociales* no. 5–6, 1994, pp. 13–46. For his part, Olivier Masclet has shown the "dishonor" and "shame" felt by Algerian immigrant fathers on becoming aware of their sons' deviance: "the arrest of unworthy sons [. . .] is the unbearable sign of the gap that has opened between them," between stable workers and sub-proletarians, between "respectable workers" and "young people without a future." O. Masclet, "Les parents immigrés pris au piège de la cité," *Cultures & Conflits* no. 46, 2002, pp. 147–173.

28. N. Elias and J. L. Scotson, *Les logiques de l'exclusion,* Fayard, Paris 1997 [1965], pp. 158 ff.

29. E. P. Thompson, *La formation de la classe ouvrière anglaise,* Paris, Gallimard–le Seuil, 1988 [1963].

30. H. Rey, Etude pour le compte de la délégation interministérielle à la ville, typed report, 2001.

31. On this subject, see G. Mauger, "La politique des bandes," *Politix* no. 14, 1991.

32. See in particular B. Pudal, *Prendre parti. Pour une sociologie historique du PCF*, Paris, Presses de Science-Po, 1989.

33. It is the PCF's failure to connect with young people from the projects that Olivier Masclet describes in great detail in *La gauche et les cités, op. cit.*

34. A. Sayad, *La double absence. Des illusions de l'émigré aux souffrances de l'immigré*, Paris, Seuil, 1999.

35. J. M. Le Pen, extreme right-wing candidate, reached to the second round, where he was opposed to Jacques Chirac. The surprise and the trauma have roused a huge mobilization (as well from the left-wing parties) in favor of J. Chirac, who has been elected with 82 percent of the votes.

36. Khaled Kelkal, a young man from Vaulx en Velin implicated in the 1995 terrorist attacks in France, is from this point of view an exception because of the strong interest taken by his family in issues relating to Algeria. At this time his father was an imam in Algeria, and very involved in political Islam.

37. For a historical overview, see M. H. Abdallah, *J'y suis, j'y reste! Les luttes de l'immigration en France depuis les années 60*, Paris, Reflex, 2001; and S. Bouamama, *Dix ans de marche des beurs. Chronique d'un mouvement avorté*, Paris, Desclée de Brouwer, 1994.

38. The prefect of the region offered this comment on the protests following the death of a teenager killed by a policeman in Toulouse in December 1998: "These rioters are not unconnected with the 19 people we've recently arrested for burglaries in commercial establishments. Apart from the legitimate sadness felt after the death of young Habib, one can see in the protests in Mirail [a neighborhood in the suburbs of Toulouse] a reaction to these arrests, which certainly did not please everyone in putting an end to all sorts of illicit trafficking." *La Croix*, December 18, 1999. On the attitude of the municipality and the prefecture during the protests in a neighborhood of Dammarie les Lys during the summer of 2002, centered around the association *Bouge qui bouge* and the *Mouvement de l'Immigration et des Banlieues (MIB)*, see *Vacarme* no. 21, Autumn 2002.

39. The example of the Stop the Violence movement, launched after the death of Stéphane Coulibaly in Bouffémont, in Val d'Oise on January 14, 1999, is emblematic. Started by a certain number of teenagers who wanted to rehabilitate the image of their friend, whom the media had presented as a delinquent, this movement—supervised from the outset by a journalist from *Nova* and a socialist city councilor (David Assouline, assistant to the mayor of Paris's 20th *arrondissement*)—quickly gained the attention of public authorities and the media. Based on a manifesto condemning "violence in the suburbs," it coincides exactly, both in content and in form, with the pertinent categories of the moment in the political arena. Special radio programs were devoted to it, and the television channel *Canal* + made a documentary that was broadcast in May, and above all, representatives of the movement were invited, with great publicity, to participate in the *Rencontres nationales des acteurs de la prévention de la délinquance* held in Montpellier in March 1999. The urban affairs' minister, Claude Bartolone, received them, while Jean-Pierre Chevènement, home office minister, sent them a message of encouragement before ordering prefects to promote the development of local groups.

40. Claude Grignon and Jean-Claude Passeron even speak of a *class racism*, understood as "the certitude peculiar to a class for monopolizing the cultural definition of a human being and thus of the people who deserve to be fully recognized as such." They also explain that this certitude "inhabits vast sectors of the dominant classes, and not necessarily the most traditional or

the most elitist." C. Grignon and J.-C. Passeron, *Le savant et le populaire. Misérabilisme et populisme en sociologie et en littérature*, Paris, Gallimard-Le Seuil, 1989, p. 32.

41. Comité d'études sur la violence, la criminalité et la délinquance, *Réponses à la violence*, Paris, Presses Pocket, 1977.

42. On the modernizing group and the transformations in the state's ways of talking and acting during the "trente glorieuses," see R. F. Kuisel, *Le capitalisme et l'Etat en France. Modernisme et dirigisme au XXème siècle*, Paris, Gallimard, 1984.

43. CERES was a Marxist-oriented group led by Jean-Pierre Chevènement, who wrote the Socialist Party's program in 1980.

44. The work of Jacques Donzelot and Philippe Estèbe (*L'Etat animateur. Essai sur la politique de la ville*, éditions Esprit, 1994) offers a good summary of their theses. On the structuring of the categories for thinking about urban policy—and the effects of these categories—see S. Tissot, "Quartiers sensibles," *Genèse d'une catégorie d'action publique*, Paris, Seuil, 2006.

45. Whereas the joyriding in Les Minguettes had been the subject of only short articles in *Le Monde, Le Figaro*, and *L'Humanité* (*Libération* did not mention it), the outburst of violence in the neighborhood of Mas du Taureau in Vaulx-en-Velin in October 1990 was the subject of 34 reports and 9 editorials in the audiovisual media, whereas the national print media devoted 60 articles to it. The volume of articles on the question of the "malaise" or "sickness" or "crisis" in the *banlieues* grew larger from that time on, and has become a journalistic "genre" of its own. On the evolution of the treatment of these questions, see A. Collovald, "Des désordres sociaux à la violence urbaine," *Actes de la recherche en sciences sociales*, no. 136–37, March 2001. The media, especially the audiovisual media, henceforth played an important role in structuring the public image of the problem by homogenizing social and geographical realities ("*les banlieues*"), population groups ("the young"), and facts ("urban violence," "riots") of very different kinds. See P. Champagne, "La construction médiatique des 'malaises sociaux'," *Actes de la recherche en sciences sociales* no. 90, December 1991, pp. 64–75.

46. Thus Philippe Juhem shows "the tendency to weaken the preeminence of politicians over journalists" connected with the political change. See P. Juhem, *SOS-Racisme, histoire d'une mobilisation " apolitique". Contribution à une analyse des transformations des représentations politiques après 1981*, Thesis in political science directed by Bernard Lacroix, Paris X-Nanterre, 1998.

47. Report on *La politique de la ville*, presented by Gérard Larcher, Sénat, session 1992–1993, p. 12.

48. *Le Parisien*, October 31, 2001.

49. Televised interview with Jacques Chirac, president of the republic, Saturday July 14, 2001.

50. See especially S. Roché, *Tolérance Zéro? Incivilités et insécurité*, Paris, Odile Jacob, 2002; "La théorie de la vitre cassée en France. Incivilités et désordres en public," *Revue française de science politique*, vol. 50, no. 3, June 2000, pp. 387–412.

51. J. Q. Wilson and G. Kelling, "Broken Windows: The Police and Neighbourhood Safety," *The Atlantic Monthly*, March 1982, pp. 29–38.

52. See for example R. Bousquet, *Insécurité : nouveaux risques. Les quartiers de tous les dangers*, Paris, L'Harmattan, 1998; and A. Bauer and X. Raufer, *Violences et insécurité urbaine*, Paris, PUF (Coll. *Que sais-je* no. 3421), 1998.

53. The cases studies on young criminals—corroborated by police and court testimony—show in most cases a decrease or even a disappearance of delinquency as soon as these adolescents find a job, found a family, and so on. See for example I. Coutant, *Délit de jeunesse. La justice face aux quartiers*, Paris, La découverte, 2005, pp. 262 ff.

54. See L. Mucchielli, *Violences et insécurité. Fantasmes et réalités dans le débat français*, Paris, La découverte, 2001; and P. Rimbert, "Les managers de l'insécurité. Production et circulation d'un discours sécuritaire," in L. Bonelli and G. Sainati (ed.), *La machine à punir. Pratiques et discours sécuritaires*, Paris, L'Esprit Frappeur, 2004.

55. Thus Salvatore Palidda speaks of a "negotiated management of the rules of disorder." See S. Palidda, *Polizia postmoderna. Etnografia del nuovo controllo sociale*, Feltrinelli, Milan, 2000.

56. The rise in the power of the categories of urban police will have effects on the other services concerned with intelligence gathering or judicial proceedings. On this process, see especially L. Bonelli, "Les Renseignements généraux et les violences urbaines," *Actes de la Recherche en Sciences Sociales*, no. 136–37, March 2001, pp. 95–103. On the tensions inherent in structuring a field for security professionals, see D. Bigo, "The Globalisation of (In)security and the Ban-Opticon," *Traces: A Multilingual Series of Cultural Theory* no. 4, University of Hong Kong Press, 2004; and *Polices en réseaux. L'expérience européenne*, Paris, Presse de Science-Po, 1996.

57. W. K. Muir, *Police: Street Corner Politicians*, Chicago, University of Chicago, 1977.

58. These offenses consist respectively of insults and violence directed at the representatives of authority. Over the period they passed from 0.64 percent to 1.37 percent of the total number of offenses registered. (*Aspects de la criminalité et de la délinquance constatée en France*, La documentation française.) These figures still remain much too general, however, for they conflate the very different realities of small and large cities. In one of the areas I investigated in the Parisian *banlieue*, the increase between 1993 and 2001 was 470 percent.

59. The law *for internal security* of March 18, 2003 (NOR: INTXD200145L) stipulates, in Article L. 126-3, that "infringement of civil liberties [. . .] or deliberate obstruction of access and freedom of movement for persons or the proper functioning of mechanisms of security and safety, when they are committed by a group of several perpetrators or accomplices, in entryways, stairways, or other common areas of collective apartment buildings, are punishable by two months' imprisonment and a fine of 3,750 Euros." For the first time, on July 8, 2003, three teenagers from the Brugnauts housing project in Bagneux were prosecuted for "occupation of a stairway." On July 25, the criminal court in Lille sentenced two 19-year-olds to a month in prison with possibility of parole for "illicit occupation of the common areas of the apartment building."

60. *Le traitement en temps réel*, DACG, Ministry of Justice, p. 3.

61. *Ibid.*, p. 4.

62. P. Mary, "Pénalité et gestion des risques: vers une justice 'actuarielle' en Europe?" *Déviance et société*, vol. 25, no. 1, 2001, p. 35.

63. See L. Bonelli and G. Sainati (eds.), *La machine à punir* (. . .), *op. cit.*, pp. 134 ff.

64. Martial arts batons.

65. *Insécurité: les nouveaux risques, op. cit.*, pp. 121–122. This kind of thing is taken up by sensationalist journalists like Christian Jelen, for example, who does not hesitate to title his work *La guerre des rues* (*The War in the Streets*) (Paris, Plon, 1999).

66. The 2002 report of the committee for rights, justice, and freedoms of Saint-Denis (Seine

Saint Denis) gives numerous testimonies to these mimetic relationships, both at the level of language ("why did you look at me?"; "okay, who's the boss?"; "come on and fight, if you're a man") and at that of practices. Other examples will be found in the report of the *Commission d'enquête sur les comportements policiers à Châtenay-Malabry, Poissy et Paris 20e* (July 2002), conducted by the Human Rights League, the French lawyers' union, and the magistrates' union.

67. See F. Jobard, *Bavures policières? La force publique et ses usages*, Paris, La découverte, 2002.

68. The CLS are local institutional structures gathering together officials from local authorities, justice system, public transportation, schools, police, and so on in order to solve security problems by sharing the tasks and the means.

69. *Contrat local de sécurité de la ville de Chalon sur Saône* – Document de travail page 66– 26 septembre 2002–Annexe 4: Note sur le suivi personnalisé des familles et mineurs signalés.

70. E. Goffman, *Asiles. Etudes sur la condition sociale des malades mentaux*, Paris, éditions de Minuit, 1968, pp. 214–18.

71. Pierre Bourdieu notes that one cannot account for the dispositions and practices of teenagers in working-class neighborhoods, especially those of the most "deviant" among them, without bringing in other factors. First of all, "the withering away or weakening of sources of mobilization such as the political and labor union organizations that in the old 'red suburbs' did not limit themselves, as is often said, to 'channeling and regulating revolt,' but provided a sort of 'continuous envelopment' of every life (notably by organizing athletic, cultural, and social activities), thus helping give meaning to revolt, but also to existence in general." P. Bourdieu (dir.), *La misère du monde*, Paris, Seuil, 1993, p. 225.

72. M. Edelman, *Pièces et règles du jeu politique*, Paris, Seuil, 1991, pp. 53 ff.

73. R. V. Ericson and K. D. Haggerty, *Policing the Risk Society*, University of Toronto Press, 1997, pp. 73 and 75.

74. R. Castel, *Les métamorphoses de la question sociale. Une chronique du salariat, op. cit.* p. 163.

75. See D. Garland, *The Culture of Control. Crime and Social Order in Contemporary Society*, Oxford, Oxford University Press, 2001; and N. Christie, *L'industrie de la punition. Prison et politique pénale en Occident*, Paris, Autrement, 2003.

76. In this, the young people differ fundamentally from organized groups, whether "criminals" or "terrorists." If arrests are made, it takes longer and is more complicated to reconstitute a group whose coherence is based on relationships of confidence that are up to dealing with the risks that are run.

77. For a presentation of these claims, see L. Wacquant, *Punir les pauvres*, Marseille, Agone, 2004; and B. E. Harcourt, *Illusion of Order. The False Promise of Broken Windows Policing*, Cambridge, Harvard University Press, 2001.

78. In 2002, the General Inspection Office of the French national police (IGPN) registered 592 complaints, up from 566 in 2001 and 548 in 2000, for an increase of 8 percent in three years. This rise is still more obvious for Paris and its nearest suburbs: 432 cases occurred in 2002, 385 in 2001, 360 in 2000, and 216 in 1997. In five years, the number of cases of complaint has doubled (*Le Monde*, February 21, 2003).

79. See D. Bigo, "Sécurité et immigration. Vers une gouvernementalité par l'inquiétude?" *Cultures & Conflits* no. 31–32, Autumn 1998.

5

Policing Ourselves:
Law and Order in the American Ghetto

SUDHIR ALLADI VENKATESH

AND ALEXANDRA K. MURPHY

There is a documented history of antagonism between African-Americans and law enforcement. Most recently, scholars and policymakers have identified a "crisis of legitimacy" in the relationships of black Americans to courts, police, and other parts of the criminal justice system.[1] Disproportionate numbers of African-Americans are in jails and prisons, and incidents of police brutality and abusive law enforcement practices in black communities are still a contemporary social problem. African-Americans have less faith than their white counterparts that police are there to serve them and protect their persons and property.

Although these criminal justice issues have received significant attention, less well understood is the manner by which African-Americans have developed mechanisms for maintaining social order and ensuring some minimal level of personal and public safety in the absence of an effective and responsive justice apparatus. This chapter examines the ways in which a poor, predominantly black urban community has developed such "indigenous" resources for resolving disputes and attending to delinquent and criminal behavior; we contrast this sphere of justice with "state-sanctioned" juridical procedures, such as community policing or conventional law enforcement prosecution via the courts. We place the development of this dynamic within a global context, both pointing to the ways in which the relationship between indigenous forms of maintaining social order and state-sanctioned law enforcement practices are shaped by global political and economic shifts and noting the rise in such developments across the globe.

Using "indigenous" means of ensuring social order is not entirely a novel practice for African-Americans. Whether as a coping device for neglectful police or an extension of differing moral and ethical precepts, the use of juridical mechanisms outside the state have been part of the black diaspora in the United States for centuries.[2] Throughout the period of black enslavement, the police were a source of harassment, not support, for blacks. Even after their emancipation, it was difficult to rely on the state for justice—as evidenced by the still-existing struggles over civil rights, fights over disproportionate police patrols in their community, anti-brutality initiatives, and so on. When police failed to respond, others in the community were called on to deal with social problems and criminality. Ministers, businesspersons, block club presidents, and other types of local stakeholders attended to conflict mediation, dispute resolution, punishment, and redress. If courts did not prove useful for achieving justice, informal venues could be pursued—such as backroom negotiations and public shaming. In this way, actors ostensibly not officially invested in enforcement and protection might assume roles that, in most communities, are commonly understood to be the responsibility of law enforcement officials (Drake and Cayton 1945; Spear 1979).

The importance of innovative juridical procedures that work outside the state or that supplement formal government mechanisms will be recognizable to anyone familiar with studies of "community justice," a broad, loose field of inquiry organized around localized procedures of deliberation and conflict mediation. Legal scholars, in particular, have looked closely at concrete programs and policies that seek to increase the legitimacy of state enforcement institutions. An example is the use of "community courts" that are placed directly in the neighborhoods of the disenfranchised in order to make the justice system appear more friendly, thereby enhancing its "legitimacy" (Meares 2000; Fagan 2002). In addition, anthropologists have studied examples of legal structures and processes in non-Western societies in which the state has a marginal or nonexistent role. They have pointed to the ways in which the state may be one of several institutional arenas for maintaining order, normative prescriptions, sentencing, and so on (Comaroff 1982; Merry 1993). Much of their attention has been drawn to "traditional" societies, in which the government's juridical structures confront religious, tribal, and other legal foundations that specify how people may act, including how these formal and informal institutions should respond to conflicts and transgressions. The U.S. case has not been studied in a similar vein.

In the context of African-American communities, studies of these types of juridical processes—whether in the United States or abroad, and whether historical or contemporary in nature—rarely focus on young people. This is noteworthy particularly since many of the dynamics that involve the use of indigenous juridical processes in these communities involve youth and adolescents. These young people are often at the heart of struggles to acquire effective law enforcement, solve conflicts creatively, and otherwise maintain social order. One such actor is the street gang. In the last few decades, the street gang has anchored the discourse on criminality in the American ghetto. Indeed, the "gang-and-drug problem" became the shorthand phrase to reference the marginalization of youth, the incapacity of police to successfully enforce laws, and the overall social alienation of the ghetto from mainstream society.

This chapter considers the emergence of indigenous versus state-sponsored justice in the contemporary American ghetto. The specific example is based on a case study of law-and-order dynamics in a predominantly African-American working-poor community in Chicago, Illinois—one in which a youth street gang plays a prominent role. For several years, one of the authors conducted fieldwork, gathering observations of the various methods of conflict resolution and mediation that local residents and stakeholders employed to maintain social order. We use this case study to document contemporary methods of creating and maintaining social order in the American ghetto but also to re-cast how we think about the factors that have led to such forms of indigenous justice.

In particular, we argue that social order in the ghetto may be understood in a global context—that is, how social order in the ghetto is established and maintained is influenced by changes in global, social dynamics, including recent transformations in the role of state representatives (lawyers, court officials, and police). On the one hand, the challenges of crime control, the reintegration of ex-offenders, and the socialization of young people must be understood as social dynamics that constrain the capacities of urban poor actors to utilize government services, and that, in so doing, limit their ability to rely on legal institutions that might assist them in keeping their neighborhoods habitable. This retrenchment of the state and a correlative move from rehabilitative to punitive urban policing have manifested throughout the Americas and Europe, as well as in certain parts of Africa and Australia (see Rob White's essay "Public Spaces, Consumption, and the Social Regulation of Young People," chapter 8 in this volume).

On the other hand, the consequences of these dynamics are also felt worldwide. Across the globe scholars have documented the process by which—as the state moves out of the business of providing public, effective, ongoing enforcement—the private or civil sector becomes faced with the burden of dealing with crime, delinquency, and social problems associated with disenfranchised populations who cannot rely on the formal economy to make ends meet. As Loader (1999) has cogently argued, the privatization of policing will differ by national contexts: in some areas, one finds gated communities with private security forces; in other ghetto areas and ethnic enclaves where religious law trumps state law, one finds local militias and self-efficacious styles of policing and redress (cf., Caldeira 2000). Finally, as we suggest below, the global character of these developments is not evidenced simply by their simultaneous occurrence in disparate parts of their world, but because actors in these places share ideas with one another and sometimes work collaboratively to forge policing and justice initiatives, often resulting in shared international policing and privatization practices. Thus, for the purposes of this chapter, we use the term *globalization* to refer both to economic and political shifts occurring at the international level as well as to the spread of ideas and practices across the world.

The substantive focus of this chapter is the youth street gang and its impact on the inner-city community. Since the early 1980s, the gang has become the most regnant symbol both of the lawlessness of the ghetto and its distance from the mainstream, civilized world in both the United States and in countries such as Lithuania and Papua New Guniea. A predator-prey discourse has dominated scholarship, characterizing the gang and other "criminals" as actors who prey upon a law-abiding or "decent" population (Anderson 1990). Indeed, gangs are, if anything, conceived of as anti-global in that they are viewed as isolated from civilized, mainstream society. In this chapter, the

American youth gang is understood in the context of the post-1970s, so-called post-Fordist era of political-economic restructuring.[3] A significant dimension of this period of social change included the social organization of "law-and-order" initiatives aimed at troubled youth in U.S. cities. As the government altered its approach to coping with youth gangs and gang-related criminality—that is, as it moved from a rehabilitative to a punitive model—inner-city communities saw in these changes possibilities for the redefinition of crime reduction and social control. The state retrenched and withdrew resources in some areas, particularly in the funding of social welfare programs, while heightening its willingness to fund so-called law-and-order initiatives aimed at mass arrest and incarceration. As we suggest below, this "punitive" turn and the correlate response by community stakeholders to cope with local problems associated with gang activity were not isolated to particular U.S. cities, but rather, were part of an international response to increased levels of inequality and to an international movement to alter the character and function of law enforcement in urban areas.

It is not possible to provide a full explication of this argument within the space of a brief essay. We draw on fieldwork in a U.S. ghetto neighborhood to illuminate the broader discussion with an empirical case. We begin by presenting an incident involving a youth gang in an inner-city Chicago neighborhood. The narrative addresses the ways in which local actors attempted to resolve the conflicts that occurred. It focuses on the ways in which the state—via its law enforcement institutions—participated in that process. The chapter then alternates between discussion and further review of this particular case. The summary discussion revisits the topic of this volume, the impact of globalization on legal institutions and youth behavior, in light of the Chicago case.

THE INCIDENT (PART I)

Two young men meet one another in a vacant lot, in the middle of Grand Boulevard, a working-poor, predominantly African-American community in the heart of Chicago's Southside ghetto. Like many of their neighbors, they float between periods of menial-wage employment, performing general labor or chores at construction sites for example, and tenures of outright joblessness where the only income is illegally derived or obtained through a quick street hustle.

In this case, they are active participants in the underground economy, that rather loose and varied sphere of exchange in which the common thread tying the income-generating activities together is that the participants do not report their income to the government. These activities are not necessarily or always heinous actions, such as burglary or drug selling; sometimes they are mundane work like selling homemade food. In this case, one man, James, is a mechanic who is fixing a car belonging to the other man (Larry). The work has been completed and payment is due to James in full.

But there is a misunderstanding. James believed the original quote, given three days before, to be $50. The client said he heard an estimate of "$30" for the requested work. In a community where poverty is chronic and there are relatively few opportunities for wage earning, a $20 discrepancy is not trivial. Larry grows weary of arguing and decides to physically assault the mechanic. He throws James to the ground, kicks him, takes his keys, and then reclaims his car and drives away. James has fixed Larry's vehicle before. James decides to seek vengeance by burglarizing Larry's house and stealing a television and VCR as restitution for the unpaid work order. While leaving Larry's house, James yells for no reason at his neighbors, who watch as he loads the goods in his car and drives away, all the while seemingly unconcerned about the threat of apprehension.

A deliberate process of adjudication ensues. James has been paying the local street gang $50 per week for the "right" to use the vacant lot for off-the-books car repair. He has worked there for several months and customers know that the gang protects their cars by watching over the lot and over James— petty robbery being a common problem among entrepreneurs, James boasted that the gang was a "security" force for his business. Indeed, per his agreement with the local gang, on occasion James calls upon the gang to settle discrepancies or conflicts that arise. If, say, the problem is contract enforcement, James asks the gang leader to find a customer who owes him money; if someone steals James's tools, the gang leader might be able to retrieve them. In the incident above, James asks the gang to help him obtain his money from Larry.

As a third party in this matter, the gang has a number of things to consider before acting on James's behalf. The gang leader must determine the terms of the original contract and whether the work was completed, discern amongst competing narratives of the incident (e.g., who started the fight), issue a ruling, obtain consent from both parties, and deliver an appropriate punishment. The gang may have to intercede, should further retaliation take place. William, the local gang leader who James has enlisted on his behalf, begins the process by sending his chief enforcer to meet with both parties and interview them about the events that have occurred.

In this incident, the gang is not the only third-party arbiter around. This is evidenced by the fact that a parallel adjudicative process is underway. Larry happens to live on a block in the Grand Boulevard community with a vibrant "block club." Like block clubs around the United States, it is a primary form of association ostensibly concerned with ensuring public safety and patrolling children's behavior. Many block clubs report signs of municipal neglect, poor policing, petty crime, domestic abuse, and other such problems to political officials and law enforcement personnel. In the last few decades (as described below), they have played a central role in the efforts of Chicago's police to gain firsthand knowledge about local problems and perpetrators. Many of the neighbors who observed the burglary dutifully wrote down the license plate of James's car as he was leaving Larry's house and they recorded his identifying features. Following the routine in place, they give the information to the local "block club leader," Melissa, in hopes that she will follow up.

Melissa may pursue the matter in one of several ways. She may, of course, call the police and report the burglary. But many residents on the block have little faith in the police and they have suffered decades of ineffective policing, so they do not necessarily believe that a call to law enforcement is going to yield much in the way of public safety. Moreover, they are themselves involved in the underground economy, making money and purchasing goods and services under the table in order to support their households, and they have made it clear to Melissa that she has to be cautious in raising police presence in the neighborhood. Some of Melissa's neighbors have underground income that stems from legitimate activities, such as home repair or hair care; others traffic in stolen social security cards and stolen/secondhand car parts. Still others do not participate directly, but have household members who do, and so may see increased police activity as a threat to household income and their capacity to make ends meet. They tell Melissa that she is not to be simply a conduit for residents' complaints, but that she must exercise discretion when asking police to become part of local affairs.

Melissa understands her neighbors' perceptions about the limits of working with police. Indeed, part of her support locally has been due to her creative ways of resolving conflicts and restoring public safety, particularly when police are not helpful. For example, over the past two years, she has been successful in convincing the gang to withhold public narcotics sales during school hours, so that children in and around her block are not walking home (or to school) past drug sellers. Direct diplomacy with the gang is not her preferred strategy, but it has increased her neighbors' sense of safety. The gang has also recovered residents' stolen cars and they have donated money to the block club for parties. And, with threats of physical punishment, the gang ensures that the local parks personnel and sanitation officials (actually) clean up the local playgrounds and streets—a feat that Melissa and her neighbors have been unable to achieve either by protest or by political lobbying. In the matter at hand, she knows that one of her options is to use the gang to help her neighbor Larry recover his television and VCR. Calling on them might entail concessions such as withholding phone calls to the police over gang-related activity for a period of time.

This case grows a little more complicated. Larry assaulted James and he has also refused to pay for services rendered. Larry is not an innocent victim. Moreover, there was legitimate repair work performed that needs to be remunerated and, so far, Larry has not made a payment. Moreover, the same gang is helping both James the mechanic and Melissa the block club leader. Everyone involved is aware of the inherent conflict of interest for the street gang, who may not be able to provide its services to one party without compromising its ability to advocate for the other.

For her part, Melissa does have other options besides William and his gang. There are other local mediators to whom she could turn besides the gang leader (and the police for that matter). There is a local barbershop owner who has a long history of helping underground entrepreneurs settle disputes. There are many pastors as well as other block club presidents and gang leaders who are trusted by grassroots actors and who could legitimately intervene. Melissa decides to call upon Minister Johnson, a local storefront pastor, for help with the retrieval of the stolen merchandise and in her negotiations with the police (who have heard about this incident and will soon be asking Melissa to coop-erate) and the gang (who Melissa must confront at some point if she is to help Larry). She is hopeful because the minister has worked with both the gang and the police over matters that involve people making money illegally.

The three incidents—assault, unfinished transaction, and burglary—must be resolved in such a way that all the parties—the mechanic James, the car owner Larry, the neighbors, the gang leader, the minister, and the police—involved can save face. This is a problem in the underground economy, where there is no single third-party arbiter. As a block club leader, Melissa must demonstrate to neighbors that she can move local police to act, but in such a way that residents do not fear their own unreported income to be in jeopardy. For its part, the police cannot officially condone residents responding to seri-ous crimes on their own, and so they must play a role. The gang leader would be rendered impotent and unable to demand "street taxes" from underground entrepreneurs if he cannot provide them contract enforcement and security—so, he must also find a way to show his value. And the pastor usually will receive a small donation to his church for his services, so he also has a mate-rial incentive to stay involved (as well as a need to reproduce his status as a moral force in the area).

Before moving forward and unraveling the incident, a few issues may be identified in terms of the relevance of these kinds of daily social processes for the larger set of questions surrounding globalization and the dynamic of "law and order" in the urban ghetto. It would be convenient to consider this case as (yet another) example of ghetto lawlessness and dys-functionality. If one were to read scholarship on American urban poverty, such conclusions would likely emerge: that is, the ghetto is socially "disorganized," residents are held hostage by street gangs, residents lack a work ethic and are entirely isolated from mainstream social institutions (such as the police), and so on. Yet this kind of "popular" or "community" justice in Grand Boulevard says much about the forms of efficacious collective action that involve local actors—action that is highly localized and responsive to immediate circumstances to be sure, but structured nonetheless. At root, these deliberative processes are a local means of restoring order, preventing instability, offering redress, and enforcing shared beliefs. They are, in other words, legal arrangements and must be conceptualized as such, even if they may be flouting conventional standards of juridical conduct that are deemed socially acceptable to those outside the ghetto.

What are their roots? Why consider them in light of a broader set of changes to the American urban social fabric in the era of globalization? These two questions anchor the following discussion. They will be interspersed with further explication of the incident described above in the Grand Boulevard community.

THE POST-CIVIL RIGHTS GHETTO

The incident above occurred in the mid-1990s, in the streets and alleyways of an alienated Midwestern ghetto community. However, it has deep historical roots and its parameters take the analyst far away from Chicago's Southside. That one could find the gang playing a role in local conflict mediation, that police were involved yet seemingly at the margins of the dispute resolution, and that local residents would support non-state actors wishing to dispense punishment and redress are elements that are best understood in the overall transformation of the social structure of the American ghetto in the post–civil rights era. And, as we have suggested, this change has been occurring in other parts of the world. Their co-temporaneous occurrence must thus be understood in terms of the refashioning of criminal justice policy in the era of globalization.

Crack Is King

After the height of the crack-cocaine epidemic in the late 1980s, urban gangs throughout the United States changed from small, neighborhood-based entities primarily involved in social and petty delinquent activities to become coordinated citywide cartels specializing in organized crime—a process neatly described as the "corporate" turn in street gang behavior (Covington and Taylor 1991). Gang leaders used girlfriends and relatives to start legitimate businesses to facilitate their own money laundering. Those shady entrepreneurs who might be carrying around several hundreds of thousands of ill-begotten dollars won the support of car dealers, modest retail stores, landlords, and investment brokers who also offered to launder money for a fee. They had also become community institutions. The gang was not only selling narcotics, it was also contributing to political campaigns and investing in socially legitimate businesses. Gangs had become local philanthropists, giving money to service providers, churches, and other community-based organizations that had few other options available to fund their programming.[4] In many ways, the gangs were emulating the political bosses of the early and mid-twentieth century who built their capital on both city patronage and illegal economies.

In the mid-1990s, the federal government utilized powers in the Racketeer Influenced and Corrupt Organizations (RICO) Act to dismantle Chicago's organized criminal network that had been developed by the city's black and Latino gangs. Several hundred gang members and their sympathizers ended up in jail for their role in drug sales, commercial extortion, tax evasion, and other crimes tied to the gang's criminal enterprises. As a consequence, the gangs could not rest their economic hopes on a coordinated infrastructure for trafficking crack cocaine. The gangs' drug-dealing operation was in tatters. Younger members did not know where the next supply of cocaine, heroin, or marijuana would come from, although there was still plenty of demand for illegal drugs both from local inner-city residents as well as from customers who drove into their neighborhoods from other parts of the city. There was little evidence to suggest that the number of gang members in Chicago was declining significantly as a result of the federal sweeps or that gangs were no longer deeply embedded in the community. For the thousands of marginalized young people with few meaningful jobs and little educational prospects, the gang still provided a source of income—however dangerous the work might have been.

The publicity that surrounded the indictments brought aspects of youth gangs and policing practices that had not been well known to the public attention. The demographics of the neighborhood gang no longer conformed to its traditional composition of teenagers and adolescents. The black gang appeared to be a bimodal association comprised of both young people from 14 to 21 years of age and a ruling elite in their late 20s and early 30s. For the younger "shorties," the gang was primarily a social center, a source of identity one obtained by using hand signals, wearing specific clothing and footwear, fighting at school events with rival gangs, and so on. Some made illegal money, but most did not. Members would usually have to wait until they were in their late teens or early 20s for any significant opportunities to do so. For the older set, the gang was an important source of personal income: even if it provided only a few hundred dollars a month, the revenue could prove significant for those minority men who had no training and for whom menial service-sector work was the primary legitimate option. As Bourgois (2002) demonstrates in his own study of Puerto Rican drug traffickers in New York City's underground economy, a young man's armor may be pierced more easily by the shame of downtown office work than the perceived independence of street trafficking; hence the choice to entertain dangerous and illegal street work is not always about money but instead about meaning and self-determinism.

By the late 1980s, the trajectory of gang members differed from the early and mid-twentieth century when individuals "aged out" of the gang as blue-collar jobs became available. Members in the post-1980s street gangs were symbols of the "truly disadvantaged," the social strata publicized in the writings of the sociologist William Julius Wilson (1987). This group was the "underclass" for whom de-industrialization led to job loss; institutional evisceration of their communities; depletion of public resources; and a rise in crime, drug addiction, and other social ills. Whereas in an earlier period the young men in Chicago's ghetto communities might have left the gang once family responsibilities and personal desires shifted and blue-collar work presented itself, the possibility for this transition to adulthood was marred by deep-seated socioeconomic shifts that no longer provided such exit avenues. There was no factory work awaiting these young men in the 1980s—as there had been for their fathers and uncles. In looking at the life histories of youth in this period who contemplated or participated in gang activity, one is immediately drawn to the absence of legitimate employment opportunities that might offset the attractions of gang-related behavior and street crime.[5]

In this way, the "local" production of gang activity and street crime can be grounded in the far-reaching global changes to American industry in the post-Fordist period. At its core, urban labor markets were transformed from manufacturing and industrial production to a service-based economy. Over several decades, the departure of large employers (e.g., auto makers and textile and food producers) from central cities to foreign shores and American suburbs took away hundreds of thousands of well-paying unionized jobs. Urban African-Americans, like those in Chicago's Southside ghettos, were disproportionately affected. For them, this industrial sector had been their primary employment sphere since their arrival into northern cities from rural communities in the U.S. South. Left in the wake of this outmigration was a burgeoning service sector that was filled largely with menial employment opportunities that paid poorly and that offered few opportunities for meaningful social advancement and personal mobility. As Bourgois (2002) and others have cogently described, many inner-city youth preferred the dangerous, though potentially economically lucrative, life of underground markets to the low remuneration in fast-food restaurants, hospitals, cleaning-service firms, and so on. Gangland became a wishful space for young people to lodge their aspirations for conspicuous consumption.

The gang during this period was also shaped by a series of realignments to U.S. criminal justice policy and institutionalized practices of law enforcement that, akin to the structural labor market transformations described above, are also at the core of global restructuring. Beginning in the early 1970s, policing strategies in inner-city America eschewed liberal programs that sought to provide services and assistance in the hopes of reintegrating young people into labor markets and educational institutions. Instead, punitive strategies received widespread public support. These strategies included mandatory criminal sentences, mass arrests of youth for petty crimes (e.g., loitering, graffiti), heightened penalties for types of drug trafficking that disproportionately involved ghetto youth, and the treatment of juvenile offenders as adults. Not only did this "punitive turn" have a noticeable effect on the ghetto because the disproportionate share of incarcerated men and women came from inner-city neighborhoods, but this punitive approach was facilitated by increasing levels of residential segregation that allowed law enforcement to target such harsh policing practices to specific communities. Youth moved from ghetto streets to prison cells and back again in a vicious cycle of warehousing that, in his criticism of American-style neoliberal governance, Loïc Wacquant (2000) has called the "deadly symbiosis" of the ghetto and prison.

The growing acceptance of punitive programs can be seen in the changing relationships of street gang members to mainstream civic and public sector institutions. From the New Deal era to the 1960s, the objective of government human service agencies and (nongovernmental) advocacy and community-based organizations has been to persuade gang members to leave their street-based organization, receive rehabilitative care and education, and enter the labor force. This "social work" approach was rooted in the collaboration of social workers, community-based employment and training agencies, and parole/probation officers that helped youth to leave the gangs and achieve stability in their employment and household (Spergel 1996). These social service supports almost disappeared after the 1970s as industrial-sector jobs withered and the public and their elected representatives grew intolerant of supporting anything that was not "tough on crime."

The gang member's public profile quickly became that of a dangerous criminal—that is, the young person involved in the gang was quickly seen as one who should be jailed not rehabilitated. The retrenchment of one arm of the welfare state—social work, education, counseling, job placement— occurred simultaneously with the growth of the state's law enforcement branch. Chicago created the nation's first specialized police unit for street gangs; this became the national model by the mid-1970s. Chicago continued as a trendsetter by merging its narcotics and gang divisions in 1978 thereby cementing in public consciousness that the street gang was an organized criminal network above all else. This move would be replicated in other U.S. cities, although most evidence suggested that urban gangs were still primarily comprised of young people engaged in social activities and petty delinquency. Policymakers and law enforcement officials ignored research showing that only a small percentage of gang members were participating in narcotics trafficking.[6]

Above, we have tried to offer a brief synopsis of the ways in which the street gang shifted during the 1980s in accordance with fundamental transformations to the U.S. economy and U.S. state practice with respect to crime control. In chapter 2 in this volume, John Muncie (2006) analyzes these developments in a comparative context, by looking at the ways in which policing of urban youth shifted in the United Kingdom and the United States. Although the character of these changes is different in each country, region, and city, Muncie (2006) demonstrates that the happenings in distant places such as inner-city Chicago and Manchester may be linked by institutionalized criminal justice approaches as well as by the shifting involvement of the state and local residents in the policing of local communities. Although not all of these developments are a result of actual coordination across nation-states,

Muncie shows that the direct contact between people and organizations in the criminal justice system has, in certain cases, manifested in the spread notions such as "zero tolerance policing" and gang-specific legislation around the globe. It is to this global character of crime control that we now turn. Muncie captures these shifts in his notion that the approach to policing and enforcement for young people has shifted from "penal welfarism" to "neoliberal governance."

Maintaining Social Order Around the Globe

The connections in place across the Atlantic can be drawn on an even broader scale. Doing so requires expanding our focus to consider the broader challenge of maintaining law and order in the globalizing metropolis. From the vantage point of distressed and economically impoverished urban neighborhoods, we have noted the relationship between global economic shifts in the labor market and increased reliance on the criminal justice system to handle unemployed, marginal, and alienated young people.

A parallel, global trend in criminal justice has been the transfer of responsibility for maintaining social order from state to local, citizen-based associations. For Muncie (2006), globalization includes not only the spread of punitive discourses and less tolerant modes of policing, but also notions of individual and community responsibility that similarly re-frame the relationship of the state to citizens in the arena of social order maintenance. He argues that coupled with the heightened use of punitive policing measures is the belief in *responsibilisation*. The sociologist David Garland (1996) developed this term to refer to a process wherein "central government seek[s] to act upon crime not in a direct fashion through state agencies (police, courts, prisons, social work, etc.) but instead by acting indirectly, seeking to activate action on the part of non-state agencies and organizations."

Consider, for example, the privatization of security functions—that is, the transfer of responsibilities for policing and social control from state to nonstate actors. In both industrialized and developing nations, it is common to hear of the creation of private security forces and the use of physical barriers such as gated communities and cul-de-sacs that separate off wealthier communities or limit their access by external actors.[7] The factors promoting privatization in this realm are several, and include fiscal crises of states (Spitzer and Scull 1977), increases in privately secured neighborhoods (Shearing and Stenning 1983), and unmet demand by public agencies for policing among the citizenry (O'Malley and Palmer 1996; Reiner 1992). This move toward privatization has been magnified by the rise in a global consumer culture, resulting in the shift of perception of security as being a public good provided by the state to being a commodity to be consumed (Loader 1999). The removal of the state monopoly in providing security has, among other things, resulted in heightened urban segregation and created an explosion in the market for private security personnel and materials.[8] Policing and security are no longer necessarily or automatically considered matters of the state, but are instead commodities to be produced and consumed via the private market. As Wacquant (2001) writes, while neoliberal policies have been largely punitive toward the lower classes, they have been decidedly "liberal" toward the better off.

An increasingly popular law enforcement strategy around the globe, in which the responsibility of policing shifts from the public to the private sector, has been the promotion of programs and policies wherein residents work collectively with police agencies to improve safety in their communities. Police officials build interactive relationships with local stakeholders—for example, block club presidents, shopkeepers—in order to prevent crime and respond to criminality. In the United States, the reigning institutional exemplification of this ethos (developed and refined in Chicago) is "community policing." In this initiative, designated police officers work with local stakeholders to identify problems and prioritize the allocation of law enforcement resources. If, for example, one neighborhood wants to target public drug sales while another wishes to highlight domestic abuse, the respective local community policing meetings would ideally provide a means for these differences in local priorities to emerge and shape local policing in that area. In return, the police are able to transfer some measure of accountability for crime prevention from their own shoulders directly onto citizens. Internationally, there are variations on this theme, such as the French system in which social service agencies play as important a role as the police do in mediating police-resident relations and dealing with the consequences of crime (Wacquant 2001).

One of the central challenges for cities adopting community policing—or other such initiatives that involve collaborations with officers and residents—

is to motivate residents to participate and accept their own responsibility for crime prevention. In effect, it signals the increasingly limited role that police are playing in social order maintenance and the need for law enforcement to be supplemented by civic actors who work apart from the police to identify and respond to criminal behavior. Where relations between police and citizens are built on trust and responsible enforcement practices, this may not be such a challenge. However, in African-American neighborhoods in Chicago, community policing often has had limited success because of the historic distrust of police and the decades of police neglect, brutality, and ineffective protection that has been provided.[9] Thus, asking residents of these areas to bear many of the responsibilities once deemed those of the police may not necessarily produce the intended result of greater collaboration with police—instead it could produce further social distance between the two parties if calls for collaboration are not made properly.

In Latin America, one can also find a similar shift from centralized law enforcement provision to "participatory urban local government" (Douglass and Friedman 1998). Challenges akin to those in Chicago with respect to implementing community policing strategies occur in this context as well, largely because this initiative requires decentralizing authority and shifting power and decision making to local agencies. In Latin American countries, achieving community policing–style governance is difficult because the police are often organized in a vertical-hierarchical manner with rigid top-down control, the ties of civilian police to the military may be deep and difficult to change, and officers may not be adequately educated to work with community stakeholders and citizenry (Neild 1998). In addition, just as in the United States, trust in the police is compromised because of the history of law enforcement corruption (McIlwaine and Moser 2001). Thus what we find is not only a global consumption of similar law enforcement strategies, largely rooted in global economic and cultural shifts, but similar challenges internationally in the implementation of such strategies.

Indigenous versus State-Sanctioned Spheres of Justice

Notwithstanding the difficulties of implementing community policing in the United States, it is important to note that police *are* present in inner-city

African-American neighborhoods and that local residents *will* participate in police-sponsored crime prevention programs. The point is, however, that the police may not be viewed by local actors as the sole guarantor of social order, nor solely as an agent whose actions promote order. Police may appear as part of the problem, as a destabilizing force, as an agency failing to respect black Americans. This perspective is only exacerbated by the consequences of the global neoliberal retrenchment of the welfare state, which has largely resulted in the implementation of harsh penal policies that are targeted at marginalized sectors of society, furthering the sentiments of distrust and antagonism that black Americans may have toward the police. In such contexts, one may find that residents have developed alternative methods of coping with crime and instability that may not involve the police at all, or the police may be only marginally involved.

In fact, we argue that—in such African-American neighborhoods where there is a crisis of legitimacy of criminal justice institutions—one can identify two distinct structures of enforcement and redress.[10] One structure is the conventional, state-sanctioned *apparti* of police, court officers, and formal rules and procedures as codified in state law. Another indigenous institutional complex is far less visible and includes alternative styles of dispute resolution and conflict mediation, alternative norms regarding proper and improper conduct, alternative accepted forms of punishment, and so on. In the example above, this indigenous complex is discernible via the role of the street gang as a third-party enforcer and the block club's willingness not to employ police (only) to address safety issues. The neighbors' understanding that the solicitation of police involvement is a decision to be made collectively, not a reflex response to transgression, itself suggests that there may be an alternative *modus operandi* for achieving justice and ensuring local safety. This indigenous sphere of enforcement is ultimately evident, however, in the deliberation among local actors about what constitutes a suitable solution to problems in the underground economy—the subject of the next section.

The distinction between state versus indigenous modes of law enforcement is less about the types of actors involved than about the strategies for pursuing justice and maintaining order. It is well known that police respond to crime both formally and informally, and that residents often take matters into their own hands instead of utilizing law enforcement resources. The rich histories of organized criminal behavior also suggest that localized extra-state juridical processes can involve public figures, such as ward bosses and police district commanders, who may be equally involved in the state-sanctioned sphere. The distinctions between state-sanctioned and indigenous spheres of enforcement emerge through the thresholds that define improper and proper behavior and the manner by which incidents and conflicts are addressed (and resolved). Whereas in the state-sanctioned sphere there are a set of procedures and legislations that stipulate what is a crime, jurisdictions, appeals processes, and so on at the community level, both the definition of a transgression and the responses to it may be contested and negotiated among multiple actors.

We would argue that it is impossible to provide a codified assessment of the "indigenous" enforcement sphere—that is, a definite survey of the constituent codes of conduct, guidelines for penalty and punishment, notions of jurisdiction, and so on. Instead, there are situations that arise and stakeholders who become involved as a response to one or another transgression. There has to be deliberative discussion among involved parties over how conflicts will be resolved. It is this process of deliberation, one in which parties are debating how best to draw on the resources of the mainstream law enforcement community, that shows that there is more than one way to adjudicate a conflict.

In the example above, when James the mechanic broke into Larry's house, it was on one level a burglary that concerned other residents who lived on the block; on the other hand, residents also understood that it was a defensive measure taken as a reaction to another violation—namely, Larry's refusal to pay for the auto repair work that James had completed. As shown below, part of the adjudication process involves specifying what occurred and its meaning in the context of normative and ethical specifications that guide local actors' behavior. Only once this has been achieved is it possible to think about mediation, punishment, and redress.

Although distinct, the two institutional juridical complexes are interrelated.[11] While the police may not be the primary arbiter, they may nevertheless be present in the deliberations and negotiations that take place. It is important to note that, unlike the state-sanctioned system wherein police have the right to become involved, in indigenous procedures, local stakeholders may make that decision themselves. This is not unique to the United States. In response to the pervasive police mistrust, corruption, and violence in Colombia and Guatemala, gangs have recently begun to take over tradi-tional police functions, such as community mediation and criminal punish-ment, and become the primary providers of community support. Untrusting of and lacking confidence in state law enforcement, gangs, such as "Los Muchachos" have been transformed into community mediators and protectors (McIlwaine and Moser 2001). Similarly, social organizations, such as social cleansing and lynching groups, have formed in order to ensure community social order through the meting out of criminal punishments in the absence of official police action. These social cleansing groups take it upon themselves to kill the community undesirables, specifically targeting street children, thieves, drug addicts, and prostitutes (McIlwaine and Moser 2001).

In the absence of state-provided law enforcement, informal social control is not always dominated by these deviant, extralegal groups, however. In many countries, religious groups and communities may take on state responsibilities where the state is absent. For example, in northern Nigeria, as state responsi-bility has declined, the response has been a rise in religious fundamentalism among Muslims as a strategy of combating and punishing such vices as pros-titution, alcoholism, and gambling. Efforts to curb social deviance have largely focused on the regulation of women. Most prevalent has been an increase in the support for early marriage as a response to the lack of employment and educational opportunities for women (Bunting and Merry 2004). For African-Americans, this use of community agency is critical because it is precisely this feeling of efficacy that is perceived to be lacking with respect to their involve-ment in the state-sanctioned arena.

Turning to our empirical example, Melissa, the block club leader, and her client Larry may request the assistance of the police at any point by filing a for-mal complaint against the mechanic who burglarized the client's home. How-ever, perhaps counterintuitively, enlisting officers in a formal way may not actually strengthen the community's relationship with the police, nor would it guarantee a more effective use of law enforcement resources. In the recent past, the success of this particular block club group in obtaining law enforcement services has partly resulted from the block club's systematic, albeit *informal,* work with police officers to address issues outside the judicial system. For example, the block club leader and police mediate domestic assaults literally at the front door; both work together by deploying "scared straight" approaches—

for example, visits to prisons—to frighten adolescents away from drug dealing; both have been known to work with the street gangs in order to locate stolen cars. Thus, part of the decision regarding the use of police involves determining the precise avenue—formal or informal—through which the request will be made. Each will afford different possibilities for enforcement, punishment, and re-constitution of a safe living environment. Further, as noted above, any such choice to enlist the official agents of law enforcement will affect the ways in which indigenous procedures of redress might be invoked. If the block club president asks the police to apprehend the burglar, avenues to work with the street gang to recover stolen goods might be closed off.

In this manner, it is possible to view our example through the lens of two arenas of law enforcement. The mechanic has forcefully decided to enlist the street gang and its methods for achieving local justice—indeed, given that his method of generating income is illegal, the state-sanctioned path is effectively precluded and so he does not have recourse to courts and police as would a legitimate economic actor. The client and block club leader have not yet made their decision about the use of indigenous versus state-sanctioned legal forums, but they are assessing the benefits of each for redress, public safety, and symbolic legitimation of the block club. And there are certainly residents on the block displeased that any such decision-making calculus is being employed: their view is that the police should be called and that the use of gangs and self-enforcement is capricious and dangerous.

The point here is not to suggest that for this community there are entirely separate "cultures" of policing or sharply discordant beliefs or perceptions of normative conduct—either among residents or between residents and the state. In fact, on most standard social science surveys and media interviews, African-American inner-city residents respond that they want "better police services," "less crime," "no gangs and drugs," and so on. Instead, the point is that there is a structure in place that defines the resources and strategies available to residents for responding to moral and legal transgressions. One critical dimension of this social structure is the parallel, somewhat overlapping, set of informal juridical mechanisms through which residents act efficaciously to reproduce social order. Integral to these mechanisms is the way in which residents can request police services and, in turn, the ways in which police choose to respond—formally or behind-the-scenes.[12]

The historical relations between African-Americans and police departments are fairly specific to their social contexts. Cities may differ significantly from one another. However, even in this apparently idiosyncratic relationship, the view cannot be entirely local. For any neighborhood, the styles of local juridical practices will take on their specific marking *relative to other neighborhoods in the city.* The community's receipt of police services is a result of its membership in a broader urban political process, aptly noted by Castells (1983) as "collective consumption" in which "localized" coalitions vie for a share of various municipal resources and services.[13] The *local* manifestation of policing, including the organization of policing (manpower allocations, beat versus tactical enforcement), the relations of enforcement officials with local stakeholders (pastors, block clubs, service agencies), and the ability of residents to garner emergency response are constituted through the citywide organization of enforcement services. Local resident-police relations will be mediated by the power of local officials to participate in municipal political contests over resource distribution.

City services are themselves always shifting in response to political winds, tax revenues, and the relative power of municipalities in the context of national politics. As David Ranney (2003) has argued, it is impossible to understand micro-level fluctuations of urban service provision—which may manifest in differential resources for local communities—outside of global patterns of investment that determine how successful city administrations are in debt issuances and external corporate investment. Changes in the attractiveness of municipal bonds and corporate investment in urban regions can affect the municipal administration's capacity to provide such a basic service as policing.

In this way, it should not be surprising that global political and economic patterns, mediated through local power relationships, can produce local social behaviors such as the turn by actors in a marginalized community toward creative ways of supplementing inadequate law enforcement and youth social control. In Chicago's Grand Boulevard community, for decades, local actors have shown the willingness to utilize indigenous means of adjudication, conflict resolution, and enforcement that are outside of the auspices of the state. The use of these means of social control is a result of both the drive for collectively efficacious behavior in the sphere of social order maintenance and the neighborhood's incapacity, relative to other areas of the city, to participate effectively in wider fields of political action that determine allocation of municipal services. Thus, even if only as an adaptation, the turn to indigenous procedures signals another way in which local social criminal justice patterns are best understood as a product of broader social structures.

What happens when not everyone participates in "community policing" as a means to address local crime and deal with troubled youth, like those in street gangs? This is a central part of the story in Chicago's urban African-American communities. As we shall see below, some will turn to other, indigenous ways of enacting "responsibilisation."

THE INCIDENT (PART II)

Melissa speaks of her position as a neighborhood leader nostalgically. Her politicking with the local gangs, police, and residents reminds her of the work of her uncle, a prominent "Ward Boss" who, in the 1950s and 1960s, played a similar role. In a conversation with me (2002), she described the benefits that her uncle's position brought to her all-black community, despite the fact that the city's black leaders were far outmatched by white ethnics who controlled Chicago's political economy.

"He knew everything that went on [in this neighborhood]. You gambling? He knew about it. You needed a job? He knew—and he'd find you work if you promised to vote for him. Everyone turned to him, even the police, even the Mayor."

"What do you mean, 'even the police turned to him'?" I asked.

"Well, you know, police never came around these parts back then—even less than they do now, so you know, black people really had it bad. But, let's say your store got robbed or your husband beat the shit out of you. You called my uncle and he got the cops involved. They may not come until he called."

"Seems to me," I interrupted, "that it's not that different from what you do?!"

"Yes, I can get the cops to come, but you know, I can't really find you a job or get you into a college or get the streets fixed. He could do that. So, yes, its like what he does, but mostly I just try to watch over people who are causing trouble, and try to make things safe when police don't come around all the time."

Whether white or black, Chicago's ward bosses were the intermediaries between neighborhood-based actors and the resources of the city administration. The allocation of government jobs, street repair services, building permits, timely sanitation collection, traffic tickets, and jury service—all could be influenced by a prominent political voice. In some communities there were elected political officials, such as aldermen and "committee men," who played this role. But, especially in black areas, there could be clergy and prominent businesspersons, even "shady" leaders like "policy kings" and gamblers, who might have such influence.[14] Into the post–World War II era, black areas of the city were still represented by white leaders who skillfully manipulated local black leaders to ensure their own capacity to win the local vote; influential African-Americans who could not easily win public office sought their power in commerce, civic, and religious organizations. The day that Melissa's neighbor's house was burglarized, it is unclear whether or not this history weighed on her mind. But, in the actions that followed, there were certainly some resonances between her work and the mid-twentieth-century political bosses who came before her.

Melissa's first decision as a block club leader was to act in such a way that she did not alienate the police. She recognized that an immediate, formal request of police to apprehend James, the car mechanic who broke into Larry's house, might not necessarily address the many issues that must be rectified in order for families to feel safe in the neighborhood. For example, the local gang might seek retribution by punishing Larry as a means of revenging his attack on James. The gang might intimidate her neighbors in hopes that they would not cooperate with police. Or the gang might shoot their guns outside Larry's house, making families unsafe. But she knew that the police had to be involved because there were two incidents—an assault and burglary—that were now public knowledge; the police could not be seen as refusing to respond to crime. She would have preferred to call them informally and work with them behind the scenes, but that would not help the police to publicly demonstrate their utility.

This strategy will certainly ring strange to those for whom the police are the primary guarantor of social order. But safety has a short- and long-term component for local residents in Grand Boulevard. In the short term, for disputes in the underground economy or gang-related activities such as shootings and drug trafficking, the police are unhelpful. They do not respond to every incident, their responses often fail to prevent future occurrences, and they manage to antagonize local residents and decrease resident faith in the police despite the existence of community policing and law enforcement outreach. So, in the short term, Melissa has developed other means of responding to crime and social problems. She may ask the gang directly to stop their drug trafficking, she may call on a prostitute to move away from her block, or she may try to settle a dispute between trader and customer on her own. For long-term stability, she believes that improved policing is the only way to help the community, so she continuously lobbies alongside her neighbors for improved law enforcement. She protests and writes letters to the mayor, but she understands that this is not a sufficient strategy without the other short-term solutions.

To figure out how to help Larry, Melissa called a friend, Minister Johnson, and asked for his advice. The local storefront pastor called on several other clergy to meet with Melissa, all of whom decided on a course of action. Melissa began by calling a local police officer, Marshall Jackson, who was a friend of the clergy. She described to him the entire incident and he said that the most important matter for the police was the burglary. The police would be less concerned about the assault, Officer Jackson suggested, because this was rooted in the underground economy—over which police had no regulatory interest. Moreover, no one was hurt badly enough to warrant police involvement. He suggested that the police could respond officially to the burglary. However, if Melissa wanted to work with the gangs directly or find a solution to the underground economic exchange gone awry, the police could provide only limited assistance. Most important, the police did not want to be seen as working alongside gang members in an enforcement capacity. Officer Jackson went with Melissa and Minister Johnson to meet with two police officials who said that their primary concern of law enforcement was the house burglary, to which they would have to respond in an official manner.

Melissa and Minister Jackson then approached the street gang to ascertain its own interested position. The gang leader, William, said that his obligation was to ensure that James the mechanic was fairly treated. The gang received money from James to provide security, so they had to honor their agreement. This meant that they must find Larry, ensure that he pay James the money owed for the repair, and punish Larry to the degree necessary—for example, by imposing a monetary fine, inflcting physical punishment, and/or demanding in-kind payment. The gang was not concerned with the house burglary.

The three mediators developed a solution. James should return the stolen goods (the TV and VCR) to Larry. Then Larry would pay James $50 for the car repair. There would be no additional punishment levied on either party because there were two grievances that offset one another: namely, Larry had beaten up James; James had broken into Larry's house.

The process would begin when Larry filed a formal complaint at the police station. James would then return the stolen merchandise to the police station directly, not to Larry or Melissa or Minister Johnson. This would enable the police to confront the perpetrator (James) and save face by fulfilling their role as the primary agent maintaining social order locally. Once he retrieved his property, Larry would agree to withdraw his complaint and the police would agree not to pursue the matter further. Then the gang, represented by their leader William, along with Melissa and Minister Johnson would accompany Larry to see James, whereupon the former would pay $50 to the latter for the completed auto repair work and issue an apology. James would then apologize for breaking into Larry's house.

The conflict was resolved as the parties had hoped. After the incident, James continued working on cars in the alleyway and paid the gang's monthly fee for "security." Larry remains one of his steady customers. Melissa, Pastor Johnson, Officer Jackson, and other stakeholders still address many incidents "off-the-books" and there remains a vibrant indigenous forum where residents can resolve local problems in an informal, non-bureaucratic manner. The final section of this chapter concludes by discussing some of the implications of these kinds of daily conflicts (and the attendant patterns of resolution) for the broader questions concerning the role of legal institutions and the relationship between the state and local levels/means of social control maintenance in an era of globalization.

DISCUSSION

The working relationships among different social actors in the case above indicate that law enforcement officials are present in community affairs in multiple ways. A critical public perception is that police in black communities act ostensibly as a force of control and containment. In other words, police neglect their duties as enforcement officials to protect person and property and instead work primarily to ensure that social problems do not spread from inner-city neighborhoods to other parts of the city. There are many problematic aspects of this view. This chapter has suggested that citizens of poor black communities have developed a relationship to the police that is neither purely antagonistic nor one that is best viewed as victimized. For decades, U.S. law enforcement officials have been neglectful in terms of their relative allocation of resources to varying parts of the city and overenthusiastic in their greater use of paramilitary strategies in black areas. However, the residents in such neglected communities are not passive actors. In the case of Chicago's Grand Boulevard community, there are alternative means by which police can become part of the overall neighborhood strategy to maintain social order, some of which are subject to resident discretion. At the local level, the varying ways in which residents and police interact hints at some of the complex arrangements that police and residents can create to respond to crime and maintain social order.

Almost any police officer will say that good policing involves building personal relationships with neighborhood actors—whether they are residents, shopkeepers, or block club presidents. This, however, should not take away from the fact that police practice is nevertheless racialized so that black urbanites experience a different relationship to this arm of the state. Even a seemingly race-neutral initiative such as "community policing" must be seen as operating in a history of contentious relationships among African-Americans and the law enforcement community. Implementing community policing in a white or Asian area in which the historical relations are different may not produce similar outcomes in terms of residents' trust of police, the collective efficacy with respect to local criminal behavior, and the effectiveness of police, court officers, social workers, and so on in helping households deal with crime and delinquency.

In the Grand Boulevard neighborhood, Melissa and her neighbors are aware of the local community policing meetings. They regularly attend in order to voice their concerns about safety problems in and around their streets. But, like many stakeholders, Melissa has developed alternative methods to supplement community policing and the wider resources that are formally available through the state. Resident-initiated self-enforcement strategies such as the one described above are a response to state neglect, a strategy to procure minimal state services and, simultaneously, a proactive declaration of local autonomy and efficacy. Law enforcement officials' willingness to work casually or "off-the-books" with residents testifies, similarly, to their own perceptions of potentially effective policing in the community, their perceptions of residents' attitudes toward the enforcement community, and their understandings of the limits of formal enforcement strategies.

We have termed such alternate strategies for social order maintenance "indigenous" in order to make them distinct from state-sanctioned juridical spheres. The codes of conduct, the methods for obtaining justice, and the actors who may act as judge and jury diverge in each arena—although there may be overlap between the two. The example above demonstrates that residents may approach any incident by appealing to customary indigenous procedures or by a direct appeal to the state. And, for any particular incident, there may be twin processes of adjudication that take place. The "burglary" on Melissa's street was investigated in an official manner by the police and in an off-the-books manner by Melissa, Minister Johnson, and the street gang. It is important to note that the form of justice that individuals derive in each arena may be different. For example, the police were able to retrieve the property that James stole from Larry's house. The burglary was a clear criminal act; the return of the stolen property was sufficient to forestall prosecution of James in the courts. But the "burglary" meant something different in terms of the underground economic exchange that had turned sour: in this context, the burglary was an act of retribution by James for the failure to receive a payment and, to some degree, it was a tolerable response by an aggrieved actor to try and recoup monies owed him for a missed payment.

The presence of multiple venues for resolving local problems and maintaining order does not mean that the two are equal in stature or utilization by local actors. Particularly for violent crime, residents will turn immediately to the police for assistance and they are not likely to pursue perpetrators on their own. But, even for less violent transgressions, residents will first attempt to secure help from law enforcement officials before trying to work through informal, customary procedures. Conflicts in the underground economy, on the other hand, tend to be adjudicated via indigenous means primarily because the constituent activities are illegal and so the use of police is very limited. Public safety problems—such as gangs congregating and dealing drugs, prostitutes soliciting johns, and homeless persons intimidating residents—are similarly ripe for indigenous enforcement because police tend not to respond in a timely manner and residents typically know the gang member, homeless person, and so on who may be endangering safety.

Although a champion of indigenous means of redress, Melissa is quick to note that, in the long run, this is not a viable option for urban poor and minority communities. "If we keep doing this ourselves, then we'll never get the police to take us seriously. This is just something we have to do—we don't want to be calling up gang members, but we'll do it until we can get police to respond." Her fear, and that of her neighbors, is that residents will grow increasingly alienated from the state if they continue to work outside the government, whether they work to pick up trash in their parks or to police gang activity. They do not perceive their participation in indigenous forms of maintaining social order to be in competition or conflict with the state over social control of their community, but rather as a necessary outgrowth of their social, political, and economic marginalization.

Thus the development of these local, "indigenous" forms of establishing community social control are shaped by global forces in two primary ways: by global political and economic shifts that have transformed inner-city labor markets and traditional state functions as well as by the spread of ideas and ideologies about the role of the welfare state and the spread of consumption throughout the world. With respect to the first aspect of global influence on local action, many of those in the Grand Boulevard neighborhood, faced with limited opportunities for legitimate work, have turned to informal means of generating income. The majority of people who make money off-the-books on Melissa's street do so not by selling drugs or stealing cars, but by petty income-generating activities such as selling homemade food or performing psychic services or preparing taxes and not reporting income. Their legitimate employment prospects have gradually declined over the past four decades as well-paying manufacturing jobs have moved out of the city and into the suburbs or abroad, transforming urban labor markets into low-wage, service sector–based work. They live in a "global city" that, as Sassen (1991) points out, is characterized by a bifurcated labor market and deep-seated inequities in wage earning. As such global inequities have risen in areas like Greater Grand Boulevard and other inner-city areas throughout the world, social, economic, residential, and political segregation has increased as well. The political consequence of this globalized stratification has been similar in countries around the globe, and is primarily manifested in the retrenchment of the welfare state.

This global political-economic shift has been accompanied by a second feature of globalization—namely, the proliferation of global consumption and the spread of ideas about the role of the state throughout the world. As the welfare state has withdrawn from many of its more liberal responsibilities, the onus of safety and policing has become privatized. For the upper classes, this has resulted in a retreat to gated communities or the purchase of private security systems. Self-protection has become an object to be consumed, fueled by the global labor market. For the more marginalized, this has resulted in the implementation of particularly harsh penal policies targeted toward the socioeconomically disadvantaged; an increase in the responsibility of local leaders and institutions, such as churches and community-based organizations, for ensuring community safety; and a complementary rise in the development of indigenous forms of social control. In this way, the local indigenous practices engaged in by Melissa, the gang, and Minister Johnson can be understood as a reaction to and a manifestation of greater, global shifts that have transformed both the formal and informal structures under which communities balance local demands and relations with those of a broader, global order.

ENDNOTES

1. See Berrien and Winship (2002); Meares (2000); Tyler and Huo (2002); and Fagan and Malkin (2003).

2. Mumford (1997); Spear (1979); Drake and Cayton (1945).

3. Debates on the nature of social changes in this period of capitalism's realignment have been addressed by numerous authors. See Davis (1992), and Mandel (1978) for two contrasting views.

4. The principal of Englewood High School awarded plaques and awards to one jailed gang leader and his associate for their help in forming a truce between warring gangs inside the school (Brown, Lane Harvey. October 30, 1993. "Community Angered by Gang Rally." *Chicago Sun-Times*). In October 1993, there were 10 gang members on the ballot for local school council

elections (October 22, 1993. "Gangs Should Heed Their Stated Goals." *Chicago Sun-Times*, p. 37). This movement attracted prominent Chicago leaders, including Reverend Jesse Jackson and former Chicago Mayor Eugene Sawyer ("A Push for Gang Peace: Jim Brown Convenes 50 Leaders in Bid to Settle Differences." August 31, 1992. *Chicago Sun-Times*). Thus, residents saw gatherings where gang members were surrounded by clergy, merchants, prominent black elected officials, schoolteachers and administrators, activists, and members of community-based organizations (Neal, Steve. March 21, 1995. "Bradley's Bid Puts Chicago in Bad Light." *Chicago Sun-Times*; and Byrne, Dennis. August 30, 1994. "Cheer, Cheer, the Gang's All Here." *Chicago Sun-Times*, p. 21). The unfolding of this story was also covered over the following series of articles: Blau, Robert. June 19, 1988. "Crack Failing to Dent Chicago Drug Markets." *Chicago Tribune*, p. 1; Shipp, E. R. December 27, 1985. "Chicago Gang Sues to Be Recognized as a Religion." *New York Times*, p. 14; Gills, Michael. March 20, 1997. "Feds Call Hoover a Modern Capone." *Chicago Sun-Times*; Pasternak, Judy. March 24, 1997. "Influence of Chicago Gang Boss Compared to Capone's." *Los Angeles Times*, p. 1; Sadovi, Carlos, and Frank Main. April 7, 2002. "Gangs Channel River of Drug Cash from Streets to Shops, Studios—Even Vegas." *Chicago Sun-Times*; and Sadovi, Carlos, and Frank Main. April 8, 2002. "Tracing Cash to Chip Away at Drug Trade." *Chicago Sun-Times*.

5. See Venkatesh and Levitt (2000); see also Spergel (1990).

6. Chicago would then develop a series of city ordinances to restrict the gang's capacity to occupy public space; use signaling devices such as clothing and hand signals in schools; and sell drugs near parks, schools, and churches. Accompanying these changes were heightened sentences for illicit substances disproportionately traded by urban minorities, the transfer of juvenile perpetrators into the adult criminal system, and lengthier sentences that lacked intensive parole/probation periods where rehabilitation and counseling might occur.

7. See Beall (2002); Blakely and Snyder (1997); and Caldeira (2000).

8. See Loader (1999).

9. See Robinson (1981).

10. *Indigenous* and *state-sanctioned* juridical forums must be differentiated from the case of *popular justice*, another related but distinct legal institutional complex that can manifest in urban poor communities. Sally Merry, in an excellent comparative review of popular justice cultural traditions, suggests that this third complex is culturally similar to indigenous law and opposite to the state, while its "procedures and sources of authority are similar to that of state law." In practice, these three constitute a "single social field"; however, Merry continues to argue that popular justice is much closer to state law empirically, because it basically replicates the functions and language of the state—tending, even, to "replicate the model of a court." See Merry (1993), pp. 35–37.

11. For a comparable empirical analysis, see Comaroff (1982).

12. By way of counterexample, there are white ethnic communities in Chicago in which police work actively to ensure that residents do not accumulate a criminal record for specific offenses: drunk driving may be forgiven, domestic abuse may be settled informally, judges may never see the face of teen shoplifting and thievery. But such informal arrangements are produced not out of racial hostility, histories of inadequate policing, and so on. Moreover, in white ethnic contexts, these practices may actually lead to better formal policing, since it cements ties between police and tenants, which is rarely the outcome in minority areas. In sum, then, these

white ethnic areas must be differentiated from areas of minority settlement where the outcomes may be similar. There are unfortunately few systematic comparative studies of community-based differences in policing and enforcement. Two noteworthy studies are Sullivan (1990) and Cicourel (1968).

13. For the most elegant theoretical framing of the ways in which urban politics are structured by patterns of uneven capitalist development, see Harvey (1985). More concrete elaborations can be found in Wilson (1981); see also Castells (1983).

14. For example, as John Muncie (2006) points out, the development of community policing and other initiatives has occurred as part of a broader restructuring of the social welfare and law enforcement arms of the Western state.

REFERENCES

Anderson, Elijah. 1990. *Streetwise: Race, Class, and Change in an Urban Community.* Chicago: University of Chicago Press.

Beall, J. 2002. "The People Behind the Walls: Insecurity, Identity, and Gated Communities in Johannesburg." Crisis States Programmer working paper no. 10, London: DRC.

Berrien, Jenny, and Christopher Winship. 2002. "An Umbrella of Legitimacy: Boston's Police Department—Ten Point Coalition Collaboration." In *Securing Our Children's Future: New Approaches to Juvenile Justice and Youth Violence.* pp. 201–228. Gary Katzmann (Ed.). Washington, DC: Brookings Institution Press.

Blakely, E. J., and M. G. Snyder. 1997. *Fortress America: Gated Communities in the United States.* Washington DC: Brookings Institution Press.

Bourgois, Pierre. 2002. *In Search of Respect: Selling Crack in El Barrio.* Cambridge: Cambridge University Press.

Bunting, Annie, and Sally Engle Merry. 2004. "Global Regulation and Local Political Struggles: Early Marriage in Northern Nigeria." DRAFT prepared for the Social Science Research Council. New York.

Caldeira, T. P. R. 2000. "Fortified Enclaves: The New Urban Segregation." In *Cities and Citizenship,* pp. 114–138. J. Holston (Ed.). Durham: Duke University Press.

Castells, Manuel. 1983. *The City and the Grassroots.* Berkeley: University of California Press.

Cicourel, Aaron. 1968. *The Social Organization of Juvenile Justice.* New York: Wiley.

Comaroff, John L. 1982. "Dialectical Systems, History, and Anthropology: Units of Study and Questions of Theory." *Journal of Southern African Studies* 8: 143–172.

Covington, Jeanette, and Ralph B. Taylor. 1991. "Fear of Crime in Urban Residential Neighborhoods: Implications of Between-and-Within Neighborhood Sources for Current Models." *Sociological Quarterly* 32: 231–249.

Davis, Mike. 1992. *City of Quartz: Excavating the Future in Los Angeles.* New York: Vintage.

Douglass, M., and J. Friedman (Eds). 1998. *Cities for Citizens: Planning and the Rise of Civil Society in a Global Age.* Chichester: Wiley.

Drake, St. Clair, and Horace R. Cayton. 1945. *Black Metropolis: A Study of Negro Life in a Northern City.* Chicago: University of Chicago Press.

Fagan, Jeffrey. 2002. "Race, Legitimacy, and Criminal Law." *Souls* 4:1, 69–72.

Fagan, Jeffrey, and Victoria Malkin. 2003. "Theorizing Community Justice through Community Courts." *Fordham Urban Law Journal* 30: 857–953.

Garland, David. 1996. "The Limits of the Sovereign State: Strategies of Crime Control in Contemporary Society." *British Journal of Contemporary Society* 36:4, 445–471.

Harvey, David. 1985. *The Urbanization of Capital.* Baltimore: Johns Hopkins University Press.

Loader, Ian. 1999. "Consumer Culture and the Commodification of Policing and Security." *Sociology* 33:2, 373–392.

Low, S. 2001. "The Edge and the Center: Gated Communities and the Discourse of Fear." *American Anthologist* 103:1, 45–58.

Mandel, Ernest. 1978. *Late Capitalism.* New York: Knopf Publishing Group.

McIlwaine, Cathy, and Caroline O. N. Moser. 2001. "Violence and Social Capital in Urban Poor Communities: Perspectives from Colombia and Guatemala." *Journal of International Development* 13, 965–984.

Meares, Tracey L. 2000. "Norms, Legitimacy, and Law Enforcement." *Oregon Law Review* 79: 391–415.

Merry, Sally. 1993. "Sorting out Popular Justice," in *The Possibility of Popular Justice: A Case Study of Community Mediation in the United States*, pp. 31–66. Sally Engle Merry and Neal Milner (Eds.). Ann Arbor: University of Michigan Press.

Mumford, Kevin J. 1997. *Interzones: Black/White Sex Districts in Chicago and New York in the Early Twentieth Century.* New York: Columbia University Press.

Muncie, John. 2006. "Youth Justice and the Governance of Young People: Global, International, National, and Local Contexts," in *Youth, Globalization, and the Law*, Chapter 2. Sudhir Alladi Venkatesh and Ron Kassimir (Eds.). Stanford, CA: Stanford University Press.

Neild, Rachel. 1998. "Themes and Debates in Public Security Reform—A Manual for Civil Society: Community Policing." Washington, DC: Washington Office on Latin America.

O'Malley, P., and P. Palmer. 1996. "Post-Keynesian Policing." *Economy and Society* 25: 137–155.

Padilla, Felix. 1992. *The Gang as an American Enterprise.* New Brunswick: Rutgers University Press.

Ranney, David. 2003. *Global Decisions, Local Collisions.* Philadelphia: Temple University Press.

Reiner, R. 1992. "Policing a Postmodern Society." *Modern Law Review* 55: 761–781.

Robinson, Cyril D. 1981. "The Production of Black Violence in Chicago," in *Crime and Capitalism: Readings in Marxist Criminology*, pp. 366–404. David F. Greenberg (Ed.). Philadelphia: Temple University Press.

Sassen, Saskia. 1991. *The Global City: New York, London, and Tokyo.* Princeton: Princeton University Press.

Shearing, C., and P. Stenning. 1983. "Private Security: Implications for Social Control." *Social Problems* 30: 493–506.

Spear, Allan H. 1979. *Black Chicago: The Making of a Negro Ghetto, 1890–1920.* Chicago: University of Chicago Press.

Spergel, I. A. 1990. "Youth Gangs: Continuity and Change," in *Crime and Justice: A Review of Research,* vol. 12, pp. 171–275. M. Tonry and N. Morris (Eds.). Chicago: University of Chicago Press.

———. 1996. *Gang Suppression and Intervention: An Assessment.* Collingdale: Diane Publishing Co.

Spitzer, S., and A. Scull. 1977. "Privatization and Capitalist Development: The Case of the Private Police." *Social Problems* 25: 18–29.

Sullivan, Mercer. 1990. *Getting Paid: Youth Crime and Work in the Inner City.* Ithaca: Cornell University Press.

Tyler, T. R., and Y. J. Huo. 2002. *Trust in the Law: Encouraging Public Cooperation with the Police and Courts.* New York: Russell Sage Foundation.

Venkatesh, Sudhir, and Steven D. Levitt. Autumn 2000. "Are We a Family or a Business? History and Disjuncture in the Urban American Gang." *Theory & Society* 29: 427–462.

Wacquant, Loïc. 2000. "Deadly Symbiosis: When Ghetto and Prison Meet and Mesh." *Punishment and Society* 3 (1): 95–134.

———. 2001. "The Penalisation of Poverty and the Rise of Neo-Liberalism." *European Journal on Criminal Policy and Research* 9: 401–412.

White, Rob. 2006. "Public Spaces, Consumption, and the Social Regulation of Young People," in *Youth, Globalization, and the Law,* Chapter 8. Sudhir Alladi Venkatesh and Ron Kassimir (Eds.). Stanford, CA: Stanford University Press.

Wilson, William Julius. 1981. *The Declining Significance of Race.* Chicago: University of Chicago Press.

———. 1987. *The Truly Disadvantaged: The Inner City, the Underclass, and Public Policy.* Chicago: University of Chicago Press.

III

Institutional Regulation and Youth Response

Globalization has amplified the challenges for states of managing youth populations and facilitating the transition of young people into adulthood. The three case studies in the preceding section described the ways in which young people engage institutions of social control. Youth laboring in Chicago's gangland, refugees moving between San Salvador and Los Angeles, and North African migrants in urban France are all interacting with state and civil society actors responsible for maintaining law and order. The chapters took the vantage point of the youth themselves and showed how, from their perspective, maintaining social order can be viewed alternatively as harassment, repression, neglect, and so on. The project of the state and that of youth collide in the global era, sometimes with few foreseeable prospects for reconciliation.

The essays in part III shift our gaze to the institutional actors who develop and carry out social policies. Each author notes how the functions of maintaining social order are shifting as regions of the world are connected. Complementing Bonelli's essay on Paris, Susan Terrio looks not at policing on the ground but at the practices of those who labor in the courts and agencies that make up the sphere of juvenile justice. Terrio describes how this judicial apparatus struggles to cope effectively with the fluid and complicated lives of young people or their parents who migrate to France, whether they are originally from North Africa or Eastern Europe. These young people come for work opportunities, but they may continue to live out their lives in multiple locations. They may never fully integrate into French society, but instead their lives may be shaped by social factors in several nations thousands of miles apart. This global movement poses a tremendous challenge for state actors, and Terrio describes in great detail the complex interactions of young people and the agencies in place ostensibly to serve them.

In chapter 2, John Muncie argues that there may be various responses to young people on the part of the state and that globalization has affected the character and texture of state practice. In her chapter, Brenda Coughlin picks up this line of reasoning with her look at the criminal justice system in the United States. Coughlin argues that the responsibility for managing youth is increasingly being allocated to agencies of incarceration. Once labor markets, social workers, schools, and churches may have taken the lead in socially controlling youth and re-integrating them into work, family, community, and so on. No longer is this the case: jails and prisons have grown considerably in industrialized societies, and they are now primary centers for warehousing marginalized youth. Coughlin's focus is on the United States, but the patterns she studies are occurring in many industrialized and developing nations.

Rob White complements Terrio's and Coughlin's work by looking at public space and the ways in which young people and police negotiate with one another to appropriate and lay claim to common areas—including parks, streetcorners, and spaces within ostensibly private areas such as shopping malls. What may appear to be a relatively confined problem of ensuring safety and access to public space is a much more telling dynamic in which the state must respond to the divergent views and aspirations of young people. White's focus is Australia, but, as he suggests, the patterns observed hold throughout industrialized nations where the notion of the public—for example, public speech and access to public space—is the hallmark of deliberative democratic governance. In the neoliberal era, White's work suggests, the status of the public is eroding as an available discursive and social space for young people to interact and express themselves.

6

Youth, (Im)migration, and Juvenile Law at the Paris Palace of Justice

SUSAN J. TERRIO

In June 2003 I attended the trial in the Paris juvenile correctional court of two 17-year-old boys, both French citizens of Antillean descent. Police reports and witness depositions gave contradictory accounts of an encounter between two groups of teenage boys, one from a vocational high school (*lycée*) and the other from a public housing project in the 20th district in Paris. Among nine witnesses there was no consensus on either the number of youth involved or their exact identities. Nonetheless, two teenagers of color were prosecuted and convicted for stealing a cell phone and phone card and for injuring three of the students.

At the end of the same year, in December 2003, I observed penal hearings in the chambers of the 11th district court where I encountered for a second time members of a family from the Central African Republic who had fled political upheaval there in 1996 to settle in France. The court had tried and acquitted their eldest son Jacques of aggravated rape in 2001 but had imposed psychiatric treatment as a condition of his release and rehabilitation. This time he and his youngest brother Michel, a nine-year-old boy, were accused of assaulting and injuring an elderly woman in a Paris municipal pool who, according to the police report, had objected to their splashing and "looked disapprovingly" at their sister. Only Michel, his mother, and his father appeared at the hearing, explaining that Jacques, now almost 18, had returned to Africa. The judge drew on social worker reports to express concern about "Michel's gang," a group of "incorrigible boys spreading terror in the neighborhood."

Michel's mother blamed her sons' problems on the overcrowded conditions in "the squalid welfare hotel" where she lived in one room with five children, a hotel similar to those in which nearly 50 residents, most women and children from Sub-Saharan Africa, burned to death in several suspicious fires in the summer of 2005. She recounted discriminatory treatment by Paris municipal authorities who dismissed her "as a dirty black" and repeatedly refused to provide public housing despite what she claimed as "her heritage" as the granddaughter of a French citizen. The judge retorted, "Madame, you need to make your children take responsibility for their mistakes and to give them proper structure in their lives. If not you will make them lifelong victims."

These vignettes center on juvenile justice in two representative venues: scheduled hearings for minor offenses in the judge's chambers and trials for serious misdemeanors and crimes in the juvenile court. The second of the cases above is representative of the charges commonly heard in the courtrooms to which I had regular access over the four years I conducted research at the court (from 2000 to 2004), the vast majority for simple theft or theft aggravated by the circumstance of assault (*avec violence*) and/or by a group (*en réunion*). The first case, that of Jacques, was exceptional with regard to the charge. It was also unusual because the accused and his mother insisted on his innocence and because the facts of the case produced a rare acquittal. Both, however, involved the usual suspects. The vast majority of defendants are French citizens of non-European ancestry, whether Maghrebi, West African, or Antillean or foreign nationals from Eastern Europe, primarily Romania, and from Africa, both from the Maghreb and the Sub-Saharan regions.

These vignettes reveal both the shifting international forces and the contradictory ideological forces at work in the adjudication of penal cases at the largest and most influential juvenile court in the nation. The Paris court lies within the heart of a massive discursive and institutional field of power housed at the Palace of Justice. It is also located at the center of a global city marked by intensifying economic disparities, uneven development, class differentiation, and increasing migratory flows that bring both adults and children in search of political asylum and economic opportunity.

The city's colonial and post-colonial histories are mirrored in the brown and black people clutching summonses who jostle for position in long lines to pass through metal detectors at the public entrance, who wait anxiously outside courtrooms, or who arrive disheveled, dirty, and in handcuffs directly from jail. The situations of these youth, like those of youth elsewhere in the world, arise out of the workings of neoliberal capitalism. The rhetoric of enfranchisement, the opportunity for waged citizenship, and the promise of full inclusion is undercut by the reality of de-industrialization, the demise of the welfare state, and the specter of permanent exclusion. Nonetheless, the issue of generation in general and of teenagers in particular is a fertile site onto which class anxieties and concerns about social reproduction are displaced (Comaroff and Comaroff 2001: 16). A sense of moral and social crisis is heightened as well given the ethnicization of immigrant identities, the perceived failure of cultural assimilation, greater vertical polarization (Friedman 2003), and the emergence of a new paradigm of violence in which the ideological struggles of the past have been superseded by local identity conflicts (Wieviorka 2003). If young white persons in the English-speaking world are considered teenagers, their black and Arab counterparts are seen as youth, "adolescents with an attitude, and almost always male" (Comaroff and Comaroff 2001: 16).

Legal discourses governing youth, whether those linked to social justice and universal rights or those associated with criminalization and law enforcement, originate in nation-states but increasingly circulate globally and are tied to neoliberalism. This whole process has complex and long-term consequences for the transition of youth into adulthood—specifically the ways in which young people are identified as normal, at risk, or delinquent, and the ways in which they are held accountable for their actions and treated within juvenile justice systems. In Western Europe the new arrival or increased visibility of stigmatized youth groups, illegal migrants, and French citizens of immigrant ancestry is causing mounting concern with issues of public safety and generating demands for more repressive regulatory mechanisms to control both spaces and populations deemed dangerous. When youth cross borders they become "matter out of place," whether in the city, the street, the school or, as in the case of the African boys described above, the municipal swimming pool; they then provoke contests over space.

The management of space and the removal of offending groups are mutually reinforcing strategies that demand penal versus social responses (Merry 2001: 17; Wacquant 1999). These are evident in border control techniques and containment strategies in transit camps such as Sangatte, France, as well as the human and civil rights violations of foreign minors detained in airport holding facilities, in police custody, and in prison. The emotional debate and diminished tolerance for asylum seekers and illegal migrants in the European Union has led to rising xenophobia and rightist political gains in Austria, Denmark, Italy, Scandinavia, the usually liberal Netherlands, and France. It has also fueled the public perception across Europe that juvenile offenders are younger and more violent than in the past and renewed calls for more punitive measures in the courts (Bitscheidt and Lindenberg 1998 quoted in Doek 2002). It is clear that ethnic minorities—such as North African youth in France; Turks in Germany; and Moroccans, Surinamese, and Turks in the Netherlands—are "over-represented both in registered [juvenile] crime" (Estrada 1999) and in European prisons (Wacquant 1999).

In this context the category of the child is an increasingly contested domain of public policy and cultural politics. Interestingly, international initiatives to increase legal protections for children over the past 20 years have engendered new conceptualizations of childhood and produced paradoxical and unintended consequences for their treatment within juvenile justice systems. For example, the Convention on the Rights of the Child conceives of children as active, rational beings capable of independent decision making. It views them not only as vulnerable and developing beings but also as competent individuals with enhanced moral and legal responsibility for their actions. Nevertheless, recognition of children's active agency has produced renewed calls for more punishment, for a lower minimum age for criminal responsibility, and for a "just deserts" approach that requires more retribution for offenders and more compensation for victims or society (Bitscheidt and Lindinberg 1998 quoted in Doek 2002). The effects of this approach have been visible in decisions at the European Court for Human Rights, which has interpreted due process principles in ways that change the role of the juvenile court judge and that diminish the protective aspects of police custody and pre-trial detention, orienting them more toward the enforcement of the public order. Thus, the progressive empowerment of children coincides with harsher repression of public order offenses and a shift away from welfare approaches to those that emphasize individual accountability and responsibility.

The energetic and disproportionate prosecution of (im)migrant youth marks the delinquent as a global subject even as it interrogates the regulatory and surveillance capabilities of the modern nation-state and the European Union. In this chapter I explore the unforeseen consequences of both shifting national circumstances and international child advocacy initiatives on judicial practices in France. I closely examine the gaps and slippages between institutional rhetoric, legal norms, and judicial practice. These gaps reveal changing understandings of deviance and the newly porous boundary between the child and the adult.

Careful analysis of cases observed in 2003 will show that the court is slowly but progressively moving away from welfare to neoliberal approaches that devolve risk, responsibility, and accountability onto individuals, families, and communities. This shift can be observed in municipal policing, prosecutorial prerogatives, and judicial decisions. It can be heard in the discourse of court personnel who focus on civility, respect, work values, and individual accountability. They admonish defendants to take initiative and to be responsible, two requirements for social integration and professional success. This is all the more striking since the majority of the defendants are poor, working class, foreign, or youth of immigrant ancestry who do not enjoy equal opportunity in housing or education.

Over the last 30 years the urban geography of French cities has been substantially transformed. Greater access to individual home ownership prompted the French version of white flight from public housing and widened the gap between those projects with higher concentrations of poor, ethnic populations clustered outside French cities or in "bad" inner-city neighborhoods such as the 19th or 20th districts in Paris in contrast to proliferating middle-class subdivisions. The segregation and ghettoization of marginal populations in the "immigrant" projects associated with crime fueled feelings of insecurity, support for right-wing candidates, and anti-immigrant—particularly anti-Arab— racism. Juveniles seeking rehabilitation face a job market characterized by high un- and under-employment rates for all but the most credentialed and an educational system in which working-class and immigrant youth routinely get identified for vocational versus academic tracks and end up in unpaid internships; part-time, temporary, minimum-wage jobs; or the unemployment line (Beaud and Pialoux 1999; Masclet 2001).

I argue that despite guarantees of equality under the law, the adjudication of cases involving immigrant and foreign children often has the unintended effect of undermining legal protections and of reinforcing existing hierarchies of class and ethnicity. Current court conditions—scarce institutional resources, overloaded dockets, staff shortages, and a rapid influx of unaccompanied children involved in criminal activity—combine with public pressure, limited economic opportunity, and anxiety about the rise of a permanent underclass of immigrant ancestry to move away from prevention and rehabilitation toward containment and punishment. It is possible to track this change by examining French sensitivity to international opinion, public understandings of delinquency in France, and new conditions within the Paris juvenile court.

A GLOBAL STAGE

Beginning with the famous 1833 study of American prisons undertaken by Alexis de Tocqueville and Gustave de Beaumont, French jurists and legislators have been keen observers and imitators of international trends in criminal justice and penal reform. They are justly proud that France's juvenile justice system now enjoys an international reputation as a viable and integrated welfare approach that privileges rehabilitation and makes no clear distinction between delinquent minors and at-risk children (Doek 2002). Many see this as consistent with France's status as a champion of human rights and as an enthusiastic signatory of international conventions advancing children's rights (Garapon and Salas 1995). At the same time, France's ratification of the Convention on the Rights of the Child in 1990 highlighted in uncomfortable ways the still significant gaps between new international imperatives and French legal codes, particularly in the area of police custody procedures and due process protections. Supranational institutions such as the European Court on Human Rights constitute a privileged arena for the examination and censure of national policies on issues ranging from policing, prisons, and deportation to adoption and civil unions. For example, the European court in separate 1992 and 1999 decisions condemned France for degrading and inhuman treatment of detainees in French police custody (Herzog-Evans 2000: 42). Over the same period the Council of Europe's Committee on the Prevention of Torture conducted inspections in 1991 and 1996 of French maximum security prisons, airport holding facilities, and police jails and concluded that "a person detained [in France] by police officers runs a substantial risk of being mistreated" (CPT 1993: 10; 1998: 9). Allegations of mistreatment included "punches, slaps, blows with telephone books, psychological pressure, insults and the withdrawal of food and medicine." Foreigners and teenagers in Paris and the provinces most commonly complained of mistreatment.

The Convention on the Rights of the Child also focused specific attention on the lack of due process protections for the accused and material witnesses. It prompted the 1994 creation of a Juvenile Defense Bureau at the Paris court under the aegis of the Paris Bar Association to recruit, train, and pay for court-appointed juvenile defense attorneys. International pressure was also pivotal in the 2000 vote by the Socialist-dominated legislature for a law on the presumption of innocence. The law of June 15, 2000, reinforcing the presumption of innocence and the rights of victims changed police custody rules by mandating, for the first time, notification of the right to remain silent, to know the legal length of detention, to immediate access to legal counsel (available before only after the 20th hour of a 24-hour detention period), and of the right to medical care, food, water, and rest. This law also introduced appeals for verdicts of the Assizes criminal court and enhanced victims' rights. In response to renewed international calls for the criminalization of human trafficking and its attendant sexual and labor exploitation, France appointed a children's rights commissioner in 2000. In 2001 the Paris juvenile court president created a special court to deal more humanely with unaccompanied foreign minors.

FROM REHABILITATION TO RETRIBUTION

Despite international pressure and a humanitarian commitment to enhance minors' rights, in the 1990s there was a marked shift in both rhetoric and practice from protection to retribution. During this period juvenile delinquency became a highly politicized public policy issue, generating moral panics and focusing public attention on a new type of youth violence, termed a "delinquency of exclusion." This was a coded reference to the children of marginalized immigrant families of non-European ancestry. French public discourses produced by journalists, politicians, social scientists, and jurists draw on the interwoven strands of ethnicity, class, masculinity, and culture to constitute "immigrant" delinquency as a newly threatening social category and an intractable social problem. This was all the more interesting given the long history of working-class French and European immigrant youth, who were labeled "immigrants" in the early twentieth century (Donzelot 1997; Fishman 2002).

Public fears of a delinquency of exclusion build on 20 years of sensationalist media coverage linking egregious and often unrepresentative acts of youth violence to the so-called immigrant housing projects (*cités*), whether in the now famously stigmatized suburbs outside French cities (*la banlieue*) or in the multi-ethnic neighborhoods of the 18th, 19th, and 20th districts within Paris (Boyer and Lochard 1998).[1] These are seen as the locus of disorder, anomie, and violence; as a signifier of the danger posed for the social body of the nation by the high concentration of ethnic Others—whether North or West African or Antillean. Media coverage in publications on both the left and the right has shifted from explaining delinquency as a socioeconomic problem to depicting delinquency as a cultural lack that threatens public order and French values (Collovald 2000: 40).

Politicians across the political spectrum astutely used the media to reinforce public fears of this "new" delinquency of exclusion. They contrast republican democratic principles and the rule of law in mainstream French society with the territorialized collective violence and the rule of the jungle in the "immigrant" projects. Successive governments have institutionalized a territorialized approach to crime, first in an anti-ghetto Suburb Marshall Plan proposed by the right in 1995, and later under the auspices of the Council of Domestic Safety created by the left in 1997.[2] As a resonant policy issue, the topic of *insécurité*—fear for public safety, another reference to youth crime—dominated French opinion polls and campaign rhetoric. This issue influenced the outcome of the 2002 presidential and legislative elections and contributed to the election of a center-right president and National Assembly. More significantly, it has produced legislative reform (1995, 1996, 2003, 2004) that has decisively reinforced the punitive versus the protective elements of juvenile law and imposed stiffer penalties for public order offenses such as loitering, begging, prostitution, loud music, gathering in public housing stairwells, and threatening or insulting public officials. New, more repressive regulatory mechanisms include enhanced prosecutorial power; fast-track adjudication procedures legislated in 1995, 1996, and 2002; more aggressive policing; stiffer controls on probation; and harsher penalties on delinquent families. By 2003 a new, "new" delinquency of exclusion perpetrated by illegal migrants from Eastern Europe, Asia, Turkey, and the Maghreb became visible. Growing numbers of young, unaccompanied Romanian boys arrested for theft and prostitution on Parisian streets challenged accepted "facts" equating crime exclusively with non-European populations. It is paradoxical that public opinion and state policy should so decisively shift in a society where serious youth violence—the majority aimed at property not at people—has remained stable and low for the past 30 years.

The delinquency of exclusion theories have found a perfect explanatory model in the 1920s Chicago School of Sociology theories that are still widely used by French social scientists and read by French judges. This cultural ecology paradigm links delinquency to environmental influences including unstable families, poor housing, poverty, drug and alcohol abuse, school truancy, and participation in an illicit underground economy. It theorizes youth crime as the product of economic marginality, social disorganization, and cultural deprivation of concentrated populations in enclaved, ethnic neighborhoods (Bailleau and Gorgeon 2001; Bauer and Raufer 1999; Body-Gendrot 2000; Dubet and Lapeyronnie 1992; Karsenty 2000; Lagrange 2001; Wieviorka 1996). French ethnographic studies specifically focusing on the projects describe uniformly shared normative codes—linguistic, familial, and social— that bind marginalized ethnic youth to a transgressive street culture at odds with mainstream French society (Bordet 1999; Duret 1995; Lepoutre 1997). The work represented by Bordet, Duret, and Lepoutre intended to counter negative public depictions of a subculture by providing the insider view and the inner logic of a genuine street culture. Nonetheless, this work masks the state's role in the production of marginality through postwar housing policies. It ignores anti-immigrant discrimination even as it naturalizes the link between deviance and lower class and minority Others (cf. Cicourel 1995: 25). It substitutes cultural explanations for economic ones in a shifting political economy (cf. Merry 2003) of limited opportunity for workers without specialized training or educational credentials.

Judges' and prosecutors' explanations for the causes and persistence of a delinquency of exclusion mirror both public perception and social scientific theory. Jurists, judges, and prosecutors now draw less on psychology and more on sociology to link a delinquency of exclusion to aberrant cultural norms and dangerous environmental influences, as we heard in the opening vignette. Their embrace of a cultural ecology model is a dramatic departure from judicial writings in the 1940s to 1970s (Baranger 2001; Hamon 2001; Maximy, Baranger, and Maximy 2000; Rosensvzeig 1999, 2002; Salas 1995). During that 30-year period of economic growth, demographic explosion, full employment, and single immigrant guest workers, judges saw delinquency as a coming-of-age phenomenon, individual pathology, or bad parenting in difficult circumstances. Currently cultural difference has been added to and conflated with psychology, class, and economics as significant risk factors.

Most significantly, judicial practices draw not only on French social scientific theory but also on popular folk categories that conceive of culture as a homogenous, geographically bounded, and internally consensual system. These categories rely on a holistic notion of society with its emphasis on integration as preconditions for the health of the social body and the maintenance of the moral order. In this understanding, ethnic or national groups—Bambara, Soninké, Antilleans, Algerians, Moroccans, Tunisians, Sri Lankans, Romanians, and so on—are categorized into a hierarchy of discrete, qualitatively different cultural systems. This is a hierarchy that nonetheless functions like race to ascribe certain immutable attributes to the peoples within them (cf. Balibar 1988; Beriss 2000). Because cultures are understood to determine the practices of people born into them, particularly "less evolved" non-Western cultures, they are thought to be stubbornly resistant to processes of adaptation, hybridization, or change. For these reasons, as we shall see, court personnel see the cultural particularity of non-Western peoples—particularly marginal Maghrebi and African Muslims—as a formidable obstacle to successful rehabilitation and integration even in cases where their children are born and schooled in France. The legal mandate for the protection of at-risk children also implies protection from the "backward" traits of non-Western cultural traditions with which the court must deal: polygamous families, female excision and the control of female sexuality, the subordination of women, patriarchal authority, belief in sorcery, and so on.

CLASS AND RACIAL BIAS AT THE PARIS JUVENILE COURT?

The juvenile court in Paris and its judges have been at the center of debates within the legal establishment on both the procedural rigor and the impartiality of its judgments. Sociologists of law (Bourdieu 1986; Donzelot 1997) criticize pervasive class bias that shapes court proceedings and produces different treatment of lower-class and minority defendants, making them more vulnerable to both state supervision and punitive correction. These critics emphasize that the dominant ideas of the "good" child, the "well-adjusted" adolescent, and the "proper" family are typically those of the mainstream middle classes. The question of the class homogeneity of judges, prosecutors, lawyers, bailiffs, and assessors at the correctional court is relevant here.[3] In 2003 all but one of the juvenile judges was from the majority population; the one exception, a Muslim, was—by virtue of his education—part of the upper middle class. Defendants at the court see few Arab and black faces at court because these groups are underrepresented in the bar, law enforcement, and that elite public institution, the Ecole Nationale de la Magistrature, that recruits, trains, and ranks judges for appointment by the Ministry of Justice. In contrast to discussions on class bias, few French scholars examine the question of racial or ethnic discrimination at the court. There is nothing new about the gap between abstract legal principles that guarantee equality under the law and the reality of criminal prosecution. What is distinctive about the French case is the silence surrounding origins—ethnic or racial—in the law even as judicial police and juvenile prosecutors prosecute disproportionate numbers of (im)migrant and foreign youth.

The legal silence on race dates to the 1789 revolution and the creation of nationality as the only legitimate category of difference for the state. French law recognizes no collective rights; the constitution rejects the notion of minority status; and the penal code prohibits the collection of data on ethnic, racial, religious, or cultural origin. In conformity with the 1789 revolutionary ideals and the Declaration of the Rights of Man, France has implemented an arsenal of antidiscrimination laws that punish overt manifestations of racism and xenophobia. Nonetheless, since only individuals can seek redress for discrimination, tying it to racial, ethnic, or religious origin is very difficult (Rudder, Poiret, and Vourc'h 2000: 8). The national narrative on France as the preeminent color-blind nation is actively and continuously reproduced within the Paris juvenile court. It silences public or scholarly discourse on race (there is no social science literature on race relations), perpetuates the myth that since France has no legal minorities it has no minority problem, and frames discrimination as a class issue. This narrative masks the very real and persistent use of ethno-cultural categories (in which foreign names and somatic differences play a significant part) in discriminatory practices aimed at immigrants and foreigners in housing (MacMaster 1991; Rudder, Poiret, and Vourc'h 2000; Silverman 1995: 259), schools (Raissiguier 1994), at work (Bataille 1997), and by the police (Chouk et al. 2002).

Once youth of immigrant ancestry assume French nationality they disappear from figures on arrest, detention, prosecution, conviction, and incarceration. The state refusal to collect statistics on racial, ethnic, or religious origin for French citizens means that there are no *de jure* mechanisms in place to assess and address their treatment in the juvenile justice system. This is all the more problematic given reports from human rights organizations and supranational institutions condemning the human and civil rights violations of minors in airport holding facilities at Roissy outside Paris, in police custody, and in prison. Recent reports have condemned abusive police tactics in two suburban departments and the 20th district in Paris, all multi-ethnic areas.[4] The reports deplored police use of excessive force, racist slurs, unwarranted detention, and recurrent identity checks for youth who were well known as tactics that produced riots and provoked arrests (Chouk et al. 2002). The omission of criteria of difference other than nationality in the law and the court stands in sharp contrast to public discourses that ethnicize delinquency and stigmatize cultural difference.

Some critics argue that the modern juvenile court, through its use of norms and diagnostics such as clinical observations, psychiatric evaluations, counseling, social worker visits, and judicial hearings, constitutes a more pervasive and intrusive form of social control than the juvenile reformatories and work camps of the early twentieth century (Donzelot 1997). In contrast, I maintain that the court's supervisory gaze is increasingly conspicuous for its absence or selective focus, which mandates less protection and more repression. Staff shortages and a serious lack of state-licensed residential facilities and service providers within Paris produce long delays in court-ordered evaluations, therapeutic interventions, and rehabilitation measures. They also mean that, in emergency cases, judges face few alternatives to incarceration. Thus, the image of the omnipotent judge and the paternalistic case worker (Donzelot 1997: 100–117) is now being eclipsed by the figures of the deputy prosecutor, the judicial police, and the prosecutorial representative who all have heightened power to detain, investigate, and prosecute offending youth. The post–9/11 context is marked by a swing to the right and a weak economy: the 2002 presidential and legislative elections produced a center-right government and National Assembly with a law-and-order agenda, rising xenophobia, crackdowns on illegal and legal immigration, more recourse to detention and deportation, low economic growth, and a stagnant youth labor market. There is also increased anxiety about the political radicalization of a resident underclass of adolescent Muslims, seen as potential Islamist terrorists. There are growing fears concerning homeless street urchins begging, stealing, and prostituting themselves on Paris streets.

PROSECUTING YOUTH AT THE JUVENILE COURT

In this section we return to the cases introduced at the outset. We move inside the formal correctional juvenile court that hears and judges the cases of juveniles 13–16 years of age who are accused of serious misdemeanors and crimes. We examine some of the relevant procedural features, judicial powers, and legal debates surrounding the court.

Juvenile judges enjoy considerable power for several reasons. First, juvenile judges operate within a criminal justice system that has always privileged the protection of the social order over individual rights. This system shows little concern for the consent of the accused who plead guilty; until 2004 it rejected plea bargains; it resorts frequently to preemptive detention pending trial; and belatedly, in response to international pressure, it legislated enhanced habeas corpus protections for the accused and material witnesses (Garapon 1997). In contrast to the adversarial system in the United States where the facts of a case emerge from a confrontation between the prosecution and defense in which the judge is an arbiter, in the French system the facts are provided by the state and not by the individual parties to a case. They presuppose a notion of the truth that is established independently of the prosecution and the defense and that puts the onus on the accused to prove his innocence. In France, prosecutors and examining magistrates enjoy more power and status than lawyers. Both the weight of accusation and its monopoly by the state exist in constant tension with due process protections and the presumption of innocence (Herzog-Evans 2000).

Second, judges in the juvenile court combine functions normally separate in the French legal system; they examine charges and prepare indictments as well as conduct trials and render judgment. Their capacity both to investigate and to judge individual cases relies on an extensive informational gathering phase centering on the minor and his family; this phase is conducted by the judges in collaboration with psychologists, social workers, psychiatrists, and ethnopsychiatrists—experts in psychiatric problems rooted in cultural difference. Because the 1945 ordinance governing juvenile law focuses on the child rather than the criminal act and mandates time for preventive and rehabilitative interventions to bear fruit, judges also have enormous discretionary power in their application of long-term rehabilitative and penal measures. The progress shown by minors between their first appearance before a juvenile judge and the court trial is of substantial interest to the court and can be used to contain, reduce, or (rarely) dismiss (through acquittal) sanctions sought by the prosecution.

In contrast to the U.S. juvenile court where the causes for offending are less important than the moral character of the youth (Emerson 1969), the French court is more concerned with root causes because of what these may reveal about the nature of the offense, the guilt of the youth, and his capacity for social insertion. In France the basis of the charges depends heavily on confessions obtained by police. The court relies heavily on this version and resists attempts to re-frame or retract it. It likewise resists attempts to undermine police credibility and integrity because these constitute an attack on the moral authority of the official legal system. Judges' rhetorical style during questioning is premised on the individual responsibility of the youth and his acknowledgment of the wrong done. Claims of innocence and belated alterations of the facts before the bar are viewed very negatively because acceptance of culpability is considered a precondition of rehabilitation. Thus, the judges' questions are conducted so that there can be no legitimate reason or justification for the act that can be maintained or defended (cf. Emerson 1969).

Juvenile judges nonetheless embody contradictory positions. On the one hand, they preside over trials, control the questions, and are at the center of all communicative exchanges. This prominence is offset by the physical presence of juvenile prosecutors whose sanction requests symbolize the power of the state to accuse. On the other hand, juvenile judges are marginalized within a legal establishment that views appointment to the court as a hardship to be only temporarily endured. Making it a career is suspect and suggests insufficient talent or ambition. Although defenders consider judges' unique contributions to be their in-depth knowledge of individual families and the trust created between children and "their" judges, the reality is often quite different. The turnover is high; the work is stressful, time-intensive, and emotionally draining; and promotion demands regular movement among different courts every two to three years. In fact, legal scholars and public opinion criticize juvenile judges precisely because their personalized judgments depart from and compromise the legal norm of impartiality.[5] In contrast to U.S. juvenile judges whose political appointments or elections to courts tends to reinforce their links to local communities, French juvenile judges are appointed by a huge centralized Ministry of Justice, and at the Paris court they rarely live in the districts they serve. Their physical separation from children and families is mirrored in their social distance.

Court proceedings begin with the adversarial debate (*débat contradictoire*) during which the defendant hears the charges against him and is asked to confirm or deny the facts surrounding the offense. Judges confront the facts with accounts of the youth's personal and family background presented by court social workers and his parents or guardians. The juvenile judge first addresses the minor, his parents or guardians, and the minor's social worker before allowing questions by the prosecutor, the lay assessors (who participate in the judgment and sentencing), and attorneys. Victims' testimony precedes the prosecutors' pleas and the defense attorneys have the last word before the court adjourns to deliberate.

The courtroom trial is perceived and constructed as a ritualized confrontation between the legal order and youth whose offense violates that order. It is organized to intimidate and accentuate the authority of its decisions through the isolation of the accused. Spatial arrangements modeled on the adult court (minus the public) dramatize the solemn nature of the proceedings. Minors are summoned to the bar facing the judge, who is flanked by her two assessors, the clerk to the right, and the prosecutor to the left, on an imposing raised podium. The formidable symbolic apparatus includes ceremonial black robes for all but the assessors (including lawyers), uniformed police and robed sheriffs who act as gatekeepers, archaic formulaic language and protocols, and the courtroom itself.

The ritual is structured for the accused to acknowledge guilt and to convey the intention to avoid offending (Garapon 1997: 152–53; cf. Emerson 1969: 175–86). For this reason, when juveniles change their stories in court and disavow earlier declarations out of fear of reprisals, shame in the presence of parents, or outrage at police excess, they provoke rebukes by judges and stiffer penalties from prosecutors. The accused must be seen to participate fully in the ritual and in the determination of their guilt. They must display a consistently appropriate and properly deferential demeanor. Prosecutors and judges pay particular attention to the behavior of juvenile defendants and their families in court. Their ability to stand straight, speak clearly and correctly, look directly at their interlocutors, wait their turn and register both respect and restraint all count. Only the combination of exemplary (middle-class) demeanor and a valid defense allow the accused to isolate the offense from his sociocultural background without challenging the social and legal order the court must defend (cf. Emerson 1969: 194).

The court's determination that a minor is receptive to rehabilitation depends heavily on the court social worker's written reports recorded in the file and oral summaries presented in court. Reports include psychological, physical, social, and scholastic evaluations of the minors and their families as well as detailed family histories. They focus on family structures within and between generations, housing, income, and life style and draw heavily on a medical-psychological discourse to evaluate the youth's personality traits and capacity for normalcy. Although social workers are by definition child advocates, and although as professionals they tend to oppose punitive approaches, most have heavy case loads and no training in culture or specialized knowledge of the immigrant or foreign peoples whose children require court supervision. Their reports often reveal the misfit between and imposition of Western psychiatric and treatment models on different kinship and belief systems from Africa and elsewhere. Their attempts to confront and manage cultural difference often result in ethnocentric stereotyping, reification, or the total elision of culture as a significant factor. When called upon to analyze conflicts or problems linked to cultural difference, many social workers simply interpreted this difference as individual abnormality, imposing the Western psychological models with which they are familiar.

Prosecutors who defend the state and the authority of the law build cases through their selective emphasis on elements taken from police reports, signed confessions, witness and victim depositions, medical examinations, and physical evidence. They create a selective biography of the stages of a delinquent career in order to recast offenders' behavior in opposition to the normal social order. This biography includes subjective commentaries that reflect their own class position and often reproduce a stigmatizing discourse on integration. Although French law recognizes only individual culpability, prosecutorial pleas tend to criminalize the cultural difference of minority groups through a focus on their families, communities, and cultures. They both reflect and reinforce public perceptions concerning juvenile offenders as dangerous predators even in cases where physical injuries were minor, and their families as both socially dysfunctional and culturally alien even when they have lived in France for many years and manifest the same problems as French working-class families. Although they acknowledge the effects of poverty, their demands predicate lesser penalties not only on the admission of guilt and evidence of the acceptance of French legal norms but also on the emulation of mainstream sociocultural codes. Prosecutors and judges, like politicians, express a liberal meritocratic ethos of equal opportunity and free choice.

Defense attorneys speak last and have the last word before the court recess. Their pleas last no more than two to three minutes, but in this time they must address and contest the facts as they have emerged during the judge's questioning and the prosecutor's plea. They walk a fine line between, on the one hand, appearing to excuse illegal behavior through their appeal to the extenuating circumstances of poverty and neglect and, on the other, building a case for the individual progress and initiative that are demanded as proof of rehabilitation and as a justification for clemency. They suggest, as do other court personnel, that the legal mandate for the protection of at-risk youth also implies protection from the negative aspects of their cultural backgrounds. Thus, defense attorneys emphasize, where possible, the initiative of young people to establish physical, psychological, and social distance from bad influences and neighborhoods.

In the cases that follow we see how the disciplinary gaze of court personnel focuses on the children of working-class immigrant families. I offer no comparative cases of middle-class youth because I saw very few children of middle- or upper-middle-class in penal hearings. The families of those children could and did mobilize substantial resources to deflect imputations of illness and deviance and to protect their children from legal sanction. Immigrant families, both working class and lower middle class, were much more vulnerable to both court supervision and punitive correction. In earlier periods the juvenile court relied on normative medical-psychological discourses to link at-risk children with "deviant" working-class habits such as indigence, neglect, sloth, instability, and promiscuity and/or "abnormal" family structures differing from middle-class social norms (Donzelot 1997; Fishman 2002). New discursive formations such as those in recent state-commissioned reports on delinquency now depict it as "a failure of socialization," "a crisis of the classic assimilation model" (Lazerges and Balduyck 1998: 19–20), and as evidence of non-Western social and cultural norms at odds with French republican values (ibid: 96).

The Case of Jacques

In the first case examined here we meet Jacques, one of the defendants in the assault case mentioned above. In 2001 he was only 13 years old and charged with the beating and sexual molestation of a six-year-old girl, also of African ancestry. They lived one floor apart in a welfare hotel in the 11th district depicted by a court social worker as "indescribable." She informed the court that Jacques had been in France only four years and was the eldest of five siblings who lived alone with their mother in one room. She emphasized Jacques's school truancy, failing grades, and difficulties with French. As a result of the serious charges and pending trial, Jacques had been removed from his family and placed in a facility outside Paris for the most serious offenders. She reported that "he reacted badly [to the separation] and took part in violent altercations there." She gave no details about who was to blame, provided no corroboration of her account, and declined to describe Jacques's injuries beyond mention of a three-week hospital stay. After his discharge he was returned to his mother. When they failed to respond to a court summons a few months later, the child protection brigade (*La Brigade des Mineurs*) was dispatched to bring him bodily to the Palace of Justice. His effort to evade them by jumping out a fourth floor window was described by the court as an attempted escape and by Jacques's mother as an aborted suicide. The court then mandated that he undergo outpatient psychiatric treatment.

When invited by the judge to defend himself, Jacques vigorously denied the charges. I noted that he was well spoken in French and demonstrated considerable presence given the circumstances. When the judge asked why the little girl not only supplied graphic detail about the attack but also bore scars, Jacques suggested that her mother and aunt neglected and beat her. He added that on several occasions the police were called because the child was allowed to "wander alone in the street after nine o'clock at night." Denunciations of this type are a risky tactic because they claim entitlement based on the integrity of the youth even as they threaten adult integrity and parental authority. In her questioning of Jacques, the prosecutor combined actual and rhetorical questions to emphasize the violent alterity, promiscuity, and mental illness of this African family. Both the prosecutor and the judge were incredulous upon learning that his mother was French by birth and language. They remained skeptical about the capacity of the family to adapt and to integrate within French society:

> *Prosecutor:* It is true that Jacques is under psychiatric care . . . it is incumbent upon us to put a name to his problem. What is his problem? He has the problem of violence he cannot control. Of course, his mother is also under psychiatric care. (Directing her question at Jacques's mother): Madame, you look quite depressed. Under such difficult circumstances why did you come to France?
>
> *Mother:* I was repatriated by the French consulate . . .
>
> *Judge:* (surprised, breaks in) So you are French?
>
> *Mother:* Yes.
>
> *Prosecutor:* In different [political] circumstances you would no doubt prefer to return to Africa?
>
> *Mother:* No, not at all. My maternal grandfather was French. I am French by blood (*français de souche*).[6]
>
> Simultaneous questions (expression of surprise):

Prosecutor: So you spoke French at home?

Judge: So Jacques spoke French at home?

Mother: Yes, we came because as a French family, we asked to be repatriated.

The facts of the case centered on a gynecological exam that revealed no trace of penetration but did show scars consistent with blows from a belt. Moreover, the little girl's mother had declined to press charges despite her insistence that Jacques had molested her daughter. Undaunted, the prosecutor made a plea for guilt mitigated by the humanitarian commitment to rehabilitation and therapy. At the same time, her rhetoric shifted from compassion to condemnation. She linked a poverty of culture to a culture of poverty and was clearly irritated by the persistent denials and protests of innocence by the mother and son. These were claims that seemed to confirm the teenager's emotional problems:

> *Prosecutor:* In cases of this type we have no formal proof. It is the girl who denounces a boy who sexually molested her while playing children's games. In this hotel, Jacques is the leader, the eldest, he has authority over the other children. The children admired him. Jacques repeats, "Why would I have done such a thing?" That is not the crux of the matter. What this does involve is the overcrowded conditions in this hotel. We are putting poverty, of several kinds, on trial in such a restricted space. Things can happen. . . . Why would this child accuse him in such an arbitrary way? We must not forget Jacques's difficulties, his cruel, brazen behavior. And then there is this brutal uprooting from Africa to France. To find oneself in a hotel with a mother who is alone with five children. I find it quite telling that this mother has asserted herself inappropriately in this courtroom [by earning a reproach from the judge for sobbing and insisting on her son's innocence]. It is true that Jacques is under psychiatric care and that troubles me. We must find a rehabilitative approach. Yet he persists in total denial. Such violent behavior against a six-year-old is very serious. It is completely unacceptable for him to treat her like a sexual object. I must insist. He must be removed from his family. We need an order of judicial protection. . . . He says no, but as for me, I believe the little girl.

In the presentation of her case the defense attorney emphasized the contradiction between the testimony of the child and that of her mother as well as changes in the child's story. She made a convincing case for the child's abuse within her own family:

Defense attorney: Was there a sexual attack? The gynecological exam was normal, indicating that there was no penetration. That's strange because the little girl said she was bleeding and there was no mention of blood on the medical certificate. What about the marks on her back? She had old scars on her arms and other parts of her body. There is evidence of punishment administered with a belt or other instrument. It is clear that she was mistreated by her own family. I ask you to acquit on the basis of doubt. This is his first time in court. Clearly, he has problems but sees his social worker and psychiatrist regularly. Therapy must continue under court-ordered social assistance (*mesure éducative*).

Jacques was acquitted, but his acquittal was predicated on court supervision and continued psychiatric treatment.

The Case of Kévin and Antoine

In the second, more recent case, we follow the hearing of Kévin and Antoine, the 17-year-olds tried for aggravated theft in the 20th district court in June 2003. This case was representative of the majority of the cases I observed from 2000 to 2004. They involved simple or aggravated theft; only one involved the use of a weapon and none produced serious bodily injury, a trend observed nationwide (Blatier 1999; Carle and Schosteck 2002). Police reports and witness depositions gave contradictory accounts of an encounter between two groups of teenage boys, one from a vocational high school (*lycée*) and the other from a housing project in the 20th district well known to the court. Among nine witness depositions there was no clear consensus on either the number of youth involved or the exact identities of the thieves. Nonetheless, Kévin and Antoine, both from the projects, were arrested and prosecuted for stealing a cell phone and a phone card from one of the high school students. The latter followed their attackers into the projects where insults and blows were exchanged, three students were injured, and one student landed in the hospital with moderate injuries. Kévin accepted responsibility for the theft but vehemently denied responsibility for the physical attack. He was accompanied by both parents, well dressed and well spoken, who advised the court that he would be returned to Martinique to finish a two-year vocational course in plumbing. In contrast, Antoine, angry, sullen, and uncooperative despite obvious coaching from his lawyer, categorically refused to admit guilt for the attack. In response to the judge's questions, he indicated that he had left school, was unemployed, and had no future career plans. He was in court with his divorced mother who expressed her frustration but attempted to deflect blame for bad parenting by presenting his problems as psychological not familial:

> *Mother:* It is so difficult to control him. I don't know what goes on in his head. At 12 years old he tried two or three times to commit suicide. (Antoine elbowed her, earning a strong reproach from the judge.) I have to say that his sister has done so well in school. It is so hard because he never looks for work.

The victim's attorney adroitly appropriated media images of the projects and insisted that Antoine, in particular, deserved to be punished despite his obvious problems:

> *Defense attorney:* Here we have yet another example of kids who defend their territory in the projects. We need to remember that in the French Republic there are no lawless zones!

Antoine's social worker gave a particularly ambivalent report in which she lamented his lack of initiative and refusal to be accountable yet failed to connect his behavior to both the familial and psychological problems with which he struggled:

> *Social worker:* I follow his case and he comes to appointments here at the court. He wants to make something happen but he cannot seem to follow through. It's hard to have confidence in him. His family tries to support him in his determination to find training (an internship) but he never finds it. He has given up since 8th grade (critical orientation year). He had ambition but was tremendously let down by his father. He does not want to talk about it. It really hurt him. He has a penal case open at the court. He does not take the necessary steps.

In his plea, the prosecutor echoed the attorney's emphasis on territorialized violence, suggesting that he was more inclined to be indulgent with Kévin, whose demeanor, two-parent family, and plans to leave Paris for Martinique favorably impressed him. Here violent conflict is indeed about control over space, both the liminal zones surrounding the projects and the stigmatized areas within them. It is telling that, although Kévin (like Antoine) was born and raised in metropolitan France, his departure for Martinique (an overseas department of France) is depicted as a "return home" (*retour au pays*). The prosecutor blames France's urban problems on "outsiders" and questions Kévin's capacity for integration even in Martinique. The rigid and distorted distinction drawn between victims from a local *lycée* and perpetrators from the projects is also revealing:

> *Prosecutor:* Siding with people like Antoine who make their own law in the projects is the world turned upside down. We hear talk about lawless zones. I say it is the territory of the Republic and it's not hoodlums who make the law. Both of them are drowning in this notion of collective violence. We have a liar and a thief. Let's talk about the two personalities. It is a different situation in each case. Kévin will leave for overseas. This confirms for us that it is kids coming from outside France who create a mess. Return home will do him good. It will allow him to cut off bad associations in the projects. So there is some hope for his reintegration. Alas, Antoine is not at all the same. He does not work. Here we are in the month of June. We ask him if he is looking for work and what does he say?? "I'm waiting until September!" [His tone rising, very angry.] So when is it time to work? I look around me, ten minutes from the Palace, you can find work. I've seen job notices with my own eyes [he is now shouting]. He refuses part-time work. It is too much to hear this!

Antoine's defense posed a particular challenge. Here the attorney led the court through the conflicting statements of nine witnesses, insisting that his client arrived at the scene only after the events and, therefore, deserved an acquittal. He was nonetheless, constrained to recycle the same trope of collective violence used so adroitly by the prosecution:

> *Defense attorney:* I understand the suffering of the victims but Antoine told you, he was not there. True, it is the same group phenomenon in the 20th district at one in the morning. There were fifteen individuals. Today you have only two brought before the court. Examination of the case does not allow us to conclude that he did the hitting. He has personal problems; he is registered with the national unemployment agency. He has a social worker and a mother who takes care of him. It's a well known [family] scenario. He is affected by the absence of a father who couldn't bother to come here today. He is waiting for an internship. He does not have the necessary tools.

Kévin's defense attorney relied on a similar tactic. The court returned a guilty verdict for both, sentencing them each to a four-month suspended prison sentence, a 150 euro fine, and required them to pay the victims' medical bills, attorney fees, and damages in the amount of 1,700 euros.

CONCLUSION

When I returned to France in December, I discovered that Kévin had remained in Martinique but Antoine had been convicted for selling drugs and had served a short prison term in the fall of 2003. In the case of Jacques and his younger brother Michel, the judge indicted nine-year-old Michel for assault but postponed judgment pending rehabilitation. She ordered a cultural mediation consultation for the whole family with an African ethno-psychiatrist, justifying this approach because of Jacques's mental fragility and Michel's growing incorrigibility. Their mother protested strongly, saying that "Jacques wasn't crazy." He had a "mother who was sick because she lived in a hotel not fit for dogs." The judge conceded that the hotel in question was so bad it had made the newspapers but reassured her that an ethno-psychiatrist was not a regular psychiatrist. He had expertise in African culture and language and could help with all their cultural difficulties. The mother acquiesced but added, "We have been abandoned, there is no one to help us, Jacques is going to turn eighteen in that hotel. I am French by blood just like you." In this instance the confrontation between the African boys and the French woman at the pool seems to have had less to do with cultural identity than the situation of contact. Although nothing justifies an attack on an elderly woman, was it their behavior or their mere presence at the municipal pool that earned them the disapproving stare of the Parisian lady? Was it cultural mediation and knowledge of African customs or better housing that were required?

Under existing court conditions of overloaded penal dockets, staff shortages, limited services for therapy, unequal opportunity, and an influx of illegal migrants, the supervisory gaze of the judicial apparatus is conspicuous for its selective focus on children of immigrant ancestry and its absence regarding unaccompanied children. The tutelary complex of intrusive intervention and supervision is being undermined by the beginning of a return to a punitive complex. This happens in a context marked by neoliberal regimes that demand more accountability and responsibility of individuals, families, and communities but deliver few viable training and employment opportunities and in Paris little access to decent and affordable housing. These regimes require more judicial efficiency with scarce resources while accelerating the pace of justice itself. The punitive trend is facilitated and masked by a legal system that has privileged the protection of the social order over individual rights and premises clemency and rehabilitation on an admission of guilt and evidence of the internalization of French legal codes and middle-class social norms. The French juvenile justice system seems to prejudice defendants of immigrant and foreign ancestry in a number of ways: by policing tactics that focus on public order violations; by shifting explanations for a delinquency of exclusion from economics to culture; and by stigmatizing cultural difference and origin while denying its relevance to the court.

The predicament of youth and the problem of generation, long neglected as a subject of scrutiny, must now be central to discussions of political economy. Youth the world over share similar struggles in many Western economies. They are excluded from local economies amidst stark de-industrialization, and they are denied the promise of full citizenship through work. The expectation that they could surpass their parents' accomplishments can no longer be fulfilled. This disrupts relations between genders and across generations even as it creates a crisis of masculinity. Because they are locked out of legitimate avenues of enterprise, youth must develop new diverse and illicit ones—from drug trafficking to the sale of stolen goods—in an effort to break into the cycles of accumulation, leisure, and livelihood. The courts give witness to the fact that the young feel their power and their powerlessness; both are born of a will to use force, to vent frustration, and to serve notice to polite French society (Comaroff and Comaroff 2001: 18). The inevitable happened when youth riots exploded in the suburbs of cities all over France in the fall of 2005 (see Ossman and Terrio 2006).

ENDNOTES

1. The term *banlieue* has a long history dating back to the thirteenth century, when it referred to the perimeter of one league beyond legal and ecclesiastical jurisdiction. Following the medieval period, a stigmatized liminal space on the city periphery became associated with

social marginals, uncontrolled movement, and territorialized poverty. Nineteenth-century industrialization and urban renewal entailing the demolition of inner-city slum dwellings forced the working classes to settle outside the city. The concentration of the "dangerous classes" in areas associated with criminality, disease, and disorder fueled the first moral panics surrounding the "zone," the code used for the suburb by a terrified urban Parisian bourgeoisie (Boyer and Lochard 1998: 45).

2. Successive Fifth Republic governments (from 1958 on) have targeted suburban areas for heightened police surveillance and systematic identity checks (for known individuals) as well as periodic police round-ups of suspected Islamic terrorists. Recent attempts by the political right to domesticate and channel Islamic belief through official, state-sanctioned Islamic institutions are linked to ongoing French fears about a rise in religious fundamentalism and increased crime in public suburban projects (*Le Monde*, December 23, 2002, and January 16, 2003; *New York Times*, April 16, 2003 and September 9, 2003).

3. Of the fourteen judges at the court in 2001, nine were women and five were men, including the president. In 2003 as a result of one retirement; one death; five promotions entailing appointments to the Bobigny, Nanterre, Créteil, and Versailles courts and four replacement appointments to the Paris court, leaving one vacancy; plus the creation of a special court to deal with unaccompanied minors, there were fourteen judges, twelve of whom were women. Of the thirteen court social workers, eight were women; of the four men, three were new arrivals. These included a female director and two men, one of Maghrebi ancestry and the other of West African ancestry.

4. In July 2002 three French associations—the leftist Union of Magistrates, Association of French Lawyers, and the League of the Rights of Man—publicized the findings of a study of police procedures in two suburban departments, Hauts-de-Seine and Yvelines, and the 20th district in Paris with multi-ethnic public housing projects. These complaints mirror those of Maghrebi activists in France who have long denounced the law enforcement system as racist. See also the 2001 and 2002 reports of the French NGO Droits de Enfants International-France.

5. For a discussion of these legal debates see Bruel 1995; Frichon-Roche 1999; Garapon 1985; Paperman 2001; and Rassat 1990.

6. The use of this term by an African immigrant woman is interesting. The anti-immigrant far-right political parties, the National Front, and the national Front/National Movement use this term to differentiate the rooted, pedigreed (white) French population, *Français de souche*, from the Arab and African people who migrated to France in the post-1945 period.

REFERENCES

Agence pour les développements des relations interculturelles. 2002. *Les mineurs étrangers isolés: les réponses des professionnels sur Paris-Ile-de-France.*

Aïchoune, Farid, ed. 1985. *La Beur génération.* Paris: Sans Frontière/Arcantère.

Aubusson de Cavarly, Bruno. 1998. "Statistiques." In *La Réponse à la délinquance des mineurs,* Christine Lazerges and Jean-Pierre Balduyck. Pp. 263–92. Paris: La documentation française.

Bailleau, Francis, and Catherine Gorgeon, eds. 2001. *Prévention et sécurité:vers un nouvel ordre social?* Paris: Editions de la Délégation interministérielle à la ville.

Balibar, Etienne. 1988. *Race, nation, classe: les identités ambiguës.* Paris: La Découverte.

Baranger, Thierry. 2001. A quels enfants allons-nous laisser le monde? Unpublished paper.

Bataille, Philippe. 1997. *Le Racisme au travail.* Paris: La Découverte.

Bauer, Alain, and Xavier Raufer.1999. *Violences et insécurité urbaines.* Paris: Presses Universitaires de France.

Beaud, Stéphane, and Michel Pialoux. 1999. *Retour sur la condition ouvrière.* Paris: Fayard.

Beriss, David. 2000. "Culture-as-Race or Culture-as-Culture. Caribbean Ethnicity and the Ambiguity of Cultural Identity in France." *French, Politics, Culture, and Society* 18(3): 18–47.

Blatier, Catherine. 1999. "Juvenile Justice in France. The Evolution of Sentencing for Children and Minor Delinquents." *British Journal of Criminology* 39(2): 240–52.

Body-Gendrot, Sophie. 2000. *The Social Control of Cities? A Comparative Perspective.* Oxford: Blackwell.

Body-Gendrot, Sophie, Nicole Le Guennec, and Michel Herrou. 1998. *Mission sur les violences urbaines.* Paris: La Documentation françaises/IHESI.

Bordet, Joëlle. 1999. *Les jeunes de la cité.* Paris: Presses Universitaires de France.

Bourdieu, Pierre. 1986. La force du droit. *Actes de recherché en sciences sociales* 64:3–19.

Boyer, Henri, and Guy Lochard. 1998. *Scènes de télévision en banlieues: 1950–1994.* Paris: l'Harmattan.

Bruel, Alain. 1995. Un bon juge ou un bon débat. In *La justice des mineurs. evolution d'un modèle,* Antoine Garapon and Denis Salas, eds. Pp. 73–81. Paris: LGDJ.

Carle, Jean-Claude, and Jean-Pierre Schosteck. 2002. *La délinquance des mineurs.* Rapport de la commission d'enquête du Sénat. Paris: Journal Officiel.

Chouk, Aidan, Laurence Gillet, Antoine Spire, and Emmanuel Terray. 2002. Enquete sur les comportements policiers. Paris:Syndicat de la Magistrature. (www.syndicat-magistrature .org/article/252.html)

Cicourel, Aaron V. 1995. *The Social Organization of Juvenile Justice.* New Brunswick: Transaction.

Collovald, Annie. 2000. Violence et délinquance dans la presse. In *Prévention et sécurité: vers un nouvel ordre social?* Francis Bailleau and Catherine Gorgeon, eds. Pp. 39–53. Paris: Editions de la Délégation interministérielle à la ville.

Comaroff, Jean, and John L. Comaroff, eds. 2001. *Millennial Capitalism and the Culture of Neoliberalism.* Durham, NC: Duke University Press.

CPT (Council of Europe, Committee on the Prevention of Torture). 1993, 1998. *Report to the Government of the French Republic Concerning the Visit Undertaken by the European Committee on the Prevention of Torture* (www.cpt.coe.int/en/states/fra.htm).

Coutin, Susan Bibler. 2000. *Legalizing Moves. Salvadoran Immigrants' Struggle for US Residency.* Ann Arbor: University of Michigan Press.

Défense des Enfants Internationale, 2001, 2002. Annual Report.

Doek, Jaap E. 2002. "Modern Juvenile Justice in Europe." In *A Century of Juvenile Justice,* Margaret K. Rosenheim, Franklin Zimring, David S. Tanenhaus, and Bernardine Dohrn, eds. Pp. 505–27. Chicago: University of Chicago Press.

Donzelot, Jacques. 1997. *The Policing of Families.* Baltimore, MD: Johns Hopkins University Press.

Dubet, François, and Didier Lapeyronnie. 1992. *Les quartiers d'exil.* Paris: Seuil.

Duret, Pascal. 1995. *Anthropologie de la fraternité dans les cités.* Paris: Presses Universitaires de France.

Emerson, Robert M. 1969. *Judging Delinquents. Context and Process in Juvenile Court.* Hawthorne, NY: Aldine.

Estrada, Felipe. 1999. "Juvenile Crime Trends in Post-War Europe." *European Journal on Criminal Policy and Research* 7: 23–42.

Fiacre, Patricia. 1995. *Les jeunes délinquants réitérants, suivi des trajectoires judiciaires d'une population de jeunes.* Paris: Institut des Hautes Etudes de la Sécurité Intérieure.

Fishman, Sarah. 2002. *The Battle for Children. World War II, Youth Crime, and Juvenile Justice in France.* Cambridge, MA: Harvard University Press.

Frichon-Roche, Anne Marie. 1999. L'impartialité du juge. In *Recueil Dalloz,* Pp. 53–57. Paris: Dalloz.

Friedman, Jonathan, ed. 2003. *Globalization, the State, and Violence.* Oxford: AltaMira Press.

Garapon, Antoine. 1985. *L'âne portent des reliques. Essai sur le rituel judiciaire.* Justice humaine/Le Centurion.

Garapon, Antoine. 1997. *Bien juger: essai sur le rituel judiciaire.* Paris: Odile Jacob.

Garapon, Antoine, and Denis Salas, eds. 1995. *Justice des mineurs: evolution d'un modèle.* Paris: LGDJ.

Hamon, Hervé. 2001. "La violence de la judiciarisation." Paper delivered at the Conference of French Association of Juvenile and Family Court Judges.

———. 2003. Interview. Juvenile Court. Paris Palace of Justice.

Herzog-Evans, Martine. 2000. *Procédure pénale.* Paris: Librairie Vuibert.

Huyette, Michel. 1999. *Guide de la protection judiciaire de l'enfant.* Paris: Dunod.

Jazouli, Adil. 1992. *Les années banlieues.* Paris: Seuil.

Karsenty, Jean-Claude, ed. 2000. *Jeunes sans foi ni loi? Retour sur la délinquance des mineurs.* Paris: Institut des Hautes Etudes de la Sécurité Intérieure.

Lagrange, Hugues. 2001. *De l'affrontement à l'esquive.* Paris: Syros.

Lazerges, Christine, and Jean-Pierre Balduyck. 1998. *Réponses à la délinquance des mineurs. Mission interministérielle sur la prévention et le traitement de la délinquance des mineurs. Rapport au Premier Ministre.* Paris: La Documentation française.

Léger, Raoul. 1990. *La colonie agricole et penitentiaire de Mettray. Souvenirs d'un Colon, 1922–27.* Paris: L'Harmattan.

Lepoutre, David. 1997. *Coeur de banlieue. Codes, rites et langages.* Paris: Odile Jacob.

MacMaster, Neil. 1991. "The 'seuil de tolérance': The Uses of a 'Scientific' Racist Concept." In *Race, Discourse, and Power in France,* Maxim Silverman, ed. Pp. 14–28. Aldershot: Avebury.

Masclet, Olivier. 2001. "Mission impossible. Ethnographie d'un club de jeunes." *Actes de la Recherche en Sciences Sociales* 136–37.

Maximy, Martine de, Thierry Baranger, and Hubert de Maximy. 2000. *L'enfant sorcier entre ses deux juges.* Paris: Odin.

Merry, Sally Engle. 2001. "Spatial Governmentality and the New Urban Order: Controlling Gender Violence Through Law." *American Anthropologist* 103(1): 16–29.

———. 2003. "Human Rights Law and the Demonization of Culture (and Anthropology Along the Way)." *Political and Legal Anthropology Review* (26)1: 55–76.

Ministry of Justice. 2003. Rapport d'Activité de la Protection Judiciaire de la Jeunesse de Paris. Année 2002.

Mucchielli, Laurent. 2002. *Violences et insécurité. Fantasmes et réalités dans le débat français.* Paris: La Découverte.

Ossman, Susan and Susan Terrio. 2006. "The French Riots: Questioning Spaces of Surveillance and Sovereignty," *International Migration* 44(2):5–19.

Paperman, Patricia. 2001. "Les faits et les personnes: impartialité et aveu dans la justice des mineurs." In *L'aveu: Histoire, sociologie, philosophie*, Renaud Dulong, ed. Pp. 223–40. Paris Presses Universitaires de France.

Preliminary Inspection Report of the SEAT, Paris (Document d'Inspection). 2003. Office of the Judicial Protection of Juveniles. Paris: Ministry of Justice.

Raissiguier, Catherine. 1994. *Becoming Women, Becoming Workers.* Albany, NY: SUNY Press.

Rassat, Marie-Laure. 1990. *Procédure pénale.* Paris: Presses Universitaires de France.

Roché, Sébastien. 2001. *La délinquance des jeunes. Les 13–19 ans racontent leurs délits.* Paris: Seuil.

Rosencvzeig, Jean-Pierre. 1999. *Justice pour les enfants.* Paris: Robert Laffont.

———. 2002. *Justice, ta mère.* Paris: Robert Laffont.

Rudder, Véronique de, Christian Poiret, and François Vourc'h. 2000. *L'inégalité raciste. L'universalité républicaine à l'épreuve.* Paris: Presses Universitaires de France.

Rufin, Michel. 1996. *Protection de la jeunesse et délinqunce juvénile.* Paris: La Documentation française.

Salas, Denis. 1995. "L'enfant paradoxal." In *Justice des mineurs, evolution d'un modèle*, Antoine Garapon and Denis Salas, eds. Pp. 41–62. Paris: LGDJ.

Silverman, Maxim. 1995. "Rights and Differences: Questions of Citizenship in France." In *Racism, Ethnicity, and Politics in Contemporary Europe*, Alec G. Hargreaves and Jeremy Leaman, eds. Pp. 253–63. London: Edward Elgar Publications Limited.

Stephens, Sharon. 1995. "Culture and the Politics of Culture in 'Late Capitalism.'" In *Children and the Politics of Culture*, Sharon Stephens, ed. Pp. 3–48. Princeton: Princeton University Press.

Wacquant, Loïc. 1999. *Les prisons de la misère.* Paris: Editions Raisons d'Agir.

Wieviorka, Michel. 1996. Violence, Culture and Democracy: A European Perspective. *Public Culture* 8: 329–54.

———. 2003. "The New Paradigm of Violence." In *Globalization, the State, and Violence*, Jonathan Friedman, ed. Pp. 107–39. Oxford: AltaMira Press.

Withol de Wenden, Catherine. 1991. "North African Immigration and the French Political Imaginary." In *Race, Discourse, and Power in France*, Maxim Silverman, ed. Pp. 98–110. Aldershot: Avebury.

7

Prison Walls Are Crumbling: The American Way of Punishment and Its Consequences

BRENDA C. COUGHLIN

CHILDREN ARE OUR FUTURE

On January 8, 2002, U.S. President George W. Bush signed into law a public education bill called the No Child Left Behind Act (NCLB) (Schemo 2002). Critics claimed that its standardized testing policies would cement, not repair, existing inequities between "low-" and "high-performing" schools (Bracey 2002). Others suggested that the bill's grand title over-reached; certain children would undoubtedly remain left behind (Taylor and Piche 2002). Education advocate Jonathan Kozol went further, arguing that NCLB aimed to cripple public education altogether: "The kind of testing we are doing today is sociopathic in its repetitive and punitive nature. Its driving motive is to highlight failure in inner-city schools as dramatically as possible in order to create a ground swell of support for private vouchers or other privatizing schemes" (Solomon 2005).

Within three years of NCLB's passage, a majority of states (including Texas) had either protested against, modified, or opted out altogether from certain NCLB provisions, with several states even suing or threatening to sue the federal government. Criticism of another sort also began to emerge from a new group: young people themselves. Students' growing protests against the U.S. war in Iraq and military presence inside their schools highlighted Section 9528 of NCLB (Gorman 2005), a provision largely unnoticed in 2002 (c.f. Rozoll 2002).[1] Section 9528 requires school officials to turn over students' home addresses and phone numbers to military recruiters unless parents specifically opt out, leading some to dub the law No Child Left Unrecruited (Goodman 2002).

In short, NCLB proved intensely controversial. The uproar, however, masks a likely point of agreement between critics and supporters of NCLB: the popular sentiment invoked by the bill's title.[2] *Leave no child behind.* The title echoes what education sociologist Henry Giroux calls "a classical principle of modern democracy in which youth both symbolized society's responsibility to the future and offered a measure of its progress" (Giroux 2004, 85). It is debatable whether any state (modern democracy or not) has fulfilled this principle, yet the ideal certainly informs thinking about the place of youth in social reproduction. Indeed, more prosaic versions of this principle topped pop music charts in the mid-1980s. "We are the world, we are the children," sang Michael Jackson at the 1985 LiveAid concerts and Whitney Houston belted out, "I believe children are our future."[3] The claim is so self-evident, so natural, so *right* that no one thinks twice about it; we just hum along.

Yet in the contemporary United States there is little evidence that state and civic institutions are taking up their "responsibility to the future" by protecting childhood and aiding the safe and fruitful transition of young people to adulthood (Polakow 2000). A variety of measures, including child poverty and hunger rates, indicate that some children and youth are in fact prevented from participating in this progressive model.[4] Instead, the horizons of their futures have been foreshortened, in large part by a set of punitive or regressive policies in the education and criminal justice systems.

Both systems figure prominently in the lives of U.S. youth, though the latter is typically unrecognized in this respect.[5] The debate about NCLB shows how schools are often under the spotlight of legislators, courts, and media. With almost 90 percent of students enrolled in public rather than private schools in at least the last 10 years, the vast majority of the U.S. population also has *direct* experience with the education system (NCES 2002, chap.1). Education is widely acknowledged as a centerpiece of childhood. The criminal justice system, on the other hand, is under far less public scrutiny and fewer people have direct contact with prisons than with schools. The justice system apparently affects only those who *deviate* from the norm. These children are presumably *not* "our future."

This chapter aims to redress this neglect of the role of incarceration in the lives of American children, families, and communities. I present existing data challenging the assumption that prisons touch only those at the margins of society. In doing so, I take seriously NCLB's implicit claim that the well-being of the youngest generations represent a measure of social progress. It is in this context that I examine the changing nature of penal practices in the United States, especially as they affect children and youth. My overall conclusion is neither new nor unique: the promise that American society makes to some children amounts to a dead-end. Following Giroux (2004), this finding suggests the United States is a failed democracy, even a "failed state" (see also Chomsky 2006).

PRISONS AT THE CROSSROADS

As this edited volume itself makes clear, there are numerous sites, institutions, practices, and policies where the issues of youth, law, and globalization intersect. In the United States, carceral institutions and penal practices together stand at one such intersection. Both merit increased attention (and a different *kind* of attention) on the part of scholars and practitioners not only in the legal field, but also in urban studies, education, and public health. America's high incarceration rates show no signs of abating or reversing, and the American way of punishment is spreading to other parts of the world. In this chapter, then, the term *globalization* figures as the simple claim that local forces alone are not determining the future of U.S. youth *or* of youth in countries now on the receiving end of U.S. forms of punishment. I also draw on debates about globalization to locate changing U.S. penal practices within shifts in the global economy starting in the late 1970s and in U.S. foreign policy after the end of the Cold War.

I do not offer original data here but instead, using available evidence, make a case for rethinking approaches to prisons—our methodologies if we are scholars, our evaluations if we are policymakers, our scope of engagement if we are advocates.[6] Under the current carceral regime in the United States, and increasingly elsewhere in the world, prison walls are not only *rising* as new facilities are built and old ones expanded, they are also figuratively *crumbling* as the consequences and effects of mass imprisonment bleed into family life, community livelihood, webs of social networks, and state institutions.[7] Consideration and study of carceral institutions can no longer be confined within concrete or barbed-wire borders. Just as the debate about education policy in the United States assumes a wide sphere of influence for schools (i.e., individual students, families, job markets, national productivity levels), so too must debates about prisons recognize the wide social orbit around individual carceral institutions and discrete penal practices.

I proceed in an unorthodox way: with a series of vignettes and short descriptions of select aspects of the U.S. carceral system. Each vignette, description, or set of data is intended to provoke a rethinking of how to approach and even conceive of prisons and the consequences of incarceration. In the first part ("American Carceral Trajectories"), I document the recent expansion of imprisonment and the predominant face of American prisoners (young, black, male). The two sections of this first part are largely descriptive and document basic trends. I aim to show how mass imprisonment has transformed the social categories of childhood and youth, and argue that this transformation requires new ways of assessing the social implications of corrections policy. Individual recidivism rates, for example, may be a necessary measure but they are no longer sufficient for capturing the effect of prison on youth. Assessing new forms of parenting across bars may offer another way to measure the social costs of imprisonment.

In the second section ("Carceral Orbits"), I turn to the carceral institution itself, and begin a methodological discussion about how to approach prisons as objects of study in the age of mass incarceration. If the category *youth* has been changed by the current carceral regime, so too has the category *prison*. Here I also incorporate a brief review of the ways in which scholars think about prisons as institutions and argue that these no longer adequately encompass the full realm of prison life or prisons' institutional scope. I follow up this discussion with a story of the Garza Unit in Beeville, Texas—one of the largest transit prisons in America. This description of Garza and Beeville highlights changes in the political economy of the prison itself since the advent of mass incarceration and suggests the global dimensions of U.S. corrections policy. Again, my intent is to provoke a reassessment of the prison as a strictly bounded or static institution and to urge comparative analysis.

In the third section ("Global Carceral Trajectories"), I offer a summary of the state of U.S. penal policy in comparison with that of other countries. Even as these data highlight America's exceptionalism, there is also evidence that other countries are following in the footsteps of American penal policy (Stern 2002). Here I suggest that where the United States goes, so goes the world. Children around the world might begin to look to the United States for more than the latest blockbuster film, but also for an indication of what their future could hold. Researchers, too, may want to look farther afield than simply within U.S. borders to understand what is taking place in remote American prison towns. If we confine study to prisons located only within the United States, for example, rather than also consider the export of U.S. practices elsewhere, we may not fully grasp the scope and consequences of American policy.

We need think only of a recent example of the spread of U.S. penal practices that came to light with the release of photographs from Abu Ghraib prison in Iraq. Students (and inmates) of American prisons were not particularly surprised by the acts of torture and abuse documented in those photos. They noted that many of the practices were familiar to them ("cruel but usual") from super-maximum and even juvenile facilities in the United States (Greene 2004). Students of U.S. intelligence services also pointed out that these techniques have a history in previous wars and against other enemies (Danner 2005; McCoy 2005). Like other social phenomenon and practices, incarceration and penal policy are articulated at local and global levels and have consequences beyond their immediate sphere. This may seem obvious, but the implications of this claim have not yet been fully incorporated in scholarly research or policy practices.

AMERICAN CARCERAL TRAJECTORIES

This section documents the simultaneously deep and wide infiltration of the criminal justice system in the lives of young people, their families, and their communities. I argue that, given the extent of this take-over, our methodologies, evaluation techniques, and understanding must change to encompass the far-reaching consequences of mass incarceration.

Children Know Their Future

The youth of America can now accurately predict their own future. If current trends continue, every boy now living in any of the poorest neighborhoods in Washington, DC, will likely be incarcerated at least once in his lifetime (Braman 2004, chap. 4 and appendix). The capital's poorest areas are all majority African-American. These boys are not alone in gaining new powers of prediction. Recent studies by the U.S. Department of Justice have found that about a third of all African-American men nationwide face the same future as the youth of Washington (Bonczar and Beck 1997; Bonczar 2003).[8] Nor are women immune. Since 1980, the number of women entering prison or jail has doubled every seven to eight years. About 85 percent of women incarcerated are mothers, most having sole custody of their children at the time of arrest. Approximately three-quarters of female inmates are African-American or Latino (LaLonde and George 2002).

Although the life course of some working-class people (especially African-Americans) and their families thus seems almost certain, this is not the result of some peculiarity of the nation's capital or even of poor urban areas. Though staggering, it is not atypical that over 75 percent of young black men in the District can expect to be incarcerated in their lifetime. The District's overall incarceration rate is about average for U.S. cities (Braman 2004, 235).[9] Instead, these carceral trajectories are part of a widespread change since the 1970s in social and political responses to crime and punishment (Garland 2001). Among a range of outcomes, this new set of responses has led to many more people imprisoned, with many more of them poor, young, black males.

Since 1950, the racial and ethnic composition of the U.S. prison population has reversed: from about 70 percent white at mid-century to more than 60 percent African-American and Latino today. As in other stages of criminal justice processing (arrest, detention, conviction, capital sentences), minorities are disproportionately incarcerated compared to their estimated actual engagement in illegal activity and their share of the national population (Cole 1999; Mauer 1999; Miller 1996; Tonry 1995). Thus the now familiar statistic from 1995 that one in three African-American males between the age of 20 and 29 years was under some form of criminal supervision on any given day only hints at what is politely termed *racial disparity* (Mauer and Huling 1995). This same figure increases to almost two in three in certain cities, with the majority of all imprisoned African-Americans coming from poor urban areas (Human Rights Watch 2002). The fivefold increase in the U.S. prison population since 1975 has thus largely centered on African-Americans.

In the face of these data, sociologist Loïc Wacquant (2000) suggests a "deadly symbiosis" between the ghetto and prison. His analysis echoes and builds on the prescient insights of many activists, scholars, and inmates active in the 1970s, who assessed the political contours of African-American life (Baldwin 1971; Burns 1973; Davis 1971; Higginbotham 1971; Jackson 1970; Shakur 1971; Staples 1974. For later works, see Davis 2003; Hirsch 1992; James 2003; Lichtenstein 1996; Oshinsky 1997). Their understanding of the relationship between slavery, racism, poverty, and incarceration preceded establishment criminology, which has only recently begun to take seriously racism in the U.S. penal system, by 20 to 30 years. As Wilbert Rideau and Ron Wikberg, inmates and editors of Louisiana's Angola prison newspaper, *The Angolite*, said: "That's the reality, and to hell with what the class-room bred, degree-toting, grant-hustling 'experts' say from their well-funded, air-conditioned offices far removed from the grubby realities of the prisoners' lives" (Richards and Ross 2001, 177).

Given the new realities born of mass incarceration, what does it mean to be young when imprisonment is guaranteed, either for a significant segment of the young themselves or for someone they know, including a parent, relative, or caretaker? How can we understand the prison as an institution or the ghetto as a distinct neighborhood when so many people, goods, and resources are now cycling between urban areas and rural prisons? What is the relationship of the family to carceral facilities in their neighborhoods or towns, or far away? What new ties, if any, are developing between prison towns and the home communities of inmates and their families?

These kinds of questions are worth considering simply because the tight grip of punition shows few signs of loosening, in turn suggesting that the consequences for families will increase. Incarceration rates in the United States are not diminishing substantially, even as crime rates overall continue to drop or level off (Blumstein and Wallman 2000). In addition to the empirical necessity, it is also vital to foreground families and communities because they are typically ignored in standard policy evaluations—at the expense of a comprehensive understanding of the role of prisons in social life. Both proponents and critics of mass incarceration tend to stick to issues of recidivism, efficiency, and costs. Mass incarceration is evaluated by whether crime is going down, arrest rates are lower, or drug treatment is cheaper than prison. The criminal justice system itself is at the center of this analysis of crime and punishment— more so than the lives of people, the indirect influences of law, or institutions outside the immediate purview of courts. Similarly, work in other fields has not yet accommodated the arrival of mass incarceration within its disciplinary borders. Wacquant (2002) notes that the field of urban studies, for example, has largely ignored the phenomenon of mass incarceration even though large sections of poor urban populations live in carceral facilities.

Icons of Youth and Law

This next section expands on this point by providing greater detail about the relationship between young people and the criminal justice system. When we comprehend the extent to which some young people's lives are deeply enmeshed in prison life, it becomes clear that we cannot rely on recidivism rates to document the resulting social upheaval in significant segments of the U.S. population and through wide swathes of the country.

The studies cited above indicate that some children have not been left behind—at least not by the U.S. prison system. For the boys of DC and many like them, adolescence is cut short with the prospect of likely imprisonment (Braman 2004; LeBlanc 2003; Rathbone 2005). Not only are youth themselves incarcerated, but their fathers and brothers, uncles and grandfathers, and increasingly their mothers (LaLonde and George 2002) may well be imprisoned for all or long stretches of their childhood (Bernstein 2005). If the children avoid imprisonment, they may spend the majority of their time in public schools guarded by corporate security firms or local police departments, with their hallways scanned by cameras and their entrances equipped with metal detectors (Giroux 2004; Polakow 2000). As in prisons, what these youth wear in school is strictly regulated and whom they associate with may be grounds for criminal conviction (Coughlin and Venkatesh 2003, 53–55).

Under the penal regime in the United States since the 1970s, the law has thus taken on a single dimension, entering the lives of certain young people mostly as an enforcer and rarely as a protector. Poor, black, young men and boys are understood by police, courts, and corporate media as the iconic case of youth and law. *Young black male* has become a stock phrase of nightly news reports (Hancock 2000). Despite important efforts to counteract this association (including by authors in this collection), the combination of the terms *youth* and *law* typically and forcefully conjures stereotypes of gangbangers, delinquents, pimps, and drug dealers—not child laborers, troubled teens, world citizens, or people with human rights.[10]

Criminal laws aimed at the poor have multiplied since the 1970s, with youth their indirect targets. Researchers find not that poverty causes crime, but that poverty has become criminal (Hudson 1999; Sampson 2000)—an old finding but one that needs repeating. Children in particular suffer from these new laws. Journalist Nell Bernstein (2005) describes how the 1997 federal Adoption and Safe Families Act (AFSA), for instance, has increased the number of children with incarcerated parents transferred into the foster care system, with little chance of reuniting with the parent upon release. AFSA mandates termination of parental rights for children in foster care for 15 months within a two-year period. Many petty or nonviolent offenses come with sentences far longer than 15 months. The national average of time served by parents in state prison is 80 months (Bernstein 2005, 148–49). The very circumstance of some children's lives results in their own or their families' criminalization or further retrenchment in what Wacquant (2002) calls the "carceral-assistential complex"—the closed loop of prison and welfare.

Since the 1970s, more youth are being incarcerated than before, more of them are being held in adult facilities, and poor, minority youth receive the harshest punishments. African-Americans aged 10 to 17 years old comprise 15 percent of the U.S. population; minority youth comprise one third of the U.S. adolescent population. African-Americans account for 31 percent of youth referred to juvenile court, 44 percent of youth detained in juvenile facilities, half of youth tried in adult court, and 58 percent of juveniles in adult prisons. Seventy-five percent of all youth held in adult facilities in 1997 were minorities (Poe-Yamagata and Jones 2000).

Scholarly research on the consequences of youth being held in adult facilities is scant. Rape and sexual assault are thought to be under-reported in all facilities (the government only started collecting data in 2004), but young men are quite literally prey in the adult system. This is a crucial yet almost completely ignored aspect of incarceration: the carceral sentence comes with a sexual torture component. Sexual assault and rape is likely prevalent in many facilities but is generally overlooked or condoned and is indeed often practiced by corrections officers (in 47 percent of cases reported to the justice department in 2004) (Beck and Hughes 2005).

For the young who are not incarcerated, adults in their lives may well be. In 1999, state and federal prisons held 721,500 parents with children under the age of 18 (this does not include jails, which may hold inmates up to a year or longer). Forty-six percent of these parents reported living with their children before they were incarcerated. At least 300,000 households with children aged 18 years and under have a father in prison and approximately 36,000 households with minor children have a mother in prison. Put differently, about one and a half million children under the age of 18 had at least one parent in a state or federal facility in 1999—an increase of more than 500,000 children since 1991 (Mumola 2000). These numbers will likely increase, given that women are the fastest growing population segment entering prison. Some reports find that 85 percent of new admittances are mothers, usually with sole custody at the time of arrest (LaLonde and George 2002).

For those families who struggle to stay intact or even in touch during the incarceration period, more than prison walls block their way. Long-term carceral facilities tend to be located quite far from the homes of inmates and in places not served by public transportation. Men's prisons, on average, are located more than 100 miles from their homes, and women's prisons average 160 miles away (Annie E. Casey Foundation 2002). Extended ethnographic studies reveal that the expense of prison visits can often be prohibitive for families (Gonnerman 2004; LeBlanc 2003). More than half of all incarcerated parents (57 percent of fathers, 54 percent of mothers) report never having a visit from their children while they are in prison (Annie E. Casey Foundation 2002).

The few who do receive visits from families generally must do so under difficult conditions. Sociologist Megan Comfort (2002) argues that these conditions—and even families' efforts to counteract them—reinforce rather than mitigate the "institutionalization" effect of prison on both inmates and their families. In other words, visits to prison bring families deeper into the carceral orbit and normalize incarceration for inmates. For those children who do not visit, most typically communicate with incarcerated parents by phone or mail. Telephones in carceral facilities are under monopoly control, and companies charge those on the receiving end of calls highly inflated rates. Journalist Lizzy Ratner (2003) reports that in New York City, "Since 1996, MCI has held a contract with the Department of Corrections that gives the company exclusive control over prison telephone services and allows it to jack prices as high as 38 cents a minute and charge $3.95 hook-up fees. In exchange, the state keeps over 60 percent of MCI's revenues. The state expected to net roughly $24 million last year [2002]." Again, those not incarcerated are not spared the consequences of imprisonment. In Braman's (2004) phrase, families are "doing time on the outside."

By any standard, this is a grim picture. More young are imprisoned, more of them in adult facilities, and more of them minorities. Their family members are also imprisoned, and barriers between children and incarcerated parents are high if not insurmountable. In addition to being grim, this picture means that the courts and penal practices have redefined childhood and the experience of being young. The expansion of the criminal justice system has shrunk childhood for some, a move running counter to a century of reforms on the national and international level aimed at protecting people under the age of 18.

CARCERAL ORBITS

This next section details the effects of expansion by examining prison towns in the age of mass incarceration. Not only the imprisoned and their communities live within the carceral orbit; so too do the imprisoners. This section also suggests that the shifts both producing and stemming from mass incarceration emerge not only from local forces but also from forces operating at a national and even global level. The rather lengthy discussion of changes in U.S. labor markets in the 1970s and 1980s and transformations in the military after the official end of the Cold War seeks to make these connections plain. These two additional elements of mass incarceration—new prison towns and the interplay of local and global forces—again demand innovation in research method-ologies and in policy implementation. Recent evaluations of the financial benefits of new prisons to small rural towns, for example, have offered a new way to measure the consequences of mass incarceration. Similar evaluations of social benefits and drawbacks would be another important measure (see, e.g., Hooks et al. 2004).

Prison Creep

The prison has become a central axis around which the lives of many U.S. communities and individuals rotate, from small rural towns where new pris-ons have been built in the last 20 years to highway rest stops that cater to women and children who travel hours from big cities to these prison towns for a weekend visit with an incarcerated father, son, or husband. Though aggre-gate data do little to convey details, a quick snapshot provides some sense of the creep of the prison system. More than 2 million people are incarcerated (Harrison and Beck 2005). Almost 5 million adults are on probation or parole (Glaze and Palla 2004). Thus the equivalent of about half the population of Florida is under some form of criminal supervision. At the end of 2001, more than 5.6 million in the general population had served time in a state or fed-eral prison (Bonczar 2003). Fourteen million people are detained for some period each year in jails and prisons (Farmer 2002, 242). Approximately 750,000 people are employed in corrections, making the industry overall one of the largest employers in the country, comparable to Wal-Mart and Man-power (Bauer and Owens 2002).

Consider that each person represented in these millions has family and friends, as well as communities where he or she lives and works. The numbers within the carceral orbit increase exponentially. Each element of the prison sys-tem—such as the facilities themselves, the equipment used to service those facilities (construction, food service, surveillance, weaponry), probation and parole programs, or officers' unions—involves another set of people who thereby develop relations with prisons. By these crude measures alone we see how, under mass incarceration, aspects of prison life have begun to reach far beyond prison walls. And this reach may well continue. In 2003, the Depart-ment of Justice predicted, "In the future, if 2001 first-incarceration rates remain unchanged, 6.6 percent of U.S. residents are projected to be confined in a state or federal prison during the course of an entire lifetime, up from 5.2 percent since estimates were produced for 1991" (Bonczar 2003).

Given this expansion, can we still think of prison as the "total institution" keen social observer Erving Goffman once compared to 1950s mental hospitals and army barracks? Goffman (1961) depicted sites cut off from the rest of the world, impermeable and isolated, altering only the lives of those on the inside. Anthropologist Lorna Rhodes notes in a review of prison research that much contemporary scholarship continues to emphasize the ways in which prisons "warehouse" a "hidden" or "second" population (Rhodes 2001, 67–68). Critics focus on the "magic" prisons make by "disappearing" entire groups of people (young black men), depopulating urban neighborhoods (removing residents to rural areas), and shrinking civic participation (through felony disenfranchisement). As poet and former inmate Jimmy Santiago Baca writes: "Most Americans remain ignorant that they live in a country that holds hostage behind bars another populous country of their fellow citizens" (Rhodes 2001, 68).

Historians of the early penitentiary have also detailed the institution's origins in isolating practices (Foucault 1977; Ignatieff 1978; Rothman 1971). Present-day super-maximum prisons and isolation units, as well as the advent of "enemy combatant" camps and the practice of "renditions," certainly retain elements of this initial impulse that equates *removal* with effective control and punishment (and, perhaps, impunity for the imprisoner). Rhodes's own extensive research on the "total confinement" of control units in U.S. high-security prisons (2004) documents that, even while incarceration has expanded and widened, it has also deepened and intensified. New technology isolates individual inmates in ways that Jeremy Bentham's panopticon could not hope to achieve.

The Louisiana State Penitentiary at Angola, once a plantation farmed by slaves and then by leased convict laborers, exemplifies this isolating characteristic of archetypal U.S. prisons (Rideau and Wikberg 1992). Very few people come and go within Angola. Even those without official life terms may stay forever: a 1998 report indicates that 85 percent of Angola's inmates die while incarcerated (Open Society 1998). With parole boards generally refusing to release long-term prisoners, this trend is duplicated elsewhere in the United States (Liptak 2005).

Nonetheless, not all carceral facilities are so isolated or hidden from view, especially not from those incarcerated in, employed at, or visiting them—these people know and see them quite well. And in many respects prisons such as Angola represent the past of American penal policy—at least regarding the question of their physical isolation and isolating effects on inmates. Starting in the 1970s, as the shift in imprisonment was just getting underway, sociologists with substantial access to prisons documented increased "flux" (Rhodes 2001) *within* prisons and *between* prisons and the outside world (Irwin 1980; Jacobs 1977). They noted the institutional shift away from the Big House model, with a single charismatic leader, toward a more porous institution, where gangs and other subgroups had greater influence within prisons and across the borders of walls or barbed wires.

Since then, as the previous section documented, the sheer numbers of people directly involved in the carceral system has greatly increased. With this uptick in inmates has come a proliferation of accompanying institutions. As different kinds of carceral facilities flourish today in neighborhoods—locked drug treatment and work release centers, boot camps, control units—the prison form is morphing into new shapes that dot national and neighborhood maps. Historian Mike Davis (1990) has shown how the very architecture of incarceration is reflected in homes and schools, libraries, and city streets. Farmers in rural Minnesota report that bright prison yard lights give their small towns an unwelcome big city feel and block out stars, but also make winter afternoon chores easier to finish because the daylight hours are effectively extended (Federal Reserve Bank 2002). If Bentham's panopticon dominated designs for penitentiaries, hospitals, and schools in eighteenth-century Europe (Foucault 1977), much more of the twenty-first-century American landscape is marked by fortresses and watchtowers (Graham 2004), barbed fences and surveillance cameras (Parenti 2003; Staples 2000), enclosed spaces (Midnight Notes 1990), and gated communities (Low 2003).

Keeping in mind this dual spreading and deepening of prisons under mass incarceration, the next section considers geopolitical relationships between prisons and their hosts—the communities, towns, businesses, and families that support these institutions through their labor, taxes, land, and resources. I describe the emergence of a new transit prison in Beeville, Texas, recently transformed into a carceral facility from its previous life as a military base. In Beeville we see the creep of prison life ever outward and the interplay of local

and global forces in everyday prison life. Again, the vignette is meant to stimulate a rethinking of the methodological implications of dramatic changes in
a well-worn object of study, the prison. Activists who have long referred to the
"military-prison-industrial complex" may not be precise, but they were certainly prescient. It remains for researchers and policymakers to document the
place of prison building more fully in renewed efforts to secure the "homeland"
in the United States, for example, or to flesh out the relationship between military contractors and corrections corporations.

Smalltown U.S.A.

If Angola represents the American prison in a national context before the
changes of the 1970s, the Garza Unit in Beeville, Texas, locates the U.S.
prison on a planetary scale since the advent of neoliberalism. *Wall Street Journal* reporter Joseph Hallinan recounts how the town of Beeville lost jobs rapidly in the 1980s when the state's oil and gas industry went bust (along with
small farming and savings and loans banks), and then again in the early 1990s
with the closings and consolidations of military bases (Hallinan 2001).[11] With
few other options for providing local jobs to replace those lost, Beeville cam-
paigned for new prisons. Town officials promised constituents new jobs, economic growth, and a better way of life. The campaign was successful. Beeville
now confines an inmate population of more than 7,000 in a town of about
13,000 people. Hallinan notes that this is one of the highest inmate-to-resi-
dent ratios in the United States.

The Garza Unit is one of two new prisons in Beeville, as well as being the
largest transit prison in the United States and one of the largest prisons of any
sort nationwide. About 4,500 inmates are held in Garza for less than a year
before being sent elsewhere to serve out their terms. The prison complex sits
at the edge of town, at Chase Field, on top of the remnants of a naval air base
closed in 1991. Skid marks remain on the aircraft runways around Garza.

Hallinan reports that when the unit opened, schoolteachers, restaurant
workers, and police left their jobs to work at Garza. The pay was better, and
everyone in town saw that prisons were a growth industry. The youth of
Beeville identified correctional services as a career-track, as did their parents,
one of whom told another reporter that he supported the new prison because:

"I want this to be the kind of town our kids won't have to leave when they grow up" (Benjaminson 1994). Along with the town's other carceral facility, McConnell Unit, Garza and prison life have in some sense taken over Beeville. Hallinan notes at the end of his trip to Beeville, while sitting at the side of the highway at night, looking back at the town and its bright prison yard lights, "It occurred to me that what I was seeing was not the light of some forgotten town, but the glow of a new American city" (Hallinan 2001, 20).

What Hallinan does not say is that this "new American city" is just as much a global city as a national one, emerging from local decision making in the face of base closures as well as from federal initiatives related to international labor markets and foreign policy. The 1980s oil and small farm bust and the 1990s restructuring of the U.S. military emerged from at least two global trends. The first was the expansion of neoliberal economic policies in the United States and elsewhere, partially as a result of the 1970s oil and financial crises and also because of popular social challenges to long-standing modes of organizing production (Midnight Notes 1990). The second trend concerns shifts in U.S. military spending after 1989 with the end of the Cold War. The primary direction of this shift was away from high numbers of active military personnel toward an increased focus (and spending) on military technology and weapons innovation (Lutz 2001). Both processes affected Beeville.

Although as a prison town Beeville is somewhat unusual in its global dimensions because of its former life as a military base, its enmeshing in nonlocal forces is typical of prison towns. In groundbreaking work, geographer Ruth Gilmore (1998–99; 2007) has carefully examined the interplay of local and global forces and shifts in land use and labor markets related to prison building in California, a state with one of the highest imprisonment rates in the United States. This kind of analysis recalls the work of urban sociologist William Julius Wilson (1996) on the relationship between the 1970s decline of manufacturing in northern U.S. metropoles and the entrenchment of ghetto poverty. Hallinan's nighttime musings alert us to the rise of new social forms (prisons) just as some were declining (Cold War military life), in a replacement process akin to what Wilson outlines for northern cities. Indeed, the answer to an implied question of Wilson's research—"What took the place of urban manufacturing?"—can be found in places like Beeville.

In the early 1980s, when the Texas oil business was flourishing—with the price of oil at a then record high $30 a barrel—Detroit was one of the largest out-of-state consumers of the *Houston Chronicle*'s thick employment classifieds section (*Houston Chronicle* 2001). The unemployed auto and manufacturing workers of concern to Wilson seemed to be looking to Texas for jobs. But oil did not long remain an option for these out-of-work northerners. When the oil boom went bust, the service economy began to blossom, providing wages far short of those in manufacturing and with less job security (Sassen 2001). Nonetheless, many people took these insecure, underpaid jobs because they were better than no job at all. For those who remained unemployed by the formal sector, the carceral system joined the service economy in taking over in northern ghettos. Through the so-called War on Drugs, the prison system locked up many who no longer had access to skilled, unionized jobs offered in manufacturing. Some had indeed turned to the underground economy to make a living, with its then burgeoning narcotics trade (Venkatesh 2000).

Documentary filmmaker and prison researcher Tracy Huling (2002) reports that before 1980, just over a third of all prisons were in rural communities, but that most new prisons have been built in non-urban areas since 1980. Texas in particular exemplifies this trend. Of all the new rural prisons built in the 1990s, 20 percent opened in Texas. The majority of prisoners are now living in rural America, though most of them come from urban America. In concurrence with Gilmore (2007), Huling argues that this transformation of rural economies is a direct result of the worldwide economic restructuring of the 1970s and 1980s. She points especially to the rise in agribusiness in the United States, which left smaller family farm workers high and dry and opened a gaping employment hole in rural areas.

In the years since these shifts, researchers have begun to evaluate whether new prisons, such as Garza and McConnell, have boosted local economies as their supporters claimed they would. A recent national study finds that prisons are basically neutral in terms of their effect on the local (county level) economy in most instances (Hooks et al. 2004). Prison development does not stimulate diverse economic growth and seems to have some benefits only for areas that are already relatively well off (King et al. 2003). As rural demographer Calvin Beale has noted, like other export businesses, prisons expect—and receive—substantial concessions from their hosts, concessions that leave other services and needs unattended (Beale 1993). Small towns commonly purchase the land and promise to build the water and sewer infrastructure necessary to accommodate a prison. The Federal Reserve Bank of Minneapolis reports that civic leaders in Rush City, Minnesota, added $700,000 to the $40,000 already contributed by the city to buy land for a prison-building site (Federal Reserve Bank 2002). Overall, then, there is little evidence for any substantial monetary gain at the county or town level as a result of new prisons.

Anthropologist Catherine Lutz (2001) describes a similar "trade imbalance" between military bases and their host towns, in which the former feeds off the latter. It is perhaps not surprising then that when military bases closed in the 1990s, federal prisons sometimes took their place. Both bases and prisons need plenty of space, sparse and ample housing, and some distance from the local town, even as they remain dependent on local services.[12] Miami's Krone Detention Center in the Florida Everglades, for instance, is the site of a former Nike missile base and was first set up to process Cuban refugees from Mariel (Dow 2004). A 1995 government report lists 23 federal prisons on deactivated bases or former military property, with another 10 facilities on active bases (U.S. GAO 1995). If the carceral industry fit into America's *economic* restructuring in the 1970s and 1980s, in the 1990s it fit into the *military* restructuring of the post–Cold War period.

The number of active personnel is one measure of this post–Cold War military restructuring that altered the life of towns like Beeville. In the early 1990s, during the first U.S.-led war in the Persian Gulf, 2 million military personnel were on active duty. Now there are about 1.4 million (not including private contractors). Lutz (2001) argues that this downsizing was not part of the heralded "peace dividend" that the fall of the Berlin Wall was supposed to bring. Rather, she suggests, the closing of military bases and resulting smaller corps was due in part to a renewed focus on research and development and the continued privatizing of military services. "[After the Cold War] bases . . . were closed or consolidated. The number of active-duty soldiers shrank by a third, and the budget gradually dropped by 18 percent. But a groundswell of aggressive lobbying by defense contractors, weapons labs, and the Pentagon repaired the damage: Budgets were projected to again reach the 1991 level by 2005. Though the Cold War had ended, the victor was none other than war itself. Reconstruction happened, but it was of weapons systems, not Cold War–recuperating communities like Fayetteville [North Carolina, next to Fort Bragg]" (Lutz 2001, 215).

When the military downsized personnel but upsized high-tech research, the prison industry beckoned to those newly unemployed as it had to family farmers and oil workers. Like the armed forces, corrections relies on laborers willing to do difficult and dangerous work for relatively low pay and few benefits. Not all or even most of those made redundant after the 1990s base closings went to work in prisons, but some did (a symbiotic relationship vividly, if anecdotally, brought to light in early 2004 with the story of military reservists stationed at the Abu Ghraib prison in Iraq having formerly worked in corrections). And at the level of cross-industry trade, prisons and the military also developed a new relationship in the 1990s. Elements of the corporate defense establishment cashed in on the rise of the penal regime to offset military cutbacks in traditional spending areas. In 1994, the *Wall Street Journal* reported that several major defense contractors, including Westinghouse and a division of the old General Dynamics corporation, were marketing high-tech prison and crowd-control equipment (Thomas 1994).

In sum, the opening of the Garza and McConnell units in Beeville, Texas, was one end point or byproduct of shifts in labor markets connected to neoliberal economic policies and shifts in military deployment at the end of the Cold War. Arguably, there are few social phenomena that escaped either of these seismic shifts, so the prison industry is not unique in this sense; nor can mass incarceration be explained as a direct consequence of neoliberalism or the Cold War. For the purposes of this chapter, the point is more suggestive—an encouragement to consider prisons as sites of labor, as trading partners at the industry level, as institutions in global markets. The next section builds on this effort by putting U.S. mass incarceration in a comparative context. Researchers, including several in this volume, are beginning to track the export of American carceral policy, primarily to Europe but also to parts of Latin America (see, e.g., Rouillan 2005).

GLOBAL CARCERAL TRAJECTORIES:
THE UNITED STATES VERSUS THE WORLD

In 1975, the United States imprisoned 380,000 people. In 1990, the U.S. imprisoned one million people. By 2002, more than two million people were in U.S. jails and prisons. The 1990s, known to U.S. Federal Reserve Bank chair Alan Greenspan and the mainstream media as the "boom years" of the U.S. economy (Swann 2004), were also boom years for prisons. From prison activists, the 1990s earned another nickname: the "punishing decade" (Justice Policy Institute 2000).

This recent prison boom differs markedly from earlier penal history in the United States. Between 1925 and 1973, the U.S. incarceration rate hardly fluctuated—never varying more than 30 percent in either direction and averaging between 110 and 120 inmates per 100,000 population (Zimring 2001). But by 2000, the United States surpassed Russia, with its gulag legacy, to lead the world in imprisonment. In 2001, the United States reached a new rate of 702 inmates per 100,000—five to twelve times rates in Canada and Europe (Stern 2002).[13]

This level of mass imprisonment means that the United States incarcerates almost one quarter of the world's 9 million imprisoned people, even though it comprises less than 5 percent of the world population. Together, Russia (760,000 incarcerated), China (at least 1.5 million), and the United States (2.1 million) account for about half of the world's imprisoned. What is the state of the more than 4 million others?

First, as with other global trends, carceral distribution is uneven. A cluster of states and territories have high rates of incarceration (above 400 per 100,000), while almost 60 percent have rates below 150 per 100,000 (Walmsley 2005). The United States is thus not alone in its high rate of incarceration, but its companions differ along other dimensions. The United States is alone among top incarcerators in being an advanced capitalist democracy, for example. Other high incarcerators, besides China and Russia, tend to be island states, often in the Caribbean. South American countries have a median incarceration rate of 152, whereas the Caribbean rate is 324. Other regions show similar variability. The median rate for southern European countries is 80, with Central and Eastern Europe at 184. Both Asia and Africa show distinct regional imbalances: the median rate for western and central Africa is 52, with southern Africa at 324 (with South Africa a notably high rate of 413); the Indian subcontinent rate is 55, with central Asian countries (generally ex-Soviet) at 386 (Walmsley 2005). This uneven distribution indicates that the U.S. way of punishment is not uniformly integrated across the planet, though it is spreading.

Nonetheless, if there is variability across geographic regions, there also remains a degree of uniformity worldwide with a second global characteristic of the prison: the volume of incarceration shows a continuing and overall increase. The United Kingdom's Home Office reports that 71 percent of all countries have shown an increase in their incarcerated population between the time of the Home Office's 2002 and 2003 studies on the world prison population (Walmsley 2003). Thus—despite occasional mass pardons (Wacquant 1999), efforts at decarceration (Stern 2002), and recent waves of early release in local American jails and state prisons to alleviate budgets (Wood 2004)— the spread of new punitive penal norms across the planet continues almost entirely unabated. As in the United States, across the world more people are being locked up.

Third, subjects rather than citizens are increasingly and disproportionately represented among the imprisoned, especially in Europe where the best comparative data are found. By *subjects*, I mean noncitizens: foreigners, immigrants, asylum seekers, and minority ethnic and racial groups, all of whom are also typically among the poor in Europe and the Commonwealth. Michael Tonry observes: "Members of minority groups are overrepresented among crime victims, arrestees, pretrial detainees, convicted offenders, and prisoners in every Western country. This is true in countries in which the largest affected groups are black or Afro-Caribbean, as in the United States and England; in countries in which the most affected groups are aboriginal occupants of colonized lands, as in Australia and Canada; in countries in which the most affected groups are of North African origins, as in France and the Netherlands; and in countries in which the most affected groups are mainly of European origin, as in Germany and Sweden" (1997, 1).

To offer some specifics: the United States now incarcerates black adult men at more than eight times the rate of apartheid South Africa (Wagner 2003). In England, blacks are seven times more likely to be incarcerated than their white or Asian counterparts (American black men are eight times more likely than whites to be incarcerated). In Germany, the proportion of foreigners awaiting detention grew from one third in 1989 to one half in 1994. More than a quarter of French inmates are foreigners (citizens and subjects alike), with most coming from North and Sub-Saharan Africa. New immigrants seem to flow almost directly into French detention centers and prisons. The substantial increase in the minority population in the French carceral system is due entirely to immigrant inmates (Wacquant 1999). In none of these countries do these figures compare to minority or immigrant proportions in the overall population. Here too we see the obvious parallels with U.S. carceral patterns.

Contemporary researchers and policymakers have repeatedly pointed out that instead of predicting the expansion of the prison system in the United States or worldwide, researchers were anticipating its demise in the 1970s. So, too, we cannot now be certain that the trends outlined above will continue unabated. Except for the decision by the Russian government to release some inmates to relieve overcrowding and slow the spread of tuberculosis, however, there are no indications that prison populations will decline significantly. And even if they do level off or decline, the United States and other countries are left with the consequences of twenty-five years of an extreme policy. These consequences have yet to be fully documented or understood. It is certain only that penal practices born in the United States have taken root elsewhere and that students of criminal justice will have to take this global spread into account.

CONCLUSION: NO END IN SIGHT

Using available information from government reports, ethnographic and statistical studies, and news reporting, this chapter has attempted to indicate that the transformation of the carceral system in the United States and elsewhere during the period of neoliberalism has had severe consequences for children, families, and their communities. But unconnected efforts to change U.S. penal policies are underway. There are challenges to the Rockefeller drug laws in New York State, for example, and the "Three Strikes and You're Out" provisions in California. DNA testing has exonerated hundreds of inmates, some on death row, and exposed the negligence of police departments from Houston to Chicago. National campaigns to end the death penalty, notably in the case of minors, have had significant victories. Still, the questions raised in this chapter and by practitioners in the field for many years have not resulted in an overall shift in practices or policy. Decarceration is not on any federal agenda in the United States.

If there is no end in sight, students of prison life and incarceration will have to adjust with new investigative techniques and comparative analyses. Scholars have long been accustomed to mirroring their studies and evaluations to the borders of the prison itself rather than to the needs of research. Studies of prison life, for example, do not tend to include former inmates but only current ones. Researchers of street gangs typically do not have access to incarcerated gang members, though there is evidence that they may remain influential in gang life while imprisoned. Explanations of high U.S. incarceration rates do not usually take into account shifts in other industries, such as energy, farming, or the military. Comparative work is difficult to conduct when access to facilities and parallel data is almost nil. However, a number of researchers and policy initiatives have already adjusted their methodologies, research agendas, and programs, laying groundwork for others to follow. It is doubtful if a more complete picture of the consequences of mass incarceration will alter current policies, but it will at least lay bare the brutality of the American way of punishment at the turn into the twenty-first century.

ENDNOTES

1. When NCLB passed in January 2002, President Bush had not yet officially declared war on Iraq, although military operations had begun in Afghanistan in October 2001 and intensified air bombing of Iraq was underway before March 2003. The little attention that Section 9528 did garner at the time of the bill's passage in 2002 focused on privacy rights and on costs associated with mailing announcements about the provision to all parents (see, e.g., Rozoll 2002). Deployment did not become a point of widespread vocal controversy until about 2004.

2. The Children's Defense Fund (CDF), for example, an advocacy group critical of NCLB, helped to introduce another youth-oriented bill in Congress in 2001, just as the Bush Administration introduced NCLB. The CDF bill (S. 448/H.R. 936) was called the Act to Leave No Child Behind.

3. "We are the world we are the children/We are the ones who make a brighter day/So let's start giving." Michael Jackson and Lionel Richie, USA for Africa, *We Are the World*, 1985. "I believe that children are our future/Teach them well and let them lead the way." Michael Masser and Lynn Creed, *The Greatest Love of All* (sung by Whitney Houston), 1985.

4. Child poverty in the United States has dropped since the late 1950s, but the rate started to rise again around 2000 and now compares with rates in the mid-1960s. As of 2004, about one-sixth (17.8 percent, or 13 million) of all American children under 18 years fall below the official poverty level (DeNavas-Walt, Proctor and Lee 2005, table 3). As of 2002, there were 22

million adults and 13 million children living in households reporting "food insecurity" or hunger at some point during the reporting year (Nord et al. 2003).

5. This chapter does not address links between punitive policies in the education and criminal justice systems. A number of activists, researchers, and education scholars are beginning to analyze what they call the *prison track* or the *school-to-prison pipeline* and have documented the structural homology of policies in schools and prisons (see, e.g., Wald and Rosen 2003). Lawyer and child advocate Bernardine Dohrn (2000) suggests that as youth are increasingly shut out from welfare programs, health services, education, and recreation, the door to jail or prison is the one always open to them.

6. Throughout this chapter, I use the term *prison* as shorthand for a range of carceral institutions. In terms of institutional practice and the social consequences of incarceration, however, jails, prisons, and other carceral and detention facilities are not necessarily interchangeable. They have different organizational structures and are managed by different state and sometimes private institutions. At the individual and group level, the effects of years spent in lockdown units, for example, are quite different from 30 days in a county jail. County jails are also sometimes taken over by national corporations or serve as detention centers for immigration cases of the Department of Homeland Security (Dow 2004). Statistics reported by the Department of Justice calculate their findings based on their own jurisdictions and for management purposes, not as a way to capture the full experience of incarceration in America. These standard reports thus offer a *limited* picture of incarceration for the purposes of this essay because they do not consistently include the full range of carceral facilities, but typically limit counts to jails and state and federal prisons. These counts do not always (but sometimes do) include Indian county jails, for example, or certain military detention facilities, local lock-ups, immigration detention facilities, or carceral facilities in overseas territories or occupied areas.

7. The chapter title and concluding section's subheading refer to lyrics by Bob Dylan. "The prison walls are crumblin', there is no end in sight" (Dylan 1974).

8. The findings in Bonczar and Beck's 1997 study are based on survey data collected in 1991, before the expansion of imprisonment in the 1990s. The authors claim that the lifetime likelihood of incarceration remained stable between 1991 and 1995 because the rate of new admissions did not change significantly. They also based their estimates on the assumption that incarceration rates would not increase substantially after 1995. Although incarceration rates overall are up, the latest reports bear out the hypothesis of the 1997 study. During 2002 the 2.6 percent growth in the number of inmates under state and federal jurisdiction was more than twice the 2001 growth (1.1 percent) but less than the average annual growth of 3.6 percent since year-end 1995. Nonetheless, it is worth noting that the 1997 report measures the experience of incarceration based on institutional jurisdiction: it counts only *new* admissions into federal and state prisons, not into other kinds of carceral facilities (including jails and juvenile detention facilities), and does not count repeat admissions. Annually there are almost thirty times more new admissions to local jails than to prisons and ex-prisoners have high rates of re-arrest. Bonczar's 2003 follow-up report estimates similar chances of incarceration as in the 1997 report: "If the 2001 rates of incarceration were to continue indefinitely, a black male in the United States would have about a 1 in 3 chance of going to prison during his lifetime, while a Hispanic male would have a 1 in 6 chance and a white male would have a 1 in 17 chance of going to prison" (Bonczar 2003).

9. Braman calculates the overall rate of incarceration in the District at 1.8 percent; Baltimore, Maryland, at 2.1 percent; and New Haven, Connecticut, at 1.7 percent (2004, 235).

10. Youth have long resisted these stereotypes. Journalist Elizabeth Martínez (2004, 589–91) tells the story of the 1993 youth-led "blowouts" throughout the California public school system. Students in junior high and high schools across the state walked out of schools to protest racism against them in their schools and poor education. They also directly challenged school administrators stereotyping them as gangbangers, as well as challenging the violence of gang members themselves—at one point turning in red and blue gang-color rags for brown ones, a symbol of Latino and minority unity. One youth at a Sacramento rally said, "The governor wants more prisons, we want schools. He wants more cops, we want more teachers. We want an education that values and includes our culture. We want all cultures to know about themselves."

11. Between 1988 and 1995, the federal government selected 97 major military bases for closure. Not all of them ended up being completely deactivated, although the Department of Defense reported that 67 had been closed by 1993 (U.S. GAO 1995).

12. The Navy sold 400 family housing units to the Beeville Redevelopment Corporation for $168,000. At the time of the initial closing of military bases starting in the late 1980s and early 1990s, the federal Bureau of Prisons was allotted to receive only 2 percent of all the disposable land compared with 50 percent for Fish and Wildlife Services, for example (U.S. GAO 1995).

13. In 1999, the Russian incarceration rate was 730 per 100,000 people and decreased to 675 in September 2000, compared with a U.S. rate, as of December 1999, of 690 per 100,000. The Russian rate declined because the Duma issued an amnesty for current inmates in order to decrease overcrowding, which had led to a tuberculosis epidemic (Stern 2002, 283).

REFERENCES

Annie E. Casey Foundation. 2002. *Fact Sheet 1: Incarceration, Families, and Communities.* Baltimore, MD: Annie E. Casey Foundation.

Baldwin, J. 1971. An open letter to my sister, Angela Davis. In *If they come in the morning: Voices of resistance,* A.Y. Davis and B. Aptheker, eds. Pp. 19–23. New York: The Third Press.

Bauer, L., and S.D. Owens. 2002. *Justice expenditure and employment in the United States, 2001; Bureau of Justice Statistics Report, U.S. Department of Justice Publication No. NDJ-202792;* www.ojp.usdoj.gov/bjs/abstract/jeeus01.htm.

Beale, C. 1993. Prisons, population, and jobs in nonmetro America. *Rural Development Perspectives* 8(3): 16–19.

Beck, A.J., and T.A. Hughes. 2005. *Sexual violence reported by correctional authorities, 2004; Bureau of Justice Statistics Report, U.S. Department of Justice Publication No. 210333;* www.ojp.usdoj.gov/bjs/pub/pdf/svrca04.pdf.

Benjaminson, W. 1994. As Beeville booms, housing is a bust. *Houston Chronicle* May 29, 1994, A1.

Bernstein, N. 2005. *All alone in the world: Children of the incarcerated.* New York: New Press.

Blumstein, A., and J. Wallman. 2000. The recent rise and fall of American violence. In *The crime drop in America*, eds. A. Blumstein and J. Wallman. Pp. 1–12. Cambridge: Cambridge Univ. Press.

Bonczar, T.P. 2003. *Prevalence of imprisonment in the U.S. population, 1974–2001; Bureau of Justice Statistics Special Report, U.S. Department of Justice Publication No. NDJ 197976*; www.ojp.usdoj.gov/bjs/pub/pdf/piusp01.pdf.

Bonczar, T.P., and A.J. Beck. 1997. *Lifetime likelihood of going to state or federal prison; Bureau of Justice Statistics Special Report, U.S. Department of Justice Publication No. NDJ 160092*; http://www.ojp.usdoj.gov/bjs/pub/pdf/llgsfp.pdf.

Bracey, G. 2002. What they did on vacation: It's not schools that are failing poor kids. *Washington Post* January 16, 2002, A19.

Braman, D. 2004. *Doing time on the outside: Incarceration and family life in urban America.* Ann Arbor: Univ. of Michigan Press.

Burns, H. 1973. Black people and the tyranny of American law. *Annals of the American Academy of Political and Social Science* 407: 156–66.

Chomsky N. 2006. *Failed states: The abuse of power and the assault on democracy.* New York: Metropolitan.

Cole, D. 1999. *No equal justice: Race and class in the American criminal justice system.* New York: New Press.

Comfort, M. 2002. "Papa's house": The prison as domestic and social satellite. *Ethnography* 3(4): 467–99.

Coughlin, B.C., and S.A. Venkatesh. 2003. The urban street gang since 1970. *Annual Review of Sociology* 29: 41–64.

Danner, M. 2005. *Torture and truth: America, Abu Ghraib, and the War on Terror.* New York: New York Review of Books.

Davis, A.Y. 1971. Political prisoners, prisons, and black liberation. See James 2003, 64–75.

———. 2003. *Are prisons obsolete?* New York: Seven Stories.

Davis M. 1990. *City of quartz: Excavating the future in Los Angeles.* London: Verso.

DeNavas-Walt, C., B.D. Proctor, and C.H. Lee. 2005. U.S. Census Bureau. Current Population Reports P60–229. Income, poverty, and health insurance coverage in the United States: 2004. Washington, DC: U.S. Government Printing Office.

Dohrn, B. 2000. Look out, kid, it's something you did: The criminalization of children. See Polakow 2000, 157–87. New York: Teachers College Press.

Dow, M. 2004. *American gulag: Inside U.S. immigration prisons.* Berkeley: Univ. of California Press.

Dylan, B. 1974. Tough Mama. *Planet Waves.* Columbia CBS.

Farmer, P. 2002. The house of the dead: Tuberculosis and incarceration. In *Invisible punishment: The collateral consequences of mass imprisonment*, eds. M. Mauer and M. Chesney-Lind. Pp. 239–57. New York: New Press.

Federal Reserve Bank of Minneapolis. 2002. *Fedgazette* 14(1); http://www.minneapolisfed.org/pubs/fedgaz/02-01/cover.cfm

Foucault M. 1977. *Discipline and punish: The birth of the prison.* New York: Pantheon.

Garland, D. 2001. *The culture of control: Crime and social order in contemporary society.* Chicago: Univ. of Chicago Press.

Gilmore, R.W. 1998. From military Keynesianism to post-Keynesian militarism: Finance capital, land, labor and opposition in the rising California prison state. PhD dissertation, Rutgers University.

———. 1998–99. Globalisation and U.S. prison growth: From military Keynesianism to post-Keynesian militarism. *Race and Class* 40(2/3): 174.

———. 2007. *Golden gulag: Prisons, surplus, crisis, and opposition in globalizing California.* Berkeley: Univ. of California Press.

Giroux, H.A. 2004. *The terror of neoliberalism: Authoritarianism and the eclipse of democracy.* Boulder, CO: Paradigm.

Glaze, L.E., and S. Palla. 2004. *Probation and parole in the United States, 2004; Bureau of Justice Statistics Bulletin, U.S. Department of Justice Publication No. 205336;* http://www.ojp.usdoj.gov/bjs/pubalp2.htm#Probation

Goffman, E. 1961. *Asylums: Essays on the social situation of mental patients and other inmates.* Garden City, NY: Anchor Books.

Gonnerman J. 2004. *Life on the outside: The prison odyssey of Elaine Bartlett.* New York: Farrar, Straus and Giroux.

Goodman, D. 2002. No child unrecruited: Should the military be given the names of every high school student in America? *Mother Jones,* Nov/Dec 2002; http://www.motherjones .com/news/outfront/2002/11/ma_153_01.html.

Gorman, A. 2005. Latino groups to fight military recruiting on campuses. *Los Angeles Times* August 30 2005, B4.

Graham S. ed. 2004. *Cities, war, and terrorism: Towards an urban geopolitics.* Malden, MA: Blackwell.

Greene, J. 2004. From Abu Ghraib to America: Examining our harsh prison culture. *Ideas for an open society: Occasional papers from OSI-US Programs* 4(1); http://www.soros.org/ resources/articles_publications/publications/ideas_20041004.

Hallinan, J.T. 2001. *Going up the river: Travels in a prison nation.* New York: Random House.

Hancock, L. 2000. Framing children in the news: The face and color of youth crime in America. See Polakow 2000, 78–100.

Harrison, P.M., and A.J. Beck. 2005. *Prison and jail inmates at midyear 2004; Bureau of Justice Statistics Bulletin, U.S. Department of Justice Publication No. 208801;* http://www.ojp .usdoj.gov/bjs/pub/pdf/pjim04.pdf.

Higginbotham, H.L. Jr. 1971. The black prisoner: America's caged canary. In *Violence: The crisis of American confidence,* ed. H.D. Graham. Pp. 103–25. Baltimore: Johns Hopkins Univ. Press.

Hirsch, A.J. 1992. *The rise of the penitentiary: Prisons and punishment in early America.* New Haven, CT: Yale Univ. Press.

Hooks, G., C. Mosher, T. Rotolo, and L. Lobao. 2004. The prison industry: Carceral expansion and employment in U.S. counties, 1969–1994. *Social Science Quarterly* 85(1): 37–57.

Houston Chronicle. 2001. 100 years: Oil bust, space tragedy and Chronicle sale. *Houston Chronicle* October 14, 2001, Special Section, 14.

Hudson, B. 1999. Punishment, poverty and responsibility: The case for a hardship defence. *Social and Legal Studies* 8(4): 583–91.

Huling, T. 2002. Building a prison economy in rural America. In *Invisible punishment: The collateral consequences of mass imprisonment*, eds. M. Mauer and M. Chesney-Lind. Pp. 197–213. New York: New Press.

Human Rights Watch. 2002. *Race and incarceration in the United States; HRW Press Backgrounder February 27, 2002*; http://www.hrw.org/backgrounder/usa/race/.

Ignatieff, M. 1978. *A just measure of pain: The penitentiary in the industrial revolution, 1750–1850*. London: Macmillan.

Irwin, J. 1980. *Prisons in turmoil*. Boston: Little, Brown.

Jackson, G. 1970. *Soledad Brother: The prison letters of George Jackson*. New York: Bantam.

Jackson, M., and L. Ritchie. 1985. USA for Africa, *We Are The World*.

Jacobs, J.B. 1977. *Stateville: The penitentiary in mass society*. Chicago, IL: Univ. of Chicago Press.

James, J. ed. 2003. *Imprisoned intellectuals: America's political prisoners write on life*. Lanham, MD: Rowman and Littlefield.

Justice Policy Institute. 2000. *The punishing decade: Prison and jail estimates at the millennium*. Washington, D.C.: Justice Policy Institute; http://www.justicepolicy.org.

King R., M. Mauer, and T. Huling. 2003. *Big prisons, small towns: Prison economics in rural America*. Washington, DC: The Sentencing Project; http://www.sentencingproject .org/pdfs/9037.pdf

Lafree G., K. Drass, and P. O'Day. 1992. Race and crime in post-war America: Determinants of African American and white rates, 1957–1988. *Criminology* 30: 157–88.

LaLonde, R.J., and S.M. George. 2002. Incarcerated mothers: The Chicago project on female prisoners and their children. Comments to the Congressional Black Caucus, September 14, 2002; http://harrisschool.uchicago.edu/Research/faculty_projects/incarcerated _mothers/.

Lawrence, S., and J. Travis. 2004. *The new landscape of imprisonment: Mapping America's prison expansion; Urban Institute Justice Policy Center Research Report CPR040121*. Washington, DC: Urban Institute; http://www.urban.org/url.cfm?ID=410994.

LeBlanc, A.N. 2003. *Random family: Love, drugs, trouble, and coming of age in the Bronx*. New York: Scribner.

Lichtenstein, A. 1996. *Twice the work of free labor: The political economy of convict labor in the New South*. London: Verso.

Liptak, A. 2005. To more inmates, life term means dying behind bars. *New York Times* October 2, 2005, A1.

Low, S.M. 2003. *Behind the gates: Life, security, and the pursuit of happiness in fortress America*. New York: Routledge.

Lutz, C. 2001. *Homefront: A military city and the American twentieth century*. Boston, MA: Beacon.

Martínez, E. 2004. Be down with the brown! In *Voices of a People's History of the United States*, eds. H. Zinn and A. Arnove. Pp. 589–91. New York: Seven Stories.

Masser, M., and L. Creed, 1986. *Whitney Houston*. Arista Records.

Mauer, M. 1999. *Race to incarcerate*. New York: New Press.

Mauer, M., and T. Huling. 1995. Young black Americans and the criminal justice system: Five years later. Washington, DC: The Sentencing Project.

McCoy A.W. 2005. The hidden history of CIA torture: America's road to Abu Ghraib; *TomDispatch*, Nation Institute; http://www.tomdispatch.com/index.mhtml?emx =x&pid=1795

Midnight Notes Collective. 1990. *The new enclosures; Midnight Notes 10.* New York: Autono-media.

Miller, J. 1996. *Search and destroy: African-American males in the criminal justice system.* Cambridge: Cambridge Univ. Press.

Mumola, C.J. 2000. *Incarcerated parents and their children; Bureau of Justice Statistics Special Report NCJ 182335, United States Department of Justice, Bureau of Justice Statistics;* http://www.ojp.usdoj.gov/bjs/pub/pdf/iptc.pdf.

NCES (National Center for Education Statistics). 2002. *Digest of education statistics, 2002; U.S. Department of Education NCES 2003-060;* http://nces.ed.gov/pubsearch/pubsinfo .asp?pubid=2003060

Nord M., M. Andres, and S. Carlson. 2003. *Household food security in the United States, 2002; Food Assistance and Nutrition Research Report (FANRR35) October 2003;* http://www.ers.usda.gov/publications/fanrr35/.

Open Society Institute. 1998. Dying in prison: A growing problem emerges from behind bars; *Project on Death in America Newsletter* 3; http://www2.soros.org/death/news3.

Oshinsky, D.M. 1997. *"Worse than slavery": Parchman Farm and the ordeal of Jim Crow justice.* New York: Free Press.

Pager, D. 2003. The mark of a criminal record. *American Journal of Sociology* 108(5): 937– 75.

Parenti, C. 2003. *The soft cage: Surveillance in America from slavery to the war on terror.* New York: Basic Books.

Poe-Yamagata, E., and M.A. Jones. 2000. *And justice for some; Report of the National Council on Crime and Delinquency;* http://www.buildingblocksforyouth.org/justiceforsome/ jfs.html.

Polakow, V. ed. 2000. *The public assault on America's children: Poverty, violence and juvenile injustice.* New York: Teachers College Press.

Rathbone, C. 2005. *A world apart: Women, prison and life behind bars.* New York: Random House.

Ratner, L. 2003. The state punishes inmates who want to make cheaper calls home. *City Limits;* http://www.citylimits.org/content/articles/articleView.cfm?articlenumber=1000.

Rhodes, L.A. 2001. Toward an anthropology of prisons. *Annual Review of Anthropology* 30: 65–83.

———. 2004. *Total confinement: Madness and reason in the maximum security prison.* Berkeley: Univ. of California Press.

Richards, J.I., and S.C. Ross. 2001. Introducing the new school of convict criminology. *Social Justice* 28(1): 177–90.

Rideau, W., and R. Wikberg. 1992. *Life sentences: Rage and survival behind bars.* New York: Times Books.

Rothman, D.J. 1971. *The discovery of the asylum: Social order and disorder in the new republic.* Boston, MA: Little, Brown.

Rouillan, J.M. 2005. France: Return of the convicts. Trans. H. Foster. *Le Monde Diplomatique* July 2005; http://MondeDiplo.com/2005/07/14prison.

Rozoll, B.W. 2002. Education aid limits privacy. *Chicago Sun-Times* January 31, 2002, 18.

Sampson, R.J. 2000. Whither the sociological study of crime? *Annual Review of Sociology* 26: 711–14.

Sassen, S. 2001. *The global city: New York, London, Tokyo.* 2nd ed. Princeton, NJ: Princeton Univ. Press.

Schemo, D.J. 2002. Education bill urges new emphasis on phonics as method for teaching reading. *New York Times* January 9 2002, A16.

Shakur, A. 1971. July 4th address. See James 2003, 117–21.

Solomon, D. 2005. The way we live now: Questions for Jonathan Kozol. *New York Times Magazine* September 4, 2005, 14.

Staples, R. 1974. White racism, black crime, and American justice: An application of the colonial model to explain crime and race. *Phylon* 36(1): 14–22.

Staples, W.G. 2000. *Everyday surveillance: Vigilance and visibility in postmodern life.* Lanham, MD: Rowman & Littlefield.

Stern, V. 2002. The international impact of U.S. policies. In *Invisible punishment: The collateral consequences of mass imprisonment,* eds. M. Mauer and M. Chesney-Lind. Pp. 279–92. New York: New Press.

Swann, C. 2004. Jobs data look as poor in quality as quantity. *Financial Times* March 10, 2004, 9.

Taylor, W.B. 1999. *Down on Parchman Farm: The great prison in the Mississippi Delta.* Columbus: Ohio State Univ. Press.

Taylor, W.T., and D.M. Piche. 2002. Will new school law really help? *USA Today* January 9, 2002, 13A.

Thomas, P. 1994. Making crime pay. *Wall Street Journal* May 12, A1.

Tonry, M.H. 1995. *Malign neglect: Race, crime and punishment in America.* New York: Oxford Univ. Press.

———. 1997. Preface. In *Ethnicity, crime, and immigration: Comparative and cross-national perspectives,* ed. M. Tonry. Pp. 1–27. Chicago: Univ. of Chicago Press.

U.S. GAO (United States General Accounting Office). 1995. *Military bases: Case studies on selected bases closed in 1988 and 1991, GAO/NSIAD-95-139;* http://www.gao.gov/archive/1995/ns95139.pdf.

Venkatesh, S.A. 2000. *American project: The rise and fall of a modern ghetto.* Cambridge, MA: Harvard Univ. Press.

Wacquant, L. 1999. "Suitable enemies": Foreigners and immigrants in the prisons of Europe. *Punishment & Society* 1(2):215–22.

———. 2000. Deadly symbiosis: When ghetto and prison meet and mesh. In *Mass imprisonment: Social causes and consequences,* ed. D. Garland. pp. 82–120. London: Sage.

———. 2002. The curious eclipse of prison ethnography in the age of mass incarceration. *Ethnography* 3(4): 371–97.

———. 2006. *Deadly symbiosis.* Cambridge, UK: Polity Press.

Wagner, P. 2003. *The prison index: Taking the pulse of the crime control industry.* Western Prison Project and Prison Policy Initiative; http://www.prisonpolicy.org/prisonindex .shtml

Wald, J., and D.J. Rosen, eds. 2003. *Deconstructing the school-to-prison pipeline: New directions for youth development, no. 99.* San Francisco, CA: Jossey-Bass.

Walmsley, R. 2003. U.K. Home Office, Research, Development and Statistics Directorate. World Prison Population List, Fourth Edition. London: U.K. Home Office. http://www.homeoffice.gov.uk/rds/pdfs2/r188.pdf.

———. 2005. International Centre for Prison Studies. World Prison Population List, Sixth Edition. London: International Centre for Prison Studies. http://www.kcl.ac.uk/depsta/ rel/icps/world-prison-population-list-2005.pdf.

Western, B. 2006. *Punishment and inequality in America.* New York: Russell Sage.

Wilson, W.J. 1996. *When work disappears: The world of the new urban poor.* New York: Random House.

Wood, D.B. 2004. Budget cuts are setting convicts free. *Christian Science Monitor* April 21, 2004; http://www.csmonitor.com/2004/0421/p01s01-usju.html.

Zimring, F. 2001. Imprisonment rates and the new politics of criminal punishment. In *Mass imprisonment: Social causes and consequences,* ed. D. Garland, pp. 145–49. London; Thousand Oaks, CA: Sage.

8

Public Spaces, Consumption, and the Social Regulation of Young People

ROB WHITE

This chapter explores the social construction of public space, and the place of youth in such spaces, through the lens of global transformations in consumerism and social regulation. The mass privatisation of public spaces, along with renewed interest in questions of public disorder and how best to control, manage, and regulate such spaces, are crucial backdrops to the discussions that follow. How the state and private security agencies respond to youth in public spaces reflects both differences in institutional imperatives (for state police, issues of public order and law enforcement; for private police, issues of consumer activity and order maintenance), and the differential treatment of youth depending upon social background and youth group formation (such as 'gangs').

There are major ambiguities associated with the presence of youth in public spaces. In Australia, for example, a major tension exists between the efforts of many local councils and private commercial ventures (such as shopping centres) to make public spaces more convivial and socially inclusive and the efforts of state authorities to exclude particular users of public space under the rubric of community safety and effective law enforcement. Young people are at the fulcrum of this tension. On the one hand, they are being welcomed and offered a place at the community table through local council youth policies and initiatives and state government youth participation strategies; on the other, they are vilified and patronised and told to stay away until further notice (that is, until they are adult) through regulatory and law enforcement activity.

Analysis of public space issues provides important insights into how the law-youth-globalisation nexus is played out at an empirical level: life is, indeed, messy and complicated. World wide significant developments are occurring with respect to public space. Whether construed as 'community' space or 'commercial' space, competing social interests construct public spaces in very different ways. Inevitably, conflict over uses, and between users, of public space leads to state and private attempts to regulate it. The regulation of space is simultaneously a statement about the place of youth, the nature of consumerism, and the role of regulatory agencies in sustaining certain forms of communal life. By analysing public space issues and the nature of urban policing, we are able to gauge better the impact of social intervention, for bad or for good, in the lives of contemporary young people.

PUBLIC SPACE IN THE CONSUMER SOCIETY

The construction of public space is a social process with a number of sociological, environmental, planning, and economic dimensions (see for example, Castells, 1989; Davis, 1990; Harvey, 1990; Stilwell, 1993). For present purposes, three key dimensions can be highlighted. These are the *ownership* of public space, *control over access* to public space, and the *designated uses* of public space.

At a formal institutional level, public space can be described in terms of the following demarcations (see White, 1996: 46):

- state-owned and open public access (e.g., walking malls and courtyards, parks, ovals, beaches)
- state-owned but some restrictions in access and use (e.g., sports grounds, some beaches, school yards, showgrounds)
- privately owned but open public access (e.g., shopping centres, malls)
- privately owned and exclusive private access (e.g., clubs, recreation areas, golf courses).

It needs to be acknowledged that the existing uses and basis for access to space vary depending upon the institutional logic surrounding its construction (e.g., private profit, community benefit). It can also be observed that certain users of public space will occupy a privileged status in particular types of public space, and that this depends upon its location, the time of day, and the functional roles associated with its use (e.g., educational or commercial purposes).

The form of urban space has fundamentally been shaped by the contours of economic development and class-related social processes over several hundred years. The types of housing and amenity in a neighbourhood, the policing of street life, and different patterns of use of parks and pavements have always been symptomatic of broader social divisions and differences. Where you live is a major indicator of economic and social well-being (Gregory & Hunter, 1995; Walmsley & Weinand, 1997). Although class relations have underpinned the social construction of space (Katznelson, 1993), the social relations of space have in turn also reflected gender, race, and ethnic differences in how different groups can or should enjoy the public domains of the city (Sassen, 1993; Trench et al., 1992).

The very definition of *public space* has been the subject of much contestation between different classes, as have the purposes and behaviours deemed to be appropriate within any such space (Worpole & Greenhalgh, 1996). In the Australian context, for example, the working-class traditions of using the street as a multi-functional social space has long been a source of middle-class consternation. Media-driven concerns about the 'larrikin pushes' (i.e., youth gangs) in Sydney and Brisbane at the turn of the nineteenth century heightened bourgeois fears about the anarchic conditions of city life and the 'depraved' condition of much working-class youth culture (Murray, 1973; Finch, 1993). The answer then, as now, was often to pursue policies of strong policing and social exclusion for selected groups (Finnane, 1994).

Finch (1993: 76) describes how the street as a multi-functional space was transformed architecturally and socially into a more circumscribed and regulated place with the advent of consumer-oriented capitalism. The new wider boulevards allowed strolling, and these were intrinsically linked to middle-class use and commercial purposes: 'The late nineteenth century metropolitan streetscape drew women out from the suburbs, turned shopping into leisure activity which occupied the entire day, and created "public women" among the respectable middle and working classes'. The modification of the cityscape thus occurred simultaneously with major changes in the production and consumption patterns of society. Narrowly defined uses for the street, the presence of female shoppers, and establishment of particular sites such as railway stations and public parks in which all classes had a presence were essential new features in the reconstitution of city life.

Consumerism

Public spaces have changed in concept and design over the years, depending upon the ebbs and flows of economic development and social conflict. In the present era, the social construction of public space is dominated by a series of inter-related developments. The first of these is the rise of consumerism as a major global phenomenon. *Consumption*—defined here as the purchase of goods and services (commodities)—has become the dominant public value in social life, at least in terms of media portrayal and political rhetoric. For example, the promotion of capital cities, particularly Sydney and Melbourne, occurs largely through appeal to mega-events and spectacles, from Grand Prix to Olympics, from Gay and Lesbian Mardi Gras to Melbourne Arts Festival. At a more mundane level, the viability of cities is increasingly portrayed as depending upon the provision of specific urban sites that are cosmopolitan, consumer-friendly enclaves in which to live; particular districts, with their huge entertainment complexes and multitudinous shops, are portrayed as the epitome of the consumer cathedrals of capitalism.

The buyer-seller nexus now appears to be the hub around which social life is meant to revolve (see Spearritt, 1994). This is reflected in political policies and planning objectives that are designed to attract retail and service-based businesses to central business districts and major regional centres. Development is paramount, and commercially created places rather than publicly planned spaces have come to dominate. This is so even in the light of the continued maintenance of publicly planned space, such as the St. Kilda foreshore in Melbourne. Public space is basically being defined by consumption activities and uses rather than other sorts of values.

Privatisation

The privileging of consumption and commercial activity has been accelerated in recent years through the privatisation of space. This privatisation occurs on several fronts. For example, it is associated with the privatisation of functions, such as the contracting out of the maintenance and management of public parks. It is linked to withdrawal of needed state financial support for certain services, as with public housing and rural train services. It is tied to the selling off of government services to private companies, as with road construction and public transport. *Privatisation* also refers to the ability of large corporations to buy into and buy up public landscapes, through state guarantees of profit or outright purchase, as with former school sites.

Privatisation in essence means to make private. And to make private is to transfer effective ownership and control out of public hands and into private ones, and to view the functional purposes of public spaces and amenities in commercial rather than community terms. Viability is not conceived in terms of meeting a particular social need; it is a cost-benefit economic calculation. Nor is accountability construed in the same way, for the bottom line is at the accountant's behest, not the community's. This construction of accountability raises big issues with respect to participatory planning, consultative mechanisms, and regulatory enforcement of public interest principles.

Under privatisation, it is 'the client' who counts. Even so, in many instances the planning of central squares, malls, and shopping complexes ends up working better for communities, as when more people congregate in convivial fashion because of the activities in such places, not all of which are commercially based. The commercial focus of such places does not mean that one can always predict how people will use them, what kind of activities will take place, or which sorts of relationships will be formed (see Beattie and Lehmann, 1994). Although unintended consequences—and community benefits—may arise from specific constructions, the rationale behind planning and design nevertheless places rough boundaries on the kinds of activities likely to happen.

Growing disparities are now manifest at broad regional levels, as evidenced in the social and spatial polarisation of Australian cities (Johnson, 1994; Troy, 1995; Gregory & Hunter, 1995). As research in the advanced industrialised countries has shown, this translates into high-income earners living in desirable suburbs, inner-city apartments, and regenerated historical areas, while the low-paid and unemployed live in decaying urban spaces (see Johnson, 1994; Davis, 1990; Castells, 1989; Wilson, 1996). The notion of leaving urban development primarily in the hands of private enterprise also implies that it is the market that will determine social outcomes, with potentially unequal community impacts. As Peel (1996: 16) comments:

Where change reduces choices or lowers amenity, for instance, the market will provide escape routes for those who can pay. The people most likely to experience the unwanted by-products—noise, pollution, rising rents—of other people's freedom to choose are also those who cannot afford to buy their way out. This includes those people who have not yet established themselves in the market: it is the next generation who will be asked to accept smaller houses and smaller private yards as standard. It is in Sydney's already under-serviced western suburbs, not the North Shore, that dual occupancy and medium-density developments are causing headaches.

The privatisation of the city implies, at one and the same time, a reconfiguration of basic social relationships and of public values.

Regulation

A third feature that characterises much of the urban renewal and redevelopment process is that of the intensification of public space regulation. Again, this takes different forms. It can be seen in the examples of gated suburbs and urban fortresses. Furthermore, the fear of crime and its attendant privatised means of security have in themselves become a commodity, selling newspapers and specific products for those who wish to pay. Urban planning thus becomes intertwined with crime prevention and security assessment.

To this we can add a few observations about the protection of commercial enterprises. Felson (1987), for example, speaks of the emergence of the 'great metropolitan quilt' in the United States, where reliance on the car has led to a patchwork of co-determinous facilities (e.g., shopping malls and centres) intervening between homes, businesses, and the larger society. Urban space, in this scenario, is divided up by a large set of corporations that, in turn, would be responsible for organising everyday movements, including security. The dominance of such facilities means that architects, security planners, and facilities managers associated with these complexes become central actors in shaping community life.

The shopping centre has evolved to be, for many, the central feature of urban social life. It has assumed a number of symbolic and functional uses for a wide and diverse range of people. For young people, in particular, it is a major site for meeting together and hanging out.

A shopping centre such as appears in the suburbs of cities (e.g., Chadstone Shopping Centre in the eastern suburbs of Melbourne) is distinct from a shopping district or shopping area such as the retail shopping strip/street (e.g., Chapel Street, Melbourne). The former is characterised by a group of architecturally unified commercial establishments, built on a site planned, developed, owned, and managed as a unit. The latter does not have an overall planned layout or unified operation, but is a district or street that is divided into separately owned units, and may vary in locations across a defined geographical area (Ellis, 1987). Some key features of shopping centres include retailing being their primary function, they are constituted on the basis of profit-making private investment, the rationale for decision-making is commercial rather than public interest per se, and there is management control over what is allowable within a shopping centre on basis of private property rights.

Shopping centres and districts have taken different forms over the years. Sandercock (1997) comments that recent developments are premised upon providing consumers with a clean, sanitised, attractive, and safe environment, but one so highly controlled as to deny the real diversity of the urban environment. As a number of critics have likewise argued, the modern shopping centre or shopping mall has a tendency to be designed, policed, and regulated in a manner that is intended to exclude particular groups, such as unemployed and homeless people, from their precincts (Davis, 1990; Worpole & Greenhalgh, 1996; White & Sutton, 1995).

Beyond Consumption

The urban landscape now is thus in many ways shaped by the dictates of consumption, which is legitimated through political rhetoric and policies that equate extensive consumption with the good of the people. It would appear that 'Consumerism, that is the active ideology that the meaning of life is to be found in buying things and pre-packaged experiences, pervades modern capitalism' (Bocock, 1993: 48). Moreover, it has been argued that what and how we consume has become an essential part of the way in which we construct a sense of who we are, our basic social identity. Be this as it may, it is still essential to recognise other ways of being beyond consumption, and to be sensitive to the different ways in which people engage in the consumption process.

For example, in examining the use of public spaces in general, it is simply not accurate to describe people exclusively as consumers. It is important not to forget the 'simple' pleasures associated with public space, pleasures that are about human relationships, networks, and non-commercial activities. Worpole and Greenhalgh (1996: 36) express this aptly in the following observation:

> As we have found time and time again in our research, what people most often value about the twice weekly visit to the library, or even the daily stroll in the park, is an opportunity to meet other people whether they are neighbours, relatives, close or casual friends, and to have their social identity confirmed in the process of these spontaneous, unorganised encounters. Our social identity is partly formed by these public appearances and relationships, and although they can also happen in private or commercial settings, there does seem to be something different about life in the free, non-instrumental sanctuary of the library or the park, where one is a citizen rather than a consumer.

The use of public spaces—such as beaches, malls, the street, bushland, and shopping centres—is therefore not entirely consumption oriented. Older people as well as younger people are prone to 'hanging out' in such spaces, regardless of the functional imperatives of commercial enterprises. Indeed, the feeling of connection, the sense of excitement, and the exhilaration of being in and around others is not unique to young people.

Much is said about the fear of crime and victimisation associated with public incivilities, crime, and homelessness. However, little is said about how the appearance of some degree of 'social disorganisation' is itself a source of pleasure. Indeed, the contrast between highly sanitised, extensively regulated spaces (as in some shopping complexes) and less pristine urban environments with less overt social controls makes the latter a desirable place to visit for many people, at least on an occasional basis. Some public spaces are likely to attract people precisely because of the unstructured, unorganised nature of the space. This is partly borne out by an Adelaide study, which found a fair degree of tolerance for misbehaviour or incivility on Hindley Street according to the people surveyed (Morgan, Pudsey & Roach Anleu, 1997). One can also think here about the 'notorious' Kings Cross in Sydney and St. Kilda in Melbourne. In other words, the use of certain public places carries with it expectations about what is likely to occur in those places, and a realistic assessment that street life, to be exciting and interesting, necessarily includes some negative features. The reality is that different people want different things in and from public spaces, at different times of the day. This holds as true for older people as it does for younger. Similarly, the over-regulation of public spaces can put people off in much the same way that a lack of appropriate social regulation can make people reluctant to visit some places.

The heterogenous nature of public space use is also reflected in activities in specific venues or locations. There is no such thing as a typical consumer. Different people exhibit very different sorts of relationships with the shopping centre environment, and they engage in substantially different kinds of activities while in such a setting (Bloch, Ridgway, & Dawson, 1994). Yet too often people are lumped together into an amorphous entity called 'the public', as if every adult (or young person) feels the same way about consumerism or public space issues, or sees the problems relating to street life the same way. This acceptance of 'the public' as a single aggregation ignores the profound social differences and social divisions that colour the ways in which parents, consumers, citizens, and residents respond to and interact with the world around them.

On the other hand, apparent public disquiet about young people's use of public space highlights the power of the media in portraying, and to some extent, creating a consensus about the nature of the youth problem (Schissel, 1997; Males, 1996). The fact that young people tend to hang around in groups, are vulnerable socially and politically, and are highly visible because of their modes of dress and sheer numbers means that they are easy targets for various kinds of 'moral panics' about their presumed behaviours. Although different communities have different perceptions and experiences when it comes to how their children and young people interact with and in the urban environment, the notion of public (rather than publics) opinion is a powerful one, one which in turn has major consequences for shaping the ideas of the populace at large.

YOUNG PEOPLE IN THE PUBLIC DOMAIN

As a place to hang out, *public space* refers to a wide range of specific locations—places where young people have a degree of room to move as well as to watch and interact with their peers and others. Conversely, it is not uncommon for young people to complain about issues such as lack of adequate seating, a feeling that they had to purchase something in order to be there, bad lighting, inadequate transport, and harassment from authority figures as factors affecting their satisfaction with public places and venues (White, 1999). Suspicion, intolerance and moral censure operate in particular ways that limit the spatial world of young people (Malone & Hasluck, 1998; 2002) even as they explore the limits and boundaries of this world.

In addition to highlighting the common issues and problems many young people experience in their uses of public space, it is also important to acknowledge the specific character of different kinds of space. One way to do this is to distinguish between youth-specific and youth-friendly amenities and to understand why each dimension plays an important part in how young people experience and use public space. *Youth-specific amenities* refer to those venues and amenities that young people themselves feel are most interesting, most accessible, and most suitable for them, and that reflect their particular needs and desires for entertainment and recreation. *Youth-friendly amenities* refer to venues or amenities of all types where the general atmosphere is one in which young people are treated with respect and dignity, and where they feel safe, secure, and welcome.

Where public amenities are located is a significant factor in how and where young people spend their time. A Brisbane study highlighted the importance of appreciating the localised nature of *access to public amenities and spaces*, for example (Lynch & Ogilvie, 1999). Young people were asked whether or not there were enough things to do in their local area for people of their age. The venues and amenities referred to included things such as swimming pools, cinemas, video arcades, and fast food outlets. It was found that ease of access to amenities was consistently related to a sense of having enough or not enough to do on the part of the young people.

In a Melbourne study, questions were asked about where young people spent most of their time (White et al., 1997). It is notable that the most frequent responses were those referring to 'home' and 'friend's place'. Here it can be emphasised that, while the public debates over young people tend to centre on their activities in public spaces, the primary place of social interaction is in fact the private space of the home. Therefore, when young people do venture out into the public domain it becomes even more important that they have youth-specific places within which to congregate. Likewise, the content of young people's activities in the public sphere has to represent something of a break from a usually more controlled and regulated home environment— that is, there has to be something of excitement or interest beyond the mundane routines and regimes of family life.

Consistent with other contemporary studies (see, for example, Crane, 2000), the Melbourne research found that shopping centres were by far the most likely place where young people hang out with their friends when they do venture out into public places. A distinction can be made here between access to a *general amenity*, such as a shopping centre, and access to a *youth-specific amenity*, such as a games arcade. This is an important distinction insofar as, although young people in the Melbourne study indicated ready access to shopping centres, they simultaneously indicated that they nevertheless get bored. Indeed, almost 80 per cent of the respondents said they get bored.

The Melbourne study found that when they go out, young people tend to hang around, in groups, in public spaces such as shopping centres, commercial venues, and the street. Where they go and how they spend their time is intimately related to a neighbourhood's level provision of amenities. The availability of public transport, leisure services, recreational facilities, parks, open-air plazas, gardens, and so on has major implications for young people's 'pride of place', their attachment to neighbourhood institutions such as schools, and their preferred social activities (White et al., 1997).

The first question of 'access', therefore, is whether or not certain amenities are actually available at a local level. A related issue is whether or not amenities, wherever they are located, are designed with youth interests or needs specifically in mind, or if they incorporate within them youth-specific activities. Ideally, youth-specific amenities would provide both activity-based venues or programmes, and more simply, social spaces in which young people can 'do nothing' in comfort and safety.

Access to amenity is not simply about the physical presence or otherwise of certain types of facilities and spaces. It also has a social dimension. A crucial issue here is the conditions under which young people can actually *use certain amenities*, and the conditions under which young people actually *view* the amenity as youth-friendly. This, in turn, revolves around questions of money and social status.

Young people participating in a Melbourne survey (Wooden, 1997), for example, were asked to identify key criteria for what makes a place youth-friendly or youth-unfriendly. Youth-friendly criteria included such things as type of people, acceptance, friendly people, environment, good entertainment, no violence or threats to safety, and cheap food and drinks. An unfriendly place was characterised by bad service and location, being treated badly by staff, fights and feeling unsafe, drugs and alcohol, police presence, and being alone as a teenager in such a place. Similar sorts of studies have also been carried out by other researchers in Australia (Malone, 1999), Italy (Salvadori, 1997), and the United States (Meucci & Redmon, 1997), using a variety of innovative conceptual techniques and field methods. In each case, children and young people have been encouraged to identify positive and negative features of their neighbourhoods in order to determine what is physically and socially most attractive, and most threatening, about where they live, play, and interact.

Part of the issue of access has to do with whether young people are made to feel that they are a *bona fide* part of a community or are perceived as threats to it. For example, part of the Brisbane research cited earlier (Lynch & Ogilvie, 1999) involved examination of the uses of the local pool in an economically disadvantaged neighbourhood. One public swimming pool existed locally, but the pool management had instituted a policy of insisting that T-shirts could not be worn in the pool. Many of those wishing to use the facility were indigenous young people, for whom wearing a T-shirt constituted a culturally appropriate expression of personal modesty. Apart from any cultural considerations, there are purely practical aspects to wearing a T-shirt as well. For example, wearing a large, baggy T-shirt constitutes a reasonably effective sun protection strategy, particularly for those who do not buy sunscreen with sun protection formula of 15+ (which in itself has important financial implications). In addition, in the middle of summer, walking home from the pool in a wet T-shirt is an eminently practical way of staying cool just that little bit longer. By forbidding T-shirts, the pool authorities immediately disenfranchised a significant proportion of the local young people. Rightly or wrongly, this policy was interpreted as a deliberate tactic of exclusion, consistent with the day-to-day racism many of these young people continually experienced. Whether or not there were sound reasons for the pool management's decision was irrelevant to the young people: the policy was interpreted by them as meaning the pool was 'not theirs'.

A consistent theme in much of the literature dealing with young people's use of public space is that young people rarely gain a sense of ownership when it comes to the use of amenities (Lynch & Ogilvie, 1999). At one level, the availability of amenities such as swimming pools, rollerblading rinks, and non-commercial public spaces allow young people to familiarise themselves with the feeling of being autonomous. That is, such venues and facilities provide an opportunity for young people to interact with their peers without close family or state control. These interactions constitute an important part of forming their identity, separate from those interactions constrained and determined by their family situation.

At another level, however, the opportunities to develop themselves and their own relationship with the wider social world are often restricted by the actions of the institutional providers of amenities and public spaces. This takes the form of unnecessarily restrictive rules in the use of some amenities, the presence of security apparatus and personnel, the active intervention of state police and private security guards in their affairs (regardless of whether or not a criminal act has occurred), and general media treatment that suggests that young people have no real value or place in the larger scheme of things. These restrictions and interventions can transform general community amenities, even youth-specific ones, into youth-unfriendly spaces.

Shaping Youth Space

Young people are not passive users of the street, nor are they often reticent about establishing a public presence. In many different ways, and on different levels, young people engage directly in social processes that are implicated in significant social change. In responding to their environments, they have also succeeded in transforming these environments. This is not always a conscious process, nor is it always intended to have the consequences that arise from certain types of activities (see White & Wyn, 2004).

Taking and making spaces of their own is thus never a straightforward or simple social process. It involves adaptation to local conditions and environments, as when skateboarders reconceptualise the physical landscape of the city to best match their perceptions and uses of street furniture and building architecture (see Snow, 1999). Somewhere to sit, a bench, is transformed into that which is skated on, over, or along. But this process too involves various types of social exclusion. I sit; therefore you cannot skate. I skate; therefore you cannot sit. Transgression is never socially neutral. It involves different understandings of the environment, but it also involves potential conflicts of interest, not only between marginalised youth and powerful adults, but also amongst and between young people generally (White & Wyn, 2004).

More often than not, young people simply want to 'do their thing' with their friends. This takes a number of different forms, among them:

- youth music scenes that shape cultural and physical spaces (for example, 'hip hop' adaptations around the globe; raves);
- street machiners and car culture (that involves the public parading and showing off of automobiles);
- street dancers and the street as stage (involving public performance and exhibition of skills);
- direct action politics focussing on music, political issues, and people power (via appropriation of public spaces by large numbers of people);
- anti-globalisation protests and social movement actions that involve large numbers of young people (as with Australian protests against the treatment of asylum seekers);
- marking of the public landscape (through graffiti art and other forms of graffiti production); and
- youth group formation and the sense of territory (usually perceived as 'gangs' of young people who hang out together and who generally share common interests or identities).

What characterises many of these types of activities is that they border on the illegal or are illegal in some way, or that they are perceived as anti-social to the extent that they run contrary to the interests and enjoyment of other users of those spaces. Furthermore, while often expressing the creative energies of youth and providing an avenue for artistic, musical, and political expression, they may include violent or criminal behaviour. For instance, street fights between groups of young people tend to be highly visible; they also disturb the peace and sense of safety of people nearby.

Many of these activities can be interpreted as meaningful attempts to 'transgress' the ordinary (see Hayward, 2002; Presdee, 2000). In a world of standardised diversity and global conformities, it is exciting and pleasurable to break the rules, to push the boundaries, to engage in risky and risk-taking activities. Transgressions of this nature are one way in which youth can attain a sense of identity and commonality, and can have fun.

However, group activities based upon transgression can become collective behaviour that is highly threatening and dangerous—for example, violence that is unpredictable, random, and unintelligible (McDonald, 1999). This is manifest, for instance, in the phenomenon of swarming—spontaneous gatherings of young people that occasionally result in serious episodes of violence. The fact is that not all street activity is desirable. In many cases it can lead to fear and insecurity on the part of other people, including young people, and involve anti-social violence. Autonomous and spontaneous activities have many different dimensions and, as such, they call forth a wide range of social responses. Young people thus become targets for various kinds of coercive and other types of regulatory intervention.

THE REGULATION OF PUBLIC SPACE

Although different institutions (public or private) generally have defined purposes relating to the use of specific places, often the rhetoric about and marketing of such areas stresses the 'general community' or universal character of such places. The message is that public places are for the 'people'. However, some people are more welcome than others in the public domain.

This raises the issue of how public space is regulated. The mix of privately owned and publicly owned places in any locality is matched by the mix of state police and private security as the key agencies of social control. The objectives of each regulatory agency may vary, from concerns with public order to enforcing dress and behaviour codes, but in practice the relationship each sector has with young people, in particular, is often beset by common problems. How public space is regulated, and how specific forms of regulation are justified or legitimated, are nevertheless shaped or conditioned by the institutional sphere within which the regulation occurs and the organisational imperatives of the agency doing the regulating.

Regulating (Mis)Behaviour

The systematic regulation of young people in public spaces has long been a key aspect of the maintenance of public order as conceived by authority figures (Finnane, 1994; Hogg & Golder, 1987; Cohen, 1979). This is largely because, historically, public space was generally publicly owned, and public order was primarily a responsibility of the state. Hence the police have been central players in the leisure and spare-time activities of young people, especially working-class young people and indigenous young people. Young people have used streets, beaches, malls, and shopping areas as prime sites for their unstructured activities, and it is these areas that have received the main attentions of state police services.

In many places the favoured approach to the regulation of public space, particularly as this pertains to young people, is the use of coercion (see White, 1998). This is sometimes reflected in the language of 'zero tolerance', which refers to the idea of 'taking crime seriously' by getting 'tough on crime' at its source. This is interpreted as taking pre-emptive police action in certain places (city 'hot spots') and against certain people ('youth gangs'). The approach essentially involves stepped-up general surveillance, the monitoring of specific areas and groups of people, and the active use of force and arrest, even in the case of relatively minor offences (street littering, offensive language). Any behaviour, activity, or group that is deemed to be anti-social is not to be tolerated by authorities (see Dixon, 1998). It is a model that has gained considerable popularity in conservative political circles worldwide in recent years. It is also reflected in the extension of 'disorder' into the street policing rulebook, as with the case of the *Crime & Disorder Act 1998* in the United Kingdom.

Zero tolerance is basically concerned with maintaining particular kinds of public order, in particular kinds of public spaces, using particular policing strategies that target particular groups of people more than others. It is the most evident and pervasive form of crime prevention pertaining to young people. Such policing effectively sees juvenile crime prevention as a matter of deterrence, usually through pro-active interventions that attempt either to stop young people from engaging in certain activities or to exclude them from being in certain kinds of public spaces at particular times. In operational terms, zero tolerance may take different guises: from a casual use of 'name-checks' (asking young people their names and addresses), 'move-on' powers (the right to ask young people to move away from certain areas), and a search for prohibited implements through to enhanced ability to take fingerprints and bodily samples of young alleged offenders.

Aggressive street policing and zero tolerance approaches have been criticised for unduly restricting the rights of young people, for being linked to racist assessments of who gets targeted for intervention, for creating resentment amongst young people towards authority figures, and for sending the wrong message about how best to resolve social conflicts (Dixon, 1998). Nevertheless, even the critics agree that selective use of coercive measures is warranted in specific situations and is an appropriate tactical measure when applied judiciously (White, 1998). For example, a shopping centre in Cairns (northern Queensland) was experiencing major problems with a small group of teenage boys who frightened patrons and caused persistent damage to the premises. For a short time only, the management worked with police and security guards to 'stamp out' the offending group, and with it the offending behaviour. Afterwards, the management strategy no longer relied upon coercive threat, but instead used much more friendly and interactive forms of social regulation (White, Kosky, & Kosky, 2001).

At a legislative and policy level, attempts to restrict the street presence of young people (especially those organised into 'gangs') also take the form of youth curfews or anti-loitering statutes. Curfews are used extensively in the United States, although the specific features of each curfew vary considerably in terms of times, activities, target populations, and enforcement (Bilchik, 1996). There has also been a recent extension of the power to impose youth curfews in England and Wales (Walsh, 2002). Street cleaning legislation such as this has long been linked to efforts of the establishment to deal with the most destitute or marginalised sections of the population. For instance, the history of vagrancy laws in the United Kingdom, Australia, and the United States is a history of social control over selected population groups—the poor, the unemployed, the ethnic minority, the indigenous, the transient (see Brown et al., 2001; Santos, 2001). Queensland's Vagrants Act, for example, has remained relatively unchanged since its enactment in 1931. Even outdated provisions such as 'insufficient lawful means of support', however, are still used today to charge and convict people for eating out of garbage bins and sleeping in public places (Walsh, 2004). The use of vagrancy laws to police and harass marginalised public-space users, particularly homeless people, is a matter of growing public concern due to the discriminatory nature of law enforcement (see Walsh, 2004).

Moral panics about youth misbehaviour, youth gangs, drugs, and incivility are associated with publicly voiced concern that governments 'do something' about the presumed lawlessness on city streets. It is young people who generally are the key targets in such law and order campaigns. The result is the production of a wide range of legal and policing interventions such as:

- offensive language provisions and public order policing (for example, prosecutions for offensive language now outstrip prosecutions for offensive behaviour in New South Wales);
- anti-weapons legislation that allows greater police powers to search people (the main targets for such searches and being told to move tend to be young people);
- anti-gang initiatives targeting groups of young people (so that, for example, groups of three or more young people are told to disband);
- youth curfews, whether on a formal or informal basis (that are designed to limit young people's use of public spaces at designated times);
- street cleaning and zero tolerance policing (concerted campaigns to pick young people up and remove them from public places); and
- laws allowing the cars or stereos of 'hoons' (loutish fast- and dangerous-driving youth) to be seized by police and confiscated (to reduce the presence of street machiners).

The consequence of these kinds of measures is the reduction of the capacity of young people to use public spaces or to engage in certain types of activities.

Regulating Consumption

Whether a site is publicly accessible while privately owned or has explicit restrictive access makes a difference in the kind of policing that will be in place. In some residential areas and sites, for example, residents are protected by private security firms. Access is controlled by the firms, as is routine patrolling of the site. The architecture and planning of such residences and residential areas tend to be designed with specific security and access objectives, which by their very nature exclude the general public. Interestingly, it has been suggested that in such circumstances, off-site areas, such as surrounding streets, become the proper domain of state police, with the implication that 'good' citizens will remain in their enclaves, while 'bad' citizens are identified by being on the streets (see Davies, 1995).

For most people, however, public space issues revolve around publicly accessible privately owned places such as shopping centres. The regulation of these spaces, however, is not driven by concerns with public order per se. Instead, most policing strategies are premised on the idea of promoting such spaces as 'consumer' spaces and doing whatever is necessary to facilitate consumption (White, 1994).

The main concern of commercial enterprises is to prevent crime in the most effective way possible and to ensure that behaviour of visitors to the site best matches the commercial objectives of the trader or corporation. This is reflected in a report that discussed the ways in which groups of young people gathering in Launceston's Mall (in the state of Tasmania) have caused concern to some citizens and business owners (Challenger, 1997). The sorts of behaviour that were identified as undesirable included:

- occasionally intimidating or harassing mall users;
- fighting with each other outside, with the fight sometimes spilling over into stores;
- causing anxiety to staff and customers when roaming within stores;
- causing damage to property;
- being nuisances in stores and jeopardising the safety of customers and staff (e.g., running through stores); and
- stealing goods from the stores.

Similar findings were also apparent in a Melbourne study, which found that retail staff in a large shopping complex felt that 'loitering', 'rowdiness', 'offensive behaviour', and 'shoplifting' were significant issues (Bruce, 1997).

In response to these kinds of undesirable activities, many site managers attempt to modify their sales environment or beef up security in some way.

Rules of access and rules of behaviour are set by site managers. These vary depending on the centre. An example of dress and behaviour codes associated with a shopping centre might be to prohibit access to patrons without a shirt or shoes, or to ban skateboarding, rollerblading, or bicycling on the premises (Youth Action and Policy Association, 1997: 50).

The clear message here is that the intended purpose of the centre is consumption, and even then to consume only that which is on offer within the centre itself. Leaving aside for the moment the social nature of shopping centres and the multiple social uses of space within them, it is notable that much of the policing of commercial public spaces is undertaken by private police. In many cases private security firms and guards work closely in tandem with state police in regulating privately owned spaces. A number of important questions can be asked about the precise relationship between private and public policing, particularly regarding issues of accountability, powers, and rights (see Blagg & Wilkie, 1995).

Because of their physical layout and construction, shopping complexes and recreational and entertainment centres are very amenable to highly intensive systems of surveillance and control. The use of security guards and closed-circuit cameras, for example, is prevalent. In some cases, laws have been passed that give private police greater powers of exclusion than are available to state police. Among other things, this means that private security officers have the power to ban young people from particular sites regardless of their training or their attitudes to young people (Murray, 1995).

Australian research has, however, also highlighted the fact that that some shopping centre managers and retail traders are developing positive and constructive methods of public space management and social regulation, in ways that include the concerns of young people themselves and that reduce instances of unfair treatment and unnecessary intervention as these pertain to young people (White, 1999; Crane, 2000). Adoption of such methods can be explained by consideration of the primary raison d'etre of commercial enterprises. Rather than an over-riding interest in law enforcement and public order maintenance or public welfare, the main interest of private capital is profit and commercial viability. Service provision in the case of commercial institutions is thus informed by considerations of money-making.

This commercial orientation translates into two main concerns. First, retail and service institutions are concerned to relate to young people as actual and potential consumers and thus to cater to their cultural needs as teenagers by creating comfortable environments within which they will purchase goods and services. Second, these institutions want to ensure that customers generally, including young people, feel safe and secure in the commercial environment and that any potential threats to the trading process are adequately dealt with. This means that, in some instances, companies will attempt to bolster their image or sales through a strategic *inclusion* of young people. This is especially the case for shopping centres and malls, particularly during day-time hours.

The presence (or absence) of youth, in this instance, is premised upon enhancing youth-specific and youth-friendly spaces for the purposes of *youth consumption*. Complicating the scenario that specifically and strategically includes young people, there is the problem of the potential damage caused by youth (both material, in the form of vandalism, and non-material, in the form of dissuading other potential customers by making noise and congregating in groups). Attempts to counteract potential losses have included taking steps to accommodate the needs of young people and their advocates within the context of commercial public space (White, Kosky & Kosky, 2001). For example, hiring a part-time youth worker is much cheaper than full-time security guards, and with potentially much greater positive effect.

Youth-friendly approaches generally include active dialogue among interested parties, including youth advocates (as in the part-time youth worker) and young people directly, support for youth services and youth workers, and the reliance upon low-key inclusive management procedures (see White, Kosky & Kosky, 2001; Crane & Marston, 1999). For instance, in Brisbane, the Myer Centre Youth Protocol was developed in 1998 as a means to deal with any potential problems that might arise from young people's use of the Centre. The protocol was developed as a collaborative effort involving a local government authority, a major retail centre, and the youth sector. Some of the principles underpinning the protocol include enhancing transparency and accountability; health and safety; access and equity; involvement of young people; minimally intrusive security provision; customer service; and redress in the case of complaints (Crane & Marston, 1999). In other words, the regulation of the public space was seen as a collaborative process, involving diverse interests and interest groups.

There are nevertheless other pressures and contingencies that work in the opposite direction—towards social segregation and exclusion rather than towards social inclusion. Here we might mention the reshaping of public street life through the new political economy of the night-time economy, one result of which is the creation of distinctive mainstream, residual, and alternative spaces, practices, and identities (see Chatterton & Hollands, 2003). The corporate commercial entertainment industries do their best to attract customers through standardised, yet variable, venues and attractions. As Chatterton and Hollands (2003: 93) point out, 'the commercial mainstream is a differentiated "playground" which offers a number of goods and spaces for the active production and reproduction of social groupings of young people, keen to refashion their night-time consumption identities in relation to their peers and their own labour market positions'.

In many places, marginalised youth are not welcome—rather, they are explicitly and publicly rejected. Social exclusion is thus not only constructed around the economic, but also around the cultural and the spatial. As British research demonstrates, 'residual youth groupings' that include the young unemployed are left to consume the residual or 'bottom end' of the nightlife market (Chatterton & Hollands, 2003: 188). For many disadvantaged young people, even these options are not available. For these young people, the street becomes a central place for socialising. Thus they are once again at the mercy of state authorities and subjected to highly intrusive and intensive public order policing.

CONCLUSION

Although by no means universally applied, there has nevertheless been a proliferation of positive and innovative practices, projects, and strategies that not only respect the rights and wishes of young people but also directly involve them in many decision-making processes (see, for example, Salvadori, 1997; White, 1999; Crane, 2000). And many older people—including shopping centre managers, local council representatives, and urban planners—who previously did little to recognise the special needs and common rights of young people now do so as a matter of course.

To address the ambivalent experiences of young people in public spaces it is essential to create 'community' spaces that are convivial and safe (see White & Sutton, 2001). This requires a careful assessment of particular sites and a weighing up of potentially competing objectives. For instance, when public space is over-regulated and 'sanitised' it tends to be less frequented, to the detriment of citizens and businesses alike. Public space that does not convey a sense of security and safety, on the other hand, will also tend to be less frequented and to be reserved for the select few who claim it as their own.

Making everyone feel welcome in a space is important to creating a sense of communal well-being and collective sharing. The challenge of social inclusion for young people is how to include them in strategic decision-making in relation to public spaces—including decisions over use, decisions over regulation, and decisions over design and planning. In a consumer society, big questions also need to be asked about how best to include the interests, needs, and desires of those without adequate money to 'consume' as such. In other words, the non-consuming citizen—especially young people who are poor and economically marginalised—have requirements for access to and use of public space too. Issues of social inequality can never be far from the surface when discussing policing and social control within urban environments.

As this chapter has demonstrated, the close association between consumption and public space has given rise to such phenomena as 'mall rats', as well as to diverse attempts to regulate how, when, and why young people use public spaces. Understanding the specific experiences of young people, along with the institutional imperatives of the organisations with which they are in contact, sheds light on the tensions and ambiguities of everyday street life. Such understanding simultaneously suggests avenues for the development of alternative ways in which to reconstruct the urban environment and spaces for youth.

REFERENCES

Beattie, N., & Lehmann, G. (1994) 'Special Places: The Nature of Urban Space and Its Significance', in L. Johnson (ed) *Suburban Dreaming: An interdisciplinary approach to Australian cities.* Geelong: Deakin University Press.

Bilchik, S. (1996) *Curfew: An answer to juvenile delinquency and victimization?* Washington, DC: Office of Juvenile Justice and Delinquency Prevention.

Blagg, H., & Wilkie, M. (1995) *Young People & Police Powers*. Sydney: Australian Youth Foundation.

Bloch, P., Ridgway, N., & Dawson, S. (1994) 'The Shopping Mall as Consumer Habitat', *Journal of Retailing*, 70(1): 23–42.

Bocock, R. (1993) *Consumption*. London: Routledge.

Brown, D., Farrier, D., Egger, S. & McNamara, L. (2001) *Criminal Laws: Materials and Commentary on Criminal Law and Process in New South Wales*. Sydney: The Federation Press.

Bruce, J. (1997) *Crime Prevention in a Suburban Shopping Centre: An Analysis of Young People's Use of the Chadstone Shopping Centre*. Honours Thesis, Department of Criminology, University of Melbourne.

Castells, M. (1989) *The Informational City: Informal Technology, Economic Restructuring, and the Urban-Regional Process*. Oxford: Blackwell.

Challenger, D. (1997) *The Launceston Mall*, Corporate Security and Loss Prevention Paper, Coles Meyer Limited. Launceston: Coles Myer.

Chatterton, P., & Hollands, R. (2003) *Urban Nightscapes: Youth Cultures, Pleasure Spaces and Corporate Power*. London: Routledge.

Cohen, P. (1979) 'Policing the Working-Class City', in B. Fine et al. (eds) *Capitalism and the Rule of Law*. London: Hutchinson.

Crane, P. (2000) 'Young People and Public Space: Developing Inclusive Policy and Practice', *Scottish Youth Issues Journal*, 1(1): 105–24.

Crane, P., & Marston, G. (1999) *The Myer Centre Youth Protocol: A Summary*. Brisbane: Brisbane City Council.

Cunneen, C., & White, R. (2002) *Juvenile Justice: Youth and Crime in Australia*. Melbourne: Oxford University Press.

Davies, J. (1995) 'Less Mickey Mouse, More Dirty Harry: Property, Policing and the Postmodern Metropolis', *Polemic*, 5(2): 63–69.

Davis, M. (1990) *City of Quartz: Excavating the Future in Los Angeles*. London: Vintage.

Dixon, D. (1998) 'Broken Windows, Zero Tolerance, and the New York Miracle', *Current Issues in Criminal Justice*, 10(1): 96–106.

Ellis, M. (1987) *The Shopping Centre as a Public Place: The Public Use of Private Property*. Masters Thesis, School of Urban Planning, McGill University, Montreal.

Felson, M. (1987) 'Routine Activities and Crime Prevention in the Developing Metropolis', *Criminology*, 25(4): 911–31.

Finch, L. (1993) 'On the Streets: Working Class Youth Culture in the Nineteenth Century', in R. White (ed) *Youth Subcultures: Theory, History and the Australian Experience*. Hobart: National Clearinghouse for Youth Studies.

Finnane, M. (1994) 'Larrikins, Delinquents and Cops: Police and Young People in Australian History', in R. White & C. Alder (eds) *The Police and Young People in Australia*. Melbourne: Cambridge University Press.

Gregory, R., & Hunter, B. (1995) *The Macro Economy and the Growth of Ghettos and Urban Poverty in Australia*. Canberra: Discussion Paper No. 325, Centre for Economic Policy Research, Australian National University.

Harvey, D. (1990) *The Condition of Postmodernity: An Inquiry into the Origins of Cultural Change.* Oxford: Blackwell.

Hayward, K. (2002) 'The Vilification and Pleasures of Youthful Transgression', in J. Muncie, G. Hughes, & E. McLaughlin (eds) *Youth Justice: Critical Readings.* London: Sage.

Hogg, R., & Golder, H. (1987) 'Policing Sydney in the Late Nineteenth Century', in M. Finnane (ed) *Policing in Australia: Historical Perspectives.* Sydney: New South Wales University Press.

Johnson, L. (1994) 'The postmodern Australian city', in L. Johnson (ed) *Suburban Dreaming: An interdisciplinary approach to Australian cities.* Geelong: Deakin University Press.

Katznelson, I. (1993) *Marxism and the City.* Oxford: Clarendon Press.

Lynch, M., & Ogilvie, E. (1999) 'Access to Amenities: The Issue of Ownership', *Youth Studies Australia,* 18(4): 17–21.

Males, M. (1996). *The Scapegoat Generation: America's War on Adolescents.* Maine: Common Courage Press.

Malone, K. (1999) 'Growing Up in Cities as a Model of Participatory Planning and 'Place-Making' with Young People', *Youth Studies Australia,* 18(2): 17–23.

Malone, K., & Hasluck, L. (1998) 'Geographies of Exclusion: Young People's Perceptions and Use of Public Space', *Family Matters,* No. 49: 20–26.

———. (2002) 'Australian Youth: Aliens in a Suburban Environment', in L. Chawla (ed) *Growing Up in an Urbanising World.* London: Earthscan.

McDonald, K. (1999) *Struggles for Subjectivity: Identity, Action and Youth Experience.* Cambridge: Cambridge University Press.

Meucci, S., & Redmon, J. (1997) 'Safe Spaces: California Children Enter a Policy Debate', *Social Justice,* 24(3): 139–51.

Morgan, M., Pudsey, J., & Roach Anleu, S. (1997) *Perceptions of Safety in the Hindley Street Area: A Research Report Prepared for the City of Adelaide.* Adelaide: Sociology Department, Flinders University of South Australia.

Murray, G. (1995) 'The Authoritarian Exclusion of Young People from the Public Domain—Prevention or Provocation?' Paper presented at the Youth and Community Preventing Crime Conference, Brisbane, 27–28 September.

Murray, J. (1973) *Larrikins: 19th Century Outrage.* Melbourne: Landsdowne Press.

Peel, M. (1996) 'Governing the Urban Future', *Australian Rationalist,* No. 40: 15–22.

Presdee, M. (2000) *Cultural Criminology and the Carnival of Crime.* London: Routledge.

Salvadori, I. (1997) 'A Dragon in the Neighbourhood: City Planning with Children in Milan, Italy', *Social Justice,* 24(3): 192–202.

Sandercock, L. (1997) 'From Main Street to Fortress: The Future of Malls as Public Spaces —OR—"Shut Up and Shop" ', *Just Policy,* No. 9: 27–34.

Santos, J. (2001) 'Down on the Corner: An Analysis of Gang-Related Anti-Loitering Laws', *Cardozo Law Review,* No. 22: 269–314.

Sassen, S. (1993) 'Rebuilding the Global City: Economy, Ethnicity and Space', *Social Justice,* 20(3&4): 32–50.

Schissel, B. (1997) *Blaming Children: Youth Crime, Moral Panics and the Politics of Hate.* Halifax: Fernwood Publishing.

Simpson, B., & Simpson, C. (1993) 'The Use of Curfews to Control Juvenile Offending in

Australia: Managing Crime or Wasting Time?', *Current Issues in Criminal Justice*, 5(2): 184–99.

Snow, D. (1999) 'Skateboarders, streets and style', in R. White (ed) *Australian Youth Subcultures: On the Margins and in the Mainstream*. Hobart: Australian Clearinghouse for Youth Studies.

Spearritt, P. (1994) 'I Shop, Therefore I Am', in L. Johnson (ed) *Suburban Dreaming: An Interdisciplinary Approach to Australian Cities*. Geelong: Deakin University Press.

Stilwell, F. (1993) *Reshaping Australia: Urban Problems and Policies*. Sydney: Pluto.

Trench, S., Tanner, O., & Tiesdell, S. (1992) 'Safer Cities for Women: Perceived Risks and Planning Measures', *Town Planning Review*, 63(3): 279–95.

Troy, P. (ed) (1995) *Australian Cities: Issues, Strategies and Policies for Urban Australia in the 1990s*. Melbourne: Cambridge University Press.

Walmsley, D., & Weinand, H. (1997) 'Well-Being and Settlement Type', *Urban Policy and Research*, 15(1): 43–50.

Walsh, C. (2002) 'Curfews: No More Hanging Around', *Youth Justice*, 2(2): 70–81.

Walsh, T. (2004) 'Who is the "Public", in "Public Space"? A Queensland perspective on poverty, homelessness and vagrancy', *Alternative Law Journal*, 29(2): 81–86.

White, R. (1994) 'Street Life: Police Practices and Youth Behaviour' in R. White & C. Alder (eds) *The Police and Young People in Australia*. Melbourne: Cambridge University Press.

———. (1996) 'No-Go in the Fortress City: Young People, Inequality and Space', *Urban Policy and Research*, 14(1): 37–50.

———. (1998) 'Curtailing Youth: A Critique of Coercive Crime Prevention', *Crime Prevention Studies*, No. 9: 93–113.

———. (1999) *Hanging Out: Negotiating Young People's Use of Public Space*. Canberra: National Campaign Against Violence and Crime.

White, R., with Aumair, M., Harris, A., & McDonnell, L. (1997) *Any Which Way You Can: Youth Livelihoods, Community Resources and Crime*. Sydney: Australian Youth Foundation.

White, R., Kosky, B., & Kosky, M. (2001*) MCS Shopping Centre Youth Project: A Youth-Friendly Approach to Shopping Centre Management*. Hobart: Australian Clearinghouse for Youth Studies.

White, R., & Sutton, A. (1995) 'Crime Prevention, Urban Space and Social Exclusion', *Australian and New Zealand Journal of Sociology*, 31(1): 82–99.

———. (2001) 'Social Planning for Mall Redevelopment: An Australian Case-Study', *Local Environment*, 6(1): 65–80.

White, R., & Wyn, J. (2004) *Youth and Society: Exploring the Social Dynamics of Youth Experience*. Melbourne: Oxford University Press.

Wilson, W.J. (1996) *When Work Disappears*. New York: Knopf.

Wooden, F. (1997) Youth Access Audit: Six Month Progress Report. Melbourne: Shire of Melton.

Worpole, K., & Greenhalgh, L. (1996) *The Freedom of the City*. London: Demos.

Youth Action and Policy Association NSW (1997) *No Standing: Young People and Community Space Project Research Report*. Sydney: YAPA.

IV

Contradictions of Youth Empowerment:
Rights and International Law

Chapters in the preceding sections of this book have focused on the ways in which laws and governing institutions impinge upon, control, and even punish young people—and how youth challenge, resist, and try to avoid these laws and institutions. In this final section, the constituent chapters examine what, at least on the surface, appears to be the opposite phenomena: the use of laws and institutions to protect, grant rights, and empower young people.

We remark that this is an opposite phenomenon "on the surface" because the legal discourse and advocacy related to the rights of children and youth draw from the same ambiguous and even contradictory wells that inform debates on juvenile justice and the merits of punishing young people for crimes or misbehaviors. For example, both empowering and punitive perspectives unavoidably are confronted with making claims about what constitutes the biological age that divides youth and adulthood, and the kinds of competencies (and thus the needs for protection) that are attached to issues of social or criminal "responsibility." Their parallel appearance in the 1990s are global processes inflected by a wide range of influences in most countries across the globe—not least national legal frameworks and cultures, but also perceptions and realities of everything from youth criminality and underage soldiering to child labor and child abuse. If, as some of the authors in this volume have argued, the criminalizing of young people is tied to the global spread of *neoliberal* economic and social policies, then the equally expansive discourse on youth and children's rights is no less tied to older, *liberal* ideologies. And, one might argue, these opposing ideological frames share an emphasis on individualism and universalism that entice and repel societies outside "the West," but also engender divisions within it.

Indeed, it could be said that an *international* language and framework of rights has arisen at a moment when *national* systems of social welfare and juvenile protection have broken down. It is this seemingly inevitable focus on the rights of young people, and the contradictory effects of this emphasis, that the authors in part IV innovatively address.

Elizabeth Heger Boyle, Trina Smith, and Katja Guenther provide a comprehensive survey of twentieth-century international legal treaties relevant to the lives and legal standing of young people. Thus, in one sense, they take what might be called a "global" perspective. At the same time, a key thrust of their chapter is that the rarified domains within which international law is developed and extended through the agreement of nation-states is also a "local" space in which particular Western notions of childhood and youth (themselves subject to change) are universalized. The authors trace the emergence of the child as a global object of legal thought throughout the twentieth century, describing how the child has become a modern *individual*. In their conclusion, the authors point to the limits of strategies for empowering young people through the institution of international treaties, especially in the face of the huge socioeconomic disparities across and within states that human rights approaches are rarely able to address.

The following two chapters, drawing on extended field research in Brazil and Nigeria, trace in detail the complex global-local interactions that shape attempts to extend universal rights to children and youth. John A. Guidry analyzes the forces behind the introduction of Brazil's Statute of the Child and Adolescent (ECA), the institutional mechanisms established for its implementation, and the successes and limits of the law as an instrument for nurturing and protecting Brazil's under-18 population. The ECA emerged as part of a range of initiatives in the areas of social policy and citizenship that drove Brazil's democratization movement in the 1980s. It was adopted in 1990, one year after the UN Convention on the Rights of the Child (CRC) was promulgated by the UN. Guidry argues that Brazilian participation in the global discussions helped shaped the CRC, thus "insert[ing] Brazil's local conditions . . . into the globalized conversation around children."

In the final chapter, Annie Bunting and Sally Engle Merry present the very different case of efforts to end "child marriage" in northern Nigeria, where parents often promise their daughters in their early teens to adult men. Interestingly, these efforts have involved much greater direct intervention by international advocacy groups than the Brazilian experience described by Guidry, and they have had relatively minimal impact thus far in affecting local practices. Indeed, the authors' narrative traces shifts in emphasis from children's and women's rights to health issues in order to make their case. This has occurred, in no small part, because the individualizing and universalizing rights discourses did not resonate with local culture (or, alternatively, the practices were seen as already part of Islamic traditions). Nor did it serve as an unambiguously positive resource for local women's activists with local social bases of support within northern Nigerian society. The "problem" of early marriage is a problem for different actors who hold different reasons. Bunting and Merry portray a complex ideological and organizational field in which there are important differences within the range of local activists as well as between them and international advocacy groups. Like the other chapters in this section, they call attention to the kinds of conditions that legal advocacy does not address directly. Importantly, they also note that changes in these conditions will be required in order for such rights-based approaches to have greater effect.

9

The Rise of the Child as an Individual in Global Society

ELIZABETH HEGER BOYLE, TRINA SMITH,
AND KATJA GUENTHER

Children provide a critical vantage point from which to explore nation-state power in the international system. Children are quintessentially local. They represent every community's most important source of cultural reproduction. Because of their inexperience and dependency, they are unlikely to participate directly in global networks, at least in their pre-teen years. When considered from the vantage of global forces, *child* is not intrinsically resonant across cultures. In fact, one might imagine the opposite. Sheltered because of their perceived vulnerability, children around the world might be expected to live radically different lives and take for granted radically different cultural assumptions. Yet recent trends in international law essentialize childhood and emphasize the commonalities among all children. Social scientists have never before studied children from a global perspective. The fact that such a study is now possible and even desirable is itself evidence of major transformations in the conception of the child. We think such a study will uncover even more than a redefinition of children—we expect to find fundamental shifts in global power relations as well.

In this chapter, we choose to study international law relating to children because law is a statement of aspirations and reflects what a society wants to be. International law is particularly interesting because its emergence coincides with the emergence of a perceived "global" community with a particular set of values. We view international treaties to determine whether the power to shape childhood and control youth has shifted over the course of the twentieth century. We are not referring simply to the impact of global capitalism and the attempt to shield children from it, but also to the incorporation of children into global cultural trends. Is there something unique about children that motivates them to fight for rights internationally? Or are children's rights simply the latest "discovery" in a path-dependent process of globalization? Have nation-states surrendered the authority to govern their youth or have they gained more power in this realm? How has the power of international actors and youth themselves changed over the same period?

To date, international law makes no distinction between *children* and *youth*. For that reason, we use these terms interchangeably. This chapter is divided into five sections. First, we discuss the history of youth, globalization, and international law. Next, we describe our methodology. We then turn to an analysis of international conventions and declarations relating to children. The first analytic section focuses on the power dynamics between youth, family, and the state. The second analytic section focuses on power dynamics between nation-states, and between international organizations and nation-states, with respect to youth and family policies. Finally, in the concluding section of the chapter, we elaborate the central conclusions suggested by our analysis.

Specifically, we find that power relations in the regulation of children in the twentieth century are characterized by two related forces: individualism and universalism. Individualism causes individuals to be treated as more "real" and important than relationships or collective actors (families; nation-states). With respect to children, global norms over time increasingly emphasize that families should provide support and love to their individual members and that states are required to take the interests of all of their citizens, including youth, into account when formulating policy.

Consider, for example, the case of children voting. Children's voting, if widely adopted, would indicate that families are losing authority over youth. It would mean that parents cannot act on their children's behalf in electing public officials. Searching the Internet, one can find dozens of websites supporting the idea that children should have the right to vote. At the first Social Science Research Council meeting on Youth, Globalization, and Law, Geraldine Van Bueren, a human rights activist, discussed the global effort to extend the franchise to children. She noted that children in many parts of the world were already voting. She argued that denying children the vote because of their "irrationality" mirrored the explanation for denying women the right to vote a century earlier. The fact that a discourse of child voting is even possible now, when it would have been impossible only a century ago, is part of the expanding reach of individualism over the course of the twentieth century.

In the social contract that Rousseau (1974 [1763]) imagined, all family members were represented by the male head of household. Only men voted—to have other family members vote would have been seen as redundant as well as irresponsible. More recently and still the dominant view, only adults need to vote—children are less able to ascertain their interests and thus their parents vote on their behalf. The recent move to extend the franchise to children takes individualism a step further. It may signal a move to a world where no one can legitimately speak on anyone else's behalf. Every individual ought to speak only for him- or herself. In contrast to individualism, which gains ground, we find that global norms about individual loyalty and commitment to families, states, or communities are rarely codified into international law.

Universalism also became a dominant theme of international youth law by the end of the twentieth century. This is the idea that a child "here" is essentially the same as a child "there," and every child is entitled to similar things—similar rights, similar protections from unequal power relations in the family. By its very existence, international law lays the framework for the universal application of certain principles—a framework that would have been inconceivable only a few centuries ago. The universalization of norms standardizes expectations for nation-states, reducing their autonomy. Thus, our findings suggest that states lose some freedom to be unique and to be distinct from all other states, but generally they gain more authority to regulate their populations. Our findings also indicate that youth mobilization emerges not from the attributes of youth themselves, but rather as part of broader trends globalizing particular cultural assumptions. Finally, in assuming similarities across individuals and states, universalism directs attention away from fundamental and important differences in economic resources. Until the injustices of the global economic order are addressed, extending "rights" will not combat children's true vulnerability.

BACKGROUND

Youth is a social construction. Phillippe Ariès (1962), in his famous study of the history of childhood, concluded that at an earlier time in Europe children were simply little adults. Childhood and adulthood were not easily distinguishable. Others have demonstrated that there is no necessary connection between physical childhood, that is, the physical ability to reproduce, and the period of dependence on one's parents. For example, Michael Mitteraurer (1992: 3) documents that in some parts of Europe menarche occurred on average four years earlier for girls in the late 1900s than it did in the late 1800s. (This was related to improvements in diet and overall health.) Nevertheless, girls in the late 1900s were entering the labor market, moving out of their parents' household, and getting married *later* than their counterparts a century earlier. Likewise, many different ideas of childhood exist simultaneously in the contemporary world. Europeans tend to enforce a socially important separation of childhood from adulthood by imposing a long period of dependence on adolescents (Myers 2001). During adolescence, children in these countries are generally discouraged from participating in many "adult" concerns, such as the economic maintenance of the family. Some other societies, in contrast, intermingle childhood and adulthood by equipping their children to play mature roles early on, stressing family unity and solidarity, and looking to children for contributions to the family livelihood (Myers 2001; see also Boyden 1997). These examples demonstrate that there is no universal categorization of children, youth, and adults that transcends time and place.

Just as there is no universal definition of youth, there is also no universal understanding of the appropriate relationship between children, families, and the state. Current Western thinking about these relationships emerged out of the Enlightenment. Philosophers from this era imagined only an indirect relationship between children and the state, a relationship that was necessarily mediated by fathers (Worsfold 1974). One of the earliest Enlightenment philosophers, Thomas Hobbes, saw only adult men lending their forces to the sovereign (Gauthier 1965). Hobbes expected children to lend whatever support they could to their fathers, out of indebtedness and fear. The primary goal of childrearing for Hobbes was ensuring submission. Jean-Jacque Rousseau and John Locke, in contrast, believed the primary object of childrearing was to develop a child's conscience and self-governance so that the child would mature into a thoughtful political participant (Worsfold 1974). Rather than fear, the relationship between parents and children was seen to be rooted in love. Neither of these two men saw the rights of family members as potentially contradictory.

John Stuart Mill (1963) agreed with earlier Western philosophers that children should be excluded from the public sphere. However, his philosophy on children differed in at least two ways from earlier writers. First, he elaborated the obligations of parents to their children. He believed that each generation had a responsibility to improve the next generation. Further, he explicitly addressed the angst of youth, arguing that it disqualified youth from political participation:

> The uncultivated cannot be competent judges of cultivation. Those who most need to be made wiser and better usually desire it the least, and if they desired it, would be incapable of finding the way to it by their own lights. (207)

Mill is acknowledging that parents and children sometimes have different interests. In his view, the more "cultivated"—that is, the parent—should have the final word. Although Mill did not endorse child rights, central tenets of the child rights movement—that families should be more egalitarian and that parents and children have independent interests—emerge in his philosophy. In sum, the foundation for children's rights discourse within international organizations is rooted in a relatively recent and Western articulation of state, family, and child relations.

The nation-state is also a social construction, and, like the child rights movement, has its roots in the Enlightenment. The modern state is expected to embody the cherished values, preferences, and goals of its citizens (see, e.g., Carothers 1999). This assumption underlies its legitimacy (Onuf 1995). However, extra-national pressures can undermine state actors' willingness and ability to respond to local constituents (Boyle 2002). Given the serious consequences, it is no surprise that social scientists have turned to the question of whether globalization is stripping away state authority by limiting states' ability to respond to local interests. In the financial sphere, most scholars agree that states cannot adequately regulate increasingly global capital (contrast Hirst and Thompson 1996 with Wade 1996).

In the cultural sphere, things are less clear. Countries ratify international treaties for a variety of reasons (Merry 2003). For example, world polity theorists have demonstrated that nation-states adopt policies, laws, and structures not because they need them or they are forced to have them, but because the policies promoted by international actors become a more important basis for nation-state legitimacy than local interests (Boyle 2002; Frank, Hironaka, and Schofer 2000; Barrett and Frank 1998). These international policies are particularly powerful when they are "institutionalized," meaning that any attempt to reject them reflects poorly on the one doing the rejecting *rather* than on the belief or concept itself (see Boyle 2002). This is certainly true of international human rights, where those who question the doctrine are typically labeled as selfish, oppressive, fascist, patriarchal, backward, and so on. Viewing these trends, Malcolm Waters (2001) argues that the rise of international institutions attenuates the state (see also Levitt 1983; Omae 1990; Rodrik 1997). On the other hand, John W. Meyer argues that globalization increases the power of nation-states by solidifying their position as leading global actors. Nation-states are at the forefront of identifying and managing problems on behalf of their societies (see also Panitch 1996: 84–86; Poulantzas 1975: 73). Our analysis sheds light on this debate.

Power is central to our analysis of the relationship between youth, the state, and the international system. We believe that a zero sum view of power cannot adequately capture the complex nature of shifts in relationship among these actors. Power is relational, and assessments of power must be broadly contextualized. It is plausible that an actor could gain power with respect to one group while simultaneously losing power to another group. For example, children could gain more power in relationships with their parents but have less power against a state. Likewise, an actor can gain one type of power (e.g., political access) but lose another type of power (e.g., the right to free healthcare). Furthermore, individuals are not the only power-holders. Groups, relationships, institutions, and history, among others, also exert power.

Because law is a statement of aspirations rather than an outline of realistic goals, international law often tackles problems that it cannot actually solve. We therefore recognize a disjuncture between law and action. Simply because an international convention *says* that children have more power in families does not make it so! This does not mean, however, that law carries no weight. International conventions do have an effect. They become the basis for the distribution of resources and the allocation of personnel—countries that have ratified the conventions get priority in the allocation of resources (Boyle 2002).

Many countries fund programs more with resources from international orga-nizations than from their own national revenue streams (see, e.g., Silliman 1999). For these countries, acquiescing to global initiatives is an essential pre-requisite for funding even basic services. This incentive structure makes it diffi-cult for such countries to reject global initiatives. Nevertheless, much is read · into states' willingness to ratify international conventions and otherwise go along with the initiatives of international organizations: their acquiescence is used as evidence of global consensus (cf. Edelman, Uggen, and Erlanger 1999). For this and other reasons, in the long run, more and more people take for granted the appropriateness of the ideals promoted by international documents.

INTERNATIONAL TREATIES RELATING TO YOUTH: DATA AND METHODS

To answer our questions about authority over youth in the twentieth century, we analyze international laws relating to youth. By *international law*, we mean the rules of conduct that direct states in their relations with other states, with their citizens, or with other individuals or organizations. Because they are linked into the universalistic discourse of international institutions, interna-tional treaties provide excellent empirical evidence to address how changing conceptions of youth correspond with changing autonomy and power rela-tions among actors in the global system.

In order to represent international law accurately, we first reviewed all 45 international and multinational conventions and declarations[1] relating to chil-dren adopted during the twentieth century (see Appendix 9A).[2] We also reviewed over 100 additional treaties from that time period that made passing reference to youth, children, or families. We turned to additional sources to provide context for these formal legal documents. To learn more about the local application of international law, we reviewed selected country reports to the Committee for the Convention on the Rights of the Child (the "Children's Committee") and that Committee's responses to those reports. We selected reports relating to the United Kingdom, Nigeria, and El Salvador because these are countries discussed by other authors in this volume.[3] We traced all refer-ences to families and/or children in the United Nations Yearbooks for each year since the organization was founded. The League of Nations did not have such systematic annual reporting, but we were able to gather a number of reports from that organization on youth and families as well.

Twenty-three of the 45 international treaties on youth emanated from the International Labour Organization (the "ILO"). The ILO's goal is to represent not only governments but also workers and employers. ILO conventions include the earliest child-related treaty from the twentieth century, the Minimum Age (Industry) Convention of 1919 (the "1919 Minimum Age Convention"). The next most common drafter of international law on children was the United Nations (the "UN"), which drafted 12 of the 45 treaties on children. The first of these was the Declaration of the Rights of the Child in 1959, which is the precursor to the better-known Convention on the Rights of the Child of 1989 (the "Children's Convention"). Another important UN convention is the Convention on Consent to Marriage; Minimum Age for Marriage and Registration of Marriages in 1962 (the "Marriage Convention"). In the analysis that follows, we use the 1919 Minimum Age Convention, the Marriage Convention, and the Children's Convention for representative indepth examples. Of the remaining ten international treaties on youth, one was adopted by the League of Nations. The other nine treaties were adopted by regional organizations, such as the Council of Europe, the Organization for African Unity, and the Association of Southeast Asian Nations.

Our review of international law focused on ideals, actors, relationships, and actions. Were universal values promoted? What actors were mentioned? What actors were empowered? With respect to whom were they empowered? Were controls imposed on actors? Who, if anyone, was doing the controlling? What was the nature of the relationships mentioned in each document? Did relationships involve enabling, defining, directing, regulating, intervening, punishing, and so on? Were the actions mentioned symbolic and ambiguous or concrete and specific?

DISCUSSION

Several clear trends emerge in the history of international treaties relating to children. At the beginning of the twentieth century, nations had autonomy over how children within their borders would be treated. At that time, most states left the treatment of children to the discretion of their families. Thus, neither international nor national bureaucracies were actively involved in children's issues early on. With the expansion of the modern welfare state, especially in the West, states became increasingly involved in the regulation of family life. By the end of the twentieth century, international law governed many aspects of children's lives, and states were increasingly subject to international pressure to protect children both within and from the family. Issues that were once considered solely within the purview of national law became universalized. Nations lost autonomy in this process, but gained more authority over families.

STATE AUTHORITY OVER YOUTH AND FAMILY

Over the course of the twentieth century, rhetoric supporting the family remains strong in international law, but specific provisions begin to erode this rhetoric. At the beginning of the century, conventions are more likely to emphasize children's service to their families; by the end of the century, conventions are more likely to emphasize the opposite—families' service to children. The same reversal appears for relations between children and states. Children are granted more autonomy from families and more political power against states over the course of the century. (These empowering reforms are accompanied by increasing responsibility and culpability for youthful misconduct). These changes translate into less family and state power over children. A parallel trend took authority from families and granted it to states: over time conventions allow states to intervene more in family affairs on behalf of children. Thus, power relationships among youth, families, and states were transformed during the century, but the direction of power shifts is varied and complex.

The Family in Rhetoric

Throughout the century, the family continuously received rhetorical support in international documents. Initially, this rhetoric was backed by substance. The League of Nations worked to find homes for World War I orphans and attempted to strengthen families by curbing paternal desertion, eliminating illegitimacy as grounds for state intervention in the family, and providing support for families facing the economic devastation of the Great Depression (Myers 1930; 1933). The League also urged nations to ensure that institutions that cared for orphans and other wards of the state, as well as for delinquents and the developmentally disabled, provide "the normal experience of home and community" in environments modeled on family life (League of Nations 1935/36: 169). As late as 1952, the family was "the natural and fundamental group unit of society," (UDHR, Article 16(3)) and state law was aligned with family interests: "No one shall be subjected to arbitrary interference with his [*sic*] . . . family. . . . Everyone has the right to the protection of the law against such interference or attacks" (UDHR, Article 12).

In the latter half of the twentieth century, however, rhetoric exalting the family was often accompanied by language suggesting that family power needed to be checked. In 1953, a convention suggested that family rights had to be balanced against other considerations:

1. Everyone has the right to respect for his [*sic*] private and family life . . .
2. There shall be no interference by a public authority with the exercise of this right *except such as is in accordance with the law and is necessary in a democratic society in the interests of national security, public safety or the economic well-being of the country, for the prevention of disorder or crime, for the protection of health or morals, or for the protection of the rights and freedoms of others* (ECHR, Article 8, emphasis added).

The general rule of family primacy was undercut by a multitude of exceptions.

In 1978, the American Convention on Human Rights went even further in regulating the family. Article 17 of the American Convention granted all men and women the right to marry and raise a family *only if* they met all conditions required by state law, such as minimum age requirements. The Article went on to require states to "take appropriate steps to ensure the equality of rights and the adequate balancing of responsibilities of the spouses as to marriage, during marriage, and in the event of its dissolution." Thus, we see the beginning of state intervention to equalize power relations within families.

Like many international agreements that came before it, the 1989 Children's Convention terms the family the "fundamental group of society." However, a close reading reveals that the Children's Convention is internally inconsistent about the family. It calls for states to "respect the responsibilities, rights and duties of parents . . . to provide, in a manner consistent with the evolving capacities of the child, appropriate direction and guidance in the exercise by the child of the rights recognized in the present Convention." At the same time, it views the family as a threat to children and places standardized limits on parental behavior. For example, it calls on states to intervene on behalf of children in cases of intra-familial abuse and neglect. International law also bans "traditional practices prejudicial to the health of children," such as female genital cutting. These interventions, conducted by the nation-state but mandated by international law, reflect a growing emphasis on families as potential violators of children's rights. This justifies increasing state control over the family. The Children's Convention simultaneously tries to protect and preserve family units *and* allow states to intervene in family life.

By the latter half of the twentieth century, provisions stripping families of some authority over children appear side-by-side with the rhetoric of family importance. Also at this time, conventions increasingly idealized the autonomy, empowerment, and responsibility of youth. To illustrate these points, we turn now to a more in-depth discussion of the 1919 Minimum Age Convention, the 1962 Marriage Convention, and the 1989 Children's Convention.

Youth and Family Authority

The 1919 Minimum Age Convention was the earliest twentieth-century convention relating to children. In it, children are passive subjects requiring protection. The point of the convention is to keep children out of industrial employment. The 1919 Minimum Age Convention had no provisions that would allow states to intervene in family relations. Implicitly, it assumed that children and parents have the same interests. For the most part, families are not mentioned in the treaty at all. In fact, families were specifically exempted from regulation. The only reference to families is as an exception to the application of the treaty: the treaty allows children to be employed in an "undertaking in which only members of the same family are employed"—that is, a family business.

At least two ideas drove this exception. The drafters believed that family employers were less likely to abuse their child employees than nonfamily employers. Thus, unrelated persons needed more regulation than related persons (see Smolin 2000). The second idea was that parents, more than the state, know what is best for their children. If parents have their children work in the family business, it would be inappropriate for the state to second guess that arrangement. This latter idea rests strongly on the idea that there is a private family sphere that the state should respect. At the time the 1919 Minimum Age Convention was written, the family was privileged as inviolable (by the state). Since then, this distinction between public and private spheres has been critiqued and broken down.[4]

Moving forward about 40 years, we next turn to the 1962 UN Marriage Convention. The Marriage Convention received considerable international support, attaining 49 ratifications. In the text of the Marriage Convention, children are still passive subjects who need protection. Two things set the Marriage Convention apart from the 1919 Minimum Age Convention, however. The first is that the Marriage Convention does not assume that parents and children have similar interests. In fact, it seems to assume the opposite. One goal of the Marriage Convention is to prevent parents from arranging their children's marriages. The preamble calls for states to "take all appropriate measures with a view to . . . ensuring . . . complete freedom in the choice of a spouse." The convention promotes the idea that individuals ought to choose their spouses independently of their parents. Implicitly, it suggests that parents will attempt to marry off their children without regard for the children's well-being, and that parents cannot be trusted to act in the best interests of their children.

The Marriage Convention also assumes a stark separation between childhood and adulthood. Marriage is always inappropriate for children. The state (with the backing of the convention) needs to protect children from marriage. But the Marriage Convention also suggests that the moment young men and women cross the threshold of legal majority (14 to 18 years old in most countries), they will be better judges of possible mates than their parents. Children move from a state requiring total protection to a state of total autonomy. More than the earlier Minimum Age Convention, the Marriage Convention emphasizes choice and, implicitly, individual independence.

Under the Marriage Convention, states assume more control over families and families lose some authority over their children. The convention requires families to register their marriages with the state, and allows states to determine whether marriages are appropriate. Thus, it specifically calls for state intervention in "private" family matters.

To round out the picture of the changing relationship between parents and children in international law, we consider one of the most important conventions for children during the last century—the United Nation's Convention on the Rights of the Child. The Children's Convention has been ratified by every country in the world except for the United States and Somalia. In a radical change from earlier conventions, it moves children from passive subjects to active individuals with rights. For example, the Convention grants children the rights of free association and free speech to "express . . . views freely in all matters affecting the child, the views of the child being given due weight in accordance with the age and maturity of the child."

Unlike either the 1919 Minimum Age Convention or the 1962 Marriage Convention, the 1989 Children's Convention explicitly discusses families and their role in ensuring the implementation of the treaty. It is the only one of the three conventions to put specific responsibilities on families. Section 18 declares that "The best interests of the child *will be* [parents'] basic concern" (emphasis added). This declaration implicitly recognizes that children and parents sometimes have different interests and attempts to resolve such conflicts in the children's favor. It does *not* suggest balancing children's interests against the collective family interest. Throughout the document, parents' responsibilities to their children are emphasized. The children's interests come first.

In this convention, the child also emerges as a modern individual— autonomous, agentic, and responsible. Consistent with the individualist ideal, the Children's Convention suggests that it is inappropriate to view families as a convenient amalgamation of individuals linked primarily to the regulation of physical and cultural reproduction; instead, the "true" purpose of every family is to provide support and love for each individual member. For example, in its preamble the Convention states that all children "should grow up in a family environment, in an atmosphere of happiness, love and understanding." And although children are granted freedom of religion in the Children's Convention, there is no requirement that they learn and value their *parents'* religion. In fact, the Convention clearly indicates that children should not be forced to follow the same religion as their parents. It does not require children to serve their families; rather it asks families to serve their children.

Youth and the State

Like many of her power dynamics we are considering in this chapter, the child-state dynamic is rife with the contradictions inherent in the modern state. A review of all international conventions relating to children over the last century confirms that change almost always has moved in the direction of expanding the definition and/or application of individual rights (see Boyle 2002; Boyle and Meyer 1998). At the same time, both the family and children lose some types of power relative to the state.

The treatment of child soldiers in international law illustrates changing power dynamics between children and the state. At the beginning of the century, nations had considerable discretion to engage in war as they liked. Whether and how they involved children in their military engagements was not a matter of international law. Thus, in 1921, the Minimum Age (Sea) Convention, which set the minimum age at which children could be employed on ships, specifically exempted "ships of war" from its requirements. The situation is now reversed. A number of recent conventions, including the ILO's Worst Forms of Child Labor (1999), the Children's Convention (1989), and its Optional Protocol on the Involvement of Children in Military Conflicts (2000), specifically ban the use of children under 18 years old in any military action. The early international conventions gave states the ultimate authority in matters of war—in contrast, the newer conventions give children's interests priority.

Similarly, although older documents encouraged service to the community, this language does not appear in the most recent conventions. The first Declaration on the Rights of the Child, adopted in 1923, had only five provisions. One was that children learn that their "talents must be devoted to the service of [their] fellow men."[5]

The term *fellow men* is ambiguous and could mean all people or primarily fellow citizens. The same term appears in the 1959 Declaration on the Rights of the Child, but in this document, the meaning is clearer. *Fellow men* is there paired with *universal brotherhood*, signifying all people: "He shall be brought up in a spirit of . . . universal brotherhood, and in full consciousness that his energy and talents should be devoted to the service of his fellow men." In contrast, the latest international document of this lineage—the Children's Convention—has no provisions about children's service to their community or nation. There is little concern in the convention with molding children into good citizens or invoking in them pride in their heritage. In fact, things operate the other way around—nations must serve their children.

There has been a move in the United States to punish youth crime more like adult crime. While the United States is exceptional in the extent of its punitiveness (it is the only industrialized country in the world that imposes the death penalty on youth), the rhetoric of instilling responsibility on youth has found some purchase in Europe and Australia as well. Early international conventions were silent about criminal law. In the middle of the century, human rights treaties—such as the Universal Declaration of Human Rights (1952) and the International Covenant on Civil and Political Rights (1978)—established standard expectations for states' enforcement of criminal law. The Children's Convention was the first international convention to explicitly apply these (and other) procedural protections to children. The special procedural justice provisions maintain a stark separation between children and adults. By implying that children are less culpable than adults for crime, these provisions go against the punitive rhetoric common today. Time will tell how this apparent conflict in international principles will ultimately be resolved.

Consistent with the trend away from an emphasis on community, the model of the family that is currently carried by the international system treats the personal fulfillment of *individual* family members as a top priority. In a "proper" family, each person, whether man, woman, or child, should be an equal partner (Meyer et al. 1988). Treating children as individuals first and as family members second protects children to some extent from the consequences of unequal power in the family. By the end of the twentieth century, international law was treating children as independent beings who needed to be empowered to assert their autonomy from their families. States, as the organizations supporting and enforcing children's rights within the family, are likewise empowered.

States are now allowed to intervene in nonfarm family businesses, and they now have the authority to ensure that children reach a particular age before they marry. Provisions such as these erode families' control over their children. The implication, especially in the Children's Convention, is that both the family and the state are responsible for the well-being of children.

In international law today, the state is intended to be perceived as a benevolent, and perhaps even empowering, guardian rather than as a malevolent tyrant. This is obviously problematic in states where children and youth may be political targets of the state. For example, Brazil has been criticized for its treatment of street children, and numerous governments (China and Ethiopia, among others) have responded to student protests with violence over the past several decades. The potential contradiction of being protected by one's persecutor does not appear in the text of international documents. Rather, international treaties require states to provide social security to children and make education compulsory (e.g., the Children's Convention and the 1959 Declaration on the Rights of the Child). Children are empowered to make claims for state intervention on their behalf within the family. States are called upon to intervene in families to prevent intra-familial abuse and neglect. These interventions reveal a growing emphasis on families as potential violators of children's rights and an increase in state control over the family.

Simultaneously, international treaties on children's rights reflect Western valuations of cultural practices and ideologies involving children, such as disciplinary techniques, sexual development, and children's rights to free expression. The international system promotes one particular "universal" standard for all nation-states. We consider the universalizing aspects of globalization in the next section.

INTERNATIONAL INSTITUTIONS AND NATION-STATE AUTHORITY OVER CHILDREN AND FAMILIES

International conventions during the twentieth century increasingly treated children as autonomous individuals. A parallel development was the universality of this perspective—over time, international doctrine on children came to apply to all children in all countries.

Dealing with Cultural Diversity

Countries are marked by dramatic differences in culture (Boyle 2002), resources (Myers 2001), and politics (Matua 2001; Kymlicka 2001), producing widely varying conceptions of children. Even within Europe, the definition, duration, and implications of childhood have undergone a sea change over time. To what extent does international law incorporate the myriad and contradictory instantiations of childhood?

Early in the century there were far fewer international conventions on children than later in the century. This probably indicates an unwillingness or perceived inability to deal with the complexity of childhood in all its forms around the world. International actors did not perceive childhood as a universal or global phenomenon, so there was little point in regulating it internationally. Later this perception changed, so international conventions dealing with children universally were seen as appropriate and necessary.

Our review of international conventions illustrates that their central principles are typically linked to recent Western philosophies of youth, family, and the state. There is no shortage of examples. The Children's Convention requires that families give children a name at birth, but in many cultures families delay naming an infant until a certain ceremony occurs, a sign is received, or a set amount of time passes. Many international conventions ask states to ensure that men and women play an equal role in childrearing.[6] This requirement may not make sense in communities with large households and extended families. In such communities, the household labor is not simply divided between husbands and wives—there are many other actors to consider. Furthermore, the requirement is obviously problematic in households where men and women are segregated for large portions of each day. The requirement also undermines the legitimacy of arrangements in which mother/father roles are purposely distinct (including even some religious communities in the United States). The Children's Convention grants children "freedom of expression" within the family; it bans "traditional practices prejudicial to the health of children," which is interpreted to mean almost exclusively non-Western practices.

Because individuals may object to these foreign childrearing requirements, one wonders to what extent international children's law is actually implemented within countries. To take just one example, contemporary research in

Tanzania suggests that anti-corporal-punishment policies are being implemented at the national level and promoted by NGOs, but they meet with resistance in local communities (Songora 2005). For example, a 72-year-old man from a rural community explained to Fortunata Songora (2005):

> I do not know why the *wazungu* [Europeans] are even telling us now how we should discipline our children. I have been caned and I have seen it working for children. I hear that the *wazungu* discipline their children by telling them to look at the wall or go sit in the corner and it is working. Maybe there is something unique or wrong in their brain. If that was the way I was disciplined I do not know where I would be now. But for the African children, we cane them, and I even think whoever signed [the Children's Convention] on our behalf, there was something wrong with him or he knew he has to do that to please *wazungu* but it will not work in Tanzania.

Statements such as this raise questions about precisely whose societal aspirations are reflected in international law, and whether the goals of international law are truly universal.

International law also tends to adopt the West's stark contrast between childhood and adulthood, with a long period of irresponsibility (termed *adolescence*) between the two. As mentioned earlier, this contrasts with the typical situation in many communities around the world where children take on important household responsibilities as soon as they are able. Country reports to the Children's Committee seem to recognize this and defensively justify their cultural practices in relation to the family. For example, Nigerian representatives, in conversation with the Children's Committee, note that children still do domestic chores in their own homes in Nigeria, as this is part of African culture. The U.K. country reports say nothing about children doing chores in the household. Songora (2005) points out a further difficulty with the Children's Convention's assumptions about adolescence. In Tanzania primary education ends at age 14 with the clear expectation that most students will not continue on to secondary education, but the Children's Convention forbids children from working until they are 16. Here again, we see a disconnect between the provisions of international law and the situations of particular individuals.

Ironically, if there were any childrearing norm that could claim universality, it would be deference to and respect for parents (see, e.g., Mitterauer 1992). Yet, this norm is generally *not* promoted by international conventions. The one telling exception is the Organization of African Unity's Charter on the Rights of the Child. Article 31 of the Charter, which became effective in the last year of the twentieth century, is titled "Responsibilities of Children." It requires each African child:

(a) to work for the cohesion of the family, to respect his parents, superiors and elders at all times and to assist them in case of need;

(b) to serve his national community by placing his physical and intellectual abilities at its service; . . .

(d) to preserve and strengthen African cultural values in his relations with other members of the society, in the spirit of tolerance, dialogue and consultation and to contribute to the moral well-being of society; . . . [and]

(f) to contribute to the best of his abilities, at all times and at all levels, to the promotion and achievement of African Unity.

The fact that the only child's convention that mentions responsibilities is not international, not European, not American, but rather African, seems a clear indication that African culture is underrepresented in documents such as the Children's Convention. Other conventions actually undermine children's deference to parents in some ways, for example by guaranteeing children the right to have a religion different from their parents and promoting children's "free expression" within the family. Substantively, we found that international conventions in the latter part of the twentieth century, while devoting some rhetoric to diversity, are generally Western in their orientation.

Universal Application

The universality of the application of international children's conventions increased over the course of the last century. Initially, international conventions acknowledged state differences and developed separate standards for certain states. For instance, the 1919 Minimum Age Convention, introduced at the height of colonialism, was not universal. The terms of the convention carved out special exceptions for Indian and Japanese children. Although the treaty protected children under 14 in other countries, it provided only for children under 12 in India and Japan. (Japan was a signator; India, a British colony at the time, was not.) Debate over Japan and India did not center on their essential inclusion, but instead on whether they could accept Western European standards (Alcock 1971: 32). There was also debate over how to deal with colonies in general (Alcock 1971). Although some believed that ILO conventions should apply only upon the consent of each country, others objected that this would not be fair to workers in the territories. Ultimately, although colonial authorities were to apply the convention to their colonies, protectorates, and possessions, there were major exceptions to this provision. Specifically, child labor protection did not have to be implemented, or could be modified, if "local conditions" made it "inapplicable." Thus, the Labor Convention established a multi-tier system that allowed some children to be treated one way while other children were treated in a different way.

By mid-century, international children's conventions were universally applicable. In contrast to the earlier ILO convention, the 1962 Marriage Convention coincided with colonialism's fading as a formal global control system. The Marriage Convention assumed that there are universal principles that apply to all children, regardless of the level of development of the country where they live. The idea in the Marriage Convention was to make sure girls in the former colonies had the same advantages—that is, culture—as girls in Europe. It rests on the assumption that children everywhere have the same types of interests and need the same types of protections.

Of course, the Marriage Convention addressed a "harmful" practice that was no longer prevalent in Europe. Therefore, although it theoretically applied to all countries, it did not require all countries to reform. The Children's Convention also discusses harmful traditional practices, and it is evident from the Children's Committee's responses to country reports that this is still aimed at developing nations. Among the countries we studied, the Children's Committee was persistent about eradicating negative cultural practices that inhibit the rights of the child: female genital cutting and early marriage in Nigeria, machismo and gender discrimination in El Salvador. On the other hand, while the problems of conflict in Northern Ireland were mentioned, there seems to be no serious cultural flaws in the United Kingdom that inhibit children's rights.

Thus, the Children's Convention carries on the "universalistic" spirit of the

Marriage Convention while, ironically, targeting primarily poorer countries. It states that everyone is entitled to all the rights and freedoms set forth in the Universal Declaration of Human Rights, and for the first time explicitly includes children in "everyone." Countries can and do make reservations to conventions such as the Children's Convention that limit the applicability of some provisions. These exceptions do not originate in the drafting process, however, and are viewed with hostility by many international activists and the Children's Committee.

Nation-States in the International System

Our findings here illustrate a contradiction in the operation of the transnational system that has become more pronounced in the last 20 years (compare Boyle 2002). On one side, the principle of representative democracy, which is imagined to go hand in hand with the rule of law, is clearly a strived-for ideal. For example, the International Bill of Rights—particularly the International Covenant on Political and Civil Rights—has representative democracy as a centerpiece. Today the UN and many cooperating NGOs put tremendous effort into promoting multiparty systems and regular elections in all countries of the world. However, at the same time that transnational actors ask nation-states to enact representative democracy and take the will of their people into account, those same transnational actors also ask the nation-state to assume certain goals and undertake particular projects that may *or may not* be consistent with local majority opinion. The transnational community goes to great lengths to put democracies into place, but then encourages governments to ignore them if the democratic processes might lead to the "wrong" result— that is, a result that does not reflect the principles promoted by the international system. This contradiction is particularly pronounced in the area of family norms. In this way, nation-states lose power because they lose autonomy.

We believe it is true that nation-states lose autonomy even though later conventions make more explicit references to nation-state discretion than earlier conventions. In fact, recent cases of deference are over relatively insignificant issues. The first several minimum age conventions, for example, identified a specific age under which children could not work (first 14, then 15). Nations had no discretion to change the age. The 1973 Minimum Age Convention, in contrast, gives countries discretion to make the minimum age *older*. In other words, countries can apply protection to more children, but not to fewer children under the 1973 convention. This constrained discretion appears frequently in recent international documents. Although the language sounds deferential to national autonomy, the principles promoted by the international system are actually never compromised.

Economic Globalization

Perhaps one of the most interesting differences in the international conventions is the disappearance of economic actors over time. The 1919 Minimum Age Convention specifically regulated businesses, for example, requiring them to file reports about their laborers. By the time of the Universal Declaration of Human Rights in 1952, rights were awarded but corresponding obligations were not imposed on businesses, states, or other actors. Children's rights included the right to adequate nutrition, housing, recreation, and medical services. The UDHR also gave children the right to free education. However, it was not clear, in that convention or later conventions, against whom children can enforce these rights or what children should do if these rights are not met.

The puzzle continues with the Children's Convention. Its child labor provisions do not mention employers at all. Article 32 of the Convention requires states to recognize the right of children to be "protected from economic exploitation and from performing any work that is likely to be hazardous or to interfere with the child's education, or to be harmful to the child's health or physical, mental, spiritual, moral or social development." Nevertheless, economic actors are conspicuously absent from the Children's Convention. The burden of keeping children from employment is placed first on families and then on states. No part of the burden is placed on employers in the Convention. This is disturbing in itself because employers are centrally complicit in the perpetuation of child labor, but there is also evidence that some international organizations create different standards and grant less autonomy if a country is a developing rather than a developed one (Stryker 1998).

This emphasis on aspirations over feasibility, of course, facilitates the spread of universalism. States with or without resources are assigned responsibility for allocating resources and funding programs. For example, although Article 4 of the Children's Convention requires states to implement the convention "to the maximum extent of their available resources," the Children's Committee indicated to the El Salvador representatives that a lack of economic resources did not justify inadequate implementation. Applying insufficient resources signified El Salvador's negative attitude toward children—not its economic difficulties. Furthermore, families with or without resources are assigned responsibility for providing children with "childhoods." Rather than respond directly to an El Salvadoran representative's point that compulsory education is costly for families, the Committee focused on whether children in El Salvador were given enough time to think about their studies and reflect broadly on important issues. Responsibilities and procedures set forth in the conventions are the same around the world; the ability to implement them is not. Nevertheless, the recent conventions we reviewed provided no remedies for this inequality.

CONCLUSION: YOUTH, GLOBALIZATION, AND LAW

Children, like the rest of the world, are caught up in the culture of globalization. Their needs, rights, and proper upbringing have become generalized and universalized so that all children—regardless of their gender, nationality, or even their parents' preferences—become entitled to similar experiences. Furthermore, children are now socially constructed as modern "individuals." They have individual interests (which spring from deep within), and these interests are privileged over their obligations (which are externally and involuntarily imposed) to their parents, community, religion, nation, and so on. In this construction, a child's duty to respect and obey his or her parents— prevalent in many societies—is assigned less value than the child's own personal fulfillment. Children, as a universalized concept, gain power over the state through international reforms; children, as embedded, contextualized cultural agents, lose power. In other words, children, like other individuals, cannot make legitimate claims to cultural uniqueness (particularly if their culture is illiberal). Children are caught up in the general trends of universalism and individualism that are inherent in modern globalization.

Our analysis of children's treaties has uncovered fundamental contradictions in the aspirations and operation of international law regarding youth. International law states that each family—rather than the state or an international organization—has the ultimate authority over its children. At the same time, international law dictates significant requirements on parents in their dealings with their children.

Likewise, international law requires that each state strive to represent the unique interests of its people, but the clear expectation of international organizations is that every state should have similar policies and government structures with respect to children and families. Former colonies gained power along with independence. None were signatories to the 1919 Minimum Age Convention. All are signatories to the Children's Convention. The inherently biased multi-tier system is gone. However, the local cultures of colonies were denigrated under colonialism and continue to be denigrated today. This was apparent in the Marriage Convention's banning of arranged marriages; it also exists in a more subtle form in the Children's Convention. The idea that individuals exist to *serve* their families or that families' primary function is cultural reproduction is excluded from the discourse. The expansion of individual rights has undercut these conceptions of family.

From the beginning, nation-states were linked into the international system in ways that outweigh their attachment to local citizenry. New states with new governments looked to the international system for resources and legitimacy. The result was a convergence around particular forms and beliefs. Among the most important universal principles to emerge during the twentieth century were the principles that children are autonomous and efficacious individuals and that states need to protect children from their families. Protecting children from families empowers states and international actors because it requires intervention. Ultimately, this leads to the conclusion that the modern nation-state has "less autonomy than earlier but it clearly has more to do" (Meyer et al. 1997: 157).

Finally, international human rights conventions, including those relating to children, do not acknowledge the crippling shortage of resources in some countries; nor by the end of the century do they hold economic actors accountable for undermining the enforcement of rights (see also Fernando 2001). International treaties are generally silent on economic differences that can greatly inhibit their equal implementation.

Appendix 9A. List of Conventions and Declarations Relating
to Children from the Twentieth Century

Year	Title	Organization	Ratifications/ Accessions (if applicable)
1919	Maternity Protection Convention	ILO	33
1919	Minimum Age (Industry) Convention	ILO	72
1919	Night Work of Young Persons (Industry) Convention	ILO	59
1920	Minimum Age (Sea) Convention	ILO	53
1921	Medical Examination of Young Persons (Sea) Convention	ILO	81
1921	Minimum Age (Agriculture) Convention	ILO	55
1921	Minimum Age (Trimmers and Strokers) Convention	ILO	69
1923	Declaration of Geneva (Declaration of the Rights of the Child)	LON[a]	—
1932	Minimum Age (Non-Industrial Employment) Convention	ILO	25
1936	Minimum Age (Sea) Convention (Revised)	ILO	51
1937	Minimum Age (Industry) Convention (Revised)	ILO	36
1937	Minimum Age (Non-Industrial Employment) Convention (Revised)	ILO	11
1946	Medical Examination of Young Persons (Industry) Convention	ILO	43
1946	Medical Examination of Young Persons (Non-Industrial Occupations) Convention	ILO	39
1946	Night Work of Young Persons (Non-Industrial Occupations) Convention	ILO	20
1948	Night Work of Young Persons (Industry) Convention (Revised)	ILO	50
1952	Maternity Protection Convention (Revised)	ILO	40
1956	Convention on the Law Applicable to Maintenance Towards Children	Hague Conference	16[b]
1959	Declaration on the Rights of the Child	UN	—
1959	Minimum Age (Fishermen) Convention	ILO	29
1962	Convention on Consent to Marriage; Minimum Age for Marriage and Registration of Marriages	UN	49
1965	Declaration on the Promotion among Youth of the Ideals of Peace, Mutual Respect, and Understanding Between Peoples	UN	—
1965	Medical Examination of Young Persons (Underground Work) Convention	ILO	41
1965	Minimum Age (Underground Work) Convention	ILO	41
1967	European Convention on the Adoption of Children	Council of Europe	17
1973	Minimum Age Convention	ILO	130
1974	Declaration on the Protection of Women and Children in Emergency and Armed Conflict	UN	—
1975	European Convention on the Legal Status of Children Born Out of Wedlock	Council of Europe	19

(continued)

Year	Title	Organization	Ratifications/ Accessions (if applicable)
1980	Convention on the Civil Aspects of Child Abduction	Hague Conference	74[c]
1981	Workers with Family Responsibilities Convention	ILO	34
1983	Declaration of Principles to Strengthening ASEAN Collaboration on Youth	ASEAN	—
1985	United Nations Standard Minimum Rules for the Administration of Juvenile Justice (The Beijing Rules)	UN	—
1986	Declaration of Social and Legal Principles Relating to the Protection and Welfare of Children, with Special Reference to Foster Placement and Adoption Nationally and Internationally	UN	—
1989	Convention on the Rights of the Child	UN	191
1990	African Charter on the Rights of the Child	OAU	21
1990	United Nations Guidelines for the Prevention of Juvenile Delinquency (The Riyadh Guidelines)	UN	—
1990	United Nations Rules for the Protection of Juveniles Deprived of Their Liberty	UN	—
1992	Plight of Street Children	UN	—
1993	Convention on Protection of Children and Cooperation of Intercountry Adoption	Hague Conference	53
1997	Kuala Lumpur Agenda on ASEAN Youth Development	ASEAN	—
1999	Worst Forms Child Labor Convention	ILO	143
2000	Maternity Protection Convention (Revised)	ILO	4
2000	Optional Protocol to the Convention on the Rights of the Child on the Involvement of Children in Armed Conflicts	UN	52
2000	Optional Protocol to the Convention on the Rights of the Child on the Sale of Children, Child Prostitution and Child Pornography	UN	50
2000	Yangon 2000 Declaration on Preparing ASEAN Youth for the Challenges of Globalisation	ASEAN	—

NOTES: a. Originally proposed by Save the Children's Alliance and adopted by League of Nations; b. This number represents signatories rather than ratifications/accessions; c. This number represents contracting states rather than ratifications/accessions.

ENDNOTES

1. *Conventions* are binding; *declarations* are nonbinding statements of aspirations.

2. To find all of the relevant international documents, we began with a general Internet search. This yielded a number of lists and repositories of international conventions and declarations relating to youth, children, and the family. We also used the United Nations treaty database and the University of Minnesota Human Rights Library database. Finally, we reviewed the websites of intergovernmental organizations such as the Organization for African Unity and the European Union.

3. Brazil has not filed any country reports with the Children's Committee.

4. In 1973, the 1919 Minimum Age Convention was superceded. Unlike the 1919 convention, the 1973 Minimum Age Convention did not generally exempt family businesses from its coverage. States can opt to exclude families, and small-scale family farms that do not hire outside workers continue to be exempt from coverage. Smolin (2000) discusses how the anti-child labor movement would have liked to include even the small-farm children within the convention.

5. The gender bias in language in this paragraph appeared in the original texts.

6. The origins of this idea, at least in its international law sense, can be traced back to a shift in Western philosophy occurring between the writings of Hobbes and Locke.

REFERENCES

Alcock, Antony. 1971. *History of the International Labour Organisation.* New York: Macmillan Press Ltd.

Ariès, Philippe. 1962. *Centuries of Childhood: A Social History of Family Life.* Translated by Robert Baldick. New York: Knopf.

Barrett, Deborah, and David John Frank. 1998. "Population Control for National Development: From World Discourse to National Policies." Pp. 198–221 in *Constructing World Culture: International Nongovernmental Organizations since 1875,* edited by John Boli and George M. Thomas. Stanford: Stanford University Press.

Berkovitch, Nitza. "The Emergence and Transformation of the International Women's Movement." Pp. 100–26 in *Constructing World Culture: International Nongovernmental Organizations since 1875,* edited by John Boli and George M. Thomas. Stanford: Stanford University Press, 1999.

Boyden, Jo. 1997. "Childhood and the Policy Makers: A Comparative Perspective on the Globalization of Childhood." Pp. 190–229 in *Constructing and Reconstructing Childhood,* edited by Allison James and Alan Prout. London: Falmer Press.

Boyle, Elizabeth Heger. 2002. *Female Genital Cutting: Cultural Conflict in the Global Community.* Baltimore: Johns Hopkins University Press.

Boyle, Elizabeth Heger, and John W. Meyer. 1998. "Modern Law as a Secularized and Global Model: Implications for the Sociology of Law," *Soziale Welt* 49: 275–94.

Carothers, Thomas. 1999. *Aiding Democracy Abroad: The Learning Curve.* Washington, DC: Carnegie Endowment for International Peace.

Cunningham, Hugh. 1991. *The Children of the Poor: Representations of Childhood since the Seventeenth Century.* Oxford: Blackwell Publishing.

Edelman, Lauren, Christopher Uggen, and Howard Erlanger. 1999. "The Endogeneity of Legal Regulation: Grievance Procedures as Rational Myth," *American Journal of Sociology* 105: 406–54.

Fernando, Jude L. 2001. "Children's Rights: Beyond the Impasse," *Annals of the American Academy of Political and Social Science* 575: 8–24.

Frank, David John, Ann Hironaka, and Evan Schofer. 2000. "The Nation-State and the Environment over the Twentieth Century," *American Sociological Review* 65: 96–116.

Freeman, M. D. A.1983. *The Rights and Wrongs of Children.* Dover: Frances Pinter Publishers.

Garrett, William. 1994. "Religio-Cultural Foundations of Western and Eastern Family Systems in a Global Age," *International Journal on World Peace* 26: 11–35.

Gauthier, David P. 1965. *The Logic of Leviathan.* Oxford: Clarendon Press.

Guillén, Mauro F. 2001. "Is Globalization Civilizing, Destructive or Feeble? A Critique of Five Key Debates in the Social Science Literature," *Annual Review of Sociology* 27: 235–60.

Hart, Stuart, Cynthia Price Cohen, Martha Farrell Erickson, and Målfrid Flekkøy, Eds. 2001. *Children's Rights in Education.* Philadelphia: Jessica Kingsley Publishers.

Hawes, Joseph M. 1991. *The Children's Rights Movement: A History of Advocacy and Protection.* Boston: Twayne Publishers.

Himes, James R., Ed. 1995. *Implementing the Convention on the Rights of the Child: Resource Mobilization in Low-Income Countries.* Cambridge: Kluwer Law International.

Hirst, Paul, and Grahame Thompson. 1996. *Globalization in Question: The International Economy and the Possibilities of Governance.* London: Polity Press.

Kassimir, Ronald. 1998. "The Social Power of Religious Organisation and Civil Society: The Catholic Church in Uganda," *Commonwealth and Comparative Politics* 36: 54–83.

Kymlicka, Will. 2001. *Politics in the Vernacular: Nationalism, Multiculturalism and Citizenship.* New York: Oxford University Press.

Levitt, Theodore. 1983. "The Globalization of Markets," *Harvard Business Review* 61: 92–102.

Lubin, Carol Riegelman, and Anne Winslow. 1990. *Social Justice for Women: The International Labor Organization and Women.* Durham: Duke University Press.

Matua, Makau. 2001. "Savages, Victims, Saviors: The Metaphor of Human Rights," *Harvard International Law Journal* 42: 201–45.

McGoldrick, Dominic. 1991. "The United Nations Convention on the Rights of the Child," *International Journal of Law and the Family* 5: 132–169.

Merry, Sally Engle. 2003. "From Law and Colonialism to Law and Globalization," *Law & Social Inquiry* 28: 569–90.

Meyer, John W., Francisco O. Ramirez, Henry A. Walker, Nancy Langton, and Sorca M. O'Connor. 1988. "The State and the Institutionalization of the Relations Between Women and Children." Pp. 137–58 in *Feminism, Children, and the New Families,* edited by Sanford M. Dornbusch and Myra H. Strober. New York: The Guilford Press.

Meyer, John W., Francisco Ramirez, John Boli, and George Thomas. 1997. "World Society and the Nation-State," *American Journal of Sociology* 103: 144–81.

Mill, John Stuart. 1963. *On Liberty.* New York: Washington Square Press.

Mitterauer, Michael. 1992 [1986]. *A History of Youth.* Translated by Graeme Dunphy. Oxford: Blackwell Publishing.

Myers, Denys P. 1930. *Handbook of the League of Nations Since 1920.* Boston: League of Nations.

———. 1935/6. *Handbook of the League of Nations.* Boston: League of Nations.

Myers, William E. 2001. "The Right Rights? Child Labor in a Globalizing World," *The Annals of the American Academy of Political and Social Science* 575: 38–55.

Ohmae, Kenichi. 1990. *The Borderless World: Power and Strategy in the Interlinked Economy.* New York: Harper Business.

O'Neill, Onora. 1992. "Children's Rights and Children's Lives," *International Journal of Law and the Family* 6: 24–42.

Onuf, Nicholas. 1995. "Intervention for the Common Good." Pp. 45–58 in *Beyond Westphalia? State Sovereignty and International Intervention,* edited by G. Lyons and M. Mastanduno. Baltimore: The Johns Hopkins University Press.

Panitch, L. 1996. "Rethinking the Role of the State." Pp. 83–113 in *Globalizations: Critical Reflections,* edited by J. H. Mittelman. Boulder: Lynne Reiner.

Poulantzas, Nicos. 1975. *Classes in Contemporary Capitalism.* Translated by David Fernbach. London: New Left Books.

Reher, David Sven. 1998. "Family Ties in Western Europe: Persistent Contrasts," *Population and Development Review* 24: 203–34.

Rodrik, Daniel. 1997. *Has Globalization Gone Too Far?* Washington: Institute on International Economics.

Rousseau, Jean-Jacques. 1974 [1763]. *Emile.* Translated by Barbara Foxley. London: Dent.

Saulle, Maria Rita, and Flaminia Kojanec, Eds. 1995. *The Rights of the Child: International Instruments.* New York: Transnational Publishers, Inc.

Silliman, Jael. 1999. "Expanding Civil Society: Shrinking Political Spaces—The Case of Women's Nongovernmental Organizations," *Social Politics* 6: 23–53.

Smolin, David M. 2000. "Strategic Choices in the International Campaign against Child Labor," *Human Rights Quarterly* 22: 942–87.

Songora, Fortunata Ghati. 2005. "Decoupling in the World Polity: The Case of Children's Education and Health in Tanzania." Paper presented at the Annual Meetings of the African Studies Association, November.

Stryker, Robin. 1998. "Globalization and the Welfare State," *International Journal of Sociology and Social Policy* 18: 1–49.

Wade, R. 1996. "Globalization and Its Limits: Reports of the Death of the National Economy Are Greatly Exaggerated." Pp. 60–88 in *National Diversity and Global Capitalism,* edited by Suzanne Berger and Ronald Dore. Ithaca: Cornell University Press.

Waters, Malcolm. 2001. *Globalization,* second edition. London: Routledge.

Worsfold, Victor L. 1974. "A Philosophical Justification for Children's Rights." Pp. 29–44 in *The Rights of Children.* Harvard Educational Review Reprint Series No. 9. Cambridge: Harvard Educational Review.

10

The Law, Institutions, and the Struggle for Social Change: Brazil's Estatuto da Criança e Adolescente

JOHN A. GUIDRY

During our research, we found that in spite of the discrimination faced by most people living in the Vila, they are happy people who like where they're living and don't think of leaving. We, as observers, are also happy to live here. We're constructing a history of this community and we're fighting to see that the Vila da Barca be recognized by the whole society. One day, we're going to turn this story around, because the Vila is our home.

— Núcleo de Defesa das Crianças e
Adolescente da Vila da Barca, 2002[1]

THE VILA DA BARCA

The Vila da Barca is one of the poorest neighborhoods in Belém, a city of about 1.2 million persons at the mouth of the Amazon River in Brazil.[2] The Vila is situated on the edge of the Bay of Guajará, a massive body of water where the Toncantins and Guamá Rivers empty into the Amazon. About 3,000 of the Vila's 5,000 residents live over the water in a maze of 600 wooden houses con-

The author wishes to thank the SSRC Working Group on Youth, Globalization, and the Law for support in the research and writing of this paper, especially Sudhir Venkatesh, Ron Kassimir, Elizabeth Heger Boyle, and Sasha Abramsky. Thanks goes also to my research assistants at Macalester College, Roland McKay and Ellie Morris, and to the press reviewers. The research for this work, from 1992 through 2004, has been supported by the SSRC and IIE Fulbright Dissertation Fellowships, other SSRC grants, and Augustana College, Rock Island.

structed on stilts. The houses are small, mostly three or four rooms; they usually measure four-by-four meters each. Multigenerational and extended-family households abound, because jobs are scarce and every working member needs to contribute. Jobs come in two basic kinds: formal-sector employment in factories, stores, or companies; and informal-sector employment washing cars, selling candy, or other such work found in the streets. Formal jobs come with benefits and pension contributions; informal jobs come with a certain amount of freedom and frequently earn as much as formal jobs. It is common for children to do informal work on the streets, either after school or in place of school altogether. For girls, in particular, informal domestic work is common, and girls as young as nine years old can start working as nannies, over time moving on to more mature jobs as cooks and maids. Overall, the wages are very low, whether in the formal or informal sector; in the Vila, working persons who are doing *well* might earn about $200 to $300 per month, and it's not unusual for less than half the members of a household to be employed.[3]

Average height, life expectancy, and education statistics in neighborhoods like the Vila are well below the national means, while rates of disease, infant mortality, and unemployment are higher than average.[4] In the Vila, crime and violence tend to be a bit lower than the average for Brazil's largest cities, such as São Paulo or Rio de Janeiro, but they are quite high by global standards. Brazil is a violent country. It has one of the world's highest homicide rates, which most people link to another notable Brazilian statistic: it's one of the world's most unequal societies as well. In 2001, the richest 10 percent of the population earned 46.1 percent of the national income, while the poorest 50 percent of the population earned only 14.8. In terms of social indicators such as child mortality, life expectancy, and literacy, Brazil closely resembles the profile of Honduras, even though Brazil's per capita GNP almost matches that of the industrialized Hungary (see Table 10.1).[5] Those most affected by poverty are the country's youth—a statistic that tends to be true around the world. In this mix, violence affects youths, particularly young males aged 15 to 24, at alarming rates (see Table 10.2). To be young and poor in Brazil means dealing with death; lower rates for girls mean that they are losing their boyfriends and the fathers of their children.

The Vila da Barca is a troubled neighborhood, and its youth, like all Brazilian youth, live in precarious situations. Tell someone in Belém, rich or poor,

Table 10.1 Comparison of Basic Social Indicators,
Selected Countries, 1990

Country	GNP per Capita (US$)[a]	Child Mortality Rate[b]	Life Expectancy	Adult Literacy (%)
Belgium	16,220	9	75	n.a.
Venezuela	5,220	43	70	88
Portugal	4,250	16	74	85
Hungary	2,590	16	71	n.a.
Brazil	2,540	83	66	81
Panama	1,760	31	72	88
Jamaica	1,260	20	73	98
Honduras	900	84	65	73
Haiti	360	130	56	53
India	340	142	59	48

SOURCE: UNICEF, *The State of the World's Children* (Oxford: Oxford University Press, 1992).
NOTES: n.a.: Not available. (a) GNP per capita is based on 1989 data; all other information is for
1990. (b) Child mortality is the number of children per 1,000 live births who die before the age
of five.

Table 10.2 Comparative Homicide Rates, Selected Cities, 2000

City	Population	Homicide Rate (per 100,000)			
		General	Youths, 15–24	Males, 15–24	Females, 15–24
Belém	1,280,614	56.1	52.7	106.5	4.0
Recife	1,422,905	95.8	221.3	424.5	28.7
Rio de Janeiro	5,857,904	56.5	131.1	252.3	12.8
São Paulo	10,434,252	64.8	138.8	269.4	14.7
Vitória	292,304	78.7	160.5	309.0	22.4

SOURCE: Instituto Brasileiro de Geografia e Estatística and Jacobo Waiselfisz, *Mapa da Violência: Os Jovens do Brasil*
(UNESCO, Instituto Ayrton Senna, Ministério da Justiça, 2000), as reported in *Relatório de Cidadania III: Os Jovens e
os Direitos Humanos* (São Paulo: Rede de Observatórios de Direitos Humanos, 2002).

that you're from the Vila, and they turn away. They may become afraid or feel
sorry for you. Even poor people regard the Vila as the end of the earth. But in
1999 something extraordinary began to occur there. The neighborhood association, which was first organized in 1984 during a wave of neighborhood
mobilization associated with the end of Brazil's military regime (1964–1985),
had a youth group that met weekly to prepare for the sacrament of confirma-

tion in the Catholic Church. A representative of the Center for the Defense of the Child and Adolescent—CEDECA, as it's called by its Portuguese acronym—came to the confirmation group and talked about Brazil's national youth legislation, the Statute of the Child and Adolescent or ECA (*Estatuto da Criança e Adolescente*), which was passed in 1990. The representative wanted the group to continue meeting after the confirmation process concluded, and a few of the youths were interested. They named their new group the *Núcleo de Defesa das Crianças e Adolescentes da Vila da Barca* (Nucleus for the Defense of the Child and Adolescent of the Vila da Barca), and the group affiliated with the Vila's Residents' Association. Every Saturday, CEDECA arranged for a speaker to come and talk to the youths about the law, their rights, neighborhood relations, sexual violence, child labor, domestic violence, their aspirations, and so on. At the beginning, some of meetings had only three participants, but the group grew over time and by 2004, the group had 67 members. Many of the group's events are now standing-room-only.

Besides the weekly meetings, the group also works with the *Conselho Tutelar* (CT), the local "protection council" mandated by the ECA. The CT is an elected body that helps to enforce the ECA by taking up cases of violence, abuse, or neglect of children in the area. There are four CTs in Belém, and the city government plans to create four more. The *Núcleo* also works with other organizations in the neighborhood—the local Elderly Group, which has existed since the mid-1980s; the Neighborhood Association and the Community Center, founded in 1981 and 1983, respectively; the Catholic Church's Pastoral of the Child; the Lutheran Church, which came to the neighborhood in the 1980s and holds weekly services; a government vocational-training program called Fundação Curro Velho, which began in 1990; Arco-íris ("rainbow"), a gay organization that came to the neighborhood in 2001; sporting groups; and others.

In March 2002, with the help of CEDECA, UNICEF, and other human rights organizations in Belém, the *Núcleo* began to participate in the *Relatório de Cidadania III* (Third Report on Citizenship), sponsored by the national Network of Human Rights Observatories. The Network brought together teams of five persons from 27 youth groups from all over Brazil. These 135 youths spent the next six months exchanging letters and researching the rights of youths in their neighborhoods. Each group chose its own specific topic, and the group in the Vila researched police violence. Their report concentrated on several incidents recounted by residents, both youths and older persons. The common theme across many of the stories was mistaken identity; when the police enter a poor neighborhood with a suspect in mind, the common practice is to find that person (or persons) and obtain a confession, frequently through the use of torture. When police cannot find the person they are looking for, they invade the houses of relatives or friends, frequently with violence or the threat of violence. In one well-known incident, police held and beat a group of youths who had been playing soccer in a schoolyard. Earlier that day, a different group of youths had been seen spray-painting graffiti on the school building. By the time the police arrived, the graffiti group had fled, leaving the soccer-players in the wrong place at the wrong time. The presumption of guilt surrounding poor youths and youths in the street is a root cause of abuse, by the police and others.

The 135 individual autobiographies, 27 group histories, research projects, and other materials were published in the *Relatório* at the end of the year as part of an ongoing project of the Network, which engages ordinary people as citizen-observers of human rights in their everyday lives. Taken together, the *Relatório* provides an in-depth, qualitative portrait of how poor youths experience abuses of their citizenship rights. The Network's goal is to create a vibrant human rights discourse and proactive citizenship practices that bring to light both the achievements of Brazilian democracy since the military left power in 1985 and the continuing gap between ideals and everyday reality in Brazil.

On March 23, 2004, journalist Sasha Abramsky and I spent half the day with the *Núcleo*. Our visit was arranged by CEDECA, where we had been interviewing persons in the children's rights movement. Abramsky was working on a series of articles that would appear in the North American press; I was working on this book chapter. Among other things, the youths talked to us about their next project, the "Second Stage of Social Mobilization against Domestic Child Labor," a program sponsored by CEDECA, UNICEF, Save the Children, Cordaid, the International Labor Organization, the Public Ministry of the State of Pará, and the Rómulo Maiorana Organization (Belém's principal daily newspaper and television channel). Like the *Relatório de Cidadania III*, the child labor program is connected to other efforts around the country. The group in the Vila had an invitation to send two representatives to a planning meeting. Each of the kids at the table, about 20 of them, wrote his or her name on a slip of paper, and the group asked Abramsky and me to choose the two representatives.

THIS CHAPTER

The situation of the Vila da Barca is fraught with contradictions that bring into sharp relief both global and local processes at work in the development of youth legislation in Brazil. On the one hand, we can easily trace the profound impact of transnational actors in shaping local law and practices, and we can also chart the ways in which the Brazilian case has influenced legislation in the rest of Latin America. We can demonstrate that, compared with the lives of youths 20 years ago, the children's rights movement has enriched the lives of youths in the Vila da Barca in important ways. Today an increasing number of youths know the law and their rights, and they teach other youths about citizenship. Gay youths in the Vila organized a soccer team with Arco-íris and play against other teams in the neighborhood, which would have been unimaginable in the not-so-distant past. Yet, at the same time, police abuse of youths remains common. Poverty and its associated problems of disease, alienation, and prejudice make it very difficult for ordinary people—especially persons under 18—to express and claim their citizenship rights. Neoliberal economic policies, fiscal austerity, and the increasing burden of international debt in Brazil make it increasingly difficult for the government to fund and grow social programs that would address the everyday conditions of neighborhoods like the Vila da Barca. At the time of this writing, the city government of Belém had plans to "urbanize" the Vila, a project that includes building dikes that will place all the neighborhood on dry land—but paved streets alone will not eliminate poverty and police abuse.

At the center of these cross-cutting currents is the ECA, a legislative framework passed in 1990 that redefined the citizenship of persons under 18 as well as the way that youths are treated by society and the state. In the struggle for the ECA's adoption and implementation, the protagonists are mainly Brazilians who aim to change their own society through reference to international standards such as the UN's 1989 Convention on the Rights of the Child. These actors bring transnational resources to their work in Brazil through relationships with UNICEF, international nongovernmental organizations (NGOs) such as Save the Children, or private foundations such as the Ford Foundation. What we might call "globalization" in this instance is in fact a multifaceted, contradictory, and frequently ill defined set of processes at work in the contemporary world that operates *through these actors,* such as the representatives of CEDECA who helped the youths in the Vila organize. Analyzing how social movements and globalization interact, Sidney Tarrow describes these actors with Kwame Anthony Appiah's term, *rooted cosmopolitans,*[6] whose work to address local problems extends the reach of transnational discourses such as "children's rights" into far-flung corners of the world. Understanding the role of rooted cosmopolitans turns our gaze to the institutions where these actors bring local and global processes to bear on the state and everyday life. These institutions, in turn, become footholds for more lasting change.

Specifically, the ECA creates new institutional bases for change in three domains of social life. First, the children's rights movement's interaction with the state shows how local and global processes *work through civil society to affect political culture and institutional practice.* Second, the structures of the law show these processes interact to *transform the state.* Third, the "council" structure of the ECA establishes *a new domain of state-society collaboration* in which state actors and civil society organizations build a new public space of democratic debate and policy development.[7] At the same time, however, the institutionalization of the ECA faces three important challenges that undermine the law. First, *entrenched cultural practices* that are prejudicial to persons under 18— manifest in the way the law is applied by some agents of the state and in the actions of police, private citizens, and parents—make the law difficult to apply. Second, the *decentralization* of policy implementation in the Brazilian state, across 27 federal units and almost 5,500 municipalities, means that the ECA is very unevenly institutionalized across the country. Third, the *neoliberalism* embraced by Brazilian politicians on the right and, increasingly, the left, together with IMF restrictions on the national budget, places severe limitations on the resources available for the development of the social policies called for by the ECA and other legislation.

This contradictory context is a conundrum that both global and local actors face, whether they are UNICEF officials, Brazilian attorneys and judges, or the youth of the Vila da Barca. This conundrum is the focus of this chapter, and what emerges from this analysis is an understanding of the importance of incremental change and social and political struggle to the development of democratic societies. Without claiming that enough change has taken place, this chapter explores the terrain of struggles for the advancement of children's rights in Brazil and, by implication, in other countries as well, in order to show *how* change takes place where the global and local meet.

The discussion of the ECA in this chapter remains, for the most part, at the national level, but I also draw upon research in the cities of Belém and São Paulo to illustrate more specific local instances of the statute's progress and the obstacles it faces.[8] These two cities represent two opposing Brazilian realities that help us understand a little bit about how the Brazilian context varies. Belém is an old colonial city, founded in 1617, and it is the capital of the state of Pará at the mouth of the Amazon River. With about 1.6 million inhabitants in the metropolitan area, it is currently one of Brazil's 10 largest cities. The Amazonian region is one of the poorest parts of the country, and Belém lacks the modern feel of central São Paulo and the industrialized south. São Paulo, founded in 1554, is South America's leading city in industrial development and wealth. The metropolitan area is home to over 20 million people and is one of the five largest urban agglomerations in the world. In São Paulo the contrast of Brazil's wealth and poverty is a daily reminder of the contradictions of industrialization in the Global South. In political terms, Belém and São Paulo provide complementary examples of the struggles between the right and left in Brazil, with examples of local governance by both sides in recent years. In 2000, voters in both cities elected the leftist Workers' Party to the mayoral administration, but in the 2004 municipal elections both were replaced by more conservative parties.

In spite of their differences, both cities were crucibles for the early development of the movement for children's rights in Brazil. In Belém during the 1970s, Fr. Bruno Sechi founded some of the earliest organizations for street children in Brazil, as well as Belém's Center for the Defense of the Minor (*Centro de Defesa do Menor*, now renamed *Centro de Defesa da Criança e Adolescente Emaús*, CEDECA), which was the first legal advocacy organization defending children's rights in Brazil. Fr. Bruno's work was replicated elsewhere in the development of the national movements for street children and children's rights. In São Paulo, journalists such as Gilberto Dimenstein and Gilberto Nascimento, as well as human rights lawyers such as Oscar Vilhena, provided a national voice for the children's rights movement in the center of the country's political and economic establishment. Their work's prominence in the *Folha de São Paulo*, one of the country's most important daily newspapers, set the standard for exposing abuses of youths and promoting new policy ideas that helped establish the ECA.

DEMOCRATIZATION AND THE EMERGENCE OF A MOVEMENT

The immediate backdrop to the children's rights movement in Brazil is the process of democratization that occurred as Brazil's military regime (1964–1985) began to lose its grip on power. In the 1970s, growing cross-class resistance to the regime's human rights abuses and the failure of its economic policies after the end of the economic "miracle" period (1967–1974) resulted in a cascade of new social movements that organized around the "master frames" of opposition to military rule, in the early going, and then citizenship, once the regime's exit from power was all but ensured by the early 1980s.[9] A "new unions movement" rejuvenated organized labor as a new generation of workers came on line after 1975. The current president of Brazil, Luis Inácio Lula da Silva, emerged at this time as a national labor leader and a founder of the Partido dos Trabalhadores (the Workers' Party, or PT), which challenged both the partisans of the regime as well as the middle-class opposition. At the same time, community movements began to swell in the poor and working-class neighborhoods of Brazilian cities. With the mandates of Vatican II (1962–1965) and the Latin American Bishops' conference of Medellín (1968), the Brazilian Catholic Church took a sharply progressive turn, influenced by the emergence of "liberation theology" in Latin America and also by the writings of Paulo Freire, a Brazilian educator whose pedagogical techniques informed progressive religious activists across the continent. The human rights movement benefited from links to all these groups, growing along with the outcry against the regime's increasingly public abuse of its citizens (through imprisonment, torture, and assassination) during the most severe years of repression from 1967 to 1975.[10]

Early Children's Rights Organizations

The movement for children's rights emerged with the establishment of the National Movement of Street Children (*Movimento Nacional de Meninos e Meninas de Rua*, MNMMR) in 1983. Although the movement for street children began as a class-specific sort of collective action, it quickly joined the master frame of citizenship that emerged in the 1980s, claiming that the MNMMR and other actors on behalf of youth (social workers, NGO and civil society actors, and the Catholic Church's Pastoral on Youth and other Church-related projects) were struggling to secure the rights of all persons under 18 in post-authoritarian Brazil. During the Constitutional Assembly of 1987–1988, the children's rights movement was able to propose and defend the passage of two articles (227 and 228) that laid the legal basis for the ECA two years later.[11] When national officials reviewed the ECA after its first decade, they described it as "the result of years of struggle by civil society [that] signifies an important milestone in the democratic trajectory of Brazil."[12] A brief outline of cases in Belém and São Paulo will help us understand how the movement's development played out at the local level.

In Belém, Fr. Bruno Sechi's Republic of Emmaus Movement (MRE, *Movimento República de Emaús*) was one of the earliest children's rights organizations established in Brazil and has served as a national model for the movement. The MRE typifies the structure of the children's rights movement in its local sites. In 1970, Fr. Bruno, an Italian Silesian priest, began working with youth street vendors in downtown Belém. Fr. Bruno helped organize the children and stimulate discussions among them of how they might address situations of poverty, exploitation, violence, and street life. The group soon organized the Republic of the Small Vendor (RPV, *República do Pequeno Vendedor*), which holds classes and other programs that aim at developing the children's identity as *workers* who have a right to work in the street and also as youths who have specific *citizenship rights* to education, healthcare, and family or social protection. In contrast to the desires of the police and business owners, who simply wish to remove the children from public space and the street, the

RPV enables them to contribute to the economic health of their families while bringing them into citizenship discourses.

In 1983, Fr. Bruno and others in Belém participated in the founding of the MNMMR at the national level. In Belém they created the Center for the Defense of the Minor (CDM, *Centro de Defesa do Menor*), which was the first such organization devoted youth legal advocacy in Brazil. At the same time, the MRE acquired 10 hectares in the neighborhood of Bengui on the outskirts of the city, where it created the Cidade de Emaús (CE, City of Emmaus) as a special school for at-risk children from poor neighborhoods. CE modeled an alternative pedagogy of empowerment and critical consciousness influenced by Paulo Freire's methods. The children in the CE operate a farm and pharmacy that produce herbal medicines that youths in the RPV can sell on the street. Later the CDM changed its name to the Center for the Defense of the Child and Adolescent (CEDECA-Emaús, *Centro de Defesa da Criança e Adolescente*), an organization whose representatives came to the Vila da Barca in 1999 to help form the *Núcleo*. One can now find CEDECAs in many states of Brazil.

The structure of the MRE is non-paternalistic and democratic in nature, and the youths in the programs are active participants in debates, discussions, and decision-making in the organization. The adults in the organization are lawyers, educators, psychologists, social workers, researchers, and others interested in advancing the rights of children. The movement counts on local networks of support in civil society mentioned above and transnational sponsors including the International Labour Organization (ILO), Save the Children Foundation (U.K.), ISCOS (Instituto Sindacale per la Cooperazione allo Sviluppo, Italy), Misereor (Germany), Kinderenindeknel (Netherlands), Terre des Hommes (France), and others.[13] UNICEF has several offices around Brazil, and the Belém office works closely with the MRE and other movement organizations, further aiding in transnational ties and links.

The Role of Journalists

The Brazilian movement also counted on committed journalists such as Gilberto Dimenstein, who built his career writing at *Folha de São Paulo*, one of the country's most prominent newspapers. In a series of widely read and well-regarded books on teenage prostitution in Amazonia, violence by and against youths, and the citizenship rights developed in Brazilian law, Dimenstein brought youth citizenship to national and international attention.[14] In 1997, Dimenstein founded the Escola Aprendiz (Learning School) in the central São Paulo neighborhood of Vila Madalena. Like Padre Bruno's Cidade de Emaús, Aprendiz seeks to establish an alternative pedagogy that draws upon John Dewey and French pedagogies of practical interaction between persons and their environments. According to Dimenstein, Aprendiz transforms the open space of the neighborhood and city into its classroom.[15] The walls, sidewalks, and alleys of Vila Madalena are filled with art projects that include graffiti-inspired murals and traditional Portuguese ceramic tiles known as *azulejos*, blending in this way a global hip-hop sensibility with long-standing elements of Brazilian culture. Aprendiz's "100 Walls Project" has placed these murals all over São Paulo, vividly affecting how ordinary people see and experience the public spaces of the city.[16] These and other activities provide creative outlets for at-risk youth that take them from the realm of destructive street life and into more structured activities through which Aprendiz's educators teach both professional skills and citizenship awareness.

Dimenstein's writing reflects his educational concerns. Beginning in the mid-1990s he began to publish a series of books on children's rights and citizenship that were aimed at primary and secondary schools, to serve as texts to teach children about their citizenship and the ECA. Esmeralda do Carmo Ortiz, a youth who entered Aprendiz's programs in 1999, has written an autobiography detailing her life as a street kid from the age of nine; it has become a popular text in São Paulo schools.[17] The book deals with subjects ranging from Esmeralda's abuse by family members to her life of crime and drug addiction on the street, and it is packaged with a classroom guide that orients readers to the citizenship issues in her story. Escola Aprendiz's funding partners include an eye-catching list of 43 private sector foundations, civil society organizations, and government agencies. Transnational partners include J. P. Morgan, the Bank of Boston, Microsoft, UNESCO, and UNICEF. Like Padre Bruno's MRE, Aprendiz exemplifies in bold terms the interaction of global and local processes in the development of the movement for children's rights in Brazil. In March of 2000, Dimenstein and other journalists created ANDI, *Agência de Notícias dos Direitos da Infância* (Children's Rights News Agency), a network of news agencies, journalists, human rights activists, and civil society organizations that seeks to "invest in a new journalistic culture that investigates and prioritizes questions related to the universe of children and youths, always through the lens of their rights."[18] ANDI works to transfer technology, develop civil society organizations, and train students and journalists to become agents of mobilization.

By establishing a focus on citizenship issues, alternative pedagogies, the transformation of space, and legal defense, the movement for children's rights expanded its constituency beyond "street children" or other youths who had run-ins with legal authority. It became a movement for the rights of *all* persons under 18 years of age, not just a movement of kids who got in trouble. This framing allowed the movement to consolidate important ties across the social work community, human rights movement, the Brazilian Bar Association, community associations, and the Catholic Church, which had long been active in promoting pastoral outreach to marginalized, disadvantaged youth, including street children.

TRANSNATIONAL INFLUENCES, LOCAL PURPOSES, AND NEW INSTITUTIONS

The emergence of a global discourse on children's rights is a relatively recent phenomenon. Geoffrey Robertson notes that children were "omitted from eighteenth-century [human rights] declarations because they were then regarded as the property of their parents."[19] Through much of the twentieth century, the concept of children's rights continued to be clouded by the role of parents, the status of the family as an institution, and problems with child labor that first gained attention in the nineteenth century. The earliest international conventions on children, such as the Minimum Age (Industry) Convention (C5) adopted by the ILO in 1919 (updated in 1973, C138), reflected these concerns. With the UN's Declaration of the Rights of Children in 1959, however, children's rights emerged on the global stage, setting off the process that resulted in the UN's Convention on the Rights of the Child in 1989. Brazil's ECA in 1990 was written by local actors as part of Brazil's process of reviewing and participating in the Convention on the Rights of the Child (CRC), and as such it inserts Brazil's local conditions—the Vila da Barca, for example—into the globalized conversation about children.[20] By 2004, all but five countries in the region had adopted new juvenile legislation that borrowed in some important way from the ECA.[21]

Transnational involvement in the development of children's rights organizations in Brazil has been substantial. Table 10.3 presents a sample of 27 organizations that are involved with the ECA in Brazil. They fall into three categories of scale: transnational, national, and local (subnational). They represent intergovernmental organizations (IGOs) such as UNICEF, international nongovernmental organizations (INGOs) such as Save the Children, civil society organizations and NGOs, private foundations, and government agencies (such as the judicial ministries of individual Brazilian states). The list in Table 10.3 is based on the groups I have visited and researched over the last few years in Belém and São Paulo; it is not comprehensive and represents only a fraction of the organizations involved across the country. Nonetheless, it suffices to demonstrate the intensity of local-transnational linkages at work in the development of the ECA, as well as the way in which the statute's structures are creating new spaces of state-society participation in the development of policy.

In local terms, the ECA's framers intended nothing less than the remaking of the country's political-cultural practices involving persons under 18 years of age and, one can argue, youth more generally.[22] As a category, "youth" in Brazil refers to persons up to about 25 to 30 years of age who are unmarried, consonant with practice throughout the Mediterranean world more generally. The general principle behind the ECA is the "integral protection" (*proteção integral*) of the person under the age of 18, embracing potential socio-political structures that can create a nurturing environment in which youths can grow into mature adults and competent citizens with the capacity to realize their own desires and talents. "Integral protection" departs radically from both the crisis-orientation and focus on youth labor that was the norm in Brazilian legal history, as well as from the neoliberal citizenship models emerging in Anglo-American "Zero Tolerance" discourse.

By defining persons under 18 as "human beings in the process of development" (art. 15), the ECA began to create the legal framework to enable both state and society to take a nurturing *and* protective role for these child-citizens. With this language, the movement for children's rights created *universal*

Table 10.3 Organizations and Agencies Involved with the ECA: Transnational Linkages

Organization	Location/Type	Scale	Activity	Transnational Connections
Associazione Amici dei Bambini	Italy NGO	transnational	advocacy support adoption	
Amnesty International	UK/USA INGO	transnational	research/advocacy	
Conectas	Brazil NGO	transnational	advocacy networking	UN Foundation UNESCO UNDP Ford Foundation
ILANUD: Instituto Latino Americano das Nações Unidas para Prevenção do Delito e Tratamento do Delinquente	Costa Rica	transnational	programmatic legislative	FIDH UN
Inter-American Children's Institute	Uruguay IGO	transnational	support research/advocacy: networking	
Interamerican Foundation	USA US Gov't	transnational	support	
Misereor	Germany Catholic/Gov't	transnational	support	
Save the Children	UK/USA INGO	transnational	support research/advocacy	
Sur	Brazil NGO	transnational	research/advocacy networking	
Terra dos Hommes	Netherlands NGO	transnational	support programmatic: community development, education	

	USA-INGO			
UNICEF		transnational	support	
World Vision/Visão Mundial	International Christian NGO	transnational	support programmatic: community development	
W. K. Kellogg Foundation	USA Foundation	transnational	support	
Amençar	Brazil Christian NGO	national	advocacy/programmatic: education, health	Kindernothilfe
ANDI	Brazil NGO	national	research/advocacy: networking	Save the Children W. K. Kellogg Foundation UNICEF
CECRIA	Brazil NGO	national	research/advocacy	Save the Children UNICEF USAID
FASE	Brazil NGO	national	support, research/advocacy	various European
Fundação Abrinq	Brazil Foundation	national	support, research/advocacy	Interamerican Foundation W. K. Kellogg Foundation
Missão Criança	Brazil NGO	national	programmatic: education	EU Japanese government UNICEF USAID
Centro de Apoio Operacional da Infância e Juventude-Ministério Público do Estado do Pará	Belém Gov't	local	programmatic: monitor ECA juridical advocacy	Save the Children UNICEF Terra des Hommes

(continued)

Table 10.3 *(continued)*

Organization	Location/Type	Scale	Activity	Transnational Connections
Centro de Apoio Operacional da Infância e Juventude-Ministério Público do Estado de São Paulo	São Paulo Gov't	local	programmatic: monitor ECA juridical advocacy	UNICEF ILO UN Instituto McDonald Amici dei Bambini ILANUD
ECOS-Comunicação em Sexualidade	São Paulo NGO	local	programmatic: health education	MacArthur Foundation International Women's Health Coalition Salud y Género
Escola Aprendiz	São Paulo NGO	local	programmatic: education	ING, JP Morgan, Bank of Boston Foundation, Intel, Microsoft, UNESCO, Unicef
Fundação Mauricio Sirotsky Sobrinho	Porto Alegre Foundation	local	support programmatic: education advocacy	UNICEF W. K. Kellogg Foundation
Meninos do Morumbi	São Paulo NGO	local	programmatic: education	Anglo American Rotary International UNICEF
Movimento República Emaús	Belém NGO	local	programmatic: education, monitor ECA, legal resources	Kinder Postzagels Misereor Save the Children
Núcleo de Defesa das Crianças e Adolescentes da Vila da Barca–Associação de Moradores da Vila da Barca	Belém NGO	local	programmatic: education, youth programs	UNICEF Save the Children ILO

citizenship rights for *all* persons under 18, including rights of expression and political participation in accordance with the law (Art. 16). At the same time, the statute's *protective* intent also stipulates the obligations of parents, families, regular citizens, and the state to provide for the material and social well-being of youths (Art. 18), including the conditions and circumstances under which parents may be legally relieved of their authority over children, as well as the process by which children and adolescents may be relocated to another home (articles 22–24, 155–70).

State-Society Participation: Oversight Councils

The ECA created participatory institutions, at all levels of government, charged with the oversight, application, and development of policies related to the statute (see Figure 10.1). These are modeled on the policy development councils mandated by the 1988 constitution in other areas, among them urban development, public security (policing), health, and women's issues. At the national, state, and municipal levels,[23] Councils for the Rights of Children and Adolescents (hereafter, Rights Councils) elaborate policies to secure the rights of children and adolescents as laid out in the ECA.[24] One half of these councils are state representatives, appointed by current executives (president, state governor, or mayor of the municipal district); the other half are representatives from organizations in civil society, such as the bar association, the MRE (in Belém), or other organizations associated with the movement. Movement representatives on the councils are supplied by the movement organizations, who meet in open forums to select their representatives. The organizations that qualify to be part of the selection process vary according to policy needs and local conditions, but in general they must be "entities devoted to infant/juvenile issues . . . such as, for example, those that include among their institutional mission the direct servicing, research, promotion, or defense of the rights of children and adolescents."[25] The total number of members varies given local conditions; in Belém, the Rights Council consisted of 18 people in 2004.

These three levels of developing and implementing the SCA mirror Brazil's federal-state-local governmental structure. The fourth type of popular participation in the statute's implementation is also at the municipal level, in

Figure 10.1 Participatory Council Structure:
Brazil's *Estatuto da Criança e Adolescente*

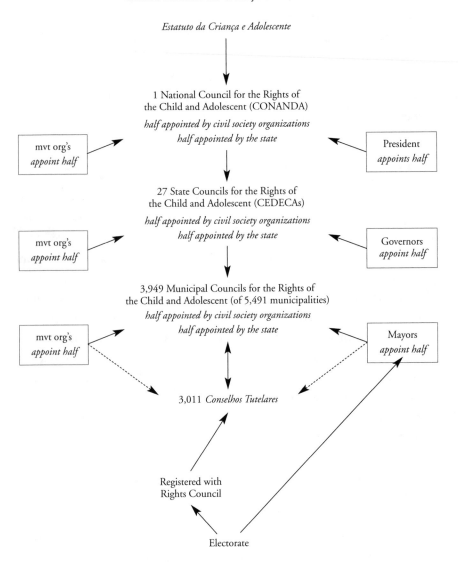

conselhos tutelares (CTs). *Conselho tutelar* translates as "protection council," emphasizing the law's intention to construct the child-citizen as a special category in need of "protection" from abuses by both the state and ordinary citizens. While the work of the Rights Councils involves the developing of policy, the CTs do actual casework that assists and accompanies claims of either the abuse of youth rights or the adjudication of youth offenders through the juvenile justice system.[26]

Each municipality is to have at least one CT with at least five councilors sitting on it; many municipalities have more than one CT.[27] Counselors are elected in small city districts and are from those districts, which ensures a familiarity with the context from which complaints emerge. They are usually movement activists, but some candidates emerge from groups that oppose the ECA. All persons over 16 are eligible to vote, but to do so they must register with the Municipal Rights Council, which coordinates the election.[28] As of 2004, CT members in Belém received a compensation of three minimum salaries (about $300 per month) for their work. By 1995, São Paulo, with about 10 million inhabitants, had 20 CTs; Franca, a smaller municipality of 250,000 in the state of São Paulo, had two; the similarly sized Maringá in the state Paraná had only one.[29] Belém, with a little over one million inhabitants, had four CTs as of 2003, with plans to develop four more.

Youth Offenders and Juvenile Justice

The sections of the law that deal with the treatment of youths who break the law were written to address the traditional manner by which adults, parents, and public authorities have "disciplined" young people. Corporal punishment has been the norm for "minors," and, in general, physical abuse by the police and parents has long been tolerated in daily life. The goal of the statute's policies toward youth offenders is to enable authorities to correct the misbehavior of young people, but to do so completely in keeping with Article 18's prohibition of inhuman and abusive treatment. In a deeper sense, these provisions of the statute are one attempt to address the violence of everyday life as it involves youths in two contradictory ways: first, the very real fact of youths who become involved in crime; and second, the general abuse of youths, whether guilty, innocent, or under suspicion, by agents of the state.

The fact that about half of the statute's articles are devoted to dealing with youth offenders and the juvenile justice system indicates the scope of the problem.

The combination of endemic poverty and the diminished status of "minor" is manifest in a general prejudice against all youths, as the *Núcleo* documented in the Vila da Barca. This is especially true for those who are poor, black, and male. A person who becomes aware of a missing wallet or purse may easily point a finger at nearby kids, who become the target of police action. The statute attempts to undermine such prejudice by providing that "no adolescent will be deprived of his freedom unless caught flagrantly in the act of infraction or by written order of the competent judicial authority" (Art. 106). When judicial authority can establish that a youth violated the law, the offender is not subject to prison in the same manner as adults (Art. 104). Rather, youth offenders are subject to "socio-educational measures" (*medidas sócio-educativas*, MSEs): (a) warning, (b) obligation to repair damages, (c) performance of community service, (d) freedom under the cognizance of others, (e) restricted freedom, (f) assignment to an educational institution, or (g) a number of more detailed regimes including removal from the family (Art. 112). The point of these detailed legal stipulations is that children and adolescents, as "human beings in the process of development," be given the guidance and supervision necessary to correct misbehavior and allow the youth the opportunity to mature in a way that would ameliorate and diminish the feelings of marginalization and discrimination that delinquent youths and gang members cite as reasons for entering "street life."

The MSEs gain concrete form in four progressively more restrictive institutions, which are utilized depending on the gravity of the crime committed and the history of the youth. In the state of Pará, these programs are administered by FUNCAP, the Foundation for Children and Adolescents of Pará. FUNCAP is an agency of the state's social services division, and it is typical of ECA implementation across the country. At the first level, youths who commit petty crimes are obligated to perform community services, which might involve cleaning public spaces, painting walls, repairing damages to property that the crime caused, or volunteering in a neighborhood organization. In Belém, FUNCAP's Center for the Provision of Community Service (*Centro de Prestação de Serviço a Comunidade*) serviced 57 adolescents in 2003, partnering with other government agencies and civil society organizations. At the second level, "assisted liberty," individual social workers work with families of youths. *Assisted liberty* is like a form of proactive probation in which youths continue to live with their families, go to school and work, and interact in the community. In 2003, FUNCAP's Center for Assisted Liberty (*Centro de Liberdade Assistida*) in Belém serviced 234 adolescents. Third, youths involved in varying degrees of violent crime may be placed in a regime of "semi-liberty," in which they live in FUNCAP-administered half-way houses but are released for school, work, and family visits on weekends or holidays. FUNCAP provides several different sites for semi-liberty programs, and in 2003 the agency serviced 174 youths. Finally, youths who commit grave crimes, including homicide and rape, may be placed in full-time institutions without freedom to come or go until they complete a proscribed period of detention and programs of evaluation or therapy. Youths who begin with a sentence to detention can work their way down the correctional ladder, to semi-liberty, assisted liberty, and finally community service. In 2003, 618 adolescents were housed in various full-time institutions.[30]

FUNCAP reports a low incidence of recidivism, but the period of post-release supervision is short and the numbers cannot reflect actual rates by which these youths may or may not return to criminal activity. Most troubling about FUNCAP's statistics in Pará is the progressively greater numbers of adolescents placed in more restrictive forms of supervision. The logic of the ECA, consistent with what is known about youth crime, is that most youths commit petty crimes and relatively few are involved in grave crimes. But we note that the numbers range from 57 in community service, 234 in assisted liberty, and 174 in semi-liberty, to 618 in full-time detention. This trend is consistent across Brazil and is one factor cited by international human rights organizations for contributing to recent riots in youth detention centers in both Belém and, more notoriously, in São Paulo.[31] People in FUNCAP, other agencies of the justice system in both Belém and São Paulo, the MRE, Escola Aprendiz, and other organizations state that judges are predisposed to recommend the most severe penalties possible to youths.

This reflects the pre-ECA culture of juvenile justice that continues to linger in the system. This culture is universally regarded as the most important impediment to the ECA's application, and it results in the higher numbers of youths sentenced to the most severe forms of MSEs. Another cause of these numbers, not considered by the officials I interviewed, is that law enforcement in Brazil concentrates on persons who commit harsher crimes, which overloads the system with these kinds of cases, while petty crimes are frequently handled informally.[32] Informal justice means violence against youths by both police officers and private citizens, whether this takes the form of shopkeepers or security guards throwing rocks at children or slapping them in public, vigilante lynchings, or "death squads" composed of off-duty officers and others that chase down street children and execute them. The persistence of informal practices, along with the higher rates of detention in full-time institutions, signals the difficulties the state and civil society face in institutionalizing the ECA.

The application and utility of the MSEs is perhaps the most controversial issue in the ECA's institutionalization. Critics charge that these measures are only a "slap on the wrist" and do little to alter the behavior of youth offenders, and the evidence is not promising in all but small number of institutions around the country. People who support the ECA, within the movement and the state, fault both the justice system (e.g., old-fashioned judges) and the limitations that neoliberal policies place on the state, especially the lack of state resources to build, staff, and fund MSE institutions in a manner sufficient to the scope of the problem. Within Brazil, supporters of the ECA have put together teams to investigate MSE practices, and in 1998 they created the *Prêmio Sócio-Educando* (Socio-Education Prize) in order to recognize the best practices of MSEs around the country. The organizations supporting the prize include a variety of civil society organizations, journalist and other professional associations, private companies and foundations, government agencies, and an array of transnational institutions including the Correctional Service of Canada, the Canadian Agency for International Development, the Kellogg Foundation, the Fundação Universitária Luis Amigo of Colombia, and the United Nations. The UN's support was organized by ILANUD, the Latin American Institute of the United Nations for the Prevention of Crime and Treatment of the Delinquent (*Instituto Latino-Americano das Nações Unidas para Prevenção do Delito e Tratamento do Delinquente*), which is based in Brazil and Costa Rica and sponsors legislative development around Latin America.[33] During 1999–2002, over 200 MSE projects around the country were nominated, with about one third of the nominations receiving finalist recognition. Both the states of São Paulo and Pará were among the most noteworthy in numbers of nominations and finalists.[34]

Still, the development of the MSEs and the struggle to recognize and disseminate best practices exemplifies the challenges faced in the institutionalization of the ECA. Entrenched social inequalities and cultural practices, decentralization, and the fiscal restraints on the neoliberal state mean that the development of institutions and policies must rely on a patchwork of state-society and local-transnational collaboration that, when it works, seems to exemplify an optimistic portrayal of the role of "rooted cosmopolitans" in helping new citizenship practices to emerge. But although the pace is slow and the change is by and large positive, the time lag allows opponents of the ECA to argue that it is an ill-advised and ineffectual law that does little to stem the problem of youth crime and violence in the country.

INSTITUTIONALIZATION AND STATE-CIVIL SOCIETY COOPERATION

As with the development of the MSEs, the council structures mandated by the ECA have developed only slowly over the first 13 years of the law's existence. Rights Councils are solidly established at the national level and in each of the 26 states and the federal district. Table 10.4 shows the municipal figures as of 2001 for the individual states, across 5,491 municipalities. At that point, there were 3,949 Municipal Rights Councils (MRCs), accounting for about 72 percent of the total, but 28 percent of Brazilian cities did not yet have the MRC implanted. Only 55 percent, or 3011, of the municipalities had implanted CTs. Although 52 percent had both MRCs and CTs, 20 percent had only MRCs, and about 3 percent had only CTs. In the latter instance, these 3 percent of Brazilian municipalities developed CTs without the appropriate MRC to oversee the CTs and the election of councilors.

As for the quality of the councils' functioning and performance, there is great variation across the country. The Rights Councils, at both the state and municipal levels, tend to reflect their executives' (governors' or mayors') stance toward the ECA.[35] Where a governor or mayor is favorable to the ECA and its

Table 10.4 Institutionalization of ECA Council Structures, 2001

State	Municipalities	Municipal Rights Councils	Conselhos Tutelares	Both MRC and CT	Only MRC	Only CT	Neither MRC nor CT
Acre	22	15 (68)	12 (55)	11 (50)	4 (18)	1 (4,50)	6 (27)
Alagoas	101	75 (74)	56 (55)	52 (51)	23 (23)	4 (4,00)	22 (22)
Amazonas	61	38 (61)	28 (45)	25 (41)	13 (21)	3 (4,90)	20 (33)
Amap	16	12 (75)	8 (50)	7 (44)	5 (31)	1 (6,30)	3 (19)
Bahia	413	228 (55)	141 (34)	114 (28)	114 (28)	27 (6,50)	158 (38)
Ceará	184	167 (91)	123 (67)	118 (64)	49 (27)	5 (2,70)	12 (6,50)
Fed. District	1	1 (100)	1 (100)	1 (100)	0	0	0
Espírito Santo	77	74 (96)	61 (79)	61 (79)	13 (17)	0	3 (3,90)
Goiás	242	192 (79)	145 (60)	139 (57)	53 (22)	6 (2,50)	44 (18)
Maranhão	217	122 (56)	61 (28)	55 (25)	67 (31)	6 (2,80)	89 (41)
Minas Gerais	848	468 (55)	329 (39)	307 (36)	161 (19)	22 (2,60)	358 (42)
Mato Grosso Sul	77	73 (95)	68 (88)	67 (87)	6 (8)	1 (1,30)	3 (3,90)
Mato Grosso N.	126	120 (95)	117 (93)	116 (92)	4 (3)	1 (0,80)	5 (4)
Pará	142	94 (66)	75 (52)	66 (46)	28 (20)	9 (6,30)	39 (27)
Paraíba	223	122 (55)	59 (26)	55 (25)	67 (30)	4 (1,80)	97 (43)
Pernambuco	185	137 (74)	64 (35)	56 (30)	81 (44)	8 (4,30)	40 (22)
Pianí	221	99 (45)	41 (19)	38 (17)	61 (28)	3 (1,40)	119 (54)
Paraná	399	390 (98)	385 (96)	378 (95)	12 (3)	7 (1,80)	2 (0,50)
Rio de Janeiro	91	86 (95)	69 (76)	67 (74)	19 (21)	2 (2,20)	3 (3,30)
Rio Grande N.	166	71 (43)	53 (32)	39 (23)	32 (19)	14 (8,40)	81 (49)
Rondônia	52	36 (69)	29 (56)	27 (52)	9 (17)	2 (3,80)	14 (27)
Roraima	15	13 (87)	6 (40)	6 (40)	7 (47)	0	2 (13)
Rio Grande Sul	467	327 (70)	286 (61)	275 (59)	52 (11)	11 (2,40)	129 (28)
Santa Catarina	293	288 (98)	280 (96)	275 (94)	13 (4)	5 (1,70)	0
Sergipe	75	66 (88)	49 (65)	46 (61)	20 (27)	3 (4,00)	6 (8)
São Paulo	643	582 (90)	438 (68)	427 (66)	155 (24)	11 (1,70)	50 (7,80)
Toncantins	134	53 (38)	27 (19)	23 (17)	30 (22)	3 (2,20)	78 (58)
Total	5491	3949 (72)	3011 (55)	2851 (52)	1098 (20)	1 (2,90)	1383 (25)

SOURCE: IBGE/CONAND.

NOTE: Numbers in parentheses are percents.

project, the Rights Councils and CTs tend to have more logistical support and more highly developed infrastructures (offices, equipment, telephones, salaries, etc.). Where a governor does not support the ECA, the councils are poorly supported, lack infrastructure, exist only on paper, or do not exist at all. Overall, executives from parties of the center and left tend to support the ECA and its structures, though this is not always the case. In some cases, conservative governors have chosen children's rights as a campaign theme and tend to provide the resources they need. Male governors tend to appoint their wives as the head of social services in the state. These wives can make sure that resources are available to the councils, even if their husbands' parties and ideological affiliations are more law-and-order oriented and tend to dismiss the ECA's goals. The greatest challenge—and hope—in the institutionalization of the ECA is the development of the CTs. In Belém, for example, Marcel Hazeu, a researcher, CEDECA/MRE activist, and member of the Municipal Rights Council (2003), referred to the CTs as "representing the arrival of the statute [ECA]" in the community, emblematic of the movement's objective of "getting involved with the institutions of the state" and "freeing up the possibility of implanting new policies."[36] Yet Hazeu also echoed the complaints of RC members, police officers, movement activists, and others that the councilors are not properly trained.

The work of the CTs is time consuming and requires great familiarity with local bureaucracies and social service agencies. João Gomes, a long-time activist in community movements and children's rights, was a CT member from the Bengui area of Belém (one of the city's poor and working-class districts) from 1995 to 1997, and he explained that most counselors in Belém heard three or four cases a day. In a 1998 interview, he provided examples of the kinds of cases they heard.[37] In one, a CT in Belém received a complaint from some children who lived in a house that also served as a neighborhood dance hall at nights and on weekends. This kind of commercial activity in households is very common in poor neighborhoods and provides a major site for leisure activities in these areas. In this case, however, the children complained of violence, drug use, and sexual activity on the premises. The CT had received other complaints about this house already, and they sent the case to a juvenile justice court after confirming the complaints. The dance hall was closed. In another case, the CT received complaints about a boy who was involved in gang fights and violence; he had injured his head. They researched the situation and found that the youth was using drugs and missing school. They oversaw his return to school and set up counseling with a psychologist to treat not only the child's behavior but also his troubled relationship with his adoptive parents. In other cases, the CTs oversee local entities, such as neighborhood crèches or daycare centers, to make sure they are executing their responsibilities. They had received, in one example, a complaint against a daycare center in the lower-class neighborhood of Terra Firme, and their research found that the daycare center had no food, irregular operating hours, and seemed to be missing much of the materials (tables, chairs, desks, food, machines, etc.) that had been provided by the government. They filed a report with FUNPAPA (*Fundação Papa João XXIII*, Pope John XXIII Foundation), the city's major social work agency involved with children. Finally, the CTs also work with the city's budget office to indicate and estimate the needs of youth service programs and lobby for these resources.

Gomes's and Hazeu's experiences in Belém have taken place in a city that has only slowly developed the councils, although support from Edmilson Rodrigues, two-term mayor for the PT (1997–2004), provided the councils with increasing support, resources, and infrastructure. In general, the state Rights Councils and broader movement organizations see the CTs as the "heart of the system of guarantees [for the rights of minors]," establishing the centrality of these bodies to the development of the law.[38] The training of new councilors is an important component of the movement organizations' activities, as well as the subject of other private-state partnerships such as Instituto Amazônia Celular's "Pró-Conselho," a five-state study (Amapá, Amazonas, Maranhão, Pará, Roraima) of CTs and MRCs in Brazil's northern region. Instituto Amazônia Celular is the social development foundation of one of the largest cell-phone companies operating in northern Brazil, and "Pró-Conselho" has the support of the State Rights Councils and the state governments' *Centros de Apoio Operacional da Infância* (Operational Support Centers, or CAOs) in the Public Ministry. The "Pró-Conselho" study was completed in late 2003, and although it showed grave cases of underdevelopment of the CTs and their elected staff, it also pinpointed areas of need that the state governments, Rights Councils, CAOs, and Instituto Amazônia Celular are addressing with training and material support.[39]

The process of supporting and developing the means to implement the ECA draws on transnational support in many forms. In the Public Ministry of Pará, the CAO for Childhood and Youth has drawn on transnational organizations (UNICEF and the Netherlands' Terra dos Hommes) as well as several local organizations across the state and civil society (including the private University of Amazônia, the national government's Eradication of Child Labor Project,[40] and the corporate foundation Instituto Amazônia Celular), in order to develop the MSEs, combat child labor, create educational programs, and promote the "Pró-Conselho" project.[41] In São Paulo, the CAO won the Socio-Education Prize, second edition, for its work in institutional development of MSEs in November of 2000, receiving international recognition from ILANUD for its work. The São Paulo CAO partners internationally with the ILO, UNICEF, the UN, the Associazione Amici dei Bambini (Italy), and the Ronald MacDonald Institute.[42] The process extends from these institutions in the state to the neighborhood associations of places such as the Vila da Barca and the murals that Escola Aprendiz has placed all over São Paulo.

In 2001, the national government of Brazil, through its Special Secretary of Human Rights and the National Council for the Rights of the Child and Adolescent (CONANDA), published a report on the country's compliance with the goals elaborated in the CRC.[43] The report notes that the ECA was the legislative structure of compliance with the CRC and goes on to detail changes over the decade 1990–2000 in the CRC's major areas: child disease, primary care and basic health services, nutrition and food security, work and income-generating opportunities, education, the situation of women's health and safety, infant and child mortality, and so forth. For example, where the goal at the adoption of the CRC in Brazil was to reduce infant and child mortality by one-third by 2000, the report notes that the country has achieved a 30.6 percent and 29.5 percent reduction, respectively, in these two areas.[44] The report's overall conclusions across all the goals established in 1990 are encouraging, but in many cases the goals have not been met or sufficient data do not exist.

The report does not evaluate the institutionalization of the ECA's council structures or the legislation's success at rehabilitating juvenile offenders. Anecdotal data and reports from some local groups such as CEDECA/MRE indicate great variance in the success of the ECA's MSEs. ILANUD's Sócio-Education Prize is the best measure to date of the kinds of programs that work well, while reports from Amnesty International, Human Rights Watch, and journalists in Brazil document the most notorious cases of failure. As with the MSEs, the council structure of the ECA is undergoing a very slow and uneven process of institutional development across the country, and this process faces the same obstacles that we noted with the development of the MSEs. Yet to focus solely on the success or failure of specific parts of the ECA, such as the MSEs—which is the preoccupation of the sensationalistic press in Brazil and elsewhere—misses the importance of the statute in developing a robust discourse around children's rights that stands in contrast to 500 years of Brazilian history since the arrival of the Europeans.

CONCLUSIONS: THE ECA, DEMOCRACY, AND THE STRUGGLE FOR CHANGE

Brazil's ECA contributes to debates about the nature of democracy in the post–Cold War era as well as to debates about the nature of globalization itself. The ECA was the product of a regionally specific redemocratization movement and became the leading edge of the CRC's impact on Latin American law. To the extent that the ECA represents a real advance in liberal democracy and citizenship in a country where these have historically been distant ideals, the statute's history and the government's efforts to implement it lend support to a "world society" thesis of increasing international norms for the rule of law.[45] The connections between local groups and transnational actors, as well as the statute's effect on legislation around the region, show how a "global civil society" emerges to nurture new norms and practices.[46] Yet to understand how these processes structure change, we must return to Vila da Barca and other places like it: the statute nurtures new norms and practices not because it promises membership in a world society to Brazilian youth, but rather because it promises the rule of law and citizenship to youths in the local spaces of Brazilian society.

In this process, local movement activists and public officials open up new spaces for democratic deliberation and policy development, bringing processes for change from civil society into the state, which Leonardo Avritzer claims is crucial to consolidating democracy in Latin America.[47] Noting that the ECA was the first legislative reform in Latin America undertaken in the context of CRC, Emilio García Mendez, an Argentine attorney who in the 1990s was a project director for UNICEF in Brazil, echoes Avritzer by stating that the ECA unleashed a "process of juridical transformation" around the region that is changing the relationship between democracy and law.[48] For García Mendez, the children's rights movement brings legal reform into the public sphere and involves actors from the bottom up, in the Vila da Barca as well as the Escola Aprendiz.

But the ECA's long-term institutionalization presents problems for analysis. At the very least, the results so far are of the "glass half-full/half-empty" variety. Much has changed in Brazil as a result of the statute's council structure and the commitment of the national government under both presidents Cardoso (1995–2002) and Lula da Silva (2003–2006). My research from 1992 on in Belém shows that the statute is widely discussed across all segments of society. Even where people have a misinformed idea of what the statute really is, there are many others who correct, or at least challenge, these incorrect ideas. Belém's Padre Bruno summed up the ECA's objectives, the challenges it faces, and some of its connections to transnational processes in an interview on March 23, 2004. Asked to summarize the changes in Brazil since the ECA became law in 1990, he outlined how the statute's ultimate objectives have always depended on a new "socialization of power" between state and society, as well as the tensions at work in that process:

> The Statute inaugurated a way of treating children and adolescents within a vision of participatory democracy. This implies a change in power relations. It implies the participation of organized [civil] society as much in the definition as the execution of public policies. . . . The power of the State has to open itself up to being shared with organized society. . . . Of course, we live in a society that tends more toward vengeance than justice. Yet justice presumes the guarantee of fundamental rights, not only in Brazil, but globally . . . [and] Brazil cannot deny that the Statute has provoked a process of change, including in mentality.

Padre Bruno went on to note that, in his view, public reactions against the statute—by "law-and-order" politicians, police officers, or others who view the ECA as protecting or coddling child-criminals—have been declining. Marga Rothe, a Lutheran minister and the state of Pará's ombudswoman for the police forces, notes that public officials and movement actors *transform the state* when they demonstrate to the police how respect for human rights benefits them in their jobs and roles in the community.[49] Padre Bruno adds that Brazil's "federal government has increasingly valued the Statute, because they perceive that elsewhere [in other countries] they value the Statute."[50] Both Padre Bruno and Rothe stress that social change is incremental and depends on developing the legal institutions that provide channels for the citizenship claims of ordinary people, who are becoming increasingly aware of the how the law can be used. The ECA is not, all by itself, social change; it is a *framework* for social change. García Mendez presses the claim further: if the law's purpose is to transform society, it must envision a world very different from the present state of affairs; in this sense, law must challenge the "realism" of those who criticize rights legislation.[51] Law establishes ideals and frameworks within which rooted cosmopolitans and other social actors, inside and outside the state, can advance toward those ideals.

For Padre Bruno, Cecilia Hamoy, CEDECA, the MNMMR, and other social movement activists, the legal framework provides a way in which they can press claims about deepening the institutionalization of the ECA. For public officials in the agencies charged with implementing the ECA, the process is similar—but it is complicated by the fact that many, if not most, entrenched politicians and bureaucrats do not lend sufficient support to developing the mechanisms that the ECA needs to achieve its goals. For transnational actors in UNICEF, Oxfam, Save the Children, or the host of organizations and donors to programs such as Escola Aprendiz, it means both continued vigilance and insertion in Brazil's national context through donations and the presence of international NGOs in the country. For these actors, the ECA is a "work in progress" that is central to their lives' work, however slow and fraught with challenge it is. For most of the children in Brazil, however, the options created by the ECA are either less apparent or available, even though we can point to vibrant examples of youth activism such as the Vila da Barca's *Núcleo*. These children face the conundrum posed at the outset of this chapter: a glimpse of hope that is daily challenged, if not outright denied, by the violence and poverty of everyday life. Across all these actors, the options for social change remain bound by struggle; what the ECA brings to the struggle is greater clarity about the legal and institutional foundations for change.

The globalized discourses that bring both neoliberalism and children's rights to the forefront of Brazilian social, economic, political life are cross-cutting; the results, in terms of daily life, are far from reassuring. But we would be remiss to ignore the excitement that Sasha and I witnessed in our conversations with youths in Belém, as well as with activists and public officials around the country. The kind of conundrum represented by the Brazilian situation does not fit well with academic or journalistic tendencies to demand conclusive and far-reaching evidence of change before allowing that any change at all is taking place. Truer to life, we take from the Brazilian situation a lesson in the ways that democracy is always characterized by political struggles to realize its ideals. Rather than searching for the finished product—which in the history of political research has tended to hold societies up to unrealistic and hypocritical appraisals of the effectiveness of the industrialized democracies in North America and Western Europe—we would do well to appreciate the incremental processes that characterize the real development of democracy as it has unfolded everywhere that people have attempted to build democratic societies.[52]

ACRONYMS

ABRAPIA	Associação Brasileira Multiprofissional de Proteção à Infância e à Adolescência (Multiprofessional Brazilian Association for the Protection of Childhood and Adolescence)
ACMD	Associação Comunidade de Mãos Dadas (Community of Giving Hands Association)
AI	Amnesty International
AiBi	Associazione Amici dei Bambini (Friends of Children Association)
ANDI	*Agência de Notícias dos Direitos da Infância* (News Agency for Children's Rights)
CAO	Center for Operational Support
CDM	*Centro de Defesa do Menor* (Center for the Defense of the Minor)
CE	Cidade de Emaús (City of Emmaus)
CECRIA	Centro De Referência, Estudos, e Ações Sobre Crianças e Adolescentes (Center for Reference, Study, and Action Concerning Children and Adolescents)
CEDECA	*Centro de Defesa da Criança e Adolescente* (Center for the Defense of the Child and Adolescent)
CONANDA	*Conselho acional dos Ireitos da Criança e Adolescente* (National Council for the Rights of the Child and Adolescent)
CRAMI	*Centro Regional de Atenção aos Maus Tratos na Inafância do ABCD* (Regional Attendance Center for Badly Treated Children in the ABCD Region [of metropolitan São Paolo])
CRC	Convention on the Rights of the Child
CTs	*conselhos tutelares* (protection councils)

ECOS   *Comunicação em Sexualidade* (Communication about Sexuality)

FUNCAP   *Fundação da Criança e Adolescente do Pará* (Foundation for Children and Adolescents of Pará)

IAF   Inter-American Foundation

IIN   Inter-American Children's Institute

ILANUD   *Instituto Latino Americano das Nações Unidas para Prevenção do Delito e Tratamento do Delinquente* (United Nations Latin American Institute for the Prevention of Crime and Treatment of Delinquents)

MNMMR   *Movimento Nacional de Meninos e Meninas de Rua* (National Movement of Street Children)

MRCs   Municipal Rights Councils

MRE   *Movimento República Emaús* (Republic of Emmaus Movement)

MSEs   *medidas sócio-educativas* (socio-educational measures)

PETI   *Projeto Eradicação de Trabalho Infantil* (Project for the Eradication of Child Labor)

PT   *Partido dos Trabalhadores* (Workers' Party)

RPV   *República do Pequeno Vendedor* (Republic of the Little Vendor)

ENDNOTES

1. *Relatório de Cidadania III: Os Jovens e os Direitos Humanos* (São Paulo: Rede de Observatórios de Direitos Humanos, 2002), p. 69. All translations, unless otherwise noted, are by the author.

2. These observations of the Vila da Barca and the story of the youth group there are based on a meeting with the *Núcleo de Defesa das Crianças e Adolescentes da Vila da Barca*, March 23, 2004, and on that group's contribution to the *Relatório de Cidadania III*, pp. 61–69.

3. The national census of 2000 indicated that the average monthly income of heads-of-households in Belém was R$859.89 (about US$472.00). In wealthier neighborhoods, the average was R$2,476.95 ($1358.72); in Telégrafo, the larger neighborhood of which the Vila da Barca is one part, the average was R$639.32 ($350.70). Most income earners are not heads-of-household, and their income is less. The conversion to U.S. dollars is based on the June 1, 2000, rate, as a general indicator of the salary value. See Instituto Brasileiro de Geografia e Estatística, *Censo Demográfico 2000* (Rio de Janeiro: IBGE, 2000).

4. In 1993, when I first began my research in Belém, several stories ran in the national press about declining average height for poor Brazilians as an indicator of poverty in the country, and the local paper published the results for Belém. "Miséria faz nanicos em Belém," ("Poverty creates dwarfs in Belém") *O Liberal* June 10, 1993. Malnutrition and basic health statistics in Brazil continue to reflect these disparities.

5. See *Pesquisa Nacional por Amostra de Domicílios* (Rio de Janeiro: IBGE, 2001); and

UNICEF, *The State of the World's Children* (Oxford: Oxford University Press, 1992). According to Gini index statistics compiled by the World Bank and the United Nations Development Program, Brazil is one of the four most unequal societies on earth, Central African Republic, Sierra Leone, and Swaziland being the others, followed closely by Guatemala, South Africa, and Paraguay. See Helmut Anheier, Marlies Glasius, and Mary Kaldor, eds., *Global Civil Society 2001* (Oxford: Oxford University Press, 2001), Table R17, pp. 276–79.

6. Sidney Tarrow, *The New Transnational Activism* (New York: Cambridge University Press, 2005), Chapter 3.

7. Sonia Alvarez characterizes the Brazilian constitutional process as "council democracy"; see "Reweaving the Fabric of Collective Action: Social Movements and Challenges 'Actually Existing Democracy' in Brazil," in R. Fox and O. Starn, eds., *Between Resistance and Revolution: Cultural Politics and Social Protest*, pp. 83–117 (New Brunswick, New Jersey: Rutgers University Press, 1997). In *Democracy and the Public Space in Latin America* (Princeton: Princeton University Press, 2002), Leonardo Avritzer compares Brazilian, Argentinean, and Mexican processes of democratization and argues that state-society partnerships are building a new "public space for democracy" in the region.

8. See Guidry, "The Useful State? Social Movements and the Citizenship of Children in Brazil," in J. A. Guidry, M. D. Kennedy, and M. N. Zald, eds., *Globalizations and Social Movements: Power, Culture and the Transnational Public Sphere* (University of Michigan Press, 2000); and J. A. Guidry, "'Trial by Space': The Spatial Politics of Citizenship and Social Movements in Urban Brazil," *Mobilization* vol. 8 (2) (2003), 189–204.

9. A *master frame* is a general motif for collective action that, in a given period or cycle of protest, can knit together several different social movement organizations and provide impetus to the wave of action in a given cycle. See David A. Snow and Robert D. Benford, "Master Frames and Cycles of Protest," in A. Morris and C. Mueller, eds., *Frontiers in Social Movement Theory* (New Haven: Yale University Press, 1992), pp. 133–55. See also David Snow, E. Burke Rochford, Jr., Steven K. Worden, and Robert Benford's "Frame Alignment Processes, Micromobilization, and Movement Participation," *American Sociological Review* 51 (4) (1986), pp. 464–81; and Snow and Benford, "Ideology, Frame Resonance, and Participant Mobilization," in B. Klandermans, H. Kriesi, and S. Tarrow, eds., *International Social Movement Research, Vol. 1, From Structure to Action*, pp. 197–217 (Greenwich, Conn.: JAI Press, 1988).

10. See Maria Helena Moreira Alves, *State and Opposition in Military Brazil* (Austin: University of Texas Press, 1985); Gay Seidman, *Manufacturing Militance: Workers' Movements in Brazil and South Africa, 1970–1985* (Berkeley: University of California Press, 1994); Margaret Keck, *The Workers' Party and Democratization in Brazil* (New Haven: Yale University Press, 1992); Paulo Freire, *Pedagogy of the Oppressed* (New York: Continuum, 1983); and Daniel H. Levine, *Popular Voices in Latin American Catholicism* (Princeton: Princeton University Press, 1992).

11. The Constitutional Assembly allowed citizens to present potential constitutional articles by petition, which led to 122 amendments bearing no less than 12,265,854 signatures. Keck, *The Workers' Party and Democratization in Brazil*, p. 225.

12. República Federativa do Brasil, *Relatório da República Federativa do Brasil sobre o Cumprimento das Metas Emanadas da Cúpula Mundial pelas Crianças* (2001), p. 6 (available at http://www.presidencia.gov.br/sedh/).

13. See http://www.emauscrianca.org.br.

14. Gilberto Dimenstein, *A Guerra dos Meninos* (São Paulo: Brasiliense, 1990); *Meninas da Noite: A Prostituição de Meninas-Escravas no Brasil* (São Paulo: Editora Ática, 1992); *O Cidadão de Papel: A Infância, A Adolescência e os Direitos Humanos no Brasil* (São Paulo: Editora Ática, 1993).

15. Interview with author, March 26, 2004.

16. See Escola Aprendiz's *100 Muros: Relato de uma Experiência* (São Paulo: Estúdio Infinito, 2003).

17. *Esmeralda: Por Que Não Dancei* (São Paulo: Editora SENAC, 2001).

18. See www.andi.org.br.

19. Geoffrey Robertson, *Crimes against Humanity* (New York: New Press, 1999), p. 101.

20. República Federativa do Brasil, *Relatório da República Federativa do Brasil*, pp. 5–7.

21. The exceptions are Argentina, Chile, Colombia, Mexico, and Uruguay. Emilio García Mendez, personal communication with the author, March 29, 2004; and Ana Celina Bentes Hamoy, interview with author, March 22, 2004.

22. In "Trial by Space," I use Henri Lefebvre's concept of the "trial by space" to demonstrate how the ECA attempts a deep transformation of concrete behaviors in both public and private space. The ECA's intervention in these spaces aims to preserve their public or private nature through citizenship standards instead of dissolving the distinction between public and private. See Henri Lefebvre, *The Production of Space*, trans. D. Nicholson-Smith (Oxford: Blackwell, [1974] 1991), pp. 416–17.

23. In territorial terms, the *município* in Brazil is roughly equivalent to the county in the U.S. system; in structure and governance, it operates like a U.S. municipality, with a mayor (*prefeito*) as the executive and a municipal council.

24. Felício Pontes, Jr., *Conselho de Direitos da Criança e do Adolescente* (São Paulo: Malheiros Editores, 1993), p. 20.

25. *Ibid.*, p. 51.

26. Specifically, the CTs are to oversee the application of the ECA's correctional provisions, where the rights of children and adolescents are violated (a) "by action or omission of the society or state," (b) "by the negligence, omission or abuse of parents or guardians," and (c) "by reason of [the youth's] own conduct" (art. 98). Functionally, the CT is one authority to whom people (of any age) may turn if, for example, they know that a neighbor is physically abusing his or her children. The CTs should also oversee the correctional measures applied to youths who break the law. As for the juvenile justice system, it is set out as an administrative apparatus to execute the statute and prevent young people from becoming mixed up in the regular penal system, where it is understood they will be abused, victimized, and inaugurated into a larger life of crime.

27. Edson Sêda, *ABC do Conselho Tutelar* (São Paulo: Centro Brasileiro da Infância e Adolescência, 1992), p. 7.

28. In Belém, elections for the CTs involve a turnout of around 2,000 to 3,000 voters in each of the four districts, which is a very small percentage of the hundreds of thousands of residents in each district. This signals that there is a great deal of work to be done in creating more proactive involvement in the ECA's implementation in society, but it is a start. As an effort to confront and change long-established relational and authoritarian traditions regarding youths,

the movement takes a long-term approach to developing greater participation. Hamoy, interview with author, May 22, 2003. Hamoy is a lawyer who has been a leading activist in the MRE and CEDECA (CDM) since the early 1980s.

29. Denise Neri Blanes, Maria do Carmo Brant de Carvalho, and Maria Cecília R. Nobre Barreira, *Trabalhando Conselhos Tutelares* (São Paulo: Instituto de Estudos Especiais, Pontífica Universidade Católica de São Paulo, n.d.), p. 21.

30. Data on FUNCAP programs is from the *Relatório Annual da FUNCAP, 2003*, which was in preparation at the time of this research but which was shared with the author. The status of the annual report and the programs were elaborated by Ana Maria Gomes Chamma, President of FUNCAP, and Paula Lisboa Dias, Coordinator of MSEs, in interviews and site visits on March 18, 2004 and March 22, 2004.

31. On São Paulo, see Amnesty International, "A Waste of Lives: FEBEM Juvenile Detention Centers, São Paulo," July 5, 2000. On riots in FUNCAP's EREC (*Espaço Recomeço*, "Space for New Beginning"), see Human Rights Watch, "Confinamento Cruel: Abusos contra Crianças detidas no norte do Brasil," *Human Rights Watch* 15 (1B), (April 2003).

32. Michael J. Mitchell and Charles H. Wood, "Ironies of Citizenship: Skin Color, Police Brutality, and the Challenge to Democracy in Brazil," *Social Forces* 77 (3) (1999), pp. 1001–20, show how the Brazilian police concentrate their efforts not only on violent crime but also on the cases in which the suspects are poor and nonwhite.

33. See ILANUD, *Sócio-Educação no Brasil: Adolescentes em Conflito com a Lei: Experiências de Medidas Sócio-Educativas* (São Paulo: ILANUD, n.d.).

34. *Ibid.*, pp. 17–20. For the first edition of the prize, the state of São Paulo had 35 nominations, with the rest of the states varying between 1 and 8 nominations. In the second edition, São Paulo again led with 34 nominations, but Pará jumped to third place with 10, and the second edition recognized that although the industrialized states of southern Brazil led the field, the northern region (Amazonia and Pará) had registered significant improvements.

35. Ronald Ahnen, "Civil Society's Push for Political Space: Child and Adolescent Rights Councils in Brazil," *International Journal of Children's Rights* 9 (2001), 15–43.

36. Interview with author, May 23, 2003.

37. Interview with author, August 13, 1998.

38. Marcel Hazeu and Rosely de Souza Moura, "Avaliação do Sistema de Garantias dos Direitos da Criança e do Adolescente no Pará," *Observatório da Cidadania Pará, Anuário 99*, pp. 83–104 (Belém: FAOR, 2000), p. 88. The "system of guarantees" is a national program within the children's rights movement to monitor the establishment of the law's mechanisms.

39. Rosidéa Moreira Borges de Cantuária, Executive Secretary of the State Council for the Rights of the Child and Adolescent, Pará, interview with author, May 26, 2003; Marcia Helena Marinho, researcher, Instituto Amazônia Celular, interview with author, May 28, 2003; and Maria do Socorro Mendo, CAO da Infância e Juventude do Ministério Público do Estado do Pará, interview with author, March 19, 2004.

40. *Projeto Eradicação de Trabalho Infantil,* PETI.

41. Maria do Socorro Mendo, CAO da Infância e Juventude do Ministério Público do Estado do Pará, interview with author, March 19, 2004.

42. Laila Said Abdel Qader Shukair and Roberto Barbosa Alves, CAO da Infância e Juventude do Ministério Público do Estado de São Paulo, interview with author, March 25, 2004.

43. República Federativa do Brasil, *Relatório da República Federativa do Brasil sobre o Cumprimento das Metas Emanadas da Cúpula Mundial pelas Crianças* (2001).

44. *Ibid.*, p. 20.

45. John W. Meyer, John Boli, George M. Thomas, and Francisco O. Ramirez, "World Society and the Nation-State," *American Journal of Sociology* 103 (1) (1997), pp. 144–81.

46. Jackie Smith and Hank Johnston, eds., *Globalization and Resistance* (Lanham, MD: Rowman and Littlefield, 2002).

47. Avritzer, *Democracy and the Public Space in Latin America*, p. 170.

48. Emilio Gárcia Mendez, "Infancia, Ley y Democracia: Una Cuestión de Justicia," pp. 9–29 in E. Gárcia Mendez and M. Beloff, eds., *Infancia, Ley y Democracia en América Latina* (Santa Fé de Bogotá and Buenos Aires: Editorial Temis and Ediciones Depalma, 1998), pp. 11–13.

49. Interview with author, March 20, 2004.

50. Interview with author, March 23, 2004.

51. García Mendez, p. 20.

52. John A. Guidry and Mark Q. Sawyer, "Contentious Pluralism: The Public Sphere and Democracy," *Perspectives on Politics* 1 (2) (2003), pp. 273–89.

11

Global Regulation and Local Political Struggles: Early Marriage in Northern Nigeria

ANNIE BUNTING AND

SALLY ENGLE MERRY

Local people want their daughter to be moral, want their daughter to be mature. The price for morality is so high, families and parents are willing to gamble. With Islamic awareness, the price is higher.

—Nigerian doctor, Kano, 2003

This chapter addresses one aspect of youth, globalization, and the law—the increasing control exercised over girls under pressures of globalization and the global legal discourses invoked to address this control. The vast increases in the dissemination of messages through the electronic media for urban young people and mushrooming migration within and among nations has produced youth cultures shaped by transnational ideas and differing significantly from the culture of parents and grandparents.[1] Such a high degree of new ideas and experiences for young people often provokes anxiety in older generations in many locations. These new youth societies also pose challenges for regulatory systems such as police and courts as they coalesce into gangs or rebellious collectivities. Male rather than female youth occupy center stage in these debates. We wanted to think about what happens to young women who are excluded from this urban, male, street-focused scenario and look at how global processes might affect them. In northern Nigeria, for example, "parents send boys to study the Qur'an under hard conditions—begging in the streets—but they don't send the girls. They would rather marry them."[2] Adolescent women in northern Nigeria always married young. Now, in response to greater civil disorder, crime, or economic uncertainty, they face marriage at even younger ages and at higher rates. For youthful wives, the implications of globalization are quite different than they are for urban male youths. They have fewer opportunities than their male counterparts to participate in public spaces from the school to the street. They may face greater restrictions rather than fewer, earlier entrance into motherhood rather than later, and an adult life more constrained than the lives of women were in the past. At the same time, a transnational human rights movement is challenging the practice of youthful marriage for girls. Globalization's impact on youth, we argue, encompasses the struggles over early marriage as well as efforts to regulate urban street youth.

This chapter is less about the incidence and implications of early marriage than about the shifting global and local politics of regulating it.[3] Northern Nigeria is one of the areas where this issue has achieved significant international visibility and attracted transnational human rights activism, particularly in recent years. Various groups inside and outside Nigeria have defined *early marriage* either as a human rights violation, a health hazard, a response to governmental crisis and economic uncertainty, or a religious duty to prevent promiscuity. There are significant differences among the groups that promote each of these perspectives. Regional variations in the importance of protecting culture and religion and promoting a human rights framework are striking. The predominantly Muslim north is turning to a revived Islamic law and religious life in order to counter the chaos of the collapsing state. The more religiously diverse south, largely Christian and secular with a significant Muslim minority, has relied more extensively on a discourse of human rights to rectify similar injustices and instabilities. Some argue that the "Shariazation" or "Islamicization" of the north is also a form of human rights, in this case the right to merge religion, culture, and politics. All regions are attempting to respond to a collapsing state and economy. The current political and economic turmoil in the country has produced the rise and fall of a human rights framework for early marriage and has had a profound effect on the cultural politics of human rights—in particular, the cultural politics of women's rights in the north. Thus, the global effort to regulate early marriage is a profoundly local activity.

As transnational, national, and local human rights activists from a variety of political positions have intervened to reduce early marriage in northern Nigeria, they have relied on a wide variety of ways of understanding this issue. The analysis in our chapter focuses on the competing discourses surrounding early marriage and the effects of these disjunctures on how the problem is understood and addressed. The contradictions between transnational views and the perspectives of local actors tend to evoke nationalist religious or cultural responses. The activists and academics with whom we talked are trying to negotiate these contradictions at various levels. They face the dilemmas of legitimating their activities and interventions locally while mobilizing the power of a global discourse—activists draw on human rights discourse, a "symbolic good" very much in global circulation.[4]

Early marriage, like female genital cutting, provokes strong critics and strong defenders. The case of early marriage, however, has not provoked the same amount of scholarly attention and international activism as female genital cutting.[5] International women's rights scholarship and activism over the past two decades has had little to say about early marriage as a women's rights issue. Marriage practices and age of marriage have not been left unexamined, of course, by policymakers interested in family reform: during colonization, colonial powers routinely criticized marriage institutions and practises as "barbaric" and in need of reform.[6] In India and Nigeria, for example, there were legislative attempts to regulate age at marriage.[7] Colonial administrators and social reformers referred to the issue as "child marriage," and contemporary international women's rights documents and advocates also refer to marriage of those under the age of 18 years as "child marriage."

Our research into human rights approaches to early marriage in northern Nigeria is based on interviews conducted in 1994, 2003, and 2005. The later research revealed much less talk of human rights violations. In the later interviews, early marriage was being addressed largely in terms of health issues. This chapter compares the way early marriage was understood by activists in the north in the early 2000s with the way it was understood in the early 1990s and suggests why the change has occurred. We begin by tracing the historical emergence of the issue over the last century in order to show the continuity between the British colonial regulation of marriage in the early 1900s and contemporary international human rights regulations. Nevertheless, despite the long history of British imperial struggles against early marriage in India and parts of the Middle East, this practice has received relatively little attention as a human rights violation until recent years. Spurred in part by concern about the health consequences of early childbirth, UNICEF recently issued a statement identifying early marriage as a human rights violation, and targeted certain countries in Africa in particular.[8] We then examine the variations in contemporary approaches to the issue among activists in Nigeria. This analysis reveals how significant local political and economic conditions are for international efforts to regulate practices such as early marriage.

HISTORICAL PERSPECTIVES AND THE EMERGENCE
OF A HUMAN RIGHTS APPROACH

Early marriage—child marriage and child brides—has been included in international conventions as a women's human rights "problem" since the 1960s, but it has not received much international attention until recently. The scrutiny and regulation of marriage customs in general and age at marriage in particular, however, dates back to the early 1900s.[9] As notions of childhood changed at the turn of the nineteenth century in England, attitudes toward age at marriage shifted. There were a number of different objections raised to early marriage, including lack of consent. Marriage customs in many colonized locales were seen as emblematic of the uncivilized nature of those cultures. In addition, reform efforts focused on girl children sold into domestic servitude in the early twentieth century included feminist arguments about sexual exploitation as well as concerns about child welfare.

The history of agitation against child marriage reveals the coexistence of multiple approaches. Some groups focused on parallels to slavery, others on the sexual exploitation of young girls and patriarchy, some on reproductive health consequences, and others on the importance of a girl's consent to her marriage. The role of international organizations such as the League of Nations and the United Nations, as well as nongovernmental organizations (NGOs) such as the Anti-Slavery Society, was crucial in raising the issue of early marriage. Although international conventions advocate national laws specifying a minimum age of marriage, they are unable to enforce such laws themselves.

Early advocacy around "child marriage" was linked to the anti-slavery movement in the 1920s. The League of Nations launched an inquiry into slavery in 1922 and appointed a Temporary Slavery Commission in 1924.[10] The commission's mandate was to seek the elimination of all forms of slavery, including forced marriage and child marriage. In 1926 the League of Nations passed the Slavery Convention. The British Anti-Slavery Society[11] remained active during the 1930s in opposition to British colonial interests. It advocated humanistic reforms in British colonies, sometimes in conjunction with an emerging women's movement in Britain. In 1929, the Child Marriage Restraint Act in India made it illegal to marry or participate in the marriage of a girl under 16 years. A permanent Advisory Committee of Experts on Slavery was established by the League of Nations in 1935 to monitor progress on the abolition of slavery.[12] The United Nations broadened the definition of slavery in the 1926 Convention to include servile forms of marriage in its Supplementary Convention on the Abolition of Slavery in 1956. The Supplementary Convention stated, in Article 2: "States Parties undertake to prescribe, where appropriate, suitable minimum ages of marriage, to encourage the use of facilities whereby the consent of both parties to a marriage may be freely expressed in the presence of a competent civil or religious authority, and to encourage the registration of marriages."[13]

One of the important struggles against forms of servitude by girl children was the campaign against the practice of *mui tsai* in Hong Kong by British activists in the 1920s and 1930s.[14] *Mui tsai* were bonded female domestic servants. British activists in the 1920s defined the practice as a feminist issue and referred to the girls as "child slaves." Feminists accused Chinese men of purchasing girls for sexual exploitation and saw the problem as one of patriarchy, while Chinese elites and British colonial officials defended *mui tsai* as a Chinese custom that should be respected. The Anti-Slavery Society actively joined the campaign against the practice of *mui tsai*. By the late 1930s, the framework of activists working on this problem had expanded to include a child welfare approach providing services for and supervision of women and children. Such humanitarian conceptions were fundamental aspects of the justifications for continued imperial rule during the 1930s as the practice of early marriage came under continued critique.[15] The intervention of the League of Nations and its Slavery Convention of 1926 was important in mobilizing international attention to the plight of girls in sexual relationships without choice. However, an Advisory Committee of Experts agreed in 1935 to differentiate between marriages or concubinage formed through payment of bride price, defined as outside slavery, and *mui tsai* and other practices that did represent slavery.[16]

In Nigeria, British colonization in the early 1900s meant the abolition of slavery but not the end of women's seclusion. In the Sokoto Caliphate,[17] free Hausa women went into *purdah* (seclusion) as opposed to working in agriculture, work which had been previously performed by slaves.[18] Barbara Cooper notes that the relationship between the decline in slavery and the increase in female seclusion is more complex than some authors may suggest. She argues that "the broader political, economic and cultural environment affects how seclusion is understood at various historical moments and therefore influences the rate at which it is adopted."[19] According to some historical accounts, the abolition of slavery also affected the status of junior wives in the compound as older and better-off wives asserted their power.[20] The colonial administrators in northern Nigeria were complicit with aristocratic men concerning female slavery and controlling female labor.[21]

Under the pre-independence Native Authority Law, 1954, of Northern Nigeria,[22] a native authority could legislate in the area of "regulating child betrothals" and "regulating and controlling the movement of children and young females from or within the area."[23] There were some attempts to use these powers in the late 1950s and early 1960s—at the time of independence—to regulate early marriage. Native Authorities passed declarations concerning minimum marriageable age for Biu, Idoma, Tiv, and Borgu marriages. The four orders had different ages: puberty, 12, 13, and 14.[24] The laws were largely ineffective at the time, but they remained on the books in Nigeria in the 1990s although they were unknown even within the legal profession.

In addition to legislative initiatives on marriage age in various countries, there were early international treaties on the issue. One international convention in 1962 called on signatory countries to pass legislation to specify a minimum marriageable age and to eliminate the marriage of girls under the age of puberty.[25] The United Nations passed a Recommendation three years later, in 1965, which advocated that the minimum marriageable age be no less than 15 years.[26] The Universal Declaration of Human Rights and both covenants enacting the declaration [27] hold that marriage should be entered into with full and free consent, but none of these define the age below which an individual lacks the requisite capacity to consent to marriage. Article 16 of the Universal Declaration does, however, refer to men and women of "full age" who have the right to marry and found a family.

The basic United Nations documents detailing the rights of women and children both include a prohibition on child marriage. The Convention on the Elimination of All Forms of Discrimination Against Women (CEDAW) was promulgated in 1979, and the Convention on the Rights of the Child (CRC) in 1989.[28] Both state that child marriage shall have no legal effect, although neither says that it is actually prohibited. Article 16 of CEDAW states: "The betrothal and the marriage of a child shall have no legal effect, and all necessary action, including legislation, shall be taken to specify a minimum age for marriage and to make the registration of marriages in an official registry compulsory."

The committee responsible for CEDAW has commented on Article 16 (marriage and family relations) on the importance of a woman's right to choose in marriage in its General Recommendation No. 21 (1994):

> A woman's right to choose a spouse and enter freely into marriage is central to her life and to her dignity and equality as a human being. An examination of States Parties' reports discloses that there are countries which, based on custom, religious beliefs or the ethnic origins of particular groups of people, permit forced marriages or remarriages. Other countries allow a woman's marriage to be arranged for payment or preferment and in others, women's poverty forces them to marry foreign nationals for financial security. Subject to reasonable restrictions based for example on a woman's youth or consanguinity with her partner, a woman's right to choose when, if, and whom she will marry must be protected and enforced at law.[29]

The committee further comments that, following the CRC, a *child* generally means every human under 18, and that,

> . . . the minimum age for marriage should be 18 years for both man and woman. When men and women marry, they assume important responsibilities. Consequently, marriage should not be permitted before they have attained full maturity and capacity to act. According to the World Health Organization, when minors, particularly girls, marry and have children, their health can be adversely affected and their education is impeded. As a result, their economic activity is restricted.[30]

The General Recommendation advocates that states themselves regulate age at marriage and set up registries for marriage.

In addition to anti-slavery and women's rights perspectives on early marriage, a health perspective emerged in the late 1970s. As early as 1958, there were international movements focusing on customs subjecting girls to ritual operations such as female circumcision. The UN Economic and Social Council asked the World Health Organization (WHO) to study the persistence of these customs at that time, leading to a subsequent focus on harmful traditional practices. The WHO held a seminar in Khartoum, Sudan, in 1979 that led to the formation of the Inter-African Committee on Traditional Practices Affecting the Health of Women and Children.[31] Along with the campaign against female genital cutting, the committee raised the issue of early marriage. "Child marriage" was explicitly included as a harmful traditional practice.[32]

The WHO linked early marriage to early childbearing and the associated risks. The African Charter on the Rights and Welfare of the Child, in effect in 1999, also prohibits the marriage and betrothal of girls and boys. The campaign against harmful traditional practices, often focusing on the health consequences for women and girls and emphasizing female genital cutting, expanded in the 1980s. It became a concern for the UN Human Rights Commission, UNICEF, UNESCO, and WHO, as well as many NGOs. In 1994, a spokesperson for Anti-Slavery International told the Working Group on Contemporary Forms of Slavery of the Human Rights Commission that there were still problems of marriage under the age of majority and a lack of women's rights in marriage, and that in some countries the situation was worsening.[33] The 1995 Beijing Declaration and Platform for Action[34] address child marriage as a harmful traditional custom from a gender discrimination and human rights perspective. In 1995, Anti-Slavery International published a report on *Servile Forms of Marriage* for the Beijing conference.

Despite these efforts over the past hundred years, little sustained commentary has been brought to bear on the issue of "child marriage" or marriageable age as a human rights violation. Concern has focused on slavery, on customs harmful to health, and on the need to develop national and international standards of minimum age and consent. Only recently has early marriage been explicitly defined as a violation of human rights. In 1998, the Forum on Marriage and the Rights of Women and Girls (the Forum) was established; its main concerns were early and forced marriage, non-consensual sex within marriage, domestic and family violence, and female genital mutilation.[35] The Forum was a coalition founded by several NGOs working on women's and children's issues, based primarily in the United Kingdom: Anti-Slavery International, CHANGE, Child Rights Information Network, International Planned Parenthood Association, and Save the Children UK. The Forum published "Early Marriage: Whose Right to Choose?" in 2000, "Early Marriage: Sexual Exploitation and the Human Rights of Girls" in 2001, and "Early Marriage and Poverty: Exploring the Links for Policy and Programme Development" in 2003.[36]

According to its mission statement:

> The Forum is a network of UK-based NGOs with international affiliates, sharing a vision of marriage as a sphere in which women and girls have inalienable rights. Our shared commitment to social justice places central importance on the need to bring principles and rights which are accepted in the public sphere into effective operation in the private sphere, particularly in marriage. As a Forum we are committed to the inalienability of the human rights of women throughout their lives, which cannot be reduced or violated by marriage and to the breaking down of barriers (including legal, social and cultural) that impact adversely on women's and girl's rights within marriage.[37]

The Forum's principle areas of concern are forced and early marriage, defined under CRC guidelines as marriage for women under 18 years, and violence against women and girls in and related to marriage. UNICEF funded the preparation of their report. Recently, Forum hosted a regional NGO conference on early marriage in Burkina Faso. The meeting drafted the Ouagadougou Declaration on Child Marriage (2003).[38]

The work of the Forum became the basis for the 2001 UNICEF publication, *Early Marriage, Child Spouses* (Innocenti Center). In this document, UNICEF notes that "despite the efforts of reformers in the early part of the 20th century, early marriage has received scant attention from the modern women's rights and children's rights movements. There has been virtually no attempt to examine the practice as a human rights violation in itself."[39] This is the approach the UNICEF authors advocate. UNICEF has turned toward a human rights focus in the late 1990s in general, and in these publications it has recast early marriage as a human rights violation. Thus, the emergence of early marriage as a human rights violation builds on the conjunction of activists working against slavery, those working against the health hazards of traditional harmful practices, feminist activism against violence against women, and established advocates of child welfare approaches. Reform efforts incorporate health concerns, feminist critiques of patriarchy, and human rights preoccupations with consent and choice. This range of approaches reflects both local politics and the influence of international perspectives.

The UNICEF Situation Report for Nigeria (2001) discusses early marriage and its consequences, placing the issue squarely in the context of CEDAW and CRC: "this is another example of large-scale violation of the basic rights of girls who are victims of marriages arranged by their parents without their consent and as a result are exposed to the health hazards of early pregnancy and deprived of educational opportunities."[40] Within northern Nigeria, by contrast, women's groups' strategies over the past decade have evolved from approaching early marriage as a women's rights issue with serious health consequences to strategies with less emphasis on women's human rights and less emphasis on women's reproductive ill-health, in particular vesico-vaginal fistulae (VVF), as a consequence of early marriage.[41] In the sections that follow we will explore the contemporary strategies adopted by women's groups in northern Nigeria and several factors that may affect them.

EARLY MARRIAGE IN NORTHERN NIGERIA: 1994–2005

In the states of northern Nigeria, a predominantly Muslim Hausa region, many girls are routinely married before they reach puberty. Their primary school education may be discontinued; they move to their husband's compound and live in *purdah* (seclusion); their knowledge of the Qur'an or other texts is very limited; and they may begin child bearing within months of their first menstruation. Statistics from the mid 1990s demonstrate the extent to which girls are married at or before puberty and certainly before the age of 18.[42] According to data from 1999, the national median age of marriage had increased slightly since 1991 while the median ages in the northwest and northeast were 14.6 years and 15.0 years respectively (NDHS, 1999).

In Kebbi State, "the average age of marriage for girls is just over 11 years."[43] "In the North West and North East, over 50 percent of girls aged 15–19 were either already mothers or pregnant, compared to about 8 percent in the southern zone."[44]

In the mid 1990s Women in Nigeria (WIN)[45] and the VVF Task Force[46] invited Human Rights Watch (HRW) to research a report on early marriage in northern Nigeria. A military government had been in power in Nigeria since 1983 and the politics of religion were interwoven with military rule. The military regimes of Generals Buhari and Idiagbon (1983–1985), General Babangida (1985–1993), and General Abacha (1993–1998) created an "atmosphere of terror and repression" in the country and banned professional, political, and student associations.[47] Buhari, Babangida, and Abacha were "Muslim military dictators from the North . . . each more corrupt than his predecessor."[48] The economic crisis that began in the 1980s in Nigeria and continued through the mid 1990s was provoked by Nigerian dependence on oil exports, the rapid decline in world oil prices in the 1980s, and state mismanagement. As Hussaina Abdullah argues, "as a consequence of this [collapse of the middle class], Nigeria witnessed a realignment of social forces in a manner that produced the three trends (religious, human rights and women's activism) . . . and which reflected a tension between the forces of secularism and parochialism, democracy and authoritarianism, and centralism and decentralization."[49]

Women's activism on the issue of early marriage, therefore, reflected the tensions in the country as well as tensions among various women's organizations, including WIN, the National Council of Women's Societies (NCWS), the VVF Task Force, and religious women's groups such as the Federation of Muslim Women's Associations of Nigeria (FOMWAN) and the Muslim Sisters Organization (MSO), which we discuss below. In examining the Nigerian women's movement, Abdullah notes that the NCWS, the "government-recognized umbrella organization for women," was "established in 1959 as a non-political and non-religious organization devoted to the promotion of the education, welfare and improved status of Nigerian women."[50] The NCWS dominated the women's movement from 1959 to the 1980s, when WIN was established in 1983.[51] Much more radical and political than NCWS, WIN was established as a national feminist organization. In contrast to both NCWS and WIN, which have membership in northern Nigeria but lack significant Muslim women's participation, FOMWAN is a Muslim women's umbrella organization.

In the early 1990s, WIN, along with the NCWS and the Nigerian Medical Association, lobbied the national government to legislate a universal minimum age of marriage of 18 years. The federal government itself acknowledged in its report to CEDAW in 1987 that there was a "crying need" to codify marriage laws and establish a marriage age.[52] These law reform efforts were not successful. WIN and the VVF Task Force, therefore, appealed to the international human rights forum. In 1994, at the time of the Human Rights Watch mission, women's rights activists were careful about how they framed the issue. During a 1994 conference organized by WIN, many participants called child marriage a human rights abuse.[53] To frame early marriage bluntly or as only a women's rights violation, however, would not be successful. The focus of the public education and policy efforts, thus, was the health repercussions of early marriage, in particular vesico-vaginal fistulae, or VVF.

The HRW research mission to northern Nigeria included interviews in five cities in northern Nigeria: Kano, Zaria, Katsina, Kaduna, and Sokoto. We conducted interviews with women about their age at first marriage, pregnancy and birth, and the circumstances of the marriage more generally. The average age of marriage of the 58 women interviewed was roughly 14 years; 27 said they were married at 13 or younger. All the women stated that they had not had sex before marriage and most said they did not feel prepared for sexual relations with their husbands. The vast majority of women interviewed experienced VVF. The 17 girls and young women who knew their husbands' ages reported an average 10-year age disparity; the widest margin was greater than 25 years. We also conducted interviews with workers in the healthcare professions, social workers, lawyers, community leaders, government officials, and women's rights activists about the strategies to address early age at first marriage in Nigeria. Early marriage was viewed by many in the north as tied to religion and proper moral behavior. An important rationale for marrying your daughter before puberty was to avoid "shame" being brought on your family name if she became pregnant outside of marriage. Further, some religious and community leaders told their constituencies that it was their religious duty to marry their daughters before puberty—thus to criticize early marriage was to criticize Islam.

The health focus in advocacy against early marriage in the north caused an interesting dilemma for Human Rights Watch because its organizational mandate did not yet include socioeconomic rights. It was clear that to address early marriage in northern Nigeria in a way that reflected the local efforts, rights to health, education, and poverty had to be addressed. HRW would also have to engage with the religious politics of the time in northern Nigeria. Further, many of the affected women did not see their marriage as problematic; they would say they consented to the marriage. For these and other reasons, the report did not see the light of day.[54]

Over eight years later, in 2003, Bunting conducted research on the ongoing efforts to address early marriage, and in 2005 Bunting and Merry did further research on this issue.[55] Although many of the same cultural dynamics were at play in the politics around women's rights, some important changes are underway. A civilian government with a southern Christian president—Olusegun Obasanjo—replaced the military government of General Abacha in May 1999, and so the politics of religion have shifted again.[56] Religious conflicts between Christians and Muslims in the country "resumed after the democratic elections in Nigeria" in 1999; these conflicts included religious riots in the northern cities of Kaduna and Kano.[57] A new hegemony is emerging in the north around Islamicization at the same time that the Nigerian state is weak to the point of possible collapse.[58] The expansion of Shari'a laws in various northern states, beginning with Zamfara State, also had a direct impact on women's activism in the north and the involvement of both southern civil liberties groups and transnational feminists. In particular, the introduction of Shari'a punishments—including flogging, hand or arm amputation, and stoning—has contributed to much greater caution about advocating feminist challenges to the status of women in society. Dramatic sanctions for pregnancy out of wedlock can have an impact on activism as well as on social practices in marriage.

For example, with the intensification of religion, the space for feminist activism is constrained. WIN no longer has a presence in the north (or is "dormant," as one WIN member said)[59] and is not active in lobbying efforts on a uniform age of marriage. The NCWS has also retreated from its position on child marriage and is not active on the issue in the north of the country.[60] Interestingly, the VVF Task Force is no longer in existence, in part, one activist stated, because of debates over whether early marriage should be seen as a determining factor in VVF.[61] The Muslim Sisters Organization (MSO), which was not mentioned to researchers in 1994 even though it was in existence at the time, has emerged as an important actor in women's debates albeit from a conservative religious perspective.[62]

In northern Nigeria, the growing interest in defining early marriage as a human rights violation in the early 1990s foundered on the politics of Islam-icization in the early 2000s along with the disintegration of the nation-state and the resistance to international secular public opinion.[63] Our study of the human rights approaches to early marriage shows how the changing approach to early marriage reflects these political and ideological changes in the coun-try. As Venkatesh writes in the introductory chapter of this volume, "this arena has been re-aligned as ideas and practices about justice, rights, and maintaining order travel the globe."[64] In the next section of this chapter we will outline in greater detail tentative explanations for why the human rights approach to early marriage has diminished since the mid 1990s. Finally, we will describe different actors involved with women's NGOs in northern Nige-ria and their positions on early marriage before concluding with a recent example of the tensions between global discourses and local politics.

THE CHANGING SOCIOECONOMIC CONTEXT OF ADVOCACY

The *Human Development Report on Globalization for Nigeria* (2000) states that "despite being the world's sixth largest exporter of petroleum, Nigeria ranks extremely low in terms of human development, making it impossible to attain the benefits of globalization." Nigeria was 148th in the 2002 Human Devel-opment Indicator ranking, with an overall index value of 0.462, compared with Kenya at 0.513 and Canada at 0.940. UNDP reports that 70 percent of the population live below the poverty line (living on less than US$1 a day). Maternal mortality ratio is over 1,000 (per 100,000 live births). These socio-economic indicators mask income inequality within Nigeria: Nigeria's income inequality is higher than income inequality in India, Ethiopia, and Russia.[65] Recent reports state that the economy is deteriorating, and more and more people are poor in Nigeria.

Many people interviewed by Bunting in 2003 stated that they experienced the economic situation as worsening in the country in general, and the north in particular. One woman who runs her own girl-child NGO and whose father was an emir said, "It is getting worse . . . I don't like to say this but the leadership is getting worse and there is no real effort to make things better. There is more pilfering."[66] The fuel crisis is mismanaged, resulting in drivers in Kano either waiting for a day in line for fuel at a station or buying fuel on the black market at the side of the road at many times the cost. "The issue of economic empowerment is big. The first issue when you go into a community is women who say 'we need money to improve our skills'. . . ."[67] Clara Ejembi, a community health worker who was active with the VVF Task Force in the 1990s, talked about research in Zaria state and the reasons why girls are married young in rural areas. She, like others, emphasized that early marriage must be seen in its socioeconomic context, a context that includes economic impoverishment and lack of education alternatives for girls.[68] Education remains inaccessible for many poor girls or nonexistent in areas.

Festus Okoye, executive director of Human Rights Monitor, is a long-time civil rights lawyer and activist. He collaborated with HRW in 1994 and subsequently was awarded an HRW fellowship. In 2003 he was the chair of a civil society coalition, the Monitoring Committee for Election 2003. He agrees that the deteriorating economic conditions of the Nigerian people are having an effect on early marriage. Okoye says the economic issue "is the really really fundamental issue: before it was easier to keep a big family." Now parents cannot keep big families. He also points to what he describes as the "movement towards/backwards/forwards to Shari'a."[69]

In her article on women's groups in Nigeria, Abdullah writes, the "deepseated crisis in the national economy has not only resulted in the collapse of real incomes for most Nigerians, and a sharp decline in social citizenship, as state-sponsored social services went into decay on account of the fiscal and government problems confronting the country. [. . .] A perceptible loss of faith in secular authorities has gone hand in hand with the rise of religious fundamentalism."[70] The comments of Bunting's interviewees confirm this statement. The people I interviewed often commented that "No, women do not perceive early marriage as a problem, no they don't." And one learned woman told me, "Women who die during delivery have free access to heaven—you don't want them to go to heaven?"[71,72]

Twelve states in northern Nigeria have passed Shari'a laws since 1999–2000. The increasing Islamicization of northern Nigeria is what some people call Islamic awareness or implementation of Shari'a. Others refer to it as rehabilitation of Shari'a. "Zamfara and all the states that have emulated its actions insist that the application of Shari'a in its entirety will stem social vices (prostitution, alcoholism, gambling, brigandage) and thus reduce society's slide into social and moral decadence."[73] In this context, activist strategies need to include consultation with religious and community leaders and be grounded in Muslim Hausa morality. Although this was also true in 1994, it is more so now as the sociopolitical context has intensified around religion in recent years.

As one of the founding figures in the women's movement in Nigeria, Ayehsa Imam is acutely aware of the changing politics of religion and women's rights. From Zaria, Imam studied in Nigeria, England, and Canada. She was active in early feminist lobbies in Nigeria and then formed BAOBOB for women's human rights. Imam is also the African and Middle East coordinator of Women Living Under Muslim Laws (WLUML). Imam states,

> there are a host of practices, with no legal basis at all, which are being imposed on society in the name of "shariaisation". These include widespread imposition of dress codes on women, attempts to force women to sit at the back of public vehicles, and a midnight curfew in Gusau. Many of these are enforced by extralegal groups of young men vigilantes—sometimes openly supported by the state government as in Zamphara, but sometimes with attempts to control and stop them from taking the law into their own hands, as in Kano state.[74]

Some activists face harassment from vigilante groups.[75] One women's rights activist who provides sex education and other reproductive health projects was warned that her work is unIslamic. She was threatened and told that she ought not take more foreign funding. Imam notes, too, that she and her colleagues at BAOBOB work in such a way as not to be dismissed as unbelievers, as infidels. Women's NGOs, therefore, operate in a highly regulated context.

Amina Sambo, the past chair of the VVF Task Force and one of HRW's hosts in 1994, said that while "the incidence of VVF are still hanging, the debates around early marriage are dying down."[76] Her own NGO, Grassroots

Health Organization of Nigeria (GHON), has moved to the prevention of HIV/AIDS among adolescents and youth. A number of women's NGOs commented that funders are interested in "RR/RH"—reproductive rights, reproductive health issues. Although one might include women's rights to consent to marry and marry at "full" age within the definition of reproductive rights, they are not so construed. More money is available for reproductive health education than for legal literacy and women's rights education. As Dr. Judith-Ann Walker explained, if more funding were available for legal literacy and women's rights, more organizations might be working in that area.[77] As it is, few women's groups based in the north are working with such a model. Let us now turn to the approaches taken by women's non-governmental organizations in northern Nigeria.

PERSPECTIVES ON EARLY MARRIAGE: A FEW VOICES

The majority of people interviewed said that rural parents or villagers do not see early marriage as a problem. Binta Karaye, a social worker on staff at the Kano VVF clinic, explained "in the villages, they don't think early marriage is a problem." Her colleague, Binta Muhammed Yakasai, elaborated: You "can't prevent them from marrying their children; it is a tradition. They are poor, they can't provide education, they have to marry their children."[78] Dr. Walker concurs: "Early marriage is not problematized" in northern Nigeria.[79] Dr. Mairo Mandara is a medical doctor who has researched VVF and is a member of FOMWAN. When asked if early marriage is seen as a women's rights issue in Nigeria, Dr. Mandara responded: "A few voices here and there but not making a lot of noise." With regard to rights-based strategies on the issue, Dr. Mandara commented that you "can't really sell this in this place . . . [you] must focus on health. NGO culture in the North is quite weak; in the South it is different—more educated, more enlightened, push more for rights."[80] Who then are the voices in the north?

The variety of women's activists working on the issue of age at marriage in northern Nigeria includes both groups working inside of Islam and those working outside of Islam. And along the spectrum of perspectives on early marriage there are transnational feminists, non-religious Nigerian feminists, religious conservative women's groups, and health promoters. Although the transnational feminist groups are those most often working outside of Islam (working within a women's rights framework characterized by deep secularism and antagonism for religion), they do not always do so. Indeed, interviews with some transnational feminists reveal their sensitivity to and respect for Islamic law and Muslim culture in Nigeria. Other transnational feminists see Islam as the problem. With religious revivalism in the north, as we have argued, the Islamic women's groups are important actors and the imperative for groups in the north to work within Islam has intensified. Space for secular human rights critiques has diminished and has shifted to transnational elite activism, while in the north the concern for girls is framed differently. Of course individuals may move between these categories at different times and in different places, but the categories represent general perspectives to early marriage and international women's rights activism. We will examine how each group sees early marriage, uses international human rights instruments and discourse in their work, and reacts to international intervention by funders or NGOs such as Amnesty International or Human Rights Watch.

Religious Northern Voices

An example of the opinions of northern religious people concerning child marriage is expressed here:

> Certainly there is a tension between the international human rights documents and the local. The way it is framed at the international level is quite a sore issue because people are not willing to look at it from an Islamic perspective. The best example I can give you is the A'isha, the Prophet's wife who came to him at nine. But the marriage was not consummated. Islam does not frown on contracting marriage at this age. The main purpose of early marriage is to protect chastity and her character. . . . One of the things that makes us so sore is not talking about early promiscuity—people should be talking about early promiscuity, pregnancy. Early marriage has not caused moral decay in society.[81]

The speaker, Emira Zubaida Ahmed, is the chairperson of the Federation of Muslim Women's Organizations (FOMWAN) in Kano state. She went on to explain that many people at the international level look only at the punitive aspects of Shari'a and not the moral foundation or other aspects of Shari'a. "There is a *rehabilitation* of the Shari'a because other aspects have been Westernized."[82] Emira Jamilla from the Muslim Sisters Organization (MSO) concurred with the religious interpretation of early marriage: "As a Muslim, early marriage is not a bad thing. Islam is encouraging early marriage."[83] Fatima Kwaku, a past Nigerian member of the CEDAW committee, which is made up of experts on women's issues, says "yes, strictly speaking there is nothing wrong with early marriage [in Islam]. Age at marriage is puberty."[84] Age at marriage is explicitly tied to the morality of daughters and the need to protect against sex outside marriage, promiscuity, and adultery. Further, there is some assertion that because girls physically mature sooner today than they did 30 years ago in Nigeria, marriage will occur sooner.

The Muslim Sisters Organization has existed since 1976; it was formally registered as an umbrella organization and NGO in 1983. Its mission is stated to be the education of children, youth, and women in Islamic principles of survival and social development. "We are most interested in survival for children not the child rights perspective."[85] The MSO programs include Arabic, Islamic, and rural schools; seminars on various topics; support of children at an orphanage that in 2003 had 37 children; and a youth wing with activities on adolescent problems, AIDs, contraceptives, and child survival and immunization. "Global economic forces have had a negative impact in Nigeria: we take more delight in presenting Fanta than fresh oranges. We take more delight in presenting processed rather than traditional food [. . .] We are really aggrieved by globalization . . . donors are paving the way for transnationals." When asked about legal literacy programs for women, the MSO Kano representative explained, "We do do projects on women's rights in the Qur'an. The rights are there, let's fight for them."[86]

Dr. Walker describes FOMWAN as a "vanguard organization in the north; they do it in a culturally sensitive way and they are out there. Not asserting international human rights but more culturally accepted."[87] Sadia Omar Bello was a founding member of FOMWAN at the national level and in Sokoto state; she was the first emira (chair) of FOMWAN for Nigeria. Bello described how she held a small NGO meeting in her house in the early 1980s before a Muslim women's conference was held in Kano in 1984. Bringing together Muslim women concerned to educate themselves about Islam, FOMWAN was formed. "We find it useful to discuss international human rights, women's rights and law."[88] FOMWAN held its 10th anniversary conference in Abuja in 1995, where participants studied the Beijing Platform for Action and came up with an alternative Platform for Muslim Women "to see where Muslim women fit, based on our faith. . . . During workshops and conferences on issues we discuss globalization: what does it mean to us? We see advantages and disadvantages to globalization. The advantages include that you can study through the Internet, technological advancement . . . disadvantages are that you don't have your own way of life, eat, think."[89] When asked about the international reach of religion, Bello replied, "Even the religion is a global religion. It has no barriers. Globalization has its roots in Islam. It has no barrier."[90]

Within organizations there will be tensions between more devout and secular strategies for cases and "enlightenment."[91] Members of FOMWAN in Kano explained that in their work they quote the Qur'an and the hadiths, but "never quote international human rights documents."[92] The VVF Task Force dissolved in part from divisions on the issue of early marriage. Some members saw early marriage as a contributing factor to be addressed in the prevention of VVF; others argued that early marriage is not causally linked to the incidence of VVF. Dr. Kees, the Dutch doctor on contract with the Kano state government to conduct surgical repairs for VVF and train Nigerian doctors, will not name early marriage as a problem. And although the MSO national office executive director stated that it does not use a children's rights perspective, she went on to say that the language of rights "is not a concept that came from the West. It has always been in our religion. We are not teaching them an alien culture."[93]

Transnational Feminist Activism

Dr. Rahmat Mohammad, the executive director of FORWARD-Nigeria, is another important voice in the early marriage debate. Unlike many of the other women's groups in the north, FORWARD-Nigeria is a branch of an international organization with an office in the United Kingdom. Although FORWARD has participated in research on early marriage as a women's rights issue with UNICEF funding and has published documents in England on the topic, they "have never come out and said we are against early marriage" within Nigeria. Without engaging the religious leaders, programs would have real problems. Dr. Rahmat's focus is on the health consequences of early marriage and addresses maternal mortality and morbidity. In other words, "there is a local definition that informs their activities and what is at stake."[94]

Women's NGOs such as the Women's Federation of Women Lawyers (FIDA) and League of Democratic Women (LEADS Nigeria) do problematize early marriage and frame it as a women's human rights issue. Although their noise may not be very loud, this quiet strategy is not unintentional. The Kaduna state office of FIDA "with Ford Foundation support works to sensitize parents on the international instruments, including the ills of early marriage and the aftermath of VVF but we did not make a strong case. . . . If you approach early marriage head on you would not make a strong impact because it is like encroaching on their religion, it is like a no go area."[95] FIDA-Nigeria, itself a national branch of an international women's NGO, has state branches. It does not have much presence in the northern states of Sokoto, Zamfara, Katsina, Kebbi, or Niger. FIDA in Kaduna state therefore sent members to core northern states to conduct workshops on women's status and access to justice issues. These initiatives met with resistance. One lawyer told the following story of going to Sokoto state:

> We were to go to the House of Assembly, the police station. And when we got there with the police commissioner, first thing when we sat down he said "are you married? But you women are funny. Where is your husband? You are coming here to fight for women's rights" and he told the police officers to escort us out—which he did. And when we got to the House of Assembly the women there were not even ready to listen to us and said "we are not complaining" so what is your problem?[96]

Both organizations are involved in litigation to challenge cases of early marriage on the grounds of lack of capacity to marry (because of age) and lack of consent. LEADS in Kaduna also "dialogues with stakeholders," educates people first, and does "enlightenment" work. LEADS's lawyer Rebecca Sako described cases where her organization challenged marriage contracts. In one case a girl, Nafisa, who was less than 13 years old, ran away before her marriage and sued her father on the grounds that she was underage and did not consent to the marriage contract. They secured a judgment in her favor from a judge of the Area Court (now Shari'a court). Ms. Sako described the judge as well versed in Shari'a and knowledgeable about the Qur'an, which he quoted in the decision. Many plaintiffs who initially challenge their marriage subsequently withdraw their cases; according to Sako, "It is not easy work." In another case, Hauwa was withdrawn from school by her father to be married. A case was filed in court against her father, a traditional ruler:

> In the petition, Hauwa described herself as "a prisoner of conscience" who has since gone into hiding, following the forceful marriage; a development she also said had put her out of school. Hauwa's education has been disrupted, she is traumatized and in hiding from her father and the so-called husband who are using their influence with the Emir of Muri and other traditional leaders to force her to remain married to the man.[97]

The man did eventually agree to dissolve the marriage under pressure from the wife of the vice-president, the news media, and other institutions.

National Negotiations

Hadiza Baba Yero is acutely aware of the cultural politics of religion in the north but, unlike some of her counterparts in Kaduna, she is respectful rather than scornful. Baba Yero is a transnational activist working within Islam. As a practicing Muslim and very much a cultural insider, she works within a sensitive yet secular context. John Hopkins University funds her *Listen Up!* informational radio and publications program. Their office is in the USAID building in Kano. She experienced early in her project the consequences of incomplete consultation with religious leaders.

> When we *started* this project, we had big problems with the Council of Ullama but we [tend to] look at obstacles as opportunities. We wrote them an invitation to the first meeting with stakeholders—of course they are stakeholders—they didn't come. And then they went on media and condemned the JHU program, a program they had not seen because it was funded by America. Through dialogue, but it wasn't easy (the media were not helpful at all and jumped on it), now we are working together with them.[98]

As part of the adolescent reproductive health project, *Listen Up!* had developed fact sheets on topics such as HIV/AIDS, unwanted pregnancy and abortion, and early childbearing. The fact sheet on the latter topic had initially been titled "Early Marriage and Early Childbearing." Baba Yero and her colleagues soon realized this "would be another scandal. . . . Why put early marriage and condemn the project?" The fact sheet is now titled "Early Pregnancy and Early Childbearing," but this change in title did not end their problems. To say "child marriage" would be even more controversial. In Zamfara state, on one occasion, the state radio decided not to air the *Listen Up!* program after seeing the logo from JHU. Baba Yero explains that the Sultan of Sokoto also asked for information about her funders. The Council of Imams was explicit in saying that they "are not fighting with you but with the U.S." "We play low," concludes Baba Yero.

The *Listen Up!* project does not prioritize a legal or rights framework for its work on adolescent reproductive health. LEADS, on the other hand, aims to increase legal awareness and rights awareness among northern Nigerian women, and it takes cases that challenge discriminatory laws and practices. WRAPA (Women's Rights Advancement and Protection Alternative) is another national organization with regional or zonal offices that provides legal services to women. The coordinator for the north central zone explained that WRAPA operates a legal clinic in each area. "We try and maintain a very good relationship wherever we go with community leaders especially District Heads and the Imams and we use our positions to achieve those aims. Because where I come from, I am highly acceptable and highly respected so whatever I bring is readily acceptable . . . I was a civil servant, a social worker. I retired and I know most of the workers."[99] The WRAPA coordinator works for free; is able to travel to the states in the north central zone four times a year; and oversees prison outreach, legal cases, and seminars.[100]

Mrs. Fatima Kwaku, a lawyer and member of FIDA who sits on the expert committee that monitors the women's convention, CEDAW, said "people do not really regard [early marriage] as anything unusual." She admitted that most people on the street in northern Nigeria do not know about the Women's Convention:

Nothing much is known about it up here. It is not domesticated. Need to make some noise for women to know. Indirectly introducing CEDAW . . . can introduce it in our own way, educate people first, sensitize people then . . .

Thus, even the most elite and transnational of women's groups and individuals (the CEDAW expert, FIDA, and FORWARD) in the north are now reticent to pursue strategies that name early marriage as a violation of girls and women's human rights.

CONCLUSIONS

A comparison between north and south in Nigeria reveals the historical, cultural, and religious factors that shape the difficulty of these negotiations. Factors that contribute to the differences include the colonial legacy, differential Christianization and education by region, the global Islamist movement, the hostility between the West and Islam, and regional politics in Nigeria—the relative poverty of the north and the loss of its political power with the end of the military dictatorship. This regional history and political context affects the way this problem is defined and examined in Nigeria. Such a contextualized perspective is quite different from the approach taken by transnational human rights activists, who tend to adopt a secular perspective and a universalistic one. For example, in the UNICEF document *Early Marriage: Whose Right to Choose?* the local complexities are lost.

The struggles over early marriage and the relevance of a human rights framework parallel the more spectacular and widely discussed use of stoning as a punishment for adultery in northern Nigeria. After a major international outcry, one of the first women convicted was released on a technicality: her indiscretion predated the initiation of Shari'a law. A second case also garnered significant international attention. There have been numerous Internet campaigns to protest the execution of Amina Lawal, who was convicted of adultery and sentenced to death by stoning in April 2002. In May 2003, an e-mail circulated globally, allegedly from a Spanish Amnesty International site, announcing that Amina was sentenced to be stoned June 3, 2003, and imploring readers to yet again sign petitions of protest.

However, soon after this e-mail, the leader of the Nigerian women's human rights group BAOBOB said that the information was inaccurate. The case was scheduled for appeal June 3, not for execution, and this was only the beginning of a long process of appeal. Moreover, the BAOBOB e-mail noted that none of the sentences for stoning have yet been carried out. Further, the e-mail continued, "the situation in Nigeria, being volatile, will not be helped by such campaigns." The international protest might be counterproductive, angering the Shari'a court judges and encouraging them to carry out the sentence more quickly and in private, as they did with another contested sentence of flogging that was carried out hurriedly in order to defy international protests and letters. "Thus, we would like you to recognise that an international protest letter campaign is not necessarily the most productive way to act in every situation. On the contrary, women's rights defenders should assess potential backlash effects before devising strategies." Further, campaigns based on inaccurate information damage the credibility of local activists, the apparent sources of such misinformation. "If we remember that it is local activists who most facilitate turning rights principles into everyday reality for people, then reducing the ability and potential of local activists to carry out women's and human rights promotion and defence is a counter-productive mode of proceeding."

The statement also warned about reinforcing colonialist rhetoric that portrays Islam and Africa as barbaric and savage, noting that "when protest letters represent negative stereotypes of Islam and Muslims, they inflame sentiments rather than encouraging reflection and strengthening local progressive movements." BAOBOB urged international supporters to provide support for Nigeria-based lawyers, safe havens for victims, and exchange of information and expertise. However, it emphasized the importance of supporting local institutions and activists and "to acknowledge and support internal dissent within the community involved, rather than engaging in a wholesale condemnation of peoples' beliefs and cultures, which is seldom accurate or effective in changing views within the affected community." Amnesty International quickly sent out an e-mail correcting the misinformation. The source of the misleading e-mail is apparently still unknown. The case has generated considerable Internet exchange surrounding this issue of the effectiveness of international pressure given local political struggles.

All these considerations affect the relevance of human rights for local struggles. Similar concerns have diminished the relevance of human rights for early marriage in northern Nigeria. The approaches to early marriage taken by women's NGOs in northern Nigeria have changed over the past decade. Transnational, secular, and religious approaches to early marriage represent a spectrum of activism in northern Nigeria. Activists use international women's rights language in various ways to various ends. The Muslim Sisters Organization and Federation of Muslim Women's Associations of Nigeria argue that the obligations in CEDAW can all be found in the Qur'an. Others ground their strategies in Muslim teachings and the Qur'an but *marry* the religious with the international, as does Salamatu Garba from the Women Farmers Association.

In contemporary northern Nigeria, international women's rights regulations are received with scepticism. The utility of global human rights discourses is limited to their resonance with local socio-political discourses. This chapter has argued that the approaches to early marriage represent historically and regionally specific strategies, strategies that cannot be generalized across Nigeria or over the past decade. Globalizing human rights strategies need to be attentive to the national and regional dynamics and consequences of such transnational activism. Thus we must be alive to the fact that global regulatory efforts around early marriage may produce multiple and even contradictory effects.

Appendix 11A. Nigerian Women's Nongovernmental Organizations

DRPC	Development Research and Policy Centre
FORWARD	Foundation for Women's Health, Research and Development
UNICEF	United Nations Children's Fund
FOMWAN	Federation of Muslim Women's Associations of Nigeria
FIDA	Federation of Women Lawyers, Nigeria
Baobab	Baobab for Women's Human Rights
CRD	Centre for Research and Documentation
CDD	Centre for Democracy & Development
GAT	Gender Action
GHON	Grassroots Health Organization of Nigeria
HRM	Human Rights Monitor
JHU	John Hopkins University (Adolescent Health)
Kano Forum	Forum on Marriage and the Rights of Women and Girls
LEADS-Nigeria	League of Democratic Women
MSO	Muslim Sisters Organization
NAWA	National Association of Women Academics
NCWS	National Council of Women's Societies
SWODEN	Society for Women and Development and Empowerment
SWECDEP	Society for Women Empowerment, Children's Development and Environmental Protection
RHWC	Raising Hope for Woman and Child
VVF Foundation	Vesico-vaginal Fistulae Foundation
WAYS	Women and Youth Services
WOFAN	Women Farmers' Association of Nigeria
WRAPA	Women's Rights and Protection, in Kano, Kaduna, and Sokoto States
WIN	Women in Nigeria

ENDNOTES

1. See Arjun Appadurai, *Modernity at Large: The Cultural Dimensions of Globalization* (Minneapolis: University of Minnesota Press, 1996).

2. Salamatu Garba, Executive Director WOFAN, interview by author, Kano, Nigeria, 10 March 2003.

3. There has been a move away from the terminology of *child marriage* to the more ambigu-

ous *early marriage.* We prefer to use the term *early marriage* because it is less steeped—although still implicated—in colonial discourse and Western judgment. On the global and local politics of early marriage, see Annie Bunting, "Stages of Development: Marriage of Girls and Teens as an International Human Rights Issue," *Social & Legal Studies* 14, no. 1 (2005): 17–38.

4. Sudhir Venkatesh, "Youth and Legal Institutions: Thinking Globally and Comparatively" in this volume.

5. See Elizabeth Heger Boyle, *Female Genital Cutting: Cultural Conflict in the Global Community* (Baltimore: John Hopkins University Press, 2002) Chapter 3 on the debates over female genital cutting.

6. "Veiling, polygamy, child-marriage, and sati were all significant points of conflict and negotiation between colonizing 'Western' culture and different Third-World cultures. In these conflicts, colonial powers often depicted indigenous practices as symptoms of the 'backwardness and barbarity' of Third-World cultures in contrast to the 'progressiveness of Western culture.'" Uma Narayan, *Dislocating Cultures: Identities, Traditions, and Third-World Feminism* (New York: Routledge, 1997), 17.

7. In 1929 the Child Marriage Restraint Act was passed in India; the same year England passed the Marriage Act, 1929 raising the minimum age of marriage from 12 to 16 years.

8. UNICEF Innocenti Research Centre, *Early Marriage, Child Spouses.* UNICEF Innocenti Digest no. 7 (Florence: UNICEF Innocenti Research Centre, March 2001), 2–3.

9. Mary Smith, *Baba of Karo: A Woman of the Moslem Hausa* (New York: Frederick Praeger, 1964), Chapter V "A girl's first marriage" [1904] 85–101 and footnote. Mary Smith lived in Kano and Zaria states between 1890 and 1951—in other words, during British colonial rule in northern Nigeria.

10. The Commission became Permanent Advisory Committee of Experts on Slavery in 1935–38. Its work was interrupted in 1938 during World War II. Anti-Slavery International, "The history of Anti-Slavery International"; available from http://www.antislavery.org/home page/antislavery/history.pdf , 11.

11. Ibid., 14.

12. Ibid., 12.

13. Quoted in Forum on Marriage and the Rights of Women and Girls (FORUM), "Early Marriage: Whose Right to Choose?" (London: Forum, 2000), 32.

14. Susan Pedersen, "The Maternalist Moment in British Colonial Policy: The Controversy over 'Child Slavery' in Hong Kong 1917–1941." *Past and Present* 171 (2001): 161–202.

15. Pedersen, 166, 202.

16. Pedersen, 189.

17. Consolidated in 1812. This was an independent political unit in northern Nigeria.

18. Barbara Cooper, "Reflections on slavery, seclusion and female labor in the Maradi region of Niger in the nineteenth and twentieth centuries," *Journal of African History* 35, no. 1 (1994): 61(18).

19. *Ibid.*

20. "All of these expressions are consistent with the hypothesis that with the decline of slavery alternative forms of 'marriage' could become a means whereby men (and through them senior aristocratic women) could continue to control the labor of junior women, who were now nominally 'free' in status." Cooper, *ibid.*

21. Complicity between the colonial administration and the male aristocracy concerning female slavery occurred in northern Nigeria. See Paul Lovejoy, "Concubinage and the status of women slaves in early colonial Northern Nigeria," *Journal of African History*, XXIX (1988): 245–66.

22. Cap. 77 Laws of Northern Nigeria, 1963. This law seems to no longer be in force in its 1954 form.

23. Sections 38(17) and 38(18) *Native Authority Law* respectively. Native Authorities are now called Local Governments in Nigeria.

24. Native Authority (Declaration of Tiv Native Marriage Law and Custom) Order 1955, s. 2(a): age of puberty; Native Authority (Declaration of Idoma Native Marriage Law and Custom) Order 1959, s. 2(I)(a): age twelve; Native Authority (Declaration of Borgu Native Marriage Law and Custom) Order 1961, s. 2(I)(a): age thirteen; Native Authority (Declaration of Biu Native Marriage Law and Custom) Order 1964, s. 1(a): age fourteen.

25. Convention on Consent to Marriage, Minimum Age for Marriage and Registration of Marriages (1962) opened for signature November 20, 1962, 521 U.N.T.S. 231. This convention is ratified by only 49 countries in 2006, not Nigeria.

26. Draft Recommendation on Consent to Marriage, Minimum Age for Marriage and Registration for Marriages G.A. Res. 2018 (XX). U.N. GAOR, 20th. Sess., Supp. No. 14 at 36, U.N. Doc A/6014 (1965).

27. International Covenant on Civil and Political Rights (ICCPR) Article 23 and International Covenant on Economic, Social and Cultural Rights (ICESCR).

28. Convention on the Rights of the Child, opened for signature Nov. 20, 1989, G.A. Res. 44/25, 44 U.N. GOAR Supp. (No. 49) at 165, U.N. Doc. A/44/736 (1989).

29. From the Division for the Advancement of Women (DAW), Department of Economic and Social Affairs, United Nations. 2000. *Assessing the Status of Women: A Guide to Reporting under the Convention on the Elimination of All Forms of Discrimination Against Women* (New York: United Nations, 2000), 69.

30. Ibid, 71.

31. This committee was formed in 1983 and started work in 1984. The committee is composed of experts designated by the Sub-Commission on Prevention of Discrimination and Protection of Minorities and representatives from concerned nongovernmental organizations, UNICEF, UNESCO, and WHO.

32. World Health Assembly resolution WHA46.18 on maternal and child health, and family planning for health.

33. www.unhchr.ch/Huridocda/Huridoca.nsf/0/3ac98c66e2ac2f85802566c2003ce975? Opendocument

34. Available at University of Minnesota Human Rights Library. www1.umn.edu/humanrts/instree/e5dplw.htm.

35. Forum, "Early Marriage: Whose Right to Choose?", 1.

36. Forum on Marriage and the Rights of Women and Girls (Forum), "Early Marriage and Poverty: Exploring the Links for Policy and Programme Development" (London: Forum, 2003).

37. Forum, "Early Marriage: Whose Right to Choose?", 1.

38. Available online: www.wluml.org.

39. UNICEF Innocenti Research Centre, 2–3.

40. UNICEF Nigeria, *Children's and Women's Rights in Nigeria: A Wake-up Call—Situation Assessment and Analysis 2001* (Abuja: National Planning Commission and UNICEF Nigeria, 2001), 245–46.

41. VVF is an abnormal communication between the bladder and the vagina resulting in continuous leakage of urine through the vagina. VVF is most often caused by prolonged, obstructed labor when the baby's head cannot pass through the pelvic bones. Although not caused solely by early childbearing, it is related to the immaturity of the pregnant woman's pelvic bones.

42. Annie Bunting, "Diversity of Contexts, Particularity of Rights: The Case of Early Marriage in Northern Nigeria" (S.J.D. dissertation, University of Toronto, 1999); see UNICEF Innocenti Research Centre.

43. UNICEF Innocenti Research Centre, 4.

44. UNICEF Nigeria, 201.

45. WIN is a national umbrella organization of women's groups in Nigeria. It has lobbied for a federal marriageable age since the late 1980s. See Ayesha Imam, "The Dynamics of WIN-ing: An Analysis of Women in Nigeria (WIN)" in *Feminist Genealogies, Colonial Legacies, Democratic Futures*, eds. Alexander and Mohanty (New York: Routledge, 1996), 280–307.

46. The MacArthur Foundation funded the VVF Task Force (Amina Smabo). VVF is the acronym for vesoci-vaginal fistulae.

47. Hussaina J. Abdullah, "Religious Revivalism, Human Rights Activism and the Struggle for Women's Rights in Nigeria" in *Cultural Transformation and Human Rights in Africa,* ed. Abdullahi An-Na'im (London: Zed Books, 2002) 151–191, 166.

48. Rhoda Howard-Hassmann, "The Flogging of Bariya Magazu: Nigerian Politics, Canadian Pressures and Women's and Children's Rights," *Journal of Human Rights* 3, no. 1 (2004): 3–20, 11.

49. Abdullah, 153.

50. *Ibid.*, 163.

51. *Ibid.*

52. In its official report to CEDAW, the Nigerian government suggested uniform marriage ages of 16 for boys and girls with the consent of their parents, 18 for boys and girls with the consent of one parent, and 21 without parental consent (Initial Report of Nigeria under Article 18 of the Convention, CEDAW/C/5/Add.49 11 May 1987 at p. 31).

53. Professor Bolanle Awe, "Women's Rights Are Human Rights," Keynote Address WIN 12th Annual General Meeting/ Conference, Katsina, April 13, 1994, 8; Mrs. H. A. Fika, acting director general, National Commission for Women, "Women Education and Human Rights," 9–10; Tokunbo Ige, executive director, Legal Research & Resource Development Centre and national coordinator WiLDAF, "Women and Human Rights Abuse in the Family/ Domestic Violence," 3. And see Mrs. Fatima Abdulrahman, "The Socio-Economic Basis of the Exploitation and Oppression of Women and Children in Nigeria," paper presented at the seminar on Rights of Women and Children and Traditional Institutions and Human Rights in northern Nigeria, Kaduna: March 24–25, 1994, 8; and Mrs. W. A. Abdulkadir, "The Rights of Women and Children," paper presented at the seminar on Rights of Women and Children, 10. All conference papers are on file with the author.

54. Apparently HRW could not agree on a minimum age of marriage.

55. I conducted 29 interviews with women's NGOs in Kano, Zaria, Kaduna, and Sokoto. I interviewed the permanent secretary for the Ministry of Women's Affairs in Kano. I also interviewed 5 women about the circumstances of their marriages, although this was not the purpose of our research. Interviews generally lasted an hour or more. Some interviews were taped and I took notes during all interviews. Tapes were then transcribed. Appendix 11A includes a list of the organizations. We returned to Nigeria in April 2005 and met with women's organizations in Kano, Kaduna, and Abuja.

56. Abdullah, 176.

57. Howard-Hassmann, 12, and see Human Rights Monitor, *Victims (Impact of Religious and Ethnic Conflicts on Women and Children in Northern Nigeria)*, ed. Festus Okoye (Kaduna: Human Rights Monitor, April 2000); Human Rights Monitor, *Ethnic and Religious Rights/Challenges* (Kaduna: Human Rights Monitor, January 2002).

58. Abdullah, 176–186.

59. Interview by author, Kano, Nigeria, March 11, 2003.

60. Interview by author, Kano, Nigeria, March 19, 2003.

61. Interview by author, Kano, Nigeria, March 20, 2003.

62. Interview by author, Kano, Nigeria, March 6, 2003.

63. See Howard-Hassman.

64. Venkatesh, chapter 1, in this volume.

65. UNDP, 2001 at 10, and *Human Development, Past Present and Future*, Chapter http://hdr.undp.org/reports/detail-reports.cfm?view=563

66. Interview by author, Kano, Nigeria, March 7, 2003.

67. *Ibid.*

68. Interview March 3, 2003; and see Bunting, 2005.

69. Interview by author, Kaduna, Nigeria, March 13, 2003.

70. Abdullah, 152.

71. Hadiza Baba Yero, interview by author, Kano, Nigeria, 2003.

72. Hadiza Baba Yero, interview by author, Kano, Nigeria, 2003.

73. Abdullah, 177.

74. Ayesha Imam, "Acceptance Speech—John Humphrey Freedom Award 2002" (Montreal, December 9, 2002), 5.

75. Abdullah, 177.

76. Interview by author, Kano, Nigeria, March 6, 2003.

77. Interview by author, March 20, 2003.

78. Interview by author, March 4, 2003.

79. Interview by author, March 20, 2003.

80. Interview by author, March 3, 2003.

81. Interview by author, March 12, 2003.

82. *Ibid.*

83. Interview by author, March 6, 2003.

84. Fatima Kwaku is a member of the Nigerian Bar, FIDA (Nigeria), and the National Human Rights Commission.

85. Interview by author, March 6, 2003.

86. *Ibid.*

87. Interview by author, March 20, 2003.

88. Interview by author, Sokoto, March 17, 2003.

89. *Ibid.*

90. *Ibid.*

91. Interview by author, March 20, 2003.

92. Interview by author, March 12, 2003.

93. Interview by author, March 6, 2003.

94. Dr. Judith-Ann Walker, interview by author, Kano, Nigeria, 20 March 2003.

95. Interview by author, March 13, 2003.

96. Interview by author, March 13, 2003.

97. Gwa'atia L. Maxwell, "A Plea for Hauwa" *Women's Advocate: A Quarterly Publication of League of Democratic Women (LEADS-Nigeria)* 5 (March 2002) 14:17.

98. Interview by author, March 11, 2003.

99. Interview by author, March 7, 2003.

100. She is also in a polygamous marriage as the senior wife. She has eight children. Interview by author, Kano, Nigeria.

REFERENCES

Abdullah, Hussaina J. (2002) "Religious Revivalism, Human Rights Activism and the Struggle for Women's Rights in Nigeria" in *Cultural Transformation and Human Rights in Africa,* ed. Abdullahi An-Na'im, London, Zed Books.

Appadurai, Arjun. (1996) *Modernity at Large: The Cultural Dimensions of Globalization,* Minneapolis, University of Minnesota Press.

Awe, Bolanle. (1994) "Women's Rights Are Human Rights," Keynote Address WIN 12th Annual General Meeting/Conference, Katsina, April 13, 1994.

Boyle, Elizabeth Heger. (2002) *Female Genital Cutting: Cultural Conflict in the Global Community,* Baltimore, John Hopkins University Press.

Bunting, Annie. (1999) "Diversity of Contexts, Particularity of Rights: The Case of Early Marriage in Northern Nigeria," S.J.D. dissertation, University of Toronto.

Bunting, Annie. (2005) "Stages of Development: Marriage of Girls and Teens as an International Human Rights Issue," *Social & Legal Studies* 14, no. 1.

Cooper, Barbara. (1994) "Reflections on Slavery, Seclusion and Female Labor in the Maradi Region of Niger in the Nineteenth and Twentieth Centuries," *Journal of African History* 35, no. 1.

Forum. (2000) Forum on Marriage and the Rights of Women and Girls, "Early Marriage: Whose Right to Choose?" London, Forum.

Forum. (2003) Forum on Marriage and the Rights of Women and Girls, "Early Marriage and Poverty: Exploring the Links for Policy and Programme Development," London, Forum.

Howard-Hassmann, Rhoda. (2004) "The Flogging of Bariya Magazu: Nigerian Politics, Canadian Pressures and Women's and Children's Rights," *Journal of Human Rights* 3, no. 1.

Human Rights Monitor. (2000) *Victims: Impact of Religious and Ethnic Conflicts on Women and Children in Northern Nigeria*, ed. Festus Okoye, Kaduna, Human Rights Monitor.

Human Rights Monitor. (2002) *Ethnic and Religious Rights/Challenges*, Kaduna, Human Rights Monitor.

Imam, Ayesha. (1996) "The Dynamics of WINing: An Analysis of Women in Nigeria (WIN)" in *Feminist Genealogies, Colonial Legacies, Democratic Futures*, ed. Alexander and Mohanty, New York, Routledge.

Imam, Ayesha. (2002) "Acceptance Speech—John Humphrey Freedom Award 2002," Montreal.

Lovejoy, Paul. (1988) "Concubinage and the Status of Women Slaves in Early Colonial Northern Nigeria," *Journal of African History*, XXIX.

Maxwell, Gwa'atia L. (2002) "A Plea for Hauwa," *Women's Advocate: A Quarterly Publication of League of Democratic Women (LEADS-Nigeria)* 5.

Narayan, Uma. (1997) *Dislocating Cultures: Identities, Traditions, and Third-World Feminism*, New York: Routledge.

Pedersen, Susan. (2001) "The Maternalist Moment in British Colonial Policy: The Controversy over 'Child Slavery' in Hong Kong 1917–1941," *Past and Present* 171.

Smith, Mary. (1964) *Baba of Karo: A Woman of the Moslem Hausa*, New York, Frederick Praeger.

UNICEF Innocenti Research Centre. (2001) "Early Marriage, Child Spouses." *UNICEF Innocenti Digest* no. 7, Florence, UNICEF Innocenti Research Centre.

UNICEF Nigeria. (2001) *Children's and Women's Rights in Nigeria: A Wake-up Call—Situation Assessment and Analysis 2001*, Abuja, National Planning Commission and UNICEF Nigeria.

United Nations, Division for the Advancement of Women (DAW), Department of Economic and Social Affairs. (2000) *Assessing the Status of Women: A Guide to Reporting under the Convention on the Elimination of All Forms of Discrimination Against Women*, New York: United Nations.

Contributors

LAURENT BONELLI is a lecturer in politics at the University of Paris X-Nanterre. He is a member of the Groupe d'analyse politique (GAP) and of the editorial board of *Cultures & Conflits* (http://www.conflits.org). He is co-editor, with Gilles Sainati, of *La machine à punir: Pratiques et discours sécuritaires* (Paris: L'Esprit Frappeur 2004). He has also recently published "The control of the enemy within? Police intelligence in the French *banlieues*" in Didier Bigo and Elspeth Guild, eds., *Controlling Frontiers: Free Movement into and within Europe* (London: Ashgate, 2005); "Un ennemi anonyme et sans visage: Renseignement, exception et suspicion après le 11 septembre 2001," *Cultures & Conflits* 58 (summer 2005); and "Les renseignements généraux et les violences urbaines," *Actes de la Recherche en Sciences Sociales* (March 2001).

ELIZABETH HEGER BOYLE is an associate professor of sociology and law at the University of Minnesota. She studies human rights, immigration, and international law. Professor Boyle is currently working on a project, funded by the National Science Foundation, that considers how Muslim immigrants deal with perceived contradictions between Islamic and American law. Professor Boyle is the author of *Female Genital Cutting: Cultural Conflict in the Global Community* (Baltimore: Johns Hopkins, 2002). Her articles have appeared in *The Law & Society Review, International Sociology, Social Problems,* the *American Sociological Review,* and other journals.

ANNIE BUNTING is an associate professor in the Law & Society program at York University, teaching in the areas of social justice and human rights. Professor Bunting is a graduate of York, having studied law at Osgoode Hall Law School (1988). She received her LL.M. from the London School of Economics and Political Science (1991) and her SJD from the Faculty of Law, University of Toronto (1999). Her research concerns questions of women's rights, culture, and family practices including early marriage. Her article on early marriage, "Stages of Development: Marriage of girls and teens as an international human rights issue" was published in 14(1) *Social and Legal Studies* (2005).

BRENDA C. COUGHLIN is a PhD candidate in the Department of Sociology at Columbia University. Her dissertation traces the historical development of organized crime as a social and political category by analyzing the content of state-sponsored public hearings held between 1929 and 1986. She has published a review of research on street gangs in the United States (with Sudhir Alladi Venkatesh) and an analysis of political regret and public apologies (with Jeffrey K. Olick). Her next research project is a prison ethnography.

KATJA M. GUENTHER is an assistant professor of sociology at California State University, Fullerton. Her current research examines the development of local women's movements in eastern Germany since the collapse of state socialism there in 1989.

JOHN A. GUIDRY is associate director for research of the Division of Public Health at the New York Academy of Medicine. He is currently working with an applied participatory-research project involving community development partnerships around the United States. He has edited, along with Mayer Zald and Michael D. Kennedy, *Globalizations and Social Movements: Culture, Power, and the Transnational Public Sphere* (Ann Arbor: University of Michigan Press, 2000) and has authored several articles and chapters on citizenship, social movements, Brazilian politics, youth law in Brazil, and democratic theory.

RONALD KASSIMIR has been associate dean of the New School for Social Research and associate professor in its Department of Political Science since September 2005. From 1996 to 2005 he was program director for Africa at the Social Science Research Council. He also directed the International Dissertation Field Research Fellowship Program and coordinated a research network on Youth and Globalization. Kassimir has published on civil society and politics in Uganda, and most recently co-edited, with Thomas Callaghy and

Robert Latham, *Intervention and Transnationalism in Africa: Global-Local Networks of Power* (Cambridge: Cambridge, 2001); and, with Lonnie Sherrod, Constance Flanagan, and Amy Syvertsen, *Youth Activism: An International Encyclopedia* (Westport, CT: Greenwood Publishing, 2006).

SALLY ENGLE MERRY is a professor in anthropology and law and society at New York University. Her work explores the role of law in urban life in the United States, in the colonizing process, and in contemporary transnationalism. She is currently doing transnational research on human rights and gender. She was previously on the faculty of Wellesley College, where she was the Marion Butler McLean Professor in the history of ideas and professor of anthropology. Her books include a study of law and American colonialism in Hawai'i, *Colonizing Hawai'i: The Cultural Power of Law* (Princeton: Princeton Univ. Press, 2000), which received the 2001 J. Willard Hurst Prize from the Law and Society Association; and *Human Rights and Gender Violence: Translating International Law into Local Justice* (Chicago: University of Chicago Press, 2005). She is the author or editor of four other books and has recently published articles on women's human rights, violence against women, and the process of localizing human rights. She is a past president of the Law and Society Association and the Association for Political and Legal Anthropology.

JOHN MUNCIE is a professor of criminology and co-director of the International Centre for Comparative Criminological Research at the Open University, United Kingdom. He has published widely in the field of youth criminology including his sole-authored work *Youth and Crime* (London: Sage, 1st edition 1999; 2nd edition 2004) and the edited collections *Comparative Youth Justice* (London: Sage, 2006), *Youth Crime and Justice* (London: Sage, 2006), and *Youth Justice: Critical Readings,* (London: Sage, 2002). In addition he is the co-editor of the best-selling *The Sage Dictionary of Criminology* (London: Sage, 1st edition 2001; 2nd edition 2005) with Eugene McLaughlin and *Criminological Perspectives: Essential Readings* (London: Sage/Open University, 2003) with Gordon Hughes and Eugene McLaughlin.

ALEXANDRA K. MURPHY is a PhD candidate in the Sociology Department at Princeton University. Her work includes qualitative and ethnographic work on the indoor sex trade in New York City, the transformation of public housing in Chicago, and the informal economy. She is co-author of the paper "Vice Careers: The Changing Contours of Sex Work in New York City," in the journal *Qualitative Sociology*, forthcoming. Alexandra is currently conducting ethnographic research on U.S. suburban ghettoes.

TRINA SMITH is a PhD candidate in sociology at the University of Minnesota. She studies gender, human rights, and inequality. Her dissertation examines discourse and advocacy of international reproductive rights organizations to assess how they represent diverse women.

SUSAN J. TERRIO is an associate professor of French and cultural anthropology at Georgetown University, where she holds a joint appointment between the departments of French and Sociology and Anthropology. She is writing a monograph on the Paris juvenile court, centering in particular on recent threats to a rehabilitative ideal and the rise of a punitive trend that disproportionately affects minors who are foreign and of immigrant ancestry.

SUDHIR ALLADI VENKATESH, director of the Center for Urban Research and Policy, is professor of sociology and the director of research in the Institute for Research in African American Studies at Columbia University. Professor Venkatesh has done extensive ethnographic work examining issues of race, poverty, youth, and underground economies in Chicago and Harlem, and is the author of *American Project: The Rise and Fall of a Modern Ghetto* (Cambridge, MA: Harvard University Press, 2000).

ROB WHITE is a professor and head of the School of Sociology & Social Work at the University of Tasmania, Australia. He has research, scholarly, and practical interests in areas such as juvenile justice, crime prevention, youth studies, corrections, and green or environmental criminology. Among his publications are *No Space of Their Own* (Melbourne: Cambridge University Press, 1990), *Australian Youth Subcultures* (Hobart: Australian Clearinghouse for Youth Studies, 1999), *Youth & Society* (with Johanna Wyn, Oxford: Oxford University Press, 2004), and *Juvenile Justice* (with Chris Cunneen, Oxford:

Oxford University Press 2002), as well as a recent book *Controversies in Environmental Sociology* (Cambridge: Cambridge University Press, 2004).

ELANA ZILBERG is an assistant professor in Culture and Communication in the Communication Department at the University of California San Diego. She writes on transnational spaces produced at the nexus of migration, security, and urban policy between Los Angeles and San Salvador. Her articles on this subject appear in *American Quarterly, Anthropological Theory, City and Society, Wide Angle,* and *Estudios Centroamericanos.* Her book in progress is entitled *Transnational Geographies of Violence: An Inter-American Encounter from the Cold War to the War on Terror.*

INDEX